"THE TOUCH OF CIVILIZATION"

"THE TOUCH OF CIVILIZATION"

Comparing American and Russian Internal Colonization

Steven Sabol

UNIVERSITY PRESS OF COLORADO
Louisville

© 2017 by University Press of Colorado

Published by University Press of Colorado
245 Century Circle, Suite 202
Louisville, Colorado 80027

All rights reserved
First paperback edition 2018

 The University Press of Colorado is a proud member of
The Association of American University Presses.

The University Press of Colorado is a cooperative publishing enterprise supported, in part, by Adams State University, Colorado State University, Fort Lewis College, Metropolitan State University of Denver, Regis University, University of Colorado, University of Northern Colorado, Utah State University, and Western State Colorado University.

ISBN: 978-1-60732-549-9 (cloth)
ISBN: 978-1-60732-869-8 (paperback)
ISBN: 978-1-60732-550-5 (ebook)

Library of Congress Cataloging-in-Publication Data

Names: Sabol, Steven, author.
Title: The touch of civilization : comparing American and Russian internal colonization / Steve Sabol.
Description: Boulder, Colorado : University Press of Colorado, [2017] | Includes bibliographical references and index.
Identifiers: LCCN 2016036164 | ISBN 9781607325499 (cloth) | ISBN 9781607328698 (pbk) | ISBN 9781607325505 (ebook)
Subjects: LCSH: Comparative civilization. | Imperialism—History. | United States—Territorial expansion. | Russia—Territorial expansion. | Collective memory—Russia. | Collective memory—United States. | Dakota Indians—History. | Kazakhs—History.
Classification: LCC CB451 .S23 2016 | DDC 909—dc23
LC record available at https://lccn.loc.gov/2016036164

An electronic version of this book is freely available, thanks to the support of libraries working with Knowledge Unlatched. KU is a collaborative initiative designed to make high-quality books open access for the public good. The open access ISBN for the PDF version of this book is 978-1-60732-698-4; for the ePUB version the open access ISBN is 978-1-60732-725-7. More information about the initiative and links to the open-access version can be found at www.knowledgeunlatched.org.

The University Press of Colorado gratefully acknowledges the generous support of the Charles Redd Center for Western Studies at Brigham Young University toward the publication of this book.

COVER PHOTO CREDITS. Front, clockwise from top left: courtesy of Central State Archives, Republic of Kazakhstan, 2-27605; courtesy of Denver Public Library; courtesy of Denver Public Library; courtesy of Central State Museum, Republic of Kazakhstan, NVF 5289/11. Back: courtesy of Central State Archives, Republic of Kazakhstan, 2-95119 (left); courtesy of National Anthropological Archives, Smithsonian Institution (right).

To my grandfather,
George O'Neal Sutton (1896–1982).

The law was his vocation,
but history was his passion.

Contents

Acknowledgments   ix

INTRODUCTION   3

CHAPTER ONE
The Sioux and the Kazakhs   33

CHAPTER TWO
Pre-Nineteenth-Century Expansion   69

CHAPTER THREE
Conquest and Martial Resistance   99

CHAPTER FOUR
Through the Colonial Looking-Glass   139

CHAPTER FIVE
Internal Colonization   171

CHAPTER SIX
Assimilation and Identity   205

CONCLUSION   235

Bibliography   245

Index   289

Acknowledgments

This book is unlike any other project I have ever undertaken and, admittedly, it is the happy coincidence of fly-fishing and history. In fact, the book ought to be subtitled "a river ran through it," but Norman Maclean beat me to it. My interest in this comparison started in 2006 while fly-fishing in Yellowstone National Park. I came across a road sign in the park by Nez Perce Creek that briefly described the flight of the Nez Perce and their incredible escape through the park. I was curious. I picked up a few books and started learning about the tragic fate of Chief Joseph and his people, but more importantly, I began to notice similarities between nineteenth-century American attitudes toward Indians in general and Russian attitudes toward the empire's minorities living in central Asia and the Caucasus. These similarities sparked a comparative curiosity. I noticed similar attitudes, imageries, stereotypes, and consequences. I am not a disciple of Marc Bloch, considered by many to be the father of comparative history, but came to this comparative study only after reading literature outside of my studies in Russian and central Asian history. I am, essentially, an accidental comparativist.

Having spent years in central Asia—chiefly in Almaty, Kazakhstan, studying the region—I had already noticed the geographic similarities between the Kazakh Steppe and the northern plains. But until 2006 I had not made the connection between the American process of expansion and colonization and Russian expansion—in particular, the colonizers' attitudes, perceptions, imagery, and typologies of colonized minorities. Donald W. Treadgold's books and articles—required reading for anyone interested in imperial Russian expansion—should have alerted me to the possible similarities, as he encouraged scholars to test Frederick Jackson Turner's frontier thesis in the Russian historical context. It did not register with me, in part because Turner and Treadgold tended to neglect American and Russian indigenous populations; they focused instead on expansion and resettlement of pioneers and peasants but gave minimal attention to the policies implemented by the United States and Russia to delimitate spaces between settler and native.

As a student, I was keen to understand Russia and its historical relationship with the Kazakhs and never considered a comparative possibility, certainly not with the United States. What comparative works I read dealt with China and its relationships with minority nationalities—especially those living in Xinjiang, such as the Kazakhs and Uighurs. In fact, I only read Turner's famous article once before, as an undergraduate, so I was somewhat blissfully unaware of the century-long debate about his thesis. Having trained in graduate school as a Russian and central Asian historian, I had a foundation for one side of this comparison, but not the other.

After thinking about the similarities and, perhaps more importantly, the differences between American expansion and colonization of the Sioux and Russian expansion and colonization of Kazakhs, I approached my American history colleagues to discuss the idea. Their enthusiastic response to this project frankly surprised me—or perhaps I was simply pleased they did not greet it with derisive laughter. The next test for this comparative study came at the 2009 Western Historical Association annual conference in Denver, where I presented a rough essay of this project. Once again, I was somewhat taken aback by the thoroughly positive response. The *Western Historical Quarterly* published a significantly revised version of that paper in 2012, which reinforced considerably my belief that this project had merit.[1] This work is an attempt to elaborate more fully on the various themes and interpretations addressed in that article.

It was not possible to complete this project without the invaluable assistance, advice, encouragement, and good humor from so many friends and colleagues. This project expanded and improved, I hope, due to their support. First, my colleagues in the History Department at the University of North Carolina at Charlotte were amazing, patient, and sincerely interested as this book evolved. Most notably, John David Smith and Carol Higham read numerous drafts, listened to my complaints and travails, gave advice, asked questions, and consistently offered inspiration during its several years' incubation. Several other colleagues offered advice and support along the way, including but certainly not limited to Jürgen Buchenau, Dan Dupre, Peter Thorsheim, and Benny

Andres. In addition, the dean of the College of Liberal Arts and Sciences at UNC Charlotte, Dr. Nancy Gutierrez, made available financial research support and time to write. I also benefited tremendously from my university's Faculty Research Grants Program, which provided further financial means to travel to archives in Kazakhstan and the United States. In addition, grants from the Charles Redd Center at Brigham Young University made it possible for me to conduct research in regional archives and libraries.

In Kazakhstan, my dear friend and colleague Sakhinur Dautova was always ready to help, and I am forever grateful. Many friends and colleagues provided welcome respites from the archives and libraries, especially the Between the Pillars Fishing Club. Thank you, Paul Roberts, John Strafford, Shahbaz Minallah, and others too numerous to mention, who seemed always ready with a smile, a beer, and good conversation.

Other colleagues offered incredible advice and support as well, and I would be negligent if I failed to express my gratitude to Clyde Ellis, Sheila McManus, Will Katerburg, Paula Michaels, and especially David Wrobel, who read the manuscript for the University Press of Colorado. Professor Wrobel identified numerous areas in the manuscript that needed reconstruction and reconfiguration. I am indebted to him for his meticulous reading and commentary. Two other anonymous readers also provided pointed and valuable comments. Any failings in this project remain, as always, with the author.

I must also thank Darrin Pratt and Jessica d'Arbonne of the University Press of Colorado. Their early interest in this project was critical to move it forward, and their steadfast patience as I worked through the various stages of research and writing was instrumental to its completion. Always they exhibited an enthusiasm and confidence in this book that just as frequently waned for me as I struggled to put the pieces of the puzzle together. To each, I offer my heartfelt thanks, though it hardly seems sufficient.

Finally, without the love and support of my family—Anita, Conor, and Sean—this project would have undoubtedly remained a work in progress. Now that it is finished, I am reminded of a seemingly innocuous conversation I had several years ago, one that makes sense to me in retrospect.

In 1996 I was in Almaty, conducting dissertation research. During a dinner conversation with leading Kazakh historian Mambet Koigeldiev, the topic turned to Russian imperialism and colonization and its consequences for Kazakh nomads. I was generally quite critical of the Russians, but not so my host. He surprised me when he commented that the Kazakh people suffered mightily under Russian rule, but he also said, "What we took from the Russians only made us stronger as a nation. We survived. Kazakhs have their own country now.

Where are your Indians?" I felt completely foolish; I mumbled something about reservations and that Native Americans too have survived, fully realizing how ignorant I was about the topic. Another friend joined the conversation, and she mentioned that the "Russians were not bad colonizers, better than the Chinese." The conversation turned to China; I was grateful for the comparative reprieve. Looking back all these years later, that conversation planted the seed for this comparative study, and the rivers in Yellowstone gave it the chance to bloom.

NOTE

1. Steven Sabol, "Comparing American and Russian Internal Colonization: The 'Touch of Civilisation' on the Sioux and Kazakhs," *Western Historical Quarterly* 43 (Spring 2012): 29–51.

"THE TOUCH OF CIVILIZATION"

Introduction

This work compares the process and practice of nineteenth-century American and Russian internal colonization—a form of contiguous, continental expansion, imperialism, and colonialism that incorporated indigenous lands and peoples. Both the republican United States and tsarist Russia exercised internal colonization, yet they remain neglected in many studies devoted to nineteenth-century imperialism and colonialism. Scholars generally ignore the United States in studies that compare empires and colonization because, as Amy Kaplan argued, "United States expansion is often treated as an entirely separate phenomenon from European colonialism of the nineteenth century."[1] Similarly, scholars often neglect Russian colonial expansion because, as Taras Hunczak noted, it was "a continental state, its expansion has been viewed largely as a process of unification and consolidation."[2] The contiguous nature of both the United States and Russia, and the proximity of colonized regions, seems to exclude each from discussions of nineteenth-century empires, colonialism, and internal colonization. Historian James Belich reiterated a slightly different element of this concept, positing that, even now, "American westward migration is seldom seen in the context of other great migrations—pan-Anglo, pan-European, or global. This is partly because it happened to be overland and 'internal,' yet in this it was no different from the Russian migration to Siberia or Chinese migration to Manchuria."[3]

The United States and Russia blurred the distinctions between their metropolitan origins and their newly incorporated territories by amalgamating them into a single polity.[4] The seamlessness to American and Russian movements reinforced perceptions of expansion rather than empire or colonization. American and Russian expansions appeared more natural—almost as organic extensions of physical and geographical boundaries. Nonetheless, American and Russian contiguous expansion echoed European overseas expansion, where every "settler frontier required the active political, military, and fiscal engagement and support of an aggrandizing state."[5] In both cases, expansion started slowly, often clumsily, but accelerated during the nineteenth century without any clear understanding of the people and their number, societies, histories, and traditions and the problems American and Russian troops, settlers, or officials might encounter. The United States and Russia were not accidental empires; instead, they were opportunistic, deliberate, and aggressive empires.

Few scholars dispute that France, Great Britain, Holland, Belgium, and, to some extent, Germany, were imperial powers. Up to and during the nineteenth century, these European empires colonized most of Africa and much of Asia, and Spain and Great Britain remained the United States' most serious imperial rivals in North and South America. Russia was clearly an imperial power in Siberia, the Caucasus, and central Asia. In comparison, however, scholars frequently neglect the United States in conversations about nineteenth-century empires. Nonetheless, the United States colonized the Louisiana Territory, Texas, California, and all the land between the oceans. The United States incorporated these territories largely through imperial negotiations with France, Great Britain, and Spain, but it also won this territory through conquest against Mexico, Great Britain, and indigenous peoples, such as the Sioux, Comanche, Iroquois, Kiowa, Navajo, and dozens of other tribes. Thus, it suggests that the nineteenth-century United States colonized, but it had no colonies. The United States was an empire but not imperial.[6] In Russia, a comparable argument emerged, in this sense at least: the Russian Empire colonized, but it had no colonies. Russia was, however, imperial.

Russia's expansion began in the fifteenth century, and, ultimately, it colonized Ukraine, Poland, Finland, the Baltics, Siberia, Alaska, the Caucasus, and central Asia. It acquired much of this territory through conquest over the Turks, Tatars, Poles, Chinese, Kazakhs, Bashkirs, Turkmen, Ossetians, and dozens of other peoples. Up until the nineteenth century, Russia's principal imperial rivals lay in Asia: the Ottoman Turks and the Qing Dynasty in China.[7] In the nineteenth century, Great Britain sporadically challenged Russia, but it had few serious imperial adversaries as it expanded across the continent. The ostensible absence of colonies during the nineteenth century should not hide the fact that both the United States and Russia colonized territories and organized internal colonization, which was the process and mechanism of American and Russian expansion and imperial rule over indigenous populations.

This work provides a critical, comparative examination of internal colonization exercised by the United States and Russia and experienced by two indigenous populations—the Sioux and the Kazakhs—to negate the "tendency to isolate the study of American history, to overemphasize the uniqueness of the American development and to exalt national pride."[8] It seeks to incorporate the United States into the wider nineteenth-century colonial and imperial "international context" typically accepted for European imperialism and colonialism.[9] This comparison is broad in scope, temporarily and geographically.

At the heart of this study is, of course, the issue of empire and internal colonization. Was the United States an empire? Did it colonize land and people? Did it exploit and hold dominion over alien peoples? Was it territorial or economic imperialism or both? Was it internal colonization? These are processes typically associated with nineteenth-century European imperialism and colonization. On the surface, the answer to all these questions appears to be yes. Certainly, Alexis de Tocqueville thought so when he wrote that their "starting-point is different, and their courses are not the same; yet each of them seems marked out by the will of Heaven to sway destinies of half the globe."[10] Yet, as Ann Laura Stoler and Carole McGranahan noted, in their introduction to the edited essay collection *Imperial Formations*, "What scholars have sometimes taken to be aberrant empires—the American, Russian, or Chinese empires—may indeed be quintessential ones, consummate producers of excepted populations, excepted spaces, and their own exception from international and domestic laws."[11] Scholars do not question that Russia was an empire, that it colonized land and peoples, that it exercised dominion over non-Russians, that it exploited its own population, or that it exerted control over the economy and exercised internal colonization. Scholars do not often compare Russia to other nineteenth-century empires.[12]

In the United States, however, it appears to be an unsettled interpretation of the American experience, although as Sandra M. Gustafson argued, the idea of an American empire "waxed and waned, but it has never been entirely absent" in American historiography.[13] In 1988 Lloyd C. Gardner explained the discrepancy in his presidential address to the Society for Historians of American Foreign Relations. He reminded his audience that the "American empire was still 'the empire that dare not speak its name'" because, he observed, "we are still very far from agreed about the circumstances of its creation, and its purpose."[14] American geographer Jedidiah Morse understood its purpose, however, when he wrote in 1792, "it is well known that empire has been travelling from east to west. Probably her last and broadest feat will be America." He exuberantly prophesized that "we cannot but anticipate the period, as not far distant, when the American Empire will comprehend millions of souls, west of the Mississippi. Judging upon probable grounds, the Mississippi was never designed as the western boundary of the American empire."[15] Thus, by comparing the United States and its expansion with tsarist Russia, this study will demonstrate more clearly Stoler and McGranahan's theory that the United States and Russia were "quintessential" empires that mirrored one another in theory and practice, but neither was an exception or exceptional.

In order to answer these questions, this work examines the process of internal colonization using the conquest and internal colonization of the Sioux and the Kazakhs as key case studies. These two nomadic, militarily powerful societies represented distinct challenges and obstacles to American and Russian expansion. That should not suggest that the Apache, Navajo, or Cheyenne easily succumbed to American power or that the Uzbeks, Chechens, or Turkmen posed any less of an obstacle to Russian expansion. This comparative study examines the process of American and Russian internal colonization to construct very different empires, which bear no relation to each other, and the subsequent comparable consequences for the Sioux and the Kazakhs during American and Russian imperial expansion.

Specifically, this study examines American and Russian internal colonization practiced against the Sioux and the Kazakhs. In particular, it examines how and why perceptions of the Sioux and Kazakhs as ostensibly uncivilized peoples, and similarly held American and Russian perceptions of the northern plains and the Kazakh Steppe as "uninhabited" regions that ought to be settled, reinforced American and Russian government sedentarization policies and land allotment programs among the Sioux and Kazakhs. In addition, it compares the processes practiced by the two empires and the various forms of Sioux and Kazakh martial, political, social, and cultural resistance evident throughout the nineteenth century.

As different as American and Russian expansion and conquest of continental interiors might initially appear, the consequences for the Sioux and the Kazakhs are remarkably similar; and the solutions devised by the United States and Russia to deal with intractable nomadic peoples share many parallels and results. In both cases, the colonizing power expressed absolute confidence in its civilizing mission and realized its own greatness through territorial expansion and the introduction of progress, prosperity, and stability and social, economic, and political order. Martial, cultural, and intellectual resistance by the Sioux and Kazakhs to the superior power and, by extension, its general civilizing tendencies, produced in the minds of Americans and Russians only two possible outcomes for the Sioux and the Kazakhs: assimilation or extermination. The process of internal colonization of the Sioux and the Kazakhs and its comparison deepens our understanding of and redirects attention to the United States and Russia as active participants in the nineteenth-century imperial conquests undertaken by other European powers in Asia and Africa. It reveals a universal struggle between civilization and savagism—between internal and external colonialism—and negates the tendency to study the United States and Russia in isolation or as singular national histories. When viewed through a comparative prism, American expansion no longer seems exceptional or a rejection of "old Europe" for something uniquely "American" but rather as part of a global process; and Russian expansion and conquest, and its subsequent treatment of its indigenous populations, no longer appears more brutal, more autocratic, more Russo-centric.

Comparing American and Russian colonization of the northern plains and the Kazakh Steppe—particularly the relationship between the expanding power and the indigenous Sioux and Kazakhs—serves to connect the conquests to the nineteenth-century global colonizing experience.[16] Trade, land, and security motivated both the United States and Russia to expand, and the greater wealth, superior technology, power, and population eventually eclipsed both Sioux and Kazakh abilities to resist colonization. Throughout the nineteenth century, intensified migration and the occupation of land by American settlers and Russian peasants on land previously, but historically, claimed by the Sioux and the Kazakhs resulted in sporadic contact and conflict in proportion to American and Russian formalized control. Contested claims to the land between colonizer and colonized critically undermined their relations.

After 1850 Americans and Russians assumed more formal control of Sioux and Kazakh indigenous sovereignty as the machineries of internal colonization subordinated Sioux and Kazakh political decision-making to the colonizers' sociopolitical and economic structures.[17] Sioux and Kazakh political, economic, social, and cultural dependence and collaboration intensified as American and Russian policies altered and eventually vitiated Sioux and Kazakh sovereignty. Motivated by stereotypes and misperceptions of the Sioux and Kazakhs, Americans and Russians created an environment that made expansion and internal colonization—and, ultimately, civilizing the nomads—part of the national mission. As Helen Carr noted, colonizing powers reformulated policies derived in part from misperceptions of the indigenous peoples and the urgency to occupy the land and settle the nomads into agriculturalists that justified "removal of land as the granting of civilization."[18]

Americans and Russians embraced numerous preconceived images of the Sioux and Kazakhs as they ventured into the plains and steppe—particularly notions of their own superior culture, society, and civilization when compared to the savage nomads.[19] In the nineteenth century, the Jeffersonian belief in agrarian social theory intensified, the "agricultural paradise" that anticipated the "imaginary figure of the wild horseman of the plains . . . replaced by that of the stout yeoman."[20] The Russian government similarly perceived Russian peasants as carriers of the agrarian ideal, the purveyors of modernity and equal to American pioneers.[21] This portrait of American pioneers appeared in an unvarnished stereotype, and Robert L. Mason's distilled imagery resonated for many readers. In 1927 he wrote,

> The frontier cabin in America should be emblazoned upon her coat of arms. The historical movement of this cabin across the whole of the American continent from the first built by the English at Jamestown in 1607 to the last built on the final frontier of Alaska has always heralded the vanguard of civilization. When we think of the frontiersman, wherever he may be, we see the cabin with its fort-like aspect and its primitive rifleman protected behind its heavy walls; of its peaceful smoke filling the valley showing a home under durance— but a home nevertheless—making a way in the wilderness for the mighty tread of civilization. . . . It suggests clean-mindedness and good citizenship. It implies the loss of sordidness which often goes hand in hand with the wealth of a country—and ours is wealthy.[22]

This elegant vision of the past reveals the mythology spawned by the American expansion westward. The frontier cabin was a home, it was protection, and it represented civilization in the wilderness. The cabin helped to conquer the frontier. Scholars, however, understand that the American expansion across the continent was more than a cabin, more than a simple expansion of civilization that defeated the wilderness. American expansion and internal colonization was complex, but often lost in the conversation was that the United States differed little from other contemporary empires.

As scholars take note of indigenous populations' reactions to colonialism and colonization, a tendency developed to neglect the ideology or motivation of the colonizing power. Yet there are complimentary narratives that make understanding both sides critical to understanding the whole. One of the consequences of colonialism and colonization was that indigenous sociopolitical or economic institutional norms that functioned in a pre-colonized era decayed and became inoperative or dysfunctional, which isolated the community from its constituent parts.[23] Expansion resulted in conflict that ultimately forced the Sioux and

Kazakhs to settle onto land deemed by the colonizer as sufficient for occupation and agriculture.[24]

American and Russian expansion and internal colonization in some cases destroyed native sovereignty and institutions, but Sioux and Kazakh social, cultural, and spiritual vestiges adapted and survived in various ways. Both the colonizer and colonized reacted and adapted to the relationship as it evolved. For example, the Americans and the Russians adopted administrative tactics that suited their colonizer sensibilities. According to Jeffrey Ostler, American power "manifested itself through reservation agencies administered by the Indian Office."[25] The government expected Sioux leaders, identified by reservation agents, to maintain order within this alien political environment. Restrictions placed on the Sioux and Kazakhs obstructed mobility and forced settlement and impoverishment, not assimilation. Russia did not establish reservations but instead confined Kazakhs to *volosty* (administrative units) and *uezdy* (districts) to raise livestock or farm—an environment just as restrictive as the American reservation system. It was two different solutions, but one similar result.

In response to American and Russian internal colonization, the imperial expansion produced diverse forms of resistance among the Sioux and Kazakhs; however, internal colonization also shaped their adaptive strategies. Adoption and adaptation meant survival. The internal colonization practices established by the United States and tsarist Russia did not exterminate the Sioux or the Kazakhs, as sundry nineteenth-century observers predicted. Sioux and Kazakh society weakened, their cultures radically altered, and individuals were economically dislocated and impoverished; yet they survived despite dispossession and the intensive cultural, social, political, and economic consequences of internal colonization. The concerns that the Sioux and the Kazakhs must perish or assimilate did not, and likely could not, predict the powerful forces that ultimately aligned to sustain greatly weakened Sioux and Kazakh communities and preserve cultural attachments and symbols, language, and religious beliefs. And yet some scholars regard American expansion as somehow worse—an unparalleled "colonial occupation" and "one of the greatest known *land thefts* in human history."[26] This inherently comparative statement assumes that no other colonial occupation was continental in scope and that American expansion was an exceptional "theft."

This comparison, at its core, is a macro rather than a micro examination. It is designed to compare how and why two nineteenth-century expanding powers colonized two different peoples, yet one is clearly understood and accepted to be an empire (Russia) and the other is not (United States). It compares two different nineteenth-century colonizing states that exercised dominion over two different peoples on two separate continents. It traces the policies to colonize different lands and peoples in order to illuminate that the United States and tsarist Russia were quintessential nineteenth-century empires, no different from Great Britain, France, Belgium, or any other imperial, colonizing power at that time. The comparative prism that examines the internal colonization by the United States and Russia changes the historical narrative, however slightly, to incorporate the two contiguous empires into nineteenth-century imperial and colonial history.

This work does not fully compare the Sioux and Kazakh peoples, although they figure prominently throughout this work. It does examine the indigenous peoples' response to American and Russian imperialism, which influenced the dynamics of nineteenth-century internal colonization. To the extent possible, this study contextualizes the Sioux and Kazakhs in their world, as they endured the loss of sovereignty and territory to the United States and Russia.

This work does not assume that the Sioux or Kazakhs were passive recipients or victims of American and Russian civilization, mere nonparticipants in the process of internal colonization. In fact, the Sioux and the Kazakhs resisted American and Russian expansion and conquest with martial vigor, and at other times, they deployed more subtle means. Both the Sioux and the Kazakhs influenced the course of events; they managed the variegated social, political, economic, and cultural changes wrought by internal colonization. Most importantly, the Sioux and the Kazakhs survived—a fate few believed possible in the nineteenth century. They lost sovereignty over various aspects of their lives but retained a small degree of autonomy and managed to sustain their society, language, culture, and, to some extent—certainly in the Kazakh case—a meager economy.

The Sioux and the Kazakhs adapted to and adopted the changes occurring all around them. The Americans and Russians incorporated the Sioux and the Kazakhs into their empires and compelled the nomads to adapt and adopt alien cultural, social, economic, and political structures. In so doing, the Sioux and Kazakhs adjusted to the new environment and survived. To paraphrase Frederick Jackson Turner, the plains and the steppe were not a land without people, but a people without land.[27] People were there, and they resisted internal colonization. The Sioux and the Kazakhs were not static societies but changed before, during, and after colonization. The typology and imagery of nomadism reinforced perceptions that extinction was the only possible outcome rather than recognition that the Sioux and the Kazakhs could adapt and survive.[28]

In the nineteenth century, travelers and visitors to the United States and tsarist Russia typically had two very different impressions of both places. America was lively and energetic, and its government was democratic, forward-looking, and progressive. The American people expressed optimism, faith in the future, and a belief in their own destiny. Russia, on the other hand, was dark and forbidding, the people quite gloomy and fatalistic. Writers often depicted the Russian peasant as backward, ignorant, dirty, and as superstitious as the land and people the empire colonized in Siberia, the Caucasus, and central Asia.[29] Foreigners often described Russia and its government as backward in the extreme: autocratic, ruthless, brutal, and despotic.[30] Indeed, these seemingly entrenched stereotypes, often expressed by Americans and Russians themselves and just as frequently contradictory, prevailed in the literature of the day.

These two opposite characterizations extend the gap for this comparison, or so it seems. How can two countries and two peoples, depicted in such contrary ways, end up in the same place: expanding empires that internally colonized indigenous peoples? What philosophies and ideologies were at work? What typologies and images pervaded American and Russian perceptions and attitudes about the Sioux and the Kazakhs? What were the principal motivations for expansion and internal colonization? What were the consequences for the Sioux and the Kazakhs? America had its "Indian Problem," Russia its "Nationality Question," and each pursued policies designed to resolve the problem or answer the question. There were clearly diverse opinions about the Sioux held by different segments of American society, and, periodically, prominent individuals and groups disagreed with the common typologies, perceptions, attitudes, and imagery used to characterize not just the Sioux but all Indians. And not all Russians— high official or lowly peasant—thought, much less cared, about the Kazakhs or the steppe. But are the United States and tsarist Russia comparable? This study seeks to demonstrate that internal colonization by the United States and tsarist Russia are indeed comparable, but not in every facet; and there were notable differences.

This work takes a broader focus than many other comparative histories, covering a wide temporal space, from the earliest contacts between the Americans and the Sioux and the Russians and the Kazakhs up to the first decade of the twentieth century. Although the starting points for American and Russian expansion occurred at different times, by the later part of the nineteenth century, the processes and mechanisms of internal colonization and resettlement reveal more similarities than differences. Chapter 1 of this study examines Sioux and Kazakh societies, at least to the extent possible, in their social, cultural, and economic milieu. Chapter 2 examines the early phases of contact between Europeans and the Sioux and Russians and the Kazakhs, up to the nineteenth century. Chapter 3 examines the American and Russian conquest, as well as Sioux and Kazakh resistance, and the early evolution of American and Russian internal colonization policies. Chapter 4 examines American and Russian perceptions and attitudes—particularly the typologies and imagery that influenced colonial policies in the steppe and plains. Chapter 5 and chapter 6 examine those policies and the consequences for the Sioux and the Kazakhs—most particularly those related to land, civilization, sedentarization, and assimilation—from the latter half of the nineteenth century to roughly the start of World War I.

The year 1914 was a global and historical turning point—unquestionably so for the United States and tsarist Russia. The consequences of the First World War changed the course of global European imperialism and colonialism. The war dramatically changed relations between the colonizer and the colonized in India, Africa, Asia, the United States, and Russia. Russian society agonized tremendously during the war and experienced untold suffering during the 1917 revolutions and Civil War. Moreover, the 1917 Russian Revolution, with the subsequent Bolshevik victory, ushered in a dramatically different relationship in the Kazakh Steppe in the 1920s and early 1930s. The Sioux, however, resided in a strong, confident United States that fully emerged economically and militarily on the world stage. By the 1930s, the Sioux and the Kazakhs existed in a different world—one that transformed the social, political, economic, and cultural landscape that existed just a decade before. The United States experienced a somewhat different revolution in the 1930s, in the midst of the Great Depression; and the federal government attempted to reform, once again, the relationship between Indians and the government with the introduction of the 1934 Indian Reorganization Act, also known as the Wheeler-Howard Act. The United States and the Soviet Union took interesting, but considerably different, approaches in the 1930s to deal with the legacies of internal colonization.

SOURCES

This work relies principally on published primary and secondary sources to interpret American and Russian typologies and imagery of the colonized lands and peoples.[31] An extensive amount of American government-related materials is available to scholars, such as Indian agent and US Army reports published by the Government Printing Office (GPO). The Russian government also produced a significant amount of material for scholars to examine, though not as broad as in the United States. Other valuable published materials include memoirs, travelogues, and the personal papers of leading officials.

In the nineteenth century, American, Russian, and foreign writers were characteristically comparative, frequently fixated on the innate weaknesses and backwardness of the indigenous populations they encountered and observed in comparison to their own. In most cases, the context for these works was comparative empire, expansion, and national pride. Nineteenth-century Americans moving westward were a more literate people than Russian peasants—a fact that is reflected in the types of sources used in this comparison. Americans wrote decidedly about the land and the people they encountered. The Sioux in the 1860s and 1870s were a particularly popular topic. Americans migrating westward, crossing the Great Plains, wrote extensively and frequently about their journeys, adventures, hardships, and encounters with Indians. Many travelers published memoirs, diaries, and histories, and others deposited their accounts with state historical societies' libraries or in university libraries. These unofficial sources and literary works remain an extensive, invaluable resource not replicated in Russian imperial history.

The meager amount of unofficial sources might frustrate a student of Russian expansion and colonization of the Kazakhs and the steppe, when compared to the richness of American materials, particularly if he or she is trying to examine and evaluate perceptions and attitudes among peasants. Russian intellectuals and writers certainly produced a copious amount of material about the Russian Empire—most notably, about the Caucasus and the Far East—but the Russian peasants who migrated eastward into Siberia and settled on the Kazakh Steppe in the nineteenth century simply did not record their journey with the same tenacity that Americans did. Russian government officials, military men, scientists, and others did produce a valuable written record of time spent among the Kazakhs—their way of life, religion, economy, etc.—but it is a profile in which the historian must tease out typologies, imagery, perceptions, and attitudes. By the 1890s, Russian officials frequently asked Russian peasants questions that usually dealt with points of origin or destination. They rarely posed an official question—"What do you think of Kazakhs?"—to Russians moving east. Moreover, Russian peasants tended to be an illiterate lot, and those sources are scant at best to understand Russian peasant perceptions and attitudes about the Kazakhs. Thus, this comparative study necessarily uses—cautiously—foreign visitors' sources (books and articles) more in the Russian case than in the American.

When foreign travelers met with Russian officials and peasants, they typically recorded those conversations and reproduced them for a European or American reading public that demonstrated a curiosity about the forbidding tsarist empire. Many of these works tend to describe Russia in decidedly harsh terms—despotic, oppressive, secretive, and suspicious of foreigners—the quintessential autocratic police state.[32] Americans too perceived the Russians in contradictory images. The publisher of the 1814 edition of *The Life of Field Marshal*

Souvarof noted, "The national character of the Russians is the subject of much animated discussion. They are represented . . . as a compound of ferocious barbarism and vicious profligacy [or] they are pictured with all the virtues as well as the strength of an infant and growing people."[33] Many of these authors viewed the Russian Empire with skepticism, and they held preconceived notions of what they expected to see and experience. Nonetheless, by sifting through the authors' biases and judgments, scholars can detect themes and tropes that reveal much about imperial and popular perceptions and attitudes about the Kazakhs. But these writers also understood that their readers had preconceived notions about the Russian Empire and the lands and people it conquered and colonized; writers used similar typologies and imageries to describe the Kazakhs that they thought readers could easily comprehend. The descriptions almost mirror each other, whether describing a Sioux or a Kazakh, a simple reference to nomadism dehumanized the individual and locked him into a specific form: backward, uncivilized, wandering, primitive, etc.

In both cases, official records are a valuable source, but as will become clear, the language used in these reports and documents requires scholars to extrapolate perceptions and attitudes and tease out the comparable meanings. Russian official documents tended to report information such as bureaucratic information and statistics; rarely are personal perceptions or attitudes overtly expressed. Official American sources, such as reservation agents' reports are, fortunately, not quite so reserved. The popular press is another source, even in Russia, from which to glean perceptions and attitudes. Scholarly works, literature, and even artistic impressions reveal a lot about American and Russian sensibilities during the nineteenth century; they reflect society and influence it. There is little debate that James Fenimore Cooper's *The Leatherstocking Tales* "established the Indian as a significant literary type" in the United States. The works of Cooper, Mayne Reid, and others were translated in French and available to Russian writers and social elites.[34] These works, as well as comparable Russian literature about colonized regions and people, unquestionably influenced Russian writers and the public. This literature helped shape perceptions and attitudes about the empire and the colonization of the Caucasus, Siberia, the Kazakh Steppe, Turkestan, and the Russian Far East.[35]

Despite the discrepancy of sources, scholars can reap sufficient information from primary and secondary sources to understand American and Russian perceptions, attitudes, typologies, and imagery about the Sioux and the Kazakhs in order to understand how and why policies were developed and implemented. Central to the perceptions and attitudes expressed by American and Russian commentators, scholars, writers, pioneers and peasants, government officials, and travelers was the idea of the other, the exotic, and a clear demarcation between "us" and "them." In her work *Imperial Eyes*, Mary Louise Pratt noted that nineteenth-century travelogues also conveyed control, dominance, and a sense of superiority over the landscapes and peoples that Europeans and Americans encountered and colonized.[36] Americans eagerly consumed these books and articles, and for "literate Americans in the antebellum period, Indians were everywhere in the print culture—in books, the journals of learned societies, and popular magazines."[37] Kazakhs, however, appear somewhat irregularly in Russian popular media of the day; Russian novelists and other writers were far more fascinated with the conquest of the Caucasus, contemporaneous to the conquest of the Kazakh Steppe.

This leads, naturally, to a question of language. This study uses both primary and secondary Russian- and Kazakh-language sources; however, when possible, it cites English-language sources instead in order to reach a broader audience. Nevertheless, in some cases, such as the collected works of certain Kazakh intellectuals or Russian government documents, no English-language version exists. For example, in the early 1830s, Aleksei Levshin traveled to the steppe and spent time with the Kazakhs observing their culture; experiencing (to the extent possible) the nomadic life; eating their food; and recording their folktales, histories, and traditions. His book *Opisanie Kirgiz-kazach'ikh, ili Kirgiz-kaisatskikh, ord i stepei*, first appeared in 1832 and was republished in 1996 after the Soviet Union collapsed. No English-language version exists.[38] A comparative study also requires a necessary understanding of the historiographical trends evident in both American and Russian history—specifically when dealing with issues of American and Russian conquest and colonization of the Sioux and the Kazakhs.

A novice to American history quickly learns that numerous historiographical diversions and interpretations tie American expansion west to Manifest Destiny, the frontier, slavery, cowboys and Indians, the different gold rushes, and so on, as well as the ubiquitous American exceptionalism. In the history of the West, it is sometimes difficult to disentangle myth and reality. That overstates the historical complexities of the American West, but the point is that American history in general, and the West in particular, seems to be in a state of constant reinvention. Professional historians, however, will call it a reinterpretation—particularly the reinterpretation of the West.[39] Writing in the early twentieth century, Frederick Jackson Turner, the father of American frontier theory, suggested that if American scholars, "with our own methods of the occupation of the frontier, we should compare those of other countries which have dealt with similar problems—such as Russia, Germany, and the English colonies in Canada, Australia, and Africa—we should undoubtedly find most fruitful results."[40]

Russian historiography of the empire's conquest and colonization of Siberia and central Asia remains equally encumbered with its myths and realities. Russia too follows its own exceptionalist historiographical path, but one that differs from the American narrative yet still remains richly embedded with nationalist, rhetorical uniqueness.[41] A student of Kazakh history soon learns that there were at least two conflicting interpretations of Russian expansion into the Kazakh Steppe and the colonization of the Kazakh people: voluntary unification or violent conquest. Soviet scholars—Russian and Kazakhs—used the term *prisoedinenie* (unification) or the more ambiguous, benign word *sblizhenie* (coming together). Both words suggest a voluntary unification of lands and peoples; they belonged together rather than apart. This interpretation was especially prominent during the Soviet period, although in the 1920s, numerous interpretations proliferated about the expansion, conquest, and internal colonization of the Kazakhs.[42] Post-Soviet Kazakh scholars generally reject both interpretations, arguing instead that it was conquest and imperialism. Consequently, to decipher Russian expansion, conquest, and internal colonization within this historiographical maze, and mapping and mining the tsarist, Soviet, and post-Soviet historiography, requires patience and perseverance. Interestingly, some Russian scholars were already comparing Russia's expansion eastward with America's expansion west.

Writing in 1905, the Russian statesman and historian P. N. Miliukov observed, "Both Russia and the United States have been colonized, not at a prehistoric stage of their existence, but in recent historic times. Hence, the settlement and the exploitation of the natural resources of the country form the very warp of their historical texture. Most of the important features of their economical, social, and political development must be referred to this process of colonization."[43] In the 1950s, American scholar Donald W. Treadgold, urged students of Russian imperial history to employ Turner's frontier thesis to the Russian case, believing that it could "serve as a basis for a general theory of frontier movements in modern times."[44]

Turner's influence on frontier and borderlands' studies in the Kazakh Steppe and Siberia received limited scholarly attention; it was too schematic and marginalized differences between the colonizing peasants and the indigenous Kazakhs. Among post-Soviet Kazakh scholars, the opportunity to cast off the restrictive Soviet interpretative shackles invigorated subsequent scholarship; however, the new interpretations generally conclude that the conquest and colonization of the Kazakhs and the steppe was violent, aggressive, and the worst sort of imperialism. It is hardly a nuanced interpretation but rather nationalist in tone and content.[45] These Kazakh scholars fail to observe what Richard White described as a "middle ground" in which a complex cultural, social, and economic exchange happened daily.[46]

American, Russian, and even Kazakh scholars, however, generally failed to embrace comparative history, except in very limited cases. Comparative nomadism frequently attracted Kazakh scholars, but, otherwise, comparative history remains an infertile field in post-Soviet historical investigations. In American history, the two topics that seem to attract the most attention from scholars working within a comparative framework are the frontier and slavery, which are still hotly debated topics, even without using comparative methodologies.[47] Nonetheless, in the last two decades, other scholars moved beyond the frontier comparisons between the United States and Russia in ways that expand the expectations for comparative history, including Peter Kolchin, Anne Lounsbery, Irena Grudzinska Gross, Margaret Ziolkowski, Mark Bassin, Sonja Luehrmann, and Kate Brown.[48]

Comparative history should illuminate that which might not be evident when examined in isolation. Many scholars referred to the United States as an empire as it crossed and colonized the continent; some scholars might reject that interpretation. What is the evidence? By comparing the United States to a state that exercised a similar process, the comparison illuminates the similarities and differences that strengthen the assertion that the United States and tsarist Russia were comparable empires. Moreover, it might illuminate why one empire implemented certain policies and practices of internal colonization that were not pursued in the other. It can further reveal colonial practices that failed in other contexts, such as Asia or Africa, but perhaps succeeded in the United States or Russia. Why did each state employ sedentarization policies? Why did the United States and Russia each establish inviolable boundaries—first to restrict their own populations and later to contain the natives? Ultimately, both the United States moved well past the Indian Territory and Russia pushed further south past the Kazakh Steppe into Turkestan. Why did the United States create reservations but not Russia? What made lands that most observers agreed was suitable chiefly for livestock suddenly appealing for settlement? The comparison reveals some answers but still masks others that this work attempts to uncover.

As scholars embark upon these new fields of investigation, it is important to situate the comparative history as a legitimate exercise within broader historical inquiry and interpretations. What is comparative history? It is not a methodology or analytical technique used by most scholars. George M. Frederickson, the most prominent advocate for comparative history, argued that it is "a way of isolating the critical factors or independent variables that account for national differences."[49] Michael Adas, another proponent, claimed that comparing the

United States with an appropriate case allows scholars to place American history in "broader global frames of reference that allow us to identify and explore underlying commonalities in major patterns of societal development across time and space."[50] Neither of these are precise definitions but rather explanations of comparative historical, methodological utility. Marc Bloch suggested there were two, perhaps more, types of comparative framework. One is the "universal comparison," in which a scholar examines two societies widely divergent in temporal and geographic space so that specific "phenomenon can obviously not be explained either by mutual influence or by a common origin."[51] The other is Bloch's frequently cited "historical comparison," which examines parallel contemporary societies "exercising a constant mutual influence, exposed throughout their development to the action of the same broad causes" but of "common origin."[52] But even Frederickson admits that there is still no clear definition, and so scholars are left to their own devices to employ a comparative structure, as Carol L. Higham suggests, in order to compare "two regions, experiences, nations, or peoples [so that] one can learn about their similarities and differences."[53]

Comparison clarifies and refutes myths and misinterpretations based upon the isolated analysis in which there is nothing to test the assumptions, theories, or historical explanations. It is, as Frederickson argued, a mechanism to compare systematically "some process or institution in two or more societies that are not usually conjoined within one of the traditional geographical areas of historical specialization."[54] The comparative prism used to examine the United States and tsarist Russia is through the mechanisms of imperialism and internal colonization of the Sioux and the Kazakhs, the plains and the steppe.

If the argument in this comparative work is that the United States was an empire comparable to the Russian Empire, that it exercised imperial control over the Sioux similar to Russian imperial control over the Kazakhs, it is necessary to define imperialism. Scholars, however, still debate what defines an empire as well as its corollary imperialism. For the purposes of this comparative study, A. Dirk Moses's relatively simple definition is best. Moses argued, "There is a consensus that empire means domination of one society by another, usually backed by military force. Imperialism is a process and set of policies to acquire such domination whether by annexation or through less formal means."[55]

The process of imperialism, colonialism, and colonization, wonderfully and somewhat brutally described—first in 1726 by Jonathan Swift, in his satirical story *Gulliver's Travels*—seems eerily familiar. According to Gulliver,

> they go on shore to rob and plunder; they see a harmless people, are entertained with kindness; they give the country a new name; they take formal

possession of it for their king; they set up a rotten plank of a stone for a memorial; they murder two or three dozen of the natives, bring away a couple more by force for a sample, return home, and get their pardon. Here commences a new dominion acquired with a title by divine right. Ships are sent with the first opportunity; the natives driven out or destroyed, their princes tortured to discover gold; a free license given to all acts of inhumanity and lust, the earth reeking with the blood of its inhabitants: and this execrable crew of butchers employed in so pious an expedition, is a modern colony sent to convert and civilize an idolatrous and barbarous people.[56]

For more than a century, scholars seriously debated the concepts of empire, imperialism, and the corollary, colonialism. In that sense, to consider what some scholars might regard as classical empires—for example, Persian, Han, Roman, Mongol, and Ottoman—they were all contiguous empires. It was the creation of modern empires through maritime expansion that began in earnest during the sixteenth century when historians and others observed the origins of both American (under Spanish, British, Dutch, and French maritime expansion) and Russian "imperialism."

In 1902 the British scholar J. A. Hobson, an unabashed critic of empire and imperialism, argued that modern imperialism, particularly the "Scramble for Africa," was an extension of excessive and aggressive nineteenth-century nationalism. Hobson insisted that it was the "debasement of . . . genuine nationalism, by attempts to overflow its natural banks and absorb the near or distant territory of reluctant and unassimilable peoples, that marks the passage from nationalism to a spurious colonialism on the one hand, Imperialism on the other."[57] He did not necessarily distinguish between external imperialism and internal expansion, nor did he apply his theories to internal colonization. But Hobson did consider the United States to be a recent imperial power, becoming one only after the Spanish-American War and the annexation of Hawaii.[58] He applied the economic motivation to imperial expansion, an element certainly emphasized later by Scott Nearing, the American economist, political activist, pacifist, and leading advocate for self-sufficient living, who argued in his book, *The American Empire* that the "chief characteristics of empire exist in the United States. Here are conquered territory; subject peoples; an imperial, ruling class, and the exploitation of that class of the people at home and abroad."[59] For Nearing, American expansion westward was clearly brazen imperialism and internal colonization, although he did not use that term. Vladimir Lenin, well before leading the Bolsheviks to power in Russia in 1917, earlier described Russia's expansion as "internal colonialism," which, he argued, was driven by the need for economic exploitation by the Russian metropole (or center) of the periphery or borderlands. He also mistakenly used Karl Marx's definition of a colony "in the political-economic sense" as "the existence of unoccupied, free lands, easily accessible to settlers," to which he acknowledged that the lands Russia conquered and colonized physically and politically occurred long before being incorporated economically into the imperial networks.[60] The point is that critics of imperialism and colonialism often referred to the United States as an empire. Russia was unquestionably one, even if these same critics only marginally examined the process of expansion across the continent as internal colonization, a concept that slowly gained some acceptance later.

In the early to mid-nineteenth century, Americans often debated the idea of an American Empire but often embedded it with other ideologies such as Manifest Destiny and the Monroe Doctrine. At various times before the American Civil War, advocates eagerly demanded actions against, for example, Mexico, Cuba, and Nicaragua. It created, as Brady Harrison argued, a "conflict between idealism and adventurism, between the desire to improve the human condition and the desire to take the land, wealth, and even life of Indians, or Mexicans, or Central Americans, [and] represents a powerful, persistent contradiction in U.S. culture."[61]

The difference in the American and Russian case was that neither was an overseas empire; rather, both expanded into contiguous territories. This fact seems to be the major obstacle to describing the American expansion as empire-building and internal colonization. In 1961 historian Thomas A. Bailey explained the obstacle this way: "Still another source of misunderstanding was the alleged absence of a far-flung American colonial empire until 1898." According to Bailey, an "authentic world power" seemingly bore the burden of "overseas liabilities, as well as huge armies, navies, and national debts." Consequently, a point often "missed during the nineteenth century was that the United States practiced internal colonialism and imperialism on a continental scale. When Western European nations expanded, they had to go overseas; when we expanded, we had to go west." Moreover, he wrote, "One reason for associating our advent as a world power with 1898 is the popular but erroneous assumption that the acquisition of the Philippines marked a complete break with the past. We are told that hitherto we had shunned colonizing (which is untrue), that we had formerly been isolated (which is untrue), and that thereafter we were internationalist (which is also untrue)."[62] Bailey used the terms in the abstract; he did not define them.

Americans portrayed themselves as reluctant "imperialists," performing a humanitarian service, a civilizing mission, to oppressed peoples—ironically mimicking British ideological and philosophical justifications for that country's civilizing, imperial missions around the globe.[63] Russians also debated the concept of empire—its civilizing mission—but prior to the nineteenth century, the expansion, usually referred to as the "gathering of the lands," suggested the reconstitution of ancient Rus' along "historical, dynastic and religious grounds."[64] Few Russians ever doubted that Russia was an empire engaged in imperialism. It was only later in the nineteenth century that Russia justified its imperialism with a civilizing mission comparable to the United States or Great Britain.[65]

In order to contextualize the United States and Russia into the community of nineteenth-century empires, it is important to recognize that both countries extended their control and domination of indigenous populations with internal colonization. This is not a new concept, but scholars still debate the definition of internal colonization. In the nineteenth century, some European officials used the term to describe Hapsburg and Prussian resettlement. By the 1930s, US scholars used the internal colonialism theory to "characterize relations between the northern and southern parts of the United States."[66] In 1946 George C. Guins, a former Russian government official who immigrated to the United States in 1941, wrote that the "development of the United States and Russia took place by means of internal colonization, which spread of itself, by the natural shifting of the population, and not because of government policy."[67] By the 1960s, social scientists in the United States employed the theory to examine the economic exploitative policies in urban areas and the western United States, Palestine, Ireland, and elsewhere.[68] As with the basic concepts of imperialism and colonialism, the notion of internal colonization lacks precision and clarity. Scholars Carol Chiago Lujan and Gordon Adams provided a basic definition best suited for this study: "Internal colonialism occurs when one group (or government) subjugates another within the same country."[69] This work modifies this definition to use the related concept—internal colonization rather than colonialism—because colonization extends to the resettlement of peoples (i.e., pioneers and peasants), "usually in frontier areas, loyal to the metropole to ensure security and encourage economic development of semi- or unoccupied land within a national or imperial territory."[70]

In both cases, the United States and Russia exerted political, social, economic, and cultural control over the Sioux and the Kazakhs. They applied direct and indirect rule strategies in order to colonize the Sioux and the Kazakhs; they used coercion, military power, and social and cultural distinctiveness designed to subjugate these indigenous populations with the goal of assimilating them into what was considered the mainstream of the colonizer's social, economic, cultural, and political structures. The United States and Russia justified this by employing other European imperial characteristics, such as humanitarianism, civilization, and Christianity. The difference between American and Russian internal colonization and European external colonialism was that the Americans and Russians considered expansion part of the national territorial integration.[71] It was, Peter Calvert argued, that "internal colonization parallels in all important respects external colonization and that in fact they are in essence the same process, differentiated only by their geographical location (the 'blue water' fallacy)."[72] Coupled with the theory of internal colonization, comparative history, as Robert J. Hind argued, should preserve "seminal value for scholars who are attracted to the comparative study of society and history. The treatment of certain metropolitan societies, or the experience of certain sections of a metropolitan society and that of their colonial counterparts, in a comparative war and within an internal colonial framework might help identify features of their respective experiences that could pass undetected, or be given insufficient emphasis, or be misinterpreted, if they were studied separately by other means."[73]

The United States and Russia were contiguous empires that paralleled a comparable process called the settler revolution manifest as well in Asia, Africa, and the Americas. According to James Belich, within the Anglo world, this revolution took three forms, but evident in both the American and Russian expansion, conquest, and internal colonization are "*networks*, the establishment of ongoing systems of long-range interaction, usually for trade; *empire*, the control of other peoples, usually through conquest; and *settlement*, the reproduction of one's own society through long-range migration."[74]

Shifting the examination of empires from individual narratives—the isolated examination that differentiates between overseas and contiguous empires or European empires from non-European empires such as the United States—allows scholars to analyze shared or common characteristics. It further unlocks different prospects to investigate various processes of empire in order to reconsider the definitions and interpretations. It might not result in a new historical narrative or historical reinterpretation of the American or Russian past; but the new prism sheds light on the nuances of empire and the common traits, processes, typologies, and tropes used to define that history. The comparative analysis further contextualizes the United States and Russia within the broader, global imperial and colonial expansion into Asia and Africa to provide greater understanding of the structural difficulties and interconnectedness that empires ultimately shared. All nineteenth-century empires and colonial regimes employed complex and sophisticated strategies to conquer and assimilate segments of colonized peoples into the colonial system: the Americans and Russians were not unique or exceptional empires, although their structures and processes frequently differed from their European counterparts in Asia and Africa.

The Indian scholar Partha Chatterjee argued that one key component to imperial, colonial governments was that the universalist claims made by the dominant regime typically excluded native peoples.[75] Colonial regimes categorized natives by differences—language, social structure, religion, governance—that required the active colonial intervention and guidance imposed by the colonizer. Empire and colonialism also revolved around a humanist ideal predicated on the belief that the social and cultural benefits justified the policies implemented by the colonizing power in order to advance the welfare of the colonized people. Anthony Pagden described this as a "language of interests and benefits" that established criteria and standards of human development and progress, from the primitive to civilized.[76]

It was, essentially, the intellectual ideologies and debates of empire that the United States and Russia shared with their nineteenth-century European contemporaries, which also severely devastated "indigenous institutions of governance" and the native "economic systems, ideologies, and identities."[77] These imperial ideologies rested on an "integrated system of beliefs, assumptions and values, not necessarily true or false, which reflects the needs and interests of a group or class at a particular time in history."[78] The European expansionist impulse, according to the conclusion of British explorer-missionary David Livingston, rested upon an ideological troika stimulated by the three C's: commerce, Christianity, and civilization.[79] Americans and Russians subscribed unabashedly to those concepts, although each perceived their imperial, expansionist missions as very different from European imperialism.

Throughout the nineteenth century, Americans emphasized assimilation far more than Russians did; however, the United States intervened much more intensively with its social, political, cultural, and economic policies against the Sioux than the Russians did with their internal colonization of the Kazakhs. The reason was because, in the United States, as John Wunder noted in his work *"Retained by the People": A History of American Indians and the Bill of Rights*, before 1871 Americans practiced an expansion and colonialism similar to the Europeans. Wunder referred to this process as "Old Colonialism," a course that had "as its primary goal the physical acquisition of valuable western and southern lands and the physical subjugation of its peoples."[80] By the 1870s, he argued, Old Colonialism gave way to "New Colonialism" after the United States had acquired its continental limits and started to experience "new settler demands for lands protected by existing treaties."[81] This New Colonialism was "an especially virulent strain" that "attacked every aspect of Native American life—religion, speech, political freedoms, economic liberty, and cultural diversity."[82] Old Colonialism was, in a sense, motivated by the desire to integrate indigenous lands; New Colonialism was the demand to assimilate indigenous peoples. By the 1870s, Russia altered its policies in the Kazakh Steppe, chiefly to make room for more peasants to settle there following the 1861 Russian serf emancipation. The Russian government also determined to integrate further the Kazakhs' social, political, and economic structures into the empire comparable to Wunder's New Colonialism. They eventually abandoned the concept of integration to the reimagined and perceived imperial need to assimilate—the so-called Russification policies in effect in the last two decades of tsarist rule.

The American and Russian alchemic strategies often manifested as just brute force, but other approaches included education, Christian missionaries, and economic integration—all grounded in the colonizers' common suppositions about nomads, about the land, and about the right of the colonizer to manage indigenous peoples. It was, therefore, assumed that the Sioux and the Kazakhs lacked the civilization and the social and political structures to advance without the direct guidance of, and the policies implemented by, the Americans and the Russians. Both deployed different strategies, with comparable objectives and outcomes. The ultimate key to American and Russian policies was, however, education, which became the blunt instrument of internal colonization's social and cultural beachhead against the Sioux and the Kazakhs.

The United States, far more than Russia, embraced a paternalistic attitude with its policies and programs. The United States intruded more deeply and broadly, with its social and cultural agenda, to guide the Sioux from dark barbarism to the enlightened path of civilization. The Russian government generally inclined to exclude the Kazakhs from the assimilative cultural and social sphere. Instead, it devoted its energies to civil and administrative mechanisms to guide the Kazakhs from their nomadic habits toward civilization rather than adopt the more intrusive cultural, social, and economic tools employed by the Americans. The Russians expressed their policies as integration rather than assimilation; they generally used the word *sblizhenie*, or "drawing together." Conquest and internal colonization was brutal and successful. At the same time, the Americans and the Russians distanced themselves from those they subjugated. It was not a physical or geographic remoteness but rather a social, cultural, and political distance between colonizers and colonized.

NOTES

1. Amy Kaplan, "'Left Alone with America': The Absence of Empire in the Study of American Culture," in *Cultures of United States Imperialism*, ed. Amy Kaplan and Donald E. Pease (Durham, NC: Duke University Press, 1993), 17.

2. Taras Hunczak, ed., *Russian Imperialism from Ivan the Terrible to the Revolution* (New Brunswick, NJ: Rutgers University Press, 1974), ix.

3. James Belich, *Replenishing the Earth: The Settler Revolution and the Rise of the Anglo-World, 1783–1939* (Oxford: Oxford University Press, 2009), 131.

4. Ewa M. Thompson, *Imperial Knowledge: Russian Literature and Colonialism* (Westport, CT: Greenwood, 2000), 15–16.

5. John F. Richards, *The Unending Frontier: An Environmental History of the Early Modern World* (Berkeley: University of California Press, 2003), 6. See also Dietrich Gerhard, "The Frontier in Comparative View," *Comparative Studies in Society and History* 1, no. 3 (1959): 205–29; Marvin W. Mikesell, "Comparative Studies in Frontier History," *Annals of the Association of American Geographers* 50, no. 1 (March 1960): 62–74; Hans Kohn, "Some Reflections on Colonialism," *Review of Politics* 18, no. 3 (July 1956): 259–64. "Reduced to its barest outline," Kohn argued, "colonialism is foreign rule imposed upon a nation" (264).

6. As Edward G. Gray noted, in the United States, "[o]ur nation, we generally believe, was forged in a war against empire, our founding principles emerged out of an intellectual assault on empire, and our individualistic citizenry has little appetite or interest in foreign conquest. Obviously rhetoric and reality are very different and historians have long recognized that elements of American imperial conduct date from the very founding of the nation." "Visions of Another Empire: John Ledyard, an American Traveler Across the Russian Empire, 1787–1788," *Journal of the Early Republic* 24, no. 3 (Autumn 2004): 348.

7. Interestingly, many scholars identify Russia's imperial expansion beginning in 1552, when it captured Kazan from the Golden Horde, the last vestige of the great Mongol Empire. In a sense, the Russian Empire was born on the carcass of its imperial predecessor. See Andreas Kappeler, *The Russian Empire: A Multiethnic History*, trans. Alfred Clayton (New York: Pearson Education, 2001), 21–32.

8. Gerhard, "Comparative View," 205.

9. See Richard White, "The American West and American Empire," in *Manifest Destinies and Indigenous Peoples*, ed. David Maybury-Lewis, Theodore Macdonald, and Biorn Maybury-Lewis (Cambridge, MA: Harvard University Press, 2009): 203–24. According to White, "Scholars working on the West and Indian policy have written much about motivations for policies toward Indians and their domestic context, but relatively little on what this relentless erosion of Indian land teaches us about the United States in a larger international context" (204).

10. Alexis de Tocqueville, *Democracy in America*, trans. Henry Reeve (New York: Century Co., 1898), 1:559. A German traveler to Russia also observed a comparative future for the United States and Russia, noting that a "time will come when the greatest part of civilized Europe, being over-peopled, will be unable to maintain its industrious inhabitants without the importation of grain; two granaries will remain from which to draw supplies, North America and the country of the black soil in the centre and south of Russia." Baron von Haxthausen, *The Russian Empire, Its People, Institutions and Resources*, trans. Robert Farie (London: Chapman & Hall, 1856), 2:54.

11. Ann Laura Stoler and Carole McGranahan, "Introduction: Reconfiguring Imperial Terrains," in *Imperial Formations*, ed. Ann Laura Stoler, Carole McGranahan, and Peter C. Perdue (Santa Fe: School for Advanced Research Press, 2007), 11. The authors define imperial formations as "polities of dislocation, process of dispersion, appropriation, and displacement." This system creates "new subjects that must be relocated to be productive and exploitable, dispossessed to be modern, disciplined to be independent, converted to be human, stripped of old cultural bearings to be citizens, coerced to be free" (11).

12. In a recent comparative essay, Russian historian Victor N. Zakharov observed that Russia's "imperial expansion does not differ either in methods or aims from the policies of other

powers." Zakharov only briefly mentioned the United States in his examination of nineteenth-century empires, noting that "[o]ne may comment on the obvious analogy between the exploration of Siberia and other fringes of the Russian Empire on the one hand, and colonization of the 'Wild West' in North America, exploration of South Africa and Australia by white colonizers etc, on the other hand." "The Russian Empire: Main Features and Particularities," in *Europe and Its Empires*, ed. Mary N. Harris and Csaba Lévai (Pisa: Plus-Pisa University Press, 2008), 49, 52.

13. Sandra M. Gustafson, "Histories of Democracy and Empire," *American Quarterly* 59, no. 1 (March 2007): 112.

14. Gardner identified the two conflicting interpretations: "One side takes as its major premise that the 'empire' (usually put inside quotation marks) was created in the postwar era, a byproduct of the Cold War. Thus it took the special circumstances of a political and military vacuum in Europe, the collapse of the classic nineteenth-century colonial empires, and the perceived menace of Russian expansionism to make an American 'empire.' All, or mostly all, are outside forces.

The other side argues that the Cold War empire was itself a manifestation of long-term trends in American expansionism. To understand what happened after 1945, therefore, one has to pursue the story back to the thrust into Asia, and still earlier to the transcontinental wars that began with the creation of an independent empire in 1776. The emphasis here, of course, is on internal forces." "Lost Empires," *Diplomatic History* 13, no. 1 (1989): 2.

15. Jedidiah Morse, *The American Geography; or, A View of the Present Situation of the United States of America. . . .*, 2nd ed. (London: John Stockdale, 1792), 469.

16. Scholars produced significant comparative work that links American expansion and internal colonization with similar processes in the nineteenth century, including but certainly not limited to Walter Prescott Webb, *The Great Frontier* (Boston: Houghton Mifflin, 1952); Ian Tyrrell, "American Exceptionalism in an Age of International History," *American Historical Review* 96, no. 4 (October 1991): 1031–55; Richards, *Unending Frontier*; David Thelen, "Of Audiences, Borderlands, and Comparisons: Toward the Internationalization of American History," *Journal of American History* 79, no. 2 (September 1992): 432–62; George M. Frederickson, "From Exceptionalism to Variability: Recent Developments in Cross-National Comparative History," *Journal of American History* 82, no. 2 (September 1995): 587–604; Peter Kolchin, "Comparing American History," *Reviews in American History* 10, no. 4 (December 1982): 64–81; Peter Kolchin, "Some Recent Works on Slavery Outside the United States: An American Perspective," *Comparative Studies in Society and History* 28, no. 4 (October 1986): 767–77; Michael Adas, "From Settler Colony to Global Hegemon: Integrating the Exceptionalist Narrative of the American Experience into World History," *American Historical Review* 106, no. 5 (December 2001): 1692–720; Gerhard, "Comparative View"; Raymond Grew, "The Case for Comparing Histories," *American Historical Review* 85, no. 4 (October 1980): 763–78; Herbert Heaton, "Other Wests than Ours," *Journal of Economic History* 6, no. S1 (January 1946): 50–62.

17. Michael W. Doyle, *Empires* (Ithaca, NY: Cornell University Press, 1986), 36.

18. Helen Carr, *Inventing the American Primitive: Politics, Gender and the Representation of Native American Literary Traditions, 1789–1936* (New York: New York University Press, 1996), 44.

19. Sherry L. Smith, *Reimagining Indians: Native Americans through Anglo Eyes, 1880–1940* (Oxford: Oxford University Press, 2000), 4–5.

20. Henry Nash Smith, *Virgin Land: The American West as Symbol and Myth* (1954; Cambridge, MA: Harvard University Press, 1978), 179.

21. Willard Sunderland, "The 'Colonization Question': Visions of Colonization in Late Imperial Russia," *Jahrbücher für Geschichte Osteuropas* 48 (2000): 219.

22. Robert L. Mason, *The Lure of the Great Smokies* (Boston: Houghton Mifflin, 1927), 107.

23. Robert K. Thomas, "Colonialism: Classic and Internal," *New University Thought* 4, no. 4 (Winter 1966–1967): 38.

24. In 1887 the Cheyenne River agent highlighted the difficulties, writing that "the drawbacks to successful agriculture are so great as not to be overcome with any reasonable amount of labor . . . Since about 1872 efforts have been put forth by every agent to make agriculturalists of these Indians, but the soil and climate will not allow it." US Department of the Interior, Office of Indian Affairs, *Annual Report of the Commissioner of Indian Affairs to the Secretary of the Interior for the Year 1887* (Washington, DC: Government Printing Office, 1887), 17.

25. Jeffrey Ostler, *The Plains Sioux and U.S. Colonialism from Lewis and Clark to Wounded Knee* (Cambridge: Cambridge University Press, 2004), 8.

26. Chip Colwell-Chanthaphonh, "When History is Myth: Genocide and the Transmogrification of American Indians," *American Indian Culture and Research Journal* 29, no. 2 (2005): 114 (emphasis added).

27. See Frederick Jackson Turner, *The Frontier in American History* (New York: Henry Holt, 1920).

28. There is an essential point about this comparative study: throughout this work, reference will be made very generally, generically even, to the Americans or the Russians as well as the Sioux or the Kazakhs. The United States and Russia were that different, but what happened to the Sioux and the Kazakhs was not. Specialists might be justified to criticize this approach, but it is an unavoidable hazard in this comparison.

29. Foreign observers were some of the most critical, perhaps none more so than Lady Frances Parthenope Verney in her book *How the Peasant Owner Lives in Parts of France, Germany, Italy, Russia*. She described the Russian peasant unflatteringly, asserting, "The peasant class comprises five-sixths of the whole population—a stolid, ignorant, utterly unprogressive mass of human beings." Even more harshly, the "Russian peasant cares neither for liberty nor politics, neither for education, nor cleanliness, nor civilization or any kind." *How the Peasant Owner Lives in Parts of France, Germany, Italy, Russia* (London: Macmillan, 1888), 138–39.

30. One example of this depiction of Russia comes from an anonymous collection, translated from German into English, that described Russia under Nicholas I as a place where the "concentrated power of a military government, which can bring to bear, through the impulse of a single will, not impeded or deterred by the slightest opposition, all the resources of an immense territory, and an almost innumerable population, against one or more of its neighbours, for the accomplishment of any aggressive purpose—which can conceal its projects, and watch its opportunities of action—must be considered, in the common course of things, a fair object of jealousy to other states, and of dislike to most free nations." Captain Anthony C. Sterling, *Russia under Nicholas the First*, trans. from German (London: John Murray, 1841), vii.

31. Peter Kolchin, in his comparative work *Unfree Labor*, referred to relying "primarily on printed sources. *Printed* does not imply *secondary*" (emphasis in original). This work adheres to a similar principal. *Unfree Labor: American Slavery and Russian Serfdom* (Cambridge, MA: Harvard University Press, 1987), 377.

32. See, for example, Anthony Jenkinson, *Early Voyages and Travels to Russia and Persia by Anthony Jenkinson and Other Englishmen. With Some Account of the First Intercourse of the English with Russia and Central Asia by Way of the Caspian Sea*, ed. E. Delmar Morgan and C. H. Coote, vol. 1 (New York: Bert Franklin, 1886); John S. Maxwell, *The Czar, His*

Court and People: Including a Tour in Norway and Sweden (New York: Baker & Scribner, 1850); Charles Rudy, "Despotic Russia, Part II, Adventures in the Steppes of Russian Asia and the Frosty Caucasus," *Reformed Quarterly Review* (July 1880), 325–55; Haxthausen, *Russian Empire*; Robert G. Latham, *The Native Races of the Russian Empire* (London: Hippolyte Bailliere, 1854); Sterling, *Russia under Nicholas the First*; Esther Singleton, ed. and trans., *Russia, As Seen and Described by Famous Writers* (New York: Dodd, Mead, 1904). Not all travel accounts were critical or pejorative. Robert Lyall, a Scottish traveler, dedicated his book *The Character of the Russians, a Detailed History of Moscow* to Tsar Alexander I. *The Character of the Russians, and a Detailed History of Moscow* (London: T. Cadell, 1823). See also Astolphe Marquis de Custine, *The Empire of the Czar; or, Observations on the Social, Political, and Religious State and Prospects of Russia, made during a Journey through that Empire*, trans. from French, 3 vols. (London: Longman, Brown, Green, & Longmans, 1843); Madame de Staël, *Ten Years' Exile; or, Memoirs of That Interesting Period of the Life of the Baroness de Staël-Holstein, Written by Herself, during the Years 1810, 1811, 1812, and 1813, and Now First Published from the Original Manuscript, by Her Son*, trans. from French (London: Treuttel & Würtz, Treuttel, Jun. & Richter, 1821).

33. Léger Marie Philippe Laverne, *The Life of Field Marshal Souvarof; with Reflections upon the Principal Events, Political and Military, Connected with the History of Russia, during Part of the Eighteenth Century*, trans. from French (Baltimore: Edward J. Coale, 1814), iii.

34. Robert F. Berkhofer, Jr., *The White Man's Indian: Images of the American Indian from Columbus to the Present* (New York: Vintage Books, 1979), 93. See also Milla Fedorova, *Yankees in Petrograd, Bolsheviks in New York: America and Americans in Russian Literary Perception* (Dekalb: Northern Illinois University Press, 2013).

35. See Susan Layton, *Russian Literature and Empire: Conquest of the Caucasus from Pushkin to Tolstoy* (Cambridge: Cambridge University Press, 1994).

36. See Mary Louise Pratt, *Imperial Eyes: Travel Writing and Transculturation* (London: Routledge, 1992).

37. Steven Conn, *History's Shadow: Native Americans and Historical Consciousness in the Nineteenth Century* (Chicago: University of Chicago Press, 2004), 127.

38. A French version appeared in 1840. Alexis de Levchine, *Description des hordes et des Steppes des Kirghiz-Kazaks ou Kirghiz-Kaissaks* (Paris: Imprimerie Royale, 1840).

39. It is not the intention of this study to analyze the historiographical and philosophical debates of New West history, which remains best left to the scholars involved. Instead, see as a seminal example, Patricia Nelson Limerick, *Something in the Soil: Legacies and Reckonings in the New West* (New York: W. W. Norton, 2000).

40. Frederick Jackson Turner, "Problems in American History," in *The Significance of Sections in American History* (New York: Peter Smith, 1950), 19.

41. In both cases, the end of the Cold War reignited the American and Russian exceptionalism rhetoric and debate. See, for example, Deborah L. Madsen, *American Exceptionalism* (Jackson: University Press of Mississippi, 1998); Peter J. Spiro, "The New Sovereigntists: American Exceptionalism and Its False Prophets," *Foreign Affairs* 79, no. 6 (November 2000): 9–15; Donald E. Pease, *The New American Exceptionalism* (Minneapolis: University of Minnesota Press, 2009); Godfrey Hodgson, *The Myth of American Exceptionalism* (New Haven, CT: Yale University Press, 2009); Vladimir Shlapentokh, "How Russians Will See the Status of Their Country by the End of the Century," *Journal of Communist Studies and Transition Politics* 13, no. 3 (1997): 1–23; Richard Sakwa, "Perestroika and the Challenge of Democracy in Russia," *Demokratizatsiya: The Journal of Post-Soviet Democratization* 13, no. 2 (Spring 2005): 255–76; Sean Cannady and Paul Kubicek, "Nationalism and Legitimation for Authoritarianism: A

Comparison of Nicholas I and Vladimir Putin," *Journal of Eurasian Studies* 5, no. 1 (January 2014): 1–9; Howard Davis and Sergey Erofeev, "Reframing Society and Culture in Post-Soviet Russia," *Comparative Sociology* 10, no. 5 (2011): 710–34.

42. For an excellent analysis of the intellectual and historiographical gymnastics evident in Soviet historical interpretations, particularly the Russian-Kazakh case, see Lowell R. Tillett, *The Great Friendship: Soviet Historians on the Non-Russian Nationalities* (Chapel Hill: University of North Carolina Press, 1969).

43. P. N. Miliukov, *Russia and Its Crisis* (1905; New York: Collier, 1962), 21.

44. Donald W. Treadgold, "Russian Expansion in the Light of Turner's Study of the American Frontier," *Agricultural History* 26, no. 4 (October 1952): 147–52; Donald W. Treadgold, *The Great Siberian Migration: Government and Peasant in Resettlement from Emancipation to the First World War* (Princeton, NJ: Princeton University Press, 1957), 4; William Wyckoff and Gary Hausladen, "Settling the Russian Frontier: With Comparisons to North America," *Soviet Geography* 30 (March 1989): 179–88.

45. For a useful historiographical essay examining recent Kazakh scholarship, see Yuriy Anatolyevich Malikov, "Formation of a Borderland Culture: Myths and Realities of Cossack-Kazakh Relations in Northern Kazakhstan in the Eighteenth and Nineteenth Centuries" (PhD diss., University of California, Santa Barbara, 2006). See also Virginia Martin, *Law and Custom in the Steppe: The Kazakhs of the Middle Horde and Russian Colonialism in the Nineteenth Century* (Richmond, UK: Curzon, 2001); Steven Sabol, *Russian Colonization and the Genesis of Kazak National Consciousness* (New York: Palgrave Macmillan, 2003).

46. Richard White, *The Middle Ground: Indians, Empires, and Republics in the Great Lakes Region, 1650–1815* (Cambridge: Cambridge University Press, 1991).

47. But, in a global perspective, Michael Adas argued that frontiers "all were ultimately subdued and subordinated by the expansive settler societies that sustained moving frontiers that threatened to deprive them of their lands and destroy their ways of life. This shared outcome not only provides intriguing possibilities for comparative research on indigenous warfare and frontier conflict, it suggests important transregional themes in the ethno-cultural history of frontiers as well as larger global processes that were exemplified by recurring outcomes in each, quite distinctive, frontier locale." "Settler Colony to Global Hegemon," 1715.

48. Margaret Ziolkowski, *Alien Visions: The Chechens and the Navajos in Russian and American Literature* (Newark: University of Delaware Press, 2005); Kolchin, *Unfree Labor*; Kate Brown, "Gridded Lives: Why Kazakhstan and Montana Are Nearly the Same Place," *American Historical Review* 106, no. 1 (February 2001): 17–48; Mark Bassin, "Turner, Solov'ev, and the 'Frontier Hypothesis': The Nationalist Significance of Open Spaces," *Journal of Modern History* 65, no. 3 (September 1993): 473–511; Sonja Luehrmann, *Alutiiq Villages under Russian and U.S. Rule* (Fairbanks: University of Alaska Press, 2008); Anne Lounsbery, *Thin Culture, High Art: Gogol, Hawthorne, and Authorship in Nineteenth-Century Russia and America* (Cambridge, MA: Harvard University Press, 2007); Dorothy Zeisler-Vralsted, *Rivers, Memory, and Nation-Building: A History of the Volga and Mississippi Rivers* (New York: Berghahn, 2015); Irena Grudzinska Gross, *The Scar of Revolution: Custine, Tocqueville, and the Romantic Imagination* (Berkeley: University of California Press, 1991). Other scholars examined the United States and Canada, which created useful structural models for successful comparative history, including Andrew R. Graybill, *Policing the Great Plains: Rangers, Mounties, and the North American Frontier, 1875–1910* (Lincoln: University of Nebraska Press, 2007); Jill St. Germain, *Broken Treaties: United States and Canadian Relations with the Lakotas and the Plains Cree, 1868–1885* (Lincoln: University of Nebraska Press, 2009); and Beth LaDow, *The Medicine Line: Life and Death on a North*

American Borderland (New York: Routledge, 2002). A final study that utilized the comparative method was James O. Gump, "The Subjugation of the Zulus and Sioux: A Comparative Study," *Western Historical Quarterly* 19, no. 1 (January 1988): 21–36. See also James O. Gump, *The Dust Rose Like Smoke: The Subjugation of the Zulu and the Sioux* (Lincoln: University of Nebraska Press, 1994).

49. Fredrickson, "From Exceptionalism to Variability," 587.

50. Adas, "Settler Colony to Global Hegemon," 1703.

51. Marc Léopold Benjamin Bloch, *Land and Work in Mediaeval Europe: Selected Papers* (Berkeley: University of California Press, 1967), 46.

52. See, for example, Alette Olin Hill and Boyd H. Hill, Jr., "Marc Bloch and Comparative History," *American Historical Review* 85, no. 4 (October 1980): 829–30; David Englander, ed., *Britain and America: Studies in Comparative History, 1760–1970* (New Haven CT: Yale University Press, 1997), xi; Martyn Lyons, *The Writing Culture of Ordinary People in Europe, c. 1860–1920* (Cambridge: Cambridge University Press, 2012), 10; Sam I. Gellens, "The Search for Knowledge in Medieval Muslim Societies: A Comparative Approach," in *Muslim Travellers: Pilgrimage, Migration, and the Religious Imagination*, ed. Dale F. Eickelman and James Piscatori (Berkeley: University of California Press, 1990), 50; Timothy Roberts and Emrah Şahin, "Construction of National Identities in Early Republics: A Comparison of the American and Turkish Cases," *Journal of the Historical Society* 10, no. 4 (December 2010): 507.

53. Carol L. Higham, "Introduction to Comparing the Two Wests," in *One West, Two Myths: A Comparative Reader*, ed. Carol L. Higham and Robert Thacker (Alberta: University of Calgary Press, 2004), ix–x.

54. George M. Fredrickson, "Comparative History," in *The Past Before Us: Contemporary Historical Writing in the United States*, ed. Michael Kammen (Ithaca, NY: Cornell University Press, 1980), 458. Put another way, "Only the comparative way of looking at the problem can reveal the underlying reasons for the phenomenon." A. A. Van den Braembussche, "Historical Explanation and Comparative Method: Towards a Theory of the History of Society," *History and Theory* 28, no. 1 (February 1989): 11.

55. A. Dirk Moses, "Empire, Colony, Genocide: Keywords and the Philosophy of History," in *Empire, Colony, Genocide: Conquest, Occupation, and Subaltern Resistance in World History*, ed. A. Dirk Moses (New York: Berghahn, 2010), 22.

56. Jonathan Swift, *Gulliver's Travels into Several Remote Nations of the World* (London: Temple Press, 1939), 288–89.

57. J. A. Hobson, *Imperialism: A Study* (London: James Nisbet, 1902), 4.

58. Ibid., 24.

59. Scott Nearing, *The American Empire* (New York: Rand School of Social Science, 1921), 23.

60. Vladimir I. Lenin, "The Development of Capitalism in Russia," in *Collected Works* (Moscow: Progress Publishers, 1960), 3:593–94.

61. Brady Harrison, "The Young Americans: Emerson, Walker, and the Early Literature of American Empire," *American Studies* 40, no. 3 (Fall 1999): 75–76.

62. Thomas A. Bailey, "America's Emergence as a World Power: The Myth and the Verity," *Pacific Historical Review* 30, no. 1 (February 1961): 9, 11.

63. See, for example, Uday Singh Mehta, *Liberalism and Empire: A Study in Nineteenth-Century British Liberal Thought* (Chicago: University of Chicago Press, 1999); David Cannadine, *Ornamentalism: How the British Saw Their Empire* (Oxford: Oxford University Press, 2001); Catherine Hall, *Civilising Subjects: Metropole and Colony in the English Imagination, 1830–1867* (Chicago: University of Chicago Press, 2002).

64. See chapter 2 in Kappeler, *Russian Empire*.

65. In fact, as historian Alfred J. Rieber alluded to in a rather short essay, during the second half of the nineteenth century and the growth of the popular press in Russia, the "proliferation of public organizations and institutions, the organization of scientific exhibitions and art exhibits created a new setting for the spread of popular culture. With them came fresh opportunities to draw the public into supporting imperialism, the one form of mass participation in politics acceptable to the autocracy, and to lionize the imperialist." Moreover, Rieber continued, "Russians systematically and self-consciously pursued and legitimized imperial aims in direct imitation of the West." "Russian Imperialism: Popular, Emblematic, Ambiguous," *Russian Review* 53, no. 3 (July 1994): 332–33.

66. John Stone, "Introduction: Internal Colonialism in Comparative Perspective," *Ethnic and Racial Studies* 2, no. 3 (July 1979): 255. This issue of *Ethnic and Racial Studies* is devoted to comparative perspectives of internal colonialism, although only one focuses on the United States (Alaska).

67. George C. Guins, "Russia and the United States in the World Economy," *American Journal of Economics and Sociology* 5, no. 2 (January 1946): 143–44.

68. See, for example, Stokely Carmichael and Charles V. Hamilton, *Black Power: The Politics of Liberation in America* (New York: Vintage, 1967); Robert Blauner, "Internal Colonialism and Ghetto Revolt," *Social Problems* 16, no. 4 (Spring 1969): 393–408; Elia T. Zureik, *The Palestinians in Israel: A Study in Internal Colonialism* (London: Routledge, 1979). For a more recent examination, see John R. Chávez, "Aliens in Their Native Lands: The Persistence of Internal Colonial Theory," *Journal of World History* 22, no. 4 (December 2011): 785–809.

69. Carol Chiago Lujan and Gordon Adams, "U.S. Colonization of Indian Justice Systems: A Brief History," *Wicazo Sa Review* 19, no. 2 (Fall 2004): 10.

70. Moses, "Empire, Colony, Genocide," 23.

71. Steven Wyn Williams writes that "[a]lthough the notions of colonialism and colonization found their most explicit development during the period of expansionist policies and overseas imperialism emanating from Western Europe in the fifteenth and sixteenth centuries and onwards, a form of colonialism (that is, internal colonialism) *within* certain countries (for example, Great Britain), seen usually as a stage of national integration, was also taking place." "Internal Colonialism, Core-Periphery Contrasts and Devolution: An Integrative Comment," *Area* 9, no. 4 (1977): 273. See also Michael Hechter, *Internal Colonialism: The Celtic Fringe in British National Development, 1536–1966* (Berkeley: University of California Press, 1975).

72. Peter Calvert, "Internal Colonisation, Development and Environment," *Third World Quarterly* 22, no. 1 (February 2001), 53. As Michael Adas argued, "Much of what nineteenth-century Americans thought, said, and wrote about the Indians of the American frontiers was shared, often with remarkably little variation, with the settler societies of the other neo-Europes, which were just as deeply committed to subduing their own indigenous peoples. Although the phrasing might differ, the 'banjo bards' of frontier expansion in all of these areas justified settler occupation and the consequent dispossession of pre-contact peoples with strikingly similar appeals to the need to 'open up' and render productive rich lands and critical resources that had long gone to waste." "Settler Colony to Global Hegemon," 1716.

73. Robert J. Hind, "The Internal Colonial Concept," *Comparative Studies in Society and History* 26, no. 3 (July 1984): 565.

74. Belich, *Replenishing the Earth*, 21.

75. See Partha Chatterjee, *The Nation and Its Fragments. Colonial and Postcolonial Histories* (Princeton, NJ: Princeton University Press, 1993).

76. Anthony Pagden, *Lords of All the World: Ideologies of Empire in Spain, Britain and France, c. 1500–c. 1800* (New Haven, CT: Yale University Press, 1995), 20.

77. Philip Pomper, "The History and Theory of Empires," *History and Theory* 44, no. 4 (December 2005), 24.

78. Barbara Bush, *Imperialism and Postcolonialism* (Harlow, UK: Pearson Longman, 2006), 22–23.

79. Livingston quoted in Thomas Pakenham, *The Scramble for Africa: The White Man's Conquest of the Dark Continent from 1876 to 1912* (New York: Random House, 1991), xxii.

80. John Wunder, *"Retained by the People": A History of American Indians and the Bill of Rights* (Oxford: Oxford University Press, 1994), 17. See esp. chap. 2, "The Old and New Colonialisms."

81. Ibid.

82. Ibid.

1

The Sioux and the Kazakhs

Throughout the nineteenth century, as expansion and colonization accelerated, Americans and Russians often resorted to stereotypes and perceptions of the Sioux and the Kazakhs to justify their objectives in the plains and steppe. They regarded nomadism as backward, but they were not the first people to confront intractable, hostile, barbaric nomads. The United States and Russia embraced an epistemological understanding of nomads built on both their own encounters and those they read about in the histories of the Greeks, Romans, and Chinese, and they applied that knowledge to their understanding of the Sioux and the Kazakhs, which led them to overgeneralize and underestimate the strength of the indigenous populations' social, cultural, political, and economic structures. Moreover, Europeans—and, subsequently, Americans—dealt with Indians from the moment of first contact and developed relatively inflexible ideas and opinions about them over the course of three centuries. The Europeans and Russians knew Turks; they knew Muslims; they conquered other nomadic peoples (and were conquered by them); and they assembled very strong opinions and ideas about what should be done with them. The Americans and Russians adopted policies designed to supervise peoples that they deemed capable of change only when administered by force and coercion because the Sioux and the Kazakhs possessed inferior cultures, societies, and religions and failed to take full advantage of abundant land and possibilities offered by American and Russian civilization. The Americans and Russians failed to understand or appreciate that Sioux

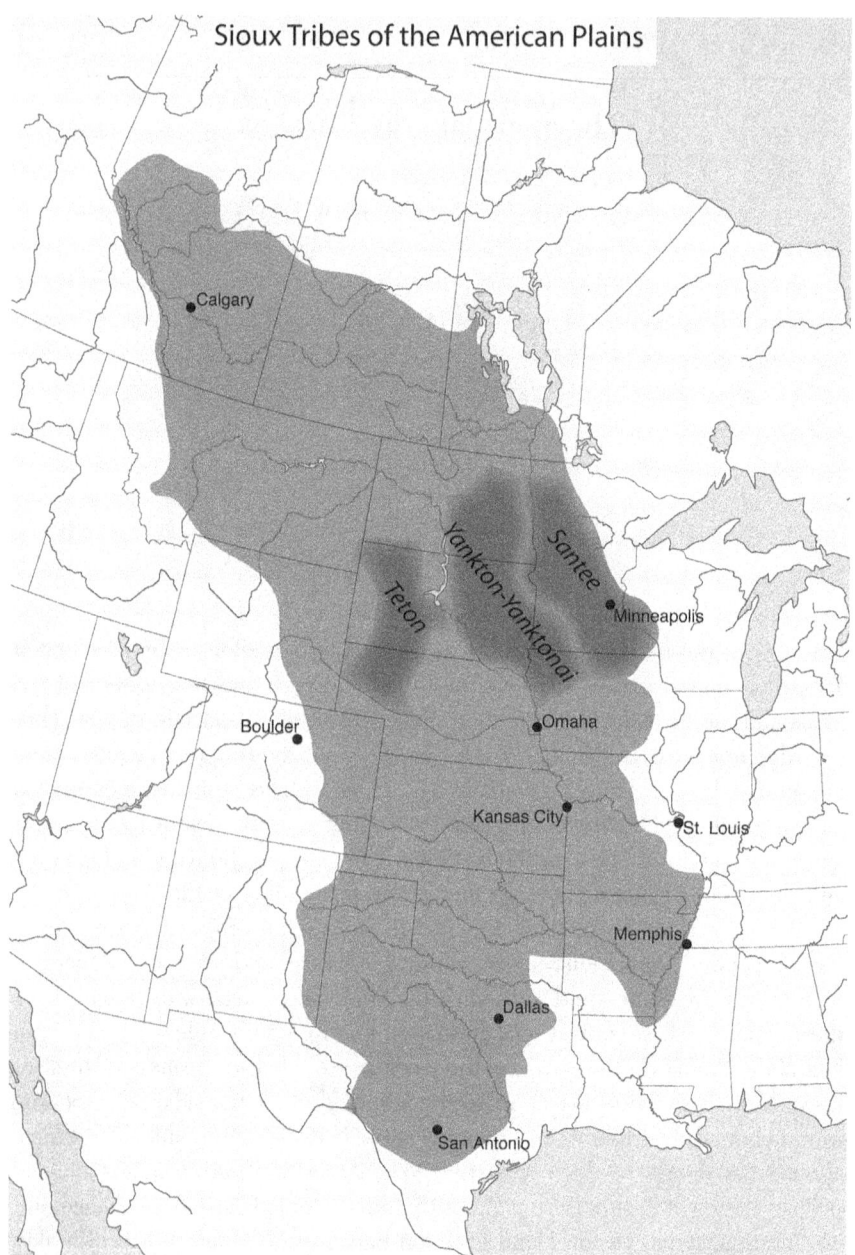

MAP 1.1. Sioux tribes of the American plains (courtesy of Department of Geography & Earth Sciences, UNC Charlotte).

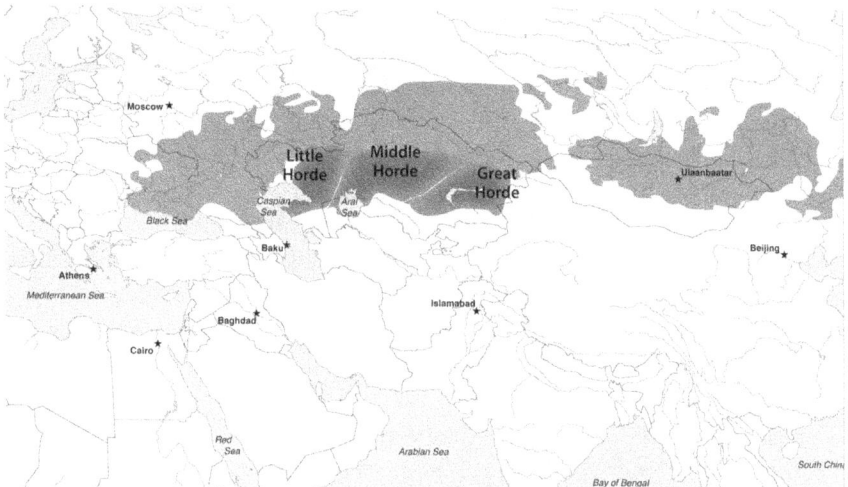

MAP 1.2 Kazakhs of the steppe (courtesy of Department of Geography & Earth Sciences, UNC Charlotte).

and Kazakh society, culture, and economy were in constant flux, and that the Sioux and the Kazakhs adopted and adapted to suit their needs and their sensibilities, however alien that might seem to the colonizers.

In order to understand American and Russian perceptions and their partial justifications for conquest, it is also necessary to situate the Sioux and the Kazakhs in their world—in their social, cultural, and economic milieu—which requires a brief overview. There is no shortage of information or scholarship to draw on to examine and understand Sioux and Kazakh nomadic cultures, societies, political or economic structures, customs, myths, religion, and even games and amusements. Unfortunately, generalizations are unavoidable in a comparative study, particularly when treating subjects as complex as "societies" and "cultures" or "customs" and "traditions."

One facet of the stereotypical image held by the Americans and the Russians was that the nomadic lifeways of Sioux and Kazakh societies made them and their economies clearly backward. But in a sense, neither the Sioux nor the Kazakhs were fully nomads; agriculture, hunting and gathering, and the trappings of sedentary life were not completely alien to them. The difference between nomadic or seminomadic peoples was that they did not live in fixed abodes or in a fixed place. Sioux and Kazakh economies were generally dependent upon mobility. The Sioux lived by the hunt; the Kazakhs raised large herds of sheep, goats, camels, and horses. The Sioux were migratory hunters and the Kazakhs were pastoral nomads.

Americans and Russians based their attitudes on superficial images and representations and somewhat subjective oversimplifications; they did not make a significant leap into some unknown universe that lacked awareness or experience with nomads. The image of nomadic culture and society was that they were static cultures and societies. American and Russian perceptions were grounded in the belief that nomads lived an ancient lifestyle. In the minds of Americans and Russians, nomadic culture and society were homogenized and easily deciphered because of universal conceptions about nomads and traits and characteristics that they believed were common to all equestrian, nomadic, warrior societies. Yet twentieth-century scholars (chiefly historians and anthropologists) demonstrated—in fact, marveled at—the global diversity of nomadic societies and cultures.

For centuries, the nomads' sedentary neighbors observed and commented upon nomadism and nomadic peoples—especially the Eurasian nomads vilified in Chinese literature. The Greeks wrote about the Scythians inhabiting the steppe lands of southern Russia. With their nomadic mode of life and seemingly endless wanderings, the Chinese and Greeks provided the stereotypical representations of nomadic peoples living beyond the boundaries of civilization whose pastimes consist of "conquest and rapine in the fat lands and rich cities of the plain." The life of the Eurasian nomad was "riding a horse[,] living in a tent[, and being] menaced by perennial uncertainty of supplies of grass and water. His temptation to maraud was strong and oft-repeated. The mobile existence of the grassland man made it easy for him to raid and pillage."[1]

Writers in sedentary societies depicted nomads as uncivilized, but they also generally perceived nomads to be very traditional, almost timeless societies that abhorred change and lacked a future: "nomads have no history; they only have geography."[2] Agrarian, non-nomadic societies relegated nomads to a peripheral social, cultural, and political status as barbarians—a "raw" people that lacked civilization and were pushed aside in "spatial terms, and to antiquity in temporal terms."[3] Geography and epoch, not society or culture, were all that seemed to distinguish between Scythians, Huns, Vandals, and other nomads such as Bedouins, Berbers, Sioux, or Kazakhs.[4]

The quintessential nomadic tribes—certainly in popular imagination—were Chingis (Genghis) Khan and his Mongol hordes thundering out of the Eurasian steppe to terrorize the civilized world with plunder and rapine. Uttering the name of the Mongols was almost a metaphor for savagery, barbarism, wanton cruelty, death, and destruction. By the end of the thirteenth century, Europeans and Russians gradually transformed the Mongol appellation into Tatars (or Tartars), convinced that classical Tartarus was their place of origin. In time, as

Devin DeWeese noted, in European consciousness, Mongols, and thus Tartars, became demonic nomads from hell sent to purify European Christendom for its many sins.[5] In a rhetorical sense, one might scratch a nomad to find a Mongol but dig deeper to find a Tartar.[6]

The simple reference to *Tartar* evoked stereotypical images, no explanation needed.[7] When Europeans encountered Indians, they invariably compared them—positively or negatively—to the ancient world cultures that they understood, such as Scythians and Tartars or the peoples of Atlantis or biblical Hebrews.[8] Early explorers and settlers in the New World, in their effort to explain the origins of Indians, noted linguistic similarities. John Joselyn, in 1673, wrote that the "Mohawks speech is a dialect of the Tartars." In 1753 Spaniard Father Venegas thought Indians resembled "Moghul Tartars."[9] Similarly, the idea of the "red" Indian evoked a specific image based on race conceptions in the nineteenth century.[10] John Foster Fraser simply described the Kazakhs as the "Red Indians of the West Siberian steppes," an image that needed no explanation or elaboration to his audience.[11] Americans employed both *Tartar* and *red* to describe Indians, such as referring to "northern plains Indians as 'the American Tartars'" or the "ruthless red Tartars of the desert."[12] This simplistic type of linguistic reference point—equating *Tartar* to *nomad*—worked to give the nineteenth-century reader an immediate sense of understanding and imagery.

Interestingly, scholars provide as many portraits of nomadic societies as they do definitions of what exactly constituted a nomadic people. Elizabeth E. Bacon, analyzing nomads in central and southwestern Asia, argued that "true" nomads are people that "dwell the year round in portable dwellings and who practice no agriculture."[13] Paul Bohannan noted that nomadism is "movement in response to the demands of animals for pasture and water."[14] Raphael Patai defined nomads as the "mode of existence of peoples who derive their livelihood from tending herds of one or more species of domesticated quadrupeds and who wander to find grazing for their cattle."[15] Nomadism, as identified by these scholars, required a symbiotic relationship between man and domesticated animals. It required movement—either seasonally or annually—and no fixed abode. But Europeans and Russians easily applied these brief definitions of nomads not just to the peoples of the Middle East, central Asia, or Africa but to the Sioux, Cheyenne, Crow, or other plains' nomads of the nineteenth century. The one major difference, of course, was between pastoral nomadism (livestock herders) and the equestrian buffalo hunters of the northern plains.

Douglas L. Johnson recognized four nomadic types based upon ecological considerations: full nomads living in steppe regions with definite changes in habitation; seminomads who bordered cultivated regions and engaged in sporadic agriculture; desert nomads who migrated between fixed water sources; and mountain nomads who used vertical, seasonal variation to pasture their herds.[16] The Sioux and the Kazakhs were a mix of the first two types. The nomadic society and economy was relatively self-sufficient; it produced almost all of the necessities to survive in the harsh plains or steppe environment, such as food, clothing, fuel, and shelter. Sioux and Kazakh nomadism provided access to resources possibly depleted in other regions, such as wood, water, and salt.

This should not suggest that nomads were completely self-sufficient or purely independent. Nomads both raided sedentary communities and traded with them, but that should not make nomads seem more violent or prone to war. History abounds with sedentary people who found time to set aside their hoe and plow to raid other settled people or go to war, and generally engage in plunder and rapine. Scholars long recognized that a symbiotic relationship existed between nomadic and sedentary peoples, and that nomads eagerly traded, attended markets, and coexisted with sedentary communities because, as Owen Lattimore noted, "it is the poor nomad who is the pure nomad."[17] Trade benefited both the nomad and the sedentary. To relieve the burden of transporting accumulated goods, nomads traded or jettisoned excess material not consumed or used, such as hides, wool, and livestock. Both the Sioux and the Kazakhs participated in trading networks; they understood that they existed within a larger, complex interacting system of exchange.[18]

The Sioux and the Kazakhs are not exact replicas—not mirror images—of nomadic peoples found in other places or other times, such as in Asia, the Middle East, or Africa. Notions about nomadism, however, were widespread in the nineteenth century and often evoked rather negative images of a people that wandered the land aimlessly and without meaning or objective. They were backward, absent a significant history, and stuck in an economic model long abandoned by civilized people. They were backward because they were not sedentary and therefore, not consistent agriculturalists.

What is clear now to scholars is that Sioux and Kazakh societies were not stagnant; they were always in transition, adopting new technologies and strategies to cope with internal and external pressures to their way of life. Many early observers considered the Sioux and the Kazakhs to be extraordinarily fine horsemen and skilled archers, but that did not stop them from adopting guns or other technology to suit their needs. The Sioux and the Kazakhs were willing traders, often enthusiastically embracing new materials and technologies. But Sioux and Kazakh nomadism differed from each other, although they shared some common elements; their social, economic, and political structures were not identical simply because they were nomads.

In order to understand the perceptions held by Americans and Russians in the nineteenth century, it is necessary to examine the sociopolitical and economic structures of the Sioux and the Kazakhs. American popular consciousness firmly affixed the image of the Sioux as the "Buffalo Nation," whether hunting throughout the plains or killing Custer. That evocative, enduring image of the mid-nineteenth-century Sioux conjured skilled horsemen and powerful warriors ready to plunder and kill white migrants along the western trails. If the Mongols— and, by later extension, the Kazakhs—created the quintessential image of the marauding Eurasian nomadic horseman thundering out of the vast and barren steppe to plunder and destroy peaceful agrarian peoples, it was an image that the Russians and other visitors to the steppe attached to the Kazakhs. But these powerful images reflected only the negative stereotypes. The reality was that the Sioux and the Kazakhs were complex societies not easily categorized; but as Brian Spooner simply noted, there were no absolute "features of culture or social organization" that are customary to all nomads or that are found exclusively among any of them.[19] Nomadic societies are as diverse as sedentary ones, perhaps even more so.

In the twentieth century, scholars also speculated about why a people might embrace nomadism, why they might abandon a semi-settled way of life and agriculture to engage in the persistent movement associated with a nomadic life, as the Sioux did in the mid-eighteenth century. Certainly, for many people in the nineteenth century, it seemed contrary to normal human progress. Most scholars agree that the adoption of equestrian hunting is what compelled the Sioux to begin their migrations, but the etiological debate about pastoral nomadism remains unresolved and likely will never be completely understood.[20] In the simplest terms, Kazakhs inherited some 2,500 years of Eurasian pastoral, equestrian nomadism; the Sioux were, in comparison, relative newcomers to equestrian nomadism.

SIOUX AND KAZAKH

The Sioux were hunting nomads whose social, economic, political, and cultural structures were in the process of changing in the eighteenth century as various bands moved west from the Minnesota and Wisconsin lakes and woodlands into the northern plains. Their language is a part of the Siouan family, which comprises fourteen "mutually unintelligible languages."[21] For this study, it is important to consider only part of that larger family order, distinguished by three dialects but two groupings, Dakota and Lakota. The Santee and Yankton/Yanktonai called themselves *Dakota* and the Teton used the variant *Lakota*. The name "Sioux," a French and English name for the Lakota and Dakota, is not the self-designation but the transliteration of an Ojibwa (Chippewa) word—*natow-essiwak*—which the French shortened to *Sioux*. Scholars still debate its meaning, most often translated as "snake" or "enemy."[22] What was more important was what they called themselves, which was Dakota or Lakota, meaning "leagued" or "allied," according to nineteenth-century American missionary Stephen R. Riggs, but perhaps intended to mean someone in union or who shared the same language, maybe a friend.[23]

Scholars are uncertain about the origins of the Sioux, based on somewhat inconclusive archaeological data, but Guy Gibbon suggests that their ancestors can be located in the northern woodland regions of Minnesota and Wisconsin around AD 800. There is no doubt that the Sioux were there by the mid-seventeenth century, so it is fair to assume that they had occupied the region for some time before the first encounter with French Jesuits in 1659 or 1660. Pierre-Esprit Radisson learned about a people that he transcribed as "Nadoueceronon," who his hosts claimed were "very strong, with whome they weare in warres with, and another wandering nation, living only upon what they could come by."[24] At the time of Radisson's visit, however, the Sioux were clearly not the stereotypical people Americans think of whenever a popular image is conjured. The Sioux society, economy, and way of life were changing, but scholars identify elements that remain vitally important to understand American-Sioux relations and the development of the powerful "Sioux Nation" of the northern plains. The Sioux embraced their own magnificent origin stories that supplied the necessary elements for Sioux society, culture, and traditions.[25]

On the other hand, the pastoral, nomadic Kazakhs remained deeply connected to centuries of central Asian nomadic social, economic, and cultural structures and heritage. Their origins are still somewhat uncertain, but most sources agree that the name "Kazakh" was in use by the sixteenth century.[26] Writing in the 1930s, Kazakh historian Sandzhar D. Asfendiarov concluded that the Kazakhs appeared as a distinct group in the steppe by the late fifteenth or early sixteenth centuries, after the Nogai-Uzbek-Kazak confederation collapsed.[27] Alfred E. Hudson suggested it designated nomadic groups in the steppe who independently established themselves or "transferred their allegiance from one to another of the numerous khans then reigning in the steppe."[28] French historian René Grousset agreed with Asfendiarov and Hudson. He referred to the Kazakhs at this time as "dissident Uzbeks."[29]

The Kazakhs emerged, by most accounts, when the "dissident" Uzbeks-Kazakhs migrated north of the Syr Darya (*Darya* means "river"; the Amu and Syr are the Oxus and Jaxartes Rivers of ancient times) and followed two brothers named Kirei and Zhanibek (who identified themselves as the "rulers" of the

Kazakhs) to become the nomadic pastoralists.[30] Others attached themselves to the Kazakhs in the steppe regions and, in time, the ethnonym "Kazakh" became the dominant identity for all of these peoples.[31] Lawrence Krader described this process of early identity formation that went from being a sort of social estate—dissidents from a ruling class—to a rudimentary political confederation inhabiting the steppe, to a people who self-identified as "Kazakh."[32]

In both the Sioux and the Kazakh case, each migrated from one place of origin—the woodlands of Wisconsin and Minnesota for the Sioux and Turkestan for the Kazakhs—into the northern plains or the Eurasian steppe to become the dominant power, displacing others or defending the newly won region against the incursions of others. They were societies in transition that Americans and Russians failed to understand because they perceived them as ancient, even static. During those migrations, however, the identities of the Sioux and the Kazakhs emerged along with the social structures that later observers and scholars identified.

In order to understand the attitudes, perceptions, typologies, and imagery that permeated nineteenth-century American and Russian thinking about the Sioux and the Kazakhs, it is necessary to juxtapose those stereotypes and clichés against what scholars, then and later, identified as the social, political, cultural, and economic structures between the two nomadic peoples. This is not an exhaustive analysis but rather is designed to contextualize and identify some features and characteristics that shaped the Sioux and Kazakh world, at least to the extent possible to reconstruct it for a comparative analysis.

OCETI SAKOWIN AND *USH ZHUZ*

Kinship relations, consanguineal units, and adoption influenced and determined Sioux social structures. The Sioux also called themselves the *Oceti Sakowin*, the "Seven Council Fires," which was a mechanism to unite through language, kinship, and culture. Scholars doubt that any sort of institution or confederacy based on the Oceti Sakowin materially existed or ever met in council or came together as the name suggests.[33] Seventeenth- and eighteenth-century visitors to various Sioux camps do not mention it, but Raymond J. DeMallie believes that the first description of it was by William Keating in 1825.[34] Nonetheless, that concept or bond held the Sioux together to reaffirm the shared language, history, culture, and traditions.

Among the Sioux, the Seven Council Fires provided that covenant to explain their commonalities, shared language and customs, history, and traditions that, according to James R. Walker, maintained peaceful relations and prevented raids and reprisals against one another.[35] Walker and other scholars were unable to find any legend or historical episode to explain the origins of the seven divisions.[36] In the eighteenth and nineteenth centuries, visitors to Sioux camps and other observers often divided the Sioux into three branches: Santee, Yankton/Yanktonai, and Teton—with the former often referred to as the eastern branch and the Teton as the western branch. Moreover, the Santee and Yankton/Yanktonai referred to themselves as Dakota and the Teton called themselves Lakota. After the Sioux western migrations began, sometime in the early to mid-eighteenth century, the Santee remained in Minnesota; the Yankton/Yanktonai occupied much of the Dakotas and northern Nebraska and Iowa; and the Teton situated in the western parts of the Dakotas, northern Nebraska, and eastern Montana and Wyoming. The Teton were the largest in population and ranged over the greater expanse of territory. The Teton also produced some of the staunchest resistance to American expansion in the nineteenth century.

The Sioux, however, existed within the *oyate* subdivision, often translated as "people," but which also corresponds somewhat to tribe or nation. The names attached to the council fires and the various bands represented the links to one's Sioux-ness—to the people's history—and situated a person in the present. These oyate are grouped to make up the Santee division: Mdewakantonwan (Spirit Lake Village), Wahpekute (Shooters Among the Leaves), Sisitonwan or Sisseton (Fish Scale Village), and Wahpetonwan or Wahpeton (Dwellers Among the Leaves). Another name for the Yankton (End Village) and Yanktonai (Little End Village) was the Middle, or Wiciyela, division; and the Teton, or Titonwan (Dwellers on the Plains), were the western division.[37] Among the Teton, there were seven sub-bands—Oglala, Brulé, Sans Arc, Hunkpapa, Miniconjou, Two Kettle, and Blackfeet.[38] According to Anthony R. McGinnis, the Oglala and Brulé were larger in population, but all were noted for their "warlike behavior" and often camped together and migrated among the Moreau, Grand, Cannonball, and Heart Rivers.[39] Geographer Joseph N. Nicollet gathered some valuable information about the various branches in 1838–1839, although he does not explain any connection to the Seven Council Fires or why the divisions occurred.[40] There was frequent contact and interaction among the various Sioux bands—linked as they were by shared language, culture, traditions, history, and intermarriage—but there is little evidence to suggest that large multiband councils or gatherings occurred before the 1850s or that the Sioux ever amalgamated into something that might resemble a unified nation before internal colonization.[41]

The division into branches existed among the Kazakhs as well: the *Ush Zhuz* or "Three Hordes." There is little debate among scholars that shortly after Kerei and

Zhanibek separated from the Uzbek confederation further fission occurred, so that by the late-sixteenth century, the Kazakhs divided into the Ush Zhuz. Each horde consisted of various clans. For the kinship relationship to operate in both social and political contexts, Kazakhs did not trace descent back to Kerai and Zhanibek but instead to the mythical *Alash* or *Alash Khan*. Scholars attempted to identify Alash to no avail.[42] More important was that Kazakhs believed it and used it to reinforce kinship, which was a link or covenant to explain what united Kazakhs as a people. Kazakhs endowed social and political configurations with a patrilineal scheme underscored by belief in a common ancestry to create consanguineal nomadic units. Kinship idioms and genealogies supplied the necessary and common principles to affirm perceptions of shared cultural heritage, confirm common territory, and establish the mutual responsibilities and rights of each member. Kazakhs, according to Krader, applied the principle of patrilineal descent that possessed rather limited political authority and was quite fluid and adaptable.[43]

The horde located geographically the furthest from the Russian line of advance was the *Uly Zhuz*, or "Great Horde." It was situated in the southeastern part of the Kazakh Steppe, close to the Turkestan khanates of Bukhara and Kokand, bordering China to the east, and in the Semirechie (Seven Rivers, in Kazakh *Zheti Su*) region, north of the Tien Shan Mountains (home of the Kirghiz nomads) and west along the north banks of the Syr Darya. To the north and west of the Great Horde was the *Orta Zhuz*, or "Middle Horde," which was the largest horde in population and considered by many to be the most powerful economically and militarily. It certainly had some of the most prominent leaders in the eighteenth and nineteenth centuries and resisted Russian expansion and colonization with a tenacity unrivaled by the other two hordes. Its territory contained some of the best pasturage and waterways in the steppe. The last horde, *Kishi Zhuz*, or "Little Horde," was second to the Middle Horde in population and geography, but it was also the closest to Russia, located in the northwest steppe above the Aral and Caspian Seas. The territory of the Little Horde was the first annexed by the Russian Empire.

Among the Kazakhs, each of the three hordes had clans, but these divisions were extremely fluid. Each clan within the horde had what Nurbulat Masanov called "traditional genealogies," from the Kazakh word *shezhere* (genealogy), used to group peoples; and each clan was apparently not rigidly bound to its own genealogy, history, or traditions. In the Great Horde, there were eleven shezhere; in the Middle Horde seven; and in the Little Horde, there were three large "unions" that formed differently than in the Middle or Great Hordes. The *Alimuly* union had six groups, the *Baiuly* union had fourteen, and the *Zhetyru* union had seven.⁴⁴ Allegiance could and often did change. Krader cited an example that illustrates this fission: when some Kazakhs of the *Kangly*, *Chaichkly*, and *Kereit* clans separated from the Great Horde and affiliated with the *Kongrad* clan of the Middle Horde. In order to assert this new genealogical right, they adopted the lineage necessary to claim membership.⁴⁵ According to Alikhan Bokeikhanov, Kazakhs rarely asserted the largest form of identity (i.e., Kazakh) unless asked by a stranger; in that case, they might also reply that they are the "children of Alash" or the "children of the three hordes." When two Kazakhs met, however, they identified the clan rather than zhuz, which they employed as expressions of their mutual relatedness and potential kinship.⁴⁶

As with the Sioux, there is little evidence to show that the Kazakhs ever united to form a single unit, although various leaders attempted to unite all Kazakhs under a single khan. Rudi Paul Lindner argued that the distance and movement between nomadic units rendered a conical clan impossible and unable to maintain rigid, segmented lineage. It might be a useful concept to study, for example, "well-defined territorial groups," but he noted that to study nomads "is to study flux and movement."⁴⁷ Consequently, there was simply no way that all Sioux or all Kazakhs could ever migrate together. Nonetheless, the Sioux and the Kazakhs affixed durable bonds to kinship, language, culture, social structure, beliefs, and traditions; but the Americans and Russians, to borrow Benedict Anderson's phrase, "imagined communities" among the nomads as political entities that simply did not exist, which often complicated relations between the colonizers and the colonized.

POPULATION

Throughout much of the nineteenth century, population estimates for the Sioux and the Kazakhs varied considerably and were largely based on lodge or yurt counts by visitors and some government officials. For example, according to Stephen Riggs, by the 1850s, the Dakotas numbered about 25,000. Riggs did not include the Lakota in his estimate. A later approximation based on some government information not available at midcentury that included the so-called western Dakota suggested that the population was closer to 40,000.⁴⁸ In the 1830s, Aleksei Levshin published one of the first demographic estimates about the Kazakhs. Levshin believed there were roughly 190,000 yurts in the Little Horde, 500,000 in the Middle Horde, and 100,000 in the Great Horde. Using a figure of six people per yurt, he concluded that there were almost 4.7 million Kazakhs.⁴⁹ This method to approximate population was similar to the lodge counting conducted by Americans to estimate the total number of Sioux. By

FIGURE 1.1. Kazakh yurt (courtesy of Central State Museum, Republic of Kazakhstan, NVF 5289/11).

the latter part of the nineteenth century, official American government statistics shed only partial light on the Sioux population. By the 1870s, some Sioux lived on reservations; other Sioux refused to settle there. In the 1870 *Annual Report of the Commissioner of Indian Affairs to the Secretary of the Interior*, the Dakota Superintendency census calculated the total population at 27,921, but it likely included various Sioux bands and non-Sioux, such as Cheyenne or Ponca.[50] By 1880, having finally forced all Sioux to live on various reservations, the report calculated that the Sioux population was 31,547.[51] That number declined during the early reservation years—between 1880 and 1910—perhaps due to infant mortality or Sioux leaving the reservations following the 1887 Dawes Act. By 1910 the Sioux numbered only 27,588.[52] The Russians, however, only conducted their first official census in 1897, and it concluded that there were 4.5 million Kazakhs in all territories of the empire, with an average of four people per yurt.[53] According to the census, 3.4 million lived in the four steppe districts, and the others lived in Turkestan and Siberia.[54] These midcentury estimates, and subsequent official American and Russian census data, demonstrate one of the major differences in this comparison: the number of Kazakhs far exceeded the number of Sioux.

Unquestionably, American Indian populations decreased significantly during American expansion and internal colonization and suffered immeasurable losses due to disease and military confrontations. This decline among American Indians, and to some extent the Sioux, fostered expectations by many contemporary observers, missionaries, government officials, and soldiers that the American Indian was on the verge of extinction. The American people readily accepted American Indian decline as the inevitable contraction of an ostensibly backward, uncivilized people confronted by civilization. The Kazakhs, on the other hand, did not endure similar population declines in the nineteenth century. Levshin's estimate appeared generally accurate based on Russian 1897 census data. Russians were much more inclined to believe that Kazakhs might integrate rather than succumb to extinction.

Although difficult to conclude with certainty, the demographics might also explain the extended period Russia required to conquer and subsequently colonize the Kazakh Steppe. From 1732, when some Kazakh khans first swore allegiance to the Russians, it took another 115 years for Russia to quell that last major Kazakh martial resistance to Russian colonization. In the United States, conquest occurred from roughly 1851 to 1890 (the Fort Laramie Treaty of 1851 to Wounded Knee, in 1891). Nonetheless, the Sioux represented the dominant force in the northern plains before 1850 and one of the largest demographically that the Americans encountered. The Kazakhs, as well, constituted a large population situated on the Russian frontier and represented a significant barrier to Russian expansion.

After the Second World War, however, Lemkin's term—*genocide*—gradually provided scholars a new interpretative framework in which to examine American internal colonization and Native American population decline.[55] Since the 1960s, many American scholars have suggested that the American government and people committed genocide against the indigenous population. Some even argued that this genocide started when the first Europeans landed in the Americas. Various American scholars equated expansion westward and the expulsion of natives as cultural genocide; others observed clear cases of physical genocide against, for example, California's natives, certainly in the years following the 1848 California gold rush. By the 1970s, Dee Brown's *Bury My Heart at Wounded Knee* thoroughly popularized the concept of genocide against American Indians, and it remains a topic of heated debate among scholars, journalists, and activists.[56] Other scholars—most notably, historian Gary Clayton Anderson—argued that it was not genocide but "ethnic cleansing."[57]

In the Kazakh case, Soviet scholars, both Russian and Kazakh, did not typically apply the term *genocide* to reinterpret Russian internal colonization. Serious discussion, however, chiefly emerged during Mikhail Gorbachev's *perestroika* and *glasnost* reforms of the 1980s and captured many Kazakh nationalists' imaginations in the years immediately following the Soviet Union's collapse in 1991. Since then, Kazakh and foreign scholars generally identified two distinct instances of possible genocide: the 1916 central Asia revolt and the Soviet collectivization famine in Kazakhstan in the 1930s and the subsequent Stalinist purges. The number of Kazakhs who died during these two tragic episodes remains uncertain, and Soviet-era interpretations further shrouded historical examination. The first work to ignite the debate was a 1989 article published in the Soviet journal *Voprosy istorii*, coauthored by two leading Kazakh historians, Zhulduzbek B. Abylkhozhin and Manash Kozybaev, and highly regarded Kazakh demographer Makash Tatimov. The article, "Kazakhstanskaia tragediia," spawned numerous scholarly articles and books in Kazakhstan that generated intense discussion in the press and popular media.[58] Most frequently, scholars identify the Soviet collectivization and Stalinist purges among the Kazakhs, in which an estimated 25 to 30 percent of the Kazakh population died, as clear evidence of state-sanctioned genocide.[59] Most Kazakh scholars believe that between 1.3 and 1.5 million Kazakhs died during the famine, which they frequently describe as genocide; but many western scholars disagree. Historian Sarah Isabel Cameron's meticulous research led her to conclude, "there is no evidence to indicate that these plans for violent modernization [collectivization] ever became transformed into a desire to eliminate Kazakhs as a group."[60]

Neither Anderson nor Cameron ignore the violence or atrocities committed against the Sioux or the Kazakhs, but, as Anderson concluded, "many Indian tribes (indeed the vast majority) survived, along with their culture . . . This weakens and perhaps makes impossible the argument for calling what happened in North American genocide of any sort."[61] In the nineteenth century, Anderson claimed, "Genocide did not occur in America, primarily because moral restraints prevented it."[62] He argued, "For either genocide or ethnic cleansing to occur, a legitimate government must plan, organize, and implement the crime . . . But other actions such as removal or diminishment of ancestral lands require a different description because they are not genocide."[63] As with Anderson's argument, the Russian government exhibited no intent to exterminate the Kazakh nation during either the 1916 central Asian revolt or Soviet collectivization. It was not the goal of the Russian government in 1916 or the 1930s to pursue ethnic cleansing either but to suppress a rebellion brought on by war and internal colonization in the former and forcefully implement Soviet modernization policies during the latter.

In the United States, Anderson noted that the absence of a clear state or government intent to eliminate indigenous peoples weakens the argument for genocide.[64] This argument is applicable in both the Sioux and Kazakh cases. Historians and others continue to debate the meaning of genocide and ethnic cleansing and identify examples or situations; but American and Russian internal colonization was not genocide. During the nineteenth century, Americans and Russians altered Sioux and Kazakh cultures, conquered Sioux and Kazakh historical territories, and consumed Sioux and Kazakh political and economic sovereignty; but the Sioux and the Kazakhs survived internal colonization. In order to contextualize Sioux and Kazakh survival, it is necessary to understand, to the extent possible, Sioux and Kazakh social, political, economic, and cultural structures as they appeared in the nineteenth century.

TIYOSPAYE AND *AUL*

The Sioux called their small nomadic communities *tiyospaye*, consisting of several camps (called *wicotipi*, or households), which joined together and were often based on actual and fictive consanguinity. During the winter months, the tiyospaye camped together; during much of the year, these camps separated for hunts but often reunited for ceremonies such as the Sun Dance. Camps generally consisted of kin but were not solely restricted to direct blood or marriage. Other kin relations included ritual adoption. Outsiders—and this typically included fur traders or members of other tribes—could acquire fictive kinship. Fur traders developed reciprocity networks, which, according to Mary K. Whelan, was an exchange "between socially defined partners" that "symbolized family relations" among the Seven Council Fires.[65] These social or even economic kinship relations were as legitimate as blood or marriage. In 1698 Father Louis Hennepin witnessed one such ritual adoption. The tribe also adopted Hennepin. He explained that after an exchange of "presents," they "adopt those" and "publicly declare them Citizens, or Children of their country; and according to their Age . . . the Savages call the adopted Persons, Sons, Brothers, Cousins, according to the degree of Relations: And they cherish them whom they have adopted, as much as if they were their own natural Brothers or Children."[66]

Kinship was an essential factor in Sioux internal relationships at all levels. The codes of conduct and behavior were firmly established, which is not to suggest violations did not occur. For example, the avoidance taboo forbade a married man to look at his mother-in-law, and a similar rule existed between a father-in-law and his son's wife.[67] This structure created a means by which the change of camp or tiyospaye by an individual or family did not require a fundamental change in behavior. Each individual, young or old, understood and complied with this system, which preserved the essential "harmonious operation" of a tiyospaye.[68] According to Ella Deloria, "kinship had everyone in a fast net of interpersonal responsibility . . . Only those who kept the rules consistently . . . thus honoring their fellows, were good Dakotas—meaning good citizens in society, meaning persons of integrity and reliability." It was, she wrote, "what men lived by."[69]

Among the Kazakhs, the smallest nomadic unit—the *aul*—consisted of relatives, usually a father and sons. The next level of kinship was the *ru*, or *taipa*, usually translated as "clan" or sometimes "tribe." Members of the clan might be related, but not necessarily. Clans conjoined into a single zhuz, or horde. As the smallest economic and social unit in Kazakh society, the aul traditionally provided the strongest connection to genealogy and was the most tangible source of wealth and security, but it could also include unrelated members. Auls generally operated as semi-independent units, gathering only for special occasions and wintering together. The economic viability hinged on self-sufficient activities, and the political structures reflected that same degree of independence.

One yurt generally consisted of the nuclear family—parents and unmarried children.[70] When a son married, he remained in the paternal aul, and the family provided him with a share of the familial property—chiefly a yurt—and some livestock. The woman's family also provided property, household goods, and some livestock as part of a dowry. Rarely did a bride remain in her natal aul. The youngest son, if there was one, usually remained in his parents' yurt after marriage, in order to care for his parents in old age. When they died, he inherited his parents' remaining property, including the livestock.[71] Both the Sioux and the Kazakhs practiced forms of exogamic marriage.

Sioux rules of exogamy required a degree of separation between potential marriage partners, discouraging marriage between a couple that shared a common grandparent. In general, it was best to marry outside the kinship group, tracing the lineage as far back as possible to ensure the appropriate separation. Arranged marriage was the norm; however, the young couple might have a say in the matter. Sioux practice also included a bride price, the *hakatakus*, which the woman's male relatives received. According to Royal B. Hassrick, the higher social status, the higher the price, usually paid in horses after the Sioux acquired them in the late eighteenth century.[72] The couple had the choice to live in the man's camp with his relatives or in the woman's camp alongside her relations. Polygamy was also an accepted practice in Sioux society, but it required a degree of wealth in order to support all of a man's wives. Levirate occurred as well, but it was not obligatory nor, it seems, frequently applied. A nuclear family shared a *tipi*, but it was the woman's property. If a man had multiple wives, each woman should occupy her own tipi.[73]

Kazakh rules of exogamy dictated that marriage could only occur between unrelated partners, traditionally by seven generations of separation. Marriage was a contractual agreement between parents, *kalym* (bride price) being paid to the girl's parents. A girl sang "weeping" or "lament" songs when departing her parents' aul to live in the aul of her new husband because she was leaving all she knew and loved behind to live among strangers in a different aul.[74] The Kazakhs practiced polygamy, but, generally, only the wealthy had up to four wives; the practice was somewhat unusual. Kazakhs also practiced levirate. A woman with no sons passed to the younger brother, but she was exempt if she had a son and inherited the property until the son or sons reached maturity.[75] Krader noted, perhaps with a little levity, that levirate was "not loved" by women because if they were compelled to marry a brother who already had one or more wives, the recently widowed woman immediately assumed a subordinate position to the others.[76] She was, simply, no longer the doyenne of her own family. Women were important social and economic partners with their husbands in both Sioux and Kazakh society.

Perceptions by outsiders in the nineteenth century typically characterized women as subordinate in Sioux and Kazakh society; the women did all the work and the men were inherently lazy. For outside observers, gender roles were an important demarcation between American and Russian women, in comparison to Sioux and Kazakh women — a clear contrast between the relative freedom American and Russian women enjoyed and the "drudgery, subservience, and patriarchal oppression" exhibited in Sioux and Kazakh societies.[77] These ideas reinforced one of the traits that colonizers detected in backward, nomadic societies: that a society's treatment of its women revealed the level of its civilization. As Sherry L. Smith commented, Americans, undoubtedly a civilized people, "pampered women; savage people enslaved them."[78] Visitors to a Kazakh aul described the women as "active and energetic, and [they] perform nearly all the labor which should devolve jointly" to men and women; but the men are "distinguished for their indolence." Another noted that the women cook and do most of the work, while the men are "too lazy to do more than look after the horses," and "lead a lazy, shiftless life."[79] Women exercised some control, but only because the men were so lazy.[80]

Among the Sioux, women served an essential role in tiyospaye functions.[81] Childbearing, food preparation, and handicrafts were all critically important. Women made the tipis, an arduous undertaking. Women typically put up and took down the tipi, which varied in size. A larger tipi often reflected the husband's ability to hunt to obtain skins. The expression "[t]he men with the fastest horses lived in the biggest tipis" revealed a husband's ability to provide for his family.[82] But, Whelan noted, the Sioux "women's ownership of 'family' tipis and the onerous nature of many of their tasks puzzled Euro-Americans because it challenged their Western gender system."[83] Later, missionaries among the Sioux on the reservations nonetheless considered the status of women to be one of servitude, and only "[t]ime alone can change this prejudice and raise Sioux women from their low condition to that of high and noble position such as is attained and held by women of civilized nations."[84]

What outside observers either neglected or failed to acknowledge was that Sioux women could speak at camp councils.[85] A Sioux woman could divorce, and she owned the major property, including furs, clothing, the cooking utensil, and other domestic implements. According to Walker, in family matters, a mother's authority exceeded that of the father. And, like male societies (warrior, dance, etc.), women had societies as well.[86]

Women in Kazakh society also played a critical role. They were never veiled or secluded. Ellsworth Huntington visited some Kazakh camps, and he remarked that women were "continually engaged in their household tasks. They converse freely with men, and make no attempt to keep themselves hidden." This is something Huntington likely expected to see because Kazakhs were Muslims, and Muslim women, in his understanding of Islamic society, were secluded and veiled.[87] Contrary to expectations, Kazakh women participated in councils and assemblies; they joined in songs and games and "respond readily to jests interchanged with men."[88]

Sioux and Kazakh women raised the children, engaged in domestic handicrafts, did the cooking and cleaning, and were fully involved in the day-to-day activities of the camp. Men guarded the herds, defended the camp, and made the political decisions; women did everything else. Despite American and Russian perceptions, Sioux and Kazakh women were not enslaved. Observations by Americans, Russians, or foreigners, however, rarely dismantled the power of nineteenth-century negative conceptions and perceptions about the Sioux and the Kazakhs, which more frequently, and typically, reinforced false beliefs.

ECONOMY

The foundation on which the Sioux way of life and economy existed was the buffalo. It played an extraordinarily important role in a culture and economy that depended on this one resource to supply almost all the material needs of the society. It constituted the principal food source, but not the only one. By the nineteenth century, the Sioux possessed large horse herds, which greatly improved their economic and material prosperity and made buffalo hunting a far more efficient undertaking. They used buffalo hides to make clothing, footwear, tipi covers, and small bullboats, and the animal later became a source of income as traders sought out the hide, meat, and fur. The Sioux used the horns and bones as cooking utensils, hide scrapers, and other functions that were both practical and ceremonial. In the arid, almost treeless plains, natives and, later, pioneers used buffalo dung as fuel. The only flaw in this structure might have been the absence of greater diversity. Certainly, the Sioux hunted other animals and willingly traded and incorporated material goods from Europeans, but the reliance on the buffalo was susceptible to overhunting and exploitation. Horses and buffaloes were valuable but vulnerable assets in the Sioux economy.

The introduction of the horse was one of two innovations adopted from Europeans that every scholar acknowledges were critical to the Sioux during the eighteenth and nineteenth centuries; the other was firearms. The Sioux functioned fine without them, if they existed in a world in which their neighbors also did not have them—but that was not the case. Plains Indians adopting the horse epitomized the "quintessential American epic" that was a "sweeping story of cultural collision and fusion." It was the story of some "obscure foot nomads . . . reinventing themselves as equestrian people [that] created one of history's most renowned horse cultures."[89] Unlike the horse-cultured nomads in other parts of the world, or even among some Native American tribes, the Sioux horse-culture nomadic existence was only seminomadic and more hunting nomadic than pastoral nomadism. The horse provided a mobility inconceivable in the seventeenth century, but that became a reality by the late eighteenth century. The introduction of the horse made the Sioux far more efficient nomads and hunters and certainly more powerful militarily.[90] The horse made hunting more individualistic and the family more independent, and acquiring horses intensified intertribal warfare to ensure unhindered access to the buffalo, which increasingly became a critical subsistence resource.[91]

As hunter-nomads, the Sioux depended on the vast buffalo herds of the Great Plains for their subsistence, but according to Robert H. Lowie and others, the horse gave the Sioux the ability to "specialize in bison subsistence."[92] The horse made the Great Plains a "place of residence rather than as a place of occasional resort" to hunt buffalo more efficiently.[93] The horse revolutionized the Sioux economy and its culture, and it transformed warfare. The Sioux had relatively small horse herds. They acquired horses, by most accounts, in the late seventeenth century, but according to Richard White, "the Sioux were hardly noted for either the abundance or quality of their herds."[94] Other scholars noted that a wealthy Sioux family might have forty horses, but that one family could do quite well with twelve.[95]

Many scholars attribute the desperation to acquire more horses to the increased frequency of conflict, as wealth was measured in horses and, according to Colin G. Calloway, "horse-raiding and war were virtually synonymous."[96] Of course, scholars will never know the frequency of warfare between Plains' Indians before the acquisition of the horse, but the animal likely improved the military capabilities of the Sioux and others who adopted it. By the nineteenth century, Sioux power on the northern plains rested on military efficiency and mobility (which prevented the devastating spread of disease that greatly weakened other tribes). In addition, as Pekka Hämäläinen noted, the Sioux developed "a functional equilibrium among horse numbers, ecological constraints, and economic, cultural, and military imperatives."[97] Popular imagination stereotypically and inextricably linked the Sioux with the horse and the buffalo. In comparison, economically, the most tangible asset the Kazakhs owned was livestock.

The typical measure of Kazakh wealth was the size of one's herds. No other animal was more important than the horse; it fulfilled material, nutritional, and symbolic needs. Kazakhs ate horse meat, but more important was *kumis*, fermented mare's milk. Every visitor, it seems, who ever visited a Kazakh aul commented about kumis. Jules Brocherel, for example, wrote, "Gulping down this liquid requires a strong digestion, for it contains a quantity of dirt and gives off such a smell that the mere sight of it arouses nausea." Another visitor wrote that the taste is "what might be expected—rancid and sour to the last degree."[98] Kazakhs, however, loved it. During summer months, they made *kurt*, a sun-dried cheese ball, and many other foodstuffs that they preserved for the long winters. Next to the horse in importance was sheep, which provided meat and wool—both of which were critical to Kazakh life. At weddings and feasts, or if a guest arrived, it was customary to slaughter a sheep for the meal. Kazakhs also kept goats, camels, and, during the nineteenth century, cattle. Thomas Witlam Atkinson, an American who traveled throughout the Kazakh Steppe in the 1850s, visited one aul and described the enormous size of the herds as he counted "one hundred and six camels, including their young; there were more than two thousand horses, one thousand oxen and cows, and six thousand sheep and goats. Even these, large as the number may appear, were far short of the total number of animals belonging to the patriarch chief; he had two other *aouls* [sic], at each of which were one thousand horses and other cattle."[99]

For both the Sioux and the Kazakhs, maintaining the herds required sufficient pasture, water, and defense against raids. The "poverty in horses" seemed to generate "constant warfare" in the northern plains. According to Hämäläinen, the Sioux (he specifically refers to the "Lakota") found the right balance of herds that encouraged them to keep their herds relatively small.[100] Lowie made a relative comparison about the role of horses in Sioux and Kazakh society, noting that among the Sioux and other Plains Indians, the horse "lacked significant features associated with Mongol and Turkic horse breeders. The Asiatic nomads gained subsistence directly from their herds—by eating the flesh of their animals and milking their mares. Few of the Plains Indian tribes ate horse flesh except in times of famine, even the Comanche used it as a distinctly subsidiary food; and no American natives ever dreamed of milking mares."[101] Lowie's statement makes

FIGURE 1.2. Plains Indians (courtesy of Denver Public Library).

it seem that meat was the only food the Sioux and the Kazakhs ate, but that was not the case.

The Sioux clearly depended on the buffalo as their principal food source, but many visitors and observers in the nineteenth century described the variety in the Sioux diet. Nonetheless, Edwin Thompson Denig stereotypically described the Sioux as "a people who depend entirely upon the chase for subsistence," despite the fact that other observers witnessed the Sioux harvest prairie turnips, wild artichokes, wild peas, red plums, and chokecherries.[102] Joseph M. Prince and Richard H. Steckel noted that the perceptions and generalizations about the Sioux ignored the reality of their food economy—particularly their use of wild plant resources such as onions, chokecherries, gooseberries, and wild rice. In addition, they noted that the Sioux "were known to use sap from the soft maple and box elder for sugar. Important cultigens such as maize, beans, squash, tobacco, and sunflowers were available to Plains nomads through a long-established intertribal trade with the more sedentary horticultural communities of Plains villagers."[103]

Among Kazakhs, meat—chiefly lamb, goat, and horse—supplied their principal diet, but they also traded for fruits and vegetables, grains, and other food with Russians and Turkestan khanates. Another industry among Kazakhs that supplied food and some income was fishing. Russian government records in the 1860s noted that in some regions—particularly those near large lakes (including the Aral Sea)—Kazakhs harvested thousands of pounds of fish and caviar annually.[104]

Stephen Riggs also observed fishing among the Sioux, as did earlier visitors to Sioux camps, but it was for subsistence rather than industry and trade.[105]

Nineteenth-century observers generally characterized the nomadic life based almost exclusively on the chase or the livestock and often ignored the diversity of Sioux and Kazakh economies. These observers equally failed to appreciate the diversity also evident within their religious practices, their leadership structures, and their cultures.

RELIGION

Embedded in the general conceptions of the Sioux are what DeMallie identified as three elementary features of Lakota traditionalism that likely applied to all Sioux and symbolized their way of life, including "land and freedom" to migrate, male pursuits such as war and hunting, and the "special relationship mankind shared with all the rest of the universe and the forces of *wakan*."[106] According to Walker, wakan was the "animating force of the universe" and "anything that was hard to understand."[107] Sioux religion had rituals and basic concepts that Sioux understood and shared but that did not include a specific structured or consistent theology. Sioux religion was not dogmatic but a belief system that made Sioux "lives and the world in which they live intelligible and acceptable."[108] Rituals gave expression to their beliefs, including the "purification lodge," also referred to as the "sweat lodge," and ceremonies such as the Sun Dance.[109] Early visitors and outside observers readily dismissed Sioux religious practices, usually decrying them as pagan and barbaric. George Catlin's description is typical and prejudiced. He was repulsed by the Sun Dance—although he admitted that he never witnessed the ceremony—as the "most extraordinary and cruel custom" practiced, which he called "looking at the sun!" He described it as a "sort of worship, or penance, of great cruelty; disgusting and painful to behold, with only one palliating circumstance about it, which is, that it is a voluntary torture and of very rare occurrence." According to Catlin, the "poor and ignorant, misguided and superstitious man who undertakes it, put his everlasting reputation at stake upon the issue," and "if he faints and falls . . . he loses his reputation as a brave or mystery-man, and suffers a signal disgrace in the estimation of the tribe."[110] Catlin's impression seems archetypal; Europeans and Americans misunderstood the purpose of the Sun Dance, but they also misunderstood Sioux religious belief and rituals. According to JoAllyn Archambault, the "Sun Dance was a focus of religious and social activities that confirmed tribal membership and helped secure a healthy, peaceful, and bountiful future for the tribe and its individual members."[111]

The Sun Dance was a ceremonial ritual rather than an artistic expression, but dance in Sioux culture was ritual rather than strictly art that Americans might recognize. According to DeMallie, "dance was a highly charged symbol . . . of religion, a ritual means to spiritual and physical betterment."[112] Samuel W. Pond described the connection between dance and religious ceremonies, such as the War Dance and the Scalp Dance, which he regarded with condescension and thought were a bit vulgar.[113] Others thought Sioux dance was beautiful and meaningful. Outside observers contextualized Sioux dance—the custom and its practice—based on their own cultural and aesthetic understanding of dance and its place in a civilized society. In the minds of most outside observers, the Sioux and their dance were primitive; if primitive was appealing to the observer, likely too was Sioux dance.

The Kazakhs, on the other hand, were Sunni Muslims. Some scholars and observers dispute the depth of Kazakh adherence to Islam. That they were Muslims is unquestioned, but the extent is unclear. According to nineteenth-century Russianized Kazakh scholar Chokan Valikhanov, "among the Kirgiz [Kazakhs] there are still many who do not know the name of Muhammed."[114] In his opinion, however, Islam was slowly replacing shamanism and pagan beliefs. L. F. Kostenko, following a journey among the Kazakhs, concluded, "Islam terrifies its people, so that not only are they incapable of development, but on the contrary they digress further still into a type of ignorance."[115] Levshin described asking two Kazakhs, "What do you believe?" They responded, perhaps somewhat confused by the question, "We don't know."[116] Eugene Schuyler received similar responses; however, he noted, "it is only externally that they are Mussulmans. On being asked what religion they have, unaccustomed to such a form of the question, they will say they do not know, but at the same time they would repel with vigour any insinuation that they were not good Mussulmans."[117]

In addition, Schuyler mistakenly attributed the Kazakhs' conversion to Islam to Russian religious policies. He claimed, "few of their sultans and chiefs had any idea of the doctrines of Islam, and there was not a mosque nor a mullah in the Steppe, but the Russians (just as they insisted on using the Tatar language in intercourse with them) insisted on treating them as though they were Mohammedans, built mosques and sent mullahs, until the whole people became outwardly Mussulman, although farther from the Russian lines, and nearer the settled populations of Central Asia, the weaker was the faith."[118] Despite what many outside observers considered a tepid embrace of Islam, most Kazakhs adhered to certain Islamic practices, such as circumcision, hygiene, and burial rituals.[119]

Americans and Russians often misunderstood Sioux and Kazakh religious practices, which influenced policies designed to manage them or weaken the nomads' seemingly stubborn adherence to them. Visitors to the Sioux often completely misunderstood and misinterpreted their religion; it was pagan, animistic, absent order, and built exclusively on superstition. In the steppe, however, Russians perceived the Kazakhs differently precisely because of Islam, which they accepted as a monotheistic faith derived from a consecrated book with something that Russians recognized as canon law. Islam advanced Kazakhs from the primitive paganism evident among the other indigenous peoples the empire encountered. Nonetheless, Russians feared the growing influence that Islam seemingly had in the steppe (Tatarization) and by the 1880s abandoned the decades-long practice of non-interference with local religious orientations. The Russians started to fear "fanatical Islam" among the Kazakhs, and the government encouraged Orthodox proselytizing among them.[120]

LEADERSHIP

Another feature of this comparison to emphasize is the role that leadership played among the Sioux and the Kazakhs. Americans and Russians frequently misunderstood the sociopolitical structures among the Sioux and the Kazakhs. Given the significant diversity in Sioux and Kazakh society, especially the fact that both were divided into three principal groups—Santee, Yankton/Yanktonai, and Teton among the Sioux and Little, Middle, and Great Hordes among the Kazakhs—political leadership was more often exercised at the clan, band, tiyospaye, and aul levels rather than at a national level.

The Sioux did not develop a centralized system of governance. The process of fission simply did not allow one to function. The Dakota and Lakota maintained political structures that fluctuated depending on need, such as an external threat or group well-being during communal hunts. Coalitions of different tiyospaye formed and when different subgroups, such as the Hunkpapa and Oglala, camped together, a camp hierarchy followed an order of "camp circles." When the Lakota and Dakota gathered together to celebrate an event, dance, hunt, or some other need, even if only in part, they maintained a specific camp order and ranking. According to Walker, the order was Teton, Santee, and Yankton/Yanktonai. Among the Teton, the order was Oglala, Miniconjou, Brulé, Two Kettle, Sans Arc, Blackfoot, and Hunkpapa.[121] American representatives were often confused and frustrated by this hierarchy because it often played out during negotiations with bands and subgroups.

Bands had chiefs, or headmen, but their political authority was limited; and a chief's principal responsibility was to carry out the will of the band. Authoritarian rule did not exist, nor did simple majority. Governance occurred through negotiation and consensus. There are some examples of leadership through descent; although hereditary right to leadership, or some form of aristocracy, was absent in Sioux society, a son could succeed a father if he had proven himself a capable warrior and exhibited wisdom and generosity. Primarily, a leader needed supporters willing to follow him. The general mechanism by which the Sioux governed themselves was through the tiyospaye councils. These councils appointed important positions, such as the *wakiconza* (camp administrator) and the *akicita* (enforcers). The council included *itancan* (elders, or, as Catherine Price translates it, "father of the band");[122] *wakicun*, which Alanson Skinner translates as "councilors";[123] and the *blotahunka*, meaning war leaders.[124] Councils permitted everyone to speak and to express an opinion. Councils did not meet regularly—generally only when an important decision confronted the band or tiyospaye, such as war or negotiations. It was a slow, deliberate process that required unanimity. If the council failed to reach consensus, it typically adjourned and, perhaps more importantly, maintained camp or band social harmony. This meant that authority or political power was never concentrated into a single individual but extended to each member of the tiyospaye. But it also meant that dissent and disagreement often resulted in splintering and fission. One disgruntled member could break away, perhaps taking allies with him to create a new tiyospaye or attract new followers.[125] The akicita enforced the council's decisions and carried out the disciplinary functions when someone disobeyed; usually akicita were noted warriors and members of warrior societies. The key to leadership was seemingly personal prestige, accumulated by age; demonstrated acts of courage; and the willingness of other Sioux to follow. There were no laws in Sioux society but rather rules that the people understood and collectively enforced. The Kazakhs differed to some extent from the Sioux in their means of governance and enforcement.

The Kazakhs had khans and others who served as leaders at all levels of society. Members of an aul or the clan followed those leaders who best protected and represented aul or clan interests. Leaders who served the welfare and survival of the group in the search for pasture or protected them against hostile neighbors attracted followers and support.[126] Political organization at the aul level was extremely fluid but usually was based on genealogical structures. The Kazakhs invested leadership in the *aksakal*, literally meaning "white beard." Because an aul usually consisted of many agnatic families, fathers, brothers, uncles, etc., the aksakal was not always the oldest male. Moreover, an aksakal was someone who inspired confidence, rendered justice, and resolved disputes. An aksakal was brave and intelligent, but wealth and social standing also attracted followers, even though they had no tangible kinship. An aksakal's authority was, according to Bacon, "directly proportionate to the willingness of the followers to accept the leader." Success in war and peace perpetuated one's rule, but failure meant replacement or abandonment.[127] The aul was an agnatic and politically organic structure that, according to Lindner, was open to all "who were willing to subordinate themselves" to an aksakal.[128] The aksakal typically decided when to move from one pasture to another, often after council with the other males in the aul. In principle, an aksakal could rule in an authoritarian manner, but that might lead to discord and fission. Another leader in Kazakh society was the *bii* (often translated as judge), who was also easily deposed or discarded by followers if he exhibited poor leadership. The next level of leadership was "sultan," probably used to identify Kazakhs claiming "white bone" descent and loosely applied to anyone who commanded respect and was considered a strong leader.[129] The khan was the leader of a horde, with an occasional hereditary structure that supported a khan's selection from father to son. But, again, a khan could both attract and lose supporters easily. Through marriage or some other relationship, it was possible that one khan might rule two different or even all three hordes, but that rarely, if ever, happened. In fact, during the eighteenth and early nineteenth centuries, when Kazakhs most strongly resisted Russian expansion into the steppe, no individual khan united all three hordes to oppose Russian imperialism.

In comparison, Sioux and Kazakh leaders generally assumed their roles due to personal merits, abilities, and political skills as opposed to a hereditary ascension to power—although that was possible. Leadership was fluid, not fixed in a structure that allowed a single individual to speak on behalf of all members of the band, clan, or horde. Therefore, in later negotiations with the Sioux and the Kazakhs, Americans and Russians demanded that agreements reached with a chief or khan be binding on all under their "authority," as understood by Americans and Russians. When the Americans and Russians expanded into the northern plains and Kazakh Steppe, the progression was clearly more than simple conquest.

The Sioux and the Kazakhs developed political structures that suited the nomadic life and shared some similarities. Americans and Russians generally misunderstood Sioux and Kazakh political structures during the nineteenth-century colonization of the northern plains and Kazakh Steppe. American and Russian expansion and internal colonization in some cases destroyed Sioux and Kazakh sovereignty and institutions, but Sioux and Kazakh social, cultural, and spiritual vestiges adapted and survived in various ways. In order to understand the process of internal colonization in the nineteenth century, however, it is important to understand the historical foundations for American and Russian expansion before 1800.

NOTES

1. J. Russell Smith, "Grassland and Farmland as Factors in the Cyclical Development of Eurasian History," *Annals of the Association of American Geographers* 33, no. 3 (September 1943): 149, 159. See also Ruth I. Meserve, "The Inhospitable Land of the Barbarian," *Journal of Asian History* 16, no. 1 (1982): 51–89; Michael Nylan, "Talk about 'Barbarians' in Antiquity," *Philosophy East and West* 62, no. 4 (October 2012): 580–601; W. R. Jones, "The Image of the Barbarian in Medieval Europe," *Comparative Studies in Society and History* 13, no. 4 (October 1971): 376–407; Denis Chernienko, "The Rulers of European Nomads and Early Mediaeval Byzantine Historiography," *Acta Orientalia* 58, no. 2 (2005): 171–78; Muzhou Pu, *Enemies of Civilization: Attitudes toward Foreigners in Ancient Mesopotamia, Egypt, and China* (Albany: State University of New York Press, 2005); W. A. P. Martin, "The Northern Barbarians in Ancient China," *Journal of the American Oriental Society* 11 (1885): 362–74; Don J. Wyatt and Nicola Di Cosmo, *Political Frontiers, Ethnic Boundaries and Human Geographies in Chinese History* (London: Routledge/Curzon, 2003).

2. Gilles Deleuze and Felix Guattari, *Nomadology: The War Machine* (New York: Semiotext(e), 1986), 73.

3. M. Fiskesjö, "On the 'Raw' and the 'Cooked' Barbarians of Imperial China," *Inner Asia* 1, no. 2 (1999): 162.

4. See chapter 4 for a brief discussion of nineteenth-century so-called scientific interpretations of primitive peoples.

5. Devin DeWeese, "The Influence of the Mongols on the Religious Consciousness of Thirteenth Century Europe," *Mongolian Studies* 5 (1978–1979): 41–78.

6. Napoleon was not being complementary when he reportedly remarked, "Scratch a Russian, find a Tartar."

7. One example of the literary link between *Tartar* and *nomad* appeared in Anne Bowman's 1861 novel, *Among the Tartar Tents; or, the Lost Father*. The author used *Tartar*, *nomad*, and *Kirghis* as synonyms. No explanation was necessary; the reader understood the context. At one point in the novel, Bowman described the Kirghis as "robbers." One character, an Afghan, was a Kirghis captive who "abhorred their life of rapine and blood." *Among the Tartar Tents; or, the Lost Father* (London: Frederick Warne, 1875), 155.

8. Robert F. Berkhofer, Jr., *The White Man's Indian: Images of the American Indian from Columbus to the Present* (New York: Vintage, 1979), 35.

9. Joselyn and Father Venegas quoted in Doane Robinson, *A History of the Dakota or Sioux Indians. . . .* (1904; Minneapolis: Ross & Haines, 1967), 16.

10. See Nancy Shoemaker, "How Indians Got to Be Red," *American Historical Review* 102, no. 3 (June 1997): 625–44.

11. John Foster Fraser, *The Real Siberia: Together with an Account of a Dash Through Manchuria* (London: Cassell, 1904), 40.

12. Henry Nash Smith, *Virgin Land: The American West as Symbol and Myth* (1954; Cambridge, MA: Harvard University Press, 1978), 286.

13. Elizabeth E. Bacon, "Types of Pastoral Nomadism in Central and Southwest Asia," *Southwestern Journal of Anthropology* 10, no. 1 (Spring 1954): 44.

14. Paul Bohannan, *Social Anthropology* (New York: Holt, Rinehart & Winston, 1963), 214–15.

15. Raphael Patai, "Nomadism: Middle Eastern and Central Asia," *Southwestern Journal of Anthropology* 7, no. 4 (Winter 1951): 401.

16. Douglas L. Johnson, *The Nature of Nomadism: A Comparative Study of Pastoral Migrations in Southwestern Asia and Northern Africa*, Department of Geography Research Paper

No. 118 (Chicago: University of Chicago, 1969), 16. The fourth type corresponds to European transhumance and is noted among the Kirghiz of the Tien Shan region in central Asia.

17. Owen Lattimore, *Inner Asian Frontiers of China* (New York: American Geographical Society, 1940), 522.

18. See, for example, Pekka Hämäläinen, "The Western Comanche Trade Center: Rethinking the Plains Indians Trade System," *Western Historical Quarterly* 29, no. 4 (Winter 1998): 485–513; M. K. Rozhkova, "Iz istorii torgovli Rossii so Srednei Aziei v 60-x godakh XIX v.," *Istoricheskie zapiski*, no. 67 (1960): 187–212.

19. Brian Spooner, *The Cultural Ecology of Pastoral Nomads* (Reading, MA: Addison-Wesley, 1973), 53.

20. See, for example, Francis Haines, "The Northward Spread of Horses among the Plains Indians," *American Anthropologist* 40, no. 3 (July/September 1938): 429–37; Guy Gibbon, *The Sioux: The Dakota and Lakota Nations* (Malden, MA: Blackwell, 2003), 77; Pekka Hämäläinen, "The Rise and Fall of Plains Indian Horse Cultures," *Journal of American History* 90, no. 3 (December 2003): 833–62; Richard White, "The Winning of the West: The Expansion of the Western Sioux in the Eighteenth and Nineteenth Centuries," *Journal of American History* 65, no. 2 (September 1978): 319–43; Clark Wissler, "The Influence of the Horse in the Development of Plains Culture," *American Anthropologist* 16, no. 1 (January/March 1914): 1–25.

21. Gibbon, *Sioux*, 35.

22. Raymond J. DeMallie argues that it never meant "snake" but derived from Proto-Algonquian languages and possibly meant someone who spoke a different language or "eastern massasauga," meaning "a small rattlesnake." See Raymond J. DeMallie, ed., vol. 13, *Plains*, part 2 of 2, *Handbook of North American Indians*, ed. William C. Sturtevant (Washington, DC: Smithsonian Institution, 2001), 749.

23. Stephen R. Riggs, *Contributions to North American Ethnology*, vol. 9, *Dakota Grammar, Texts and Ethnography*, ed. James Owen Dorsey (Washington, DC: Government Printing Office, 1893), 156, 183.

24. "Radisson's Account of His Third Journey, 1658–1660 [1654–1656?]," in *Early Narratives of the Northwest, 1634–1699*, ed. Louise Phelps Kellogg (New York: Charles Scribner's Sons, 1917), 46.

25. See Elaine A. Jahner, "Lakota Genesis: The Oral Tradition," in *Sioux Indian Religion*, ed. Raymond J. DeMallie and Douglas R. Parks (Norman: University of Oklahoma Press, 1987), 45–65.

26. Prior to that time, Vasilii Radlov, a nineteenth-century Turkologist and noted linguist who spent a lot of time among the Kazakhs, claimed the word *Kazak* is of Turkish origin and means "wanderer, freeman, vagabond, and tramp." Major-General S. B. Bronevskii thought the word meant "one who is cautious." Well-known Russian Orientalist Vasilii Bartold traced the word's origin to the late fourteenth century Timurid (Tamerlane) period and used to contrast pretenders, called "Kazak," from legitimate rulers. Sometime later, Uzbeks who abandoned their loyalty to their one ruler were designated "Uzbek-Kazak," or simply "Kazak." See V. V. Radlov, *Opyt' slovaria tiurkskikh' narechii* (St. Petersburg: Akademii nauk, 1899), 2:364; S. B. Bronevskii, "O Kirgiz'-Kaisakakh' Srednei Ordy'," *Otechestvennyi zapiski* (1830), 400; V. V. Bartold, "Kazak," *Sochineniia* (Moscow: Vostochnoi literatury, 1968), 5:535.

27. Sandzhar D. Asfendiarov, *Istoriia Kazakhstana (s drevneishikh vremen)* (Alma-Ata: Kazakstanskoe kraevoe izd-vo, 1935), 80–81.

28. Alfred E. Hudson, *Kazak Social Structure* (New Haven, CT: Yale University Press), 12.

29. René Grousset, *The Empire of the Steppes: A History of Central Asia*, trans. from French by Naomi Walford (New Brunswick, NJ: Rutgers University Press, 1970), 478–80.

30. Ney Elias, ed., *The Tarikh-i-Rashidi of Mirza Muhammad Haidar, Dughlát: A History of the Moghuls of Central Asia*, trans. E. Denison Ross, repr. ed. (Patna: Academica Asiatica, 1973), 272–73; T. I. Sultanov, "Nekotorye zamechaniia o nachale Kazakhskoi gosudarstvennosti," *Izvestiia AN Kaz SSR, seriia obshchestvennaia*, no. 1 (1971): 55–56. The author estimates that by the mid-fifteenth century, their followers numbered almost two hundred thousand.

31. K. A. Pishchulina, *Iugo-vostochnyi Kazakhstana v seredine XIV-nachale XVI veka* (Alma-Ata: Nauka, 1977), 210–24.

32. Lawrence Krader, *Peoples of Central Asia* (Bloomington: Indiana University Press, 1971), 66.

33. DeMallie, *Plains*, 6; Jeffrey Ostler, *The Plains Sioux and U.S. Colonialism from Lewis and Clark to Wounded Knee* (Cambridge: Cambridge University Press, 2004), 21.

34. James R. Walker, *Lakota Society*, ed. Raymond J. DeMallie (Lincoln: University of Nebraska Press, 1992), 10.

35. Ibid., 10.

36. Ibid., 15.

37. Stephen E. Feraca and James H. Howard, "The Identity and Demography of the Dakota or Sioux Tribe," *Plains Anthropologist* 8, no. 20 (1963): 81.

38. According to Ostler, Feraca and Howard, and other sources, the names for these seven Teton divisions are translated as follows: Oglalas (scatter one's own), Sicangus (burned thighs, thus the French term *Brulés*), Minneconjous (plant by water), Itazipcos (without bows, thus the French term *Sans Arcs*), Oohenunpas (two boilings, thus Two Kettles), Sihasapas (blackfeet), and Hunkpapas (head of camp circle entrance). See Ostler, *Plains Sioux and U.S. Colonialism*, 23; Feraca and Howard, "Identity and Demography," 83.

39. Anthony R. McGinnis, *Counting Coup and Cutting Horses: Intertribal Warfare on the Northern Plains, 1738–1889* (Lincoln: University of Nebraska Press, 2010), 76.

40. See, for example, Joseph N. Nicollet, *Joseph N. Nicollet on the Plains and Prairies: The Expeditions of 1838–39, With Journals, Letters, and Notes on the Dakota Indians*, ed. and trans. Edmund C. Bray and Martha Coleman Bray (St. Paul: Minnesota Historical Society Press, 1976).

41. DeMallie, *Plains*, 801; Ella Deloria, *Speaking of Indians* (New York: Friendship Press, 1944), 15.

42. M. Tynyshpaev, *Materialy k istorii kirgiz-kazakskogo naroda. (Chitany v Turkestanskom Otdele Russkogo Geograficheskogo Obshchestva v 1924 i 1925 gg.)* (Tashkent: Vost. Otd. Kirgizsk. Gos. Izd., 1925), 28; Elias, *Tarikh-i-Rashidi*, 121. Elias speculated that Alash might have been the Moghal Ahmad Khan, called *Ilacha* by the Kalmuks and others, but there is no tangible evidence linking Kazakh Alash to Ahmad Khan.

43. Lawrence Krader, *Social Organization of the Mongol-Turkic Pastoral Nomads* (The Hague: Mouton, 1963), 4–5; Maurizio Tosi, "Theoretical Considerations on the Origins of Pastoral Nomadism," in *Foundations of Empire: Archaeology and Art of the Eurasian Steppes*, ed. Gary Seaman (Los Angeles: Ethnographics, 1992), 27–28.

44. Nurbulat Masanov, *Kochevaia tsivilizatsiia Kazakhov* (Almaty: Sotsinvest, 1995), 56–59; N. A. Aristov, "Opyt vyiasneniia etnicheskogo sostav Kirgiz-kazakov Bol'shoi ordy i kara-kirgizov na osnovanii rodoslovnykh skazanii i svedenii o rodovykh tamgakh, a takzhe istroicheskikh dannykh i nachinaiushchikhsia antropologichecskikh issledovanii," *Zhivaia starina*, vyp. 3–4 (St. Petersburg, 1894) 400; Shakarim Qudaiberdiuly, *Turik, Qyrghyz-Qazaq ham khandar shezheresi* (1911; Almaty: Qazaqstan i Sana, 1991): 34–35.

45. Krader, *Social Organization*, 192–93.

46. Alikhan Bokeikhanov, "Kirgizy," in *Formy natsional'nago dvizheniia v sovremennykh gosudarstvakh. Avstro-vengriia. Rossiia. Germaniia*, ed. A. I. Kastelianskii (St. Petersburg: Obshchestvennaia pol'za, 1910), 591.

47. Rudi Paul Lindner, "What Was a Nomadic Tribe?," *Comparative Studies in Society and History* 24, no. 4 (October 1982): 693–95.

48. Riggs, *Dakota Grammar, Texts and Ethnography*, 155.

49. Aleksei Levshin, *Opisanie Kirgiz-kazach'ikh, ili Kirgiz-kaisatskikh, ord i stepei* (1832; Almaty: Sanat, 1996), 288. A yurt was the nomads' abode, a felt tent similar to the Sioux tipi or lodge.

50. US Department of the Interior, Office of Indian Affairs, *Annual Report of the Commissioner of Indian Affairs to the Secretary of the Interior for the Year 1870* (Washington, DC: Government Printing Office, 1870), 796–97 (hereafter *Annual Report*, year).

51. *Annual Report*, 1880, 240–55.

52. *Annual Report*, 1910, 63–66. A 1915 Department of Commerce report estimated the total in 1910 to be 22,778. See US Bureau of the Census, *The Indian Population in the United States and Alaska, 1910* (Washington, DC: Government Printing Office, 1915), 15.

53. Zhambyl Artykbaev, *Kazakhskoe obshchestvo: traditsii i innovatsii* (Karaganda: Poligrafiia, 1993), 26–27; G. V. Glinka, ed., *Aziatskaia Rossiia* (1914; St. Petersburg: Obshchestvenniia pol'za, 1974), 1:153.

54. Nurbulat Masanov, *Istoriia Kazakhstana: narody i kultury* (Almaty: Daik, 2001), 72.

55. In his seminal work, *Axis Rule in Occupied Europe*, Lemkin defined genocide to have two phases, the first destroyed the "national pattern of the oppressed group" and the second, the "imposition of the national pattern of the oppressor." The second phase is what many American scholars suggest happened in the United States because, as Lemkin argued, that "imposition" forced "upon the oppressed population which is allowed to remain, or upon the territory alone, after removal of the population and the colonization of the area by the oppressor's own nationals." See Raphael Lemkin, *Axis Rule in Occupied Europe* (Washington, DC: Carnegie Council, 1944), 79.

56. See, for example, Dee Brown, *Bury My Heart at Wounded Knee: An Indian History of the American West* (New York: Holt, Rinehart & Winston, 1972); Russell Thornton, *American Indian Holocaust and Survival: A Population History since 1492* (Norman: University of Oklahoma Press, 1987); George E. Tinker, *Missionary Conquest: The Gospel and Native American Cultural Genocide* (Minneapolis: Fortress Press, 1993); Clifford E. Trafzer and Joel R. Hyer, eds., *Exterminate Them: Written Accounts of the Murder, Rape, and Enslavement of Native Americans during the California Gold Rush* (East Lansing: Michigan State University Press, 1999); Ward Churchill, *Kill the Indian, Save the Man: The Genocidal Impact of American Indian Residential Schools* (San Francisco: City Lights, 2004); Lyman H. Legters, "The American Genocide," *Policy Studies Journal* 16, no. 4 (Summer 1988): 768–77; David E. Stannard, *American Holocaust: The Conquest of the New World* (Oxford: Oxford University Press, 1993); Michael A. McDonnell and A. Dirk Moses, "Raphael Lemkin as Historian of Genocide in the Americas," *Journal of Genocide Research* 7, no. 4 (December 2005): 501–29.

57. See Gary Clayton Anderson, *Ethnic Cleansing and the Indian: The Crime that Should Haunt America* (Norman: University of Oklahoma Press, 2014), 11–14.

58. See Zhulduzbek B. Abylkhozhin, Manash K. Kozybaev, and Makash B. Tatimov, "Kazakhstanskaia Tragediia," *Voprosy istorii*, no. 7 (1989): 53–71.

59. See, for example, Larisa Zh. Kuderina, *Genotsid v Kazakhstane* (Moscow: Skorpian, 1994); Kushbek Usenbaev, *1916: Geroicheskie i tragicheskie stranitsy* (Bishkek: Sham, 1997). Generally, most Western scholars examined the famine in Ukraine, but Kazakhstan

is often considered in that discussion. The best known is Robert Conquest, *The Harvest of Sorrow: Soviet Collectivization and the Terror-Famine* (New York: Oxford University Press, 1986). See also Nazira Nurtazina, "Great Famine of 1931–1933 in Kazakhstan: A Contemporary's Reminiscences," *Acta Slavica Iaponica* 32 (2012): 105–29; Nicolas Werth, "Stalinist State Violence: A Reappraisal Twenty Years after the Archival Revolution," *Tijdschrift voor Geschiedenis* 124, no. 4 (December 2011): 480–91; Kurt Jonassohn with Karin Solveig Björnson, *Genocide and Gross Human Rights Violations: In Comparative Perspective* (Piscataway, NJ: Transaction, 1998).

60. Sarah Isabel Cameron, "The Hungry Steppe: Soviet Kazakhstan and the Kazakh Famine, 1921–1934" (PhD diss., Yale University, 2010), 19. See also Isabelle Ohayon, *La sédentarisation des Kazakhs dans l'URSS de Staline: Collectivisation et changement social (1928–1945)* (Paris: Maisonneuve et Larose, 2006); Niccolò Pianciola, "The Collectivization Famine in Kazakhstan, 1931–33," *Harvard Ukrainian Studies* 25 (Fall 2001): 237–51; Niccolò Pianciola and Susan Finnel, "Famine in the Steppe: The Collectivization of Agriculture and the Kazakh Herdsmen, 1928–1934," *Cahiers du monde russe* 45, nos. 1–2 (2004): 137–92. Among Kazakh scholars, see S. Abdairaeiymov, ed., *Golod v Kazakhskoi Stepi: pisma trevogi i boli* (Almaty: Kazakh Universiteti, 1991); M. K. Kozybaev, ed., *Nasil'stvennaia kollektivizatsiia i golod v Kazakhstane 1931–1933gg. Sbornik dokumentov i materialov* (Almaty: XXI Vek, 1998); Gul'nar Nurbetova, *Istoriia "Krasnogo terror" v Kazakhstane (20–30 e gg. XX veka)* (Almaty: Mezhdunarodnogo Kazakhsko-Turestkogo universiteta imeni Kh. A. Iasavi, 2003).

61. Anderson, *Ethnic Cleansing and the Indian*, 13.

62. Ibid.

63. Ibid.

64. For a reasoned argument on this very subject, see Guenter Lewy, "Can There Be Genocide Without the Intent to Commit Genocide?," *Journal of Genocide Research* 9, no. 4 (2007): 661–74. According to Lewy, "The perpetrator must have had *special* or *specific* intent, he must have desired and specifically intended the result of genocide" (661).

65. See Mary K. Whelan, "Dakota Indian Economics and the Nineteenth-Century Fur Trade," *Ethnohistory* 40, no. 2 (Spring 1993): 246–76.

66. Louis Hennepin, *A New Discovery of a Vast Country in America. . .* , ed. Reuben Gold Thwaites (Chicago: A. C. McClurg, 1903), 2:476–77.

67. Royal B. Hassrick, *The Sioux: Life and Customs of a Warrior Society* (Norman: University of Oklahoma Press, 1964), 98.

68. Raymond J. DeMallie, "Sioux Ethnohistory: A Methodological Critique," *Journal of Ethnic Studies* 4, no. 3 (Fall 1976): 80–82.

69. Deloria, *Speaking of Indians*, 31–32.

70. The yurt consisted of a circular, lattice-worked frame covered in thick felt. A hole in the top allowed smoke to escape. In summer the felt walls were pulled back to let air flow through. One door, usually made of wood (or, sometimes, just a felt flap), was small and required a person to bend over to walk through. In the center of the yurt was the fire pit. Honored guests sat opposite, facing the door.

71. Elizabeth E. Bacon, *OBOK: A Study of Social Structure in Eurasia* (New York: Wenner-Gren Foundation for Anthropological Research, 1958), 68–69.

72. Hassrick, *Sioux*, 117.

73. Walker, *Lakota Society*, 53.

74. Thomas Winner, *The Oral Art and Literature of the Kazakhs of Russian Central Asia* (Durham, NC: Duke University Press, 1958), 36–41.

75. Victor Dingelstedt and N. I. Grodekoff, *Le régime patriarchal et le droit coutumier des Kirghiz* (Paris: Ernest Thorin, 1891), 21.

76. Lawrence Krader, "Principles and Structures in the Organization of the Asiatic Steppe-Pastoralists," *Southwestern Journal of Anthropology* 11, no. 2 (Summer 1955): 73.

77. See Barbara Bush, *Imperialism and Postcolonialism* (Harlow, UK: Pearson Longman, 2006), 85.

78. Sherry L. Smith, *The View from Officers' Row: Army Perceptions of Western Indians* (Tucson: University of Arizona Press, 1990), 57.

79. "An American in Turkistan," *Scribner's Monthly*, December 13, 1876, 211–23.

80. According to Mrs. E. B. Duffy, the men "assume to treat them [women] as servants, but are so indolent themselves that an energetic Kirghiz wife easily assumes the reins of the household and her husband soon learns to make no protest as long as he is allowed to recline idly on his silken cushion." See Mrs. E. B. Duffy, "The Women of all Nations: The Women of Western Asia," *Arthur's Illustrated Home Magazine*, February 1874, 88–92.

81. See, for example, Patricia Albers and Beatrice Medicine, eds., *The Hidden Half: Studies of Plains Indian Women* (Lanham, MD: University Press of America, 1983).

82. Quoted in Hassrick, *Sioux*, 187.

83. Whelan, "Dakota Indian Economics," 247.

84. Warren K. Moorehead, "The Life of an Indian Woman," *Ladies' Home Journal*, September 1891, 9.

85. Catherine Price, "Lakotas and Euroamericans: Contrasted Concepts of 'Chieftainship' and Decision-Making Authority," *Ethnohistory* 41, no. 3 (Summer 1994): 449.

86. Walker, *Lakota Society*, 42–43, 56–57, 63–65.

87. Ellsworth Huntington, "The Mountains and Kibitkas of Tian Shan," *Bulletin of the American Geographical Society* 37, no. 9 (1905): 527.

88. Raphael Patai, "Nomadism: Middle Eastern and Central Asia," *Southwestern Journal of Anthropology* 7, no. 4 (Winter 1951): 410.

89. Hämäläinen, "Plains Indian Horse Cultures," 833.

90. See Clark Wissler, "The Influence of the Horse in the Development of Plains Culture," *American Anthropologist* 16, no. 1 (January/March 1914): 1–25. On page 17, Wissler wrote, "Hence, we may formulate for further consideration the proposition that while no important Plains traits except those directly associated with the horse seem to have come into existence, the horse is largely responsible for such modification and realignments as give us the typical Plains culture of the nineteenth century, or which differentiate it from the subtypes in the same area."

91. According to sources cited by the authors, the Great Plains tribes were "85 percent dependent on hunting as their primary subsistence mode." Joseph M. Prince and Richard H. Steckel, "Nutritional Success on the Great Plains: Nineteenth-Century Equestrian Nomads," *Journal of Interdisciplinary History* 33, no. 3 (Winter 2003): 365.

92. W. W. Newcomb Jr., "A Re-Examination of the Causes of Plains Warfare," *American Anthropologist* 52, no. 3 (July/September 1950), 321; Robert H. Lowie, "Reflections on the Plains Indians," *Anthropological Quarterly* 28, no. 2 (April 1955): 66.

93. Robert M. Utley, *The Indian Frontier, 1846–1890*, rev. ed. (1984; Albuquerque: University of New Mexico Press, 2003), 14. According to Hämäläinen, "raiding was for the Plains pastoralists primarily an act of resource extraction." "Plains Indian Horse Cultures," 843.

94. According to White, "the Sioux had to replenish them by raiding or trading farther to the south. In this sense the economy of the Sioux depended on warfare to secure horses needed for the hunt." White, "Winning of the West," 331.

95. According to Prince and Steckel, the horses were assigned specific tasks: "one to carry the lodge and accessories; two to drag lodge poles; two to carry meat and miscellaneous food; three to carry the women and children; two for the men to ride; and two specially trained to hunt bison." Prince and Steckel, "Nutritional Success," 366.

96. Colin G. Calloway, "The Inter-tribal Balance of Power on the Great Plains, 1760–1850," *Journal of American Studies* 16, no. 1 (1982): 30.

97. Hämäläinen, "Plains Indian Horse Cultures," 859.

98. Jules Brocherel, "The Kirghiz," *Scottish Geographical Magazine* 18, no. 8 (1902): 399. The visitor to the sultan's aul compared drinking kumis in terms that an American understood: "Koumis is to the Kirghis what lager beer is to the German, ale to the Englishman, and cider to the 'down-east' Yankee." "Incidents of a Journey in Middle Asia: The Aoul of a Kirghis Sultan," *Youth's Companion* (June 24, 1875), 197.

99. Thomas Witlam Atkinson, *Oriental and Western Siberia: A Narrative of Seven Years Explorations and Adventures in Siberia, Mongolia, the Kirghis Steppes, Chinese Tartary, and a Part of Central Asia* (New York: Harper & Bros., 1858), 245, emphasis in original.

100. Hämäläinen, "Plains Indian Horse Cultures," 851, 861.

101. Robert H. Lowie, *Indians of the Plains* (1954; Lincoln: University of Nebraska Press, 1982), 42

102. Edwin Thompson Denig, *Five Indian Tribes of the Upper Missouri: Sioux, Arickaras, Assiniboines, Crees, Crows*, ed. John C. Ewers (Norman: University of Oklahoma Press, 1961), 11–12.

103. Prince and Steckel, "Nutritional Success on the Great Plains," 363.

104. *Tsentral'nyi gosudarstvennyi arkiv, Respublika Kazakhstana* (Central State Archive, Republic of Kazakhstan, Almaty. fond. 4, opis. 1, dela. 3629, list. 39–42, 83.

105. Riggs, *Dakota Grammar, Texts and Ethnography*, 159–60.

106. Raymond J. DeMallie, "Lakota Traditionalism: History and Symbol," in *Native American Interaction Patterns*, ed. Regna Darnell (Ottawa: National Museum of Canada, 1988), 5, emphasis in original.

107. Walker quoted in Raymond J. DeMallie, "Lakota Belief and Ritual in the Nineteenth Century," *Sioux Indian Religion*, 28.

108. DeMallie, "Lakota Belief and Ritual," 33.

109. See, for example, Raymond A. Bucko, *The Lakota Ritual of the Sweat Lodge: History and Contemporary Practice* (Lincoln: University of Nebraska Press, 1998).

110. George Catlin, *North American Indians*, ed. Peter Matthiessen (1841; New York: Penguin, 2004), 226–27.

111. JoAllyn Archambault, "Sun Dance," in DeMallie, *Plains*, 983. See also Arthur Amiotte, "The Lakota Sun Dance: Historical and Contemporary Perspectives," in *Sioux Indian Religion*, 75–89.

112. Raymond J. DeMallie, "The Lakota Ghost Dance: An Ethnohistorical Account," *Pacific Historical Review* 51, no. 4 (November 1982): 392.

113. Samuel W. Pond, *Dakota Life in the Upper Midwest* (1908; St. Paul: Minnesota Historical Society, 1986), 120–21.

114. Chokan Valikhanov, *Izbrannye proizvedeniia* (Alma-Ata: Kazakhskoe izd-vo khudozh. lit-ry, 1958): 187.

115. L. F. Kostenko, *Sredniaia Aziia i vodvorenie v nei russkoi grazhdanstvennosti* (St. Petersburg: Tip V. Bezobrazova, 1871), 85.

116. Levshin, *Opisanie Kirgiz-kazach'ikh*, 313.

117. Eugene Schuyler, *Turkistan: Notes of a Journey in Russian Turkistan, Khokand, Bukhara, and Kuldja* (New York: Scribner, Armstrong), 1:37–38.

118. Schuyler, *Turkistan*, 1:38. Steppe tribes embraced Islam by the twelfth century, if not earlier; however, it remains difficult to say with any precision how influential Islam was among Kazakhs prior to and during Russian colonization. Interestingly, Schuyler also claims that Russian policies fostered Buddhism among the Buriats in Siberia.

119. Typically, only rich Kazakhs had more than one wife. Each woman occupied her own yurt and managed her own children. Because the man had to provide a dowry, the cost usually excluded the average Kazakh from such luxuries. Kazakh marriage rituals often entailed *qalym* (*qalyng* in Kazakh), a bride price. See, for example, Kh. Argynbaev, "Marriage and Marriage Rites Among the Kazakhs in the Nineteenth and Twentieth Centuries," in *The Nomadic Alternative: Modes and Models of Interaction in the African-Asian Deserts and Steppes*, ed. Wolfgang Weissleder (The Hague: Mouton, 1978): 331–41; N. A. Kisliakov, *Ocherki po istorii sem'i i braka u narodov Srednei Azii i Kazakhstana* (Leningrad: Nauka, 1969): 65–98; Levshin, *Opisanie Kirgiz-kazach'ikh*, 334–39.

120. See Chokan Vailkhanov, *Izbrannye proizvedeniia* (Alma-Ata: Kazakhskoe izd-vo khudozh. lit-ry, 1952), 187–95; Mark Batunskii, "Islam i Russkaia kul'tura XVIII Veka: Opyt istoriko-epistemologicheskogo issledovanniakh," *Cahiers du monde russe et soviétique* 27 (January/March 1986): 45–69; Robert D. Crews, "Empire and the Confessional State: Islam and Religious Politics in Nineteenth-Century Russia," *American Historical Review* 108, no. 1 (February 2003): 50–83; Robert P. Geraci and Michael Khodarkovsky, eds., *Of Religion and Empire: Missions, Conversion, and Tolerance in Tsarist Russia* (Ithaca, NY: Cornell University Press, 2001).

121. Walker, *Lakota Society*, 18–19.

122. Price, "Lakotas and Euroamericans," 449.

123. Alanson Skinner, "A Sketch of Eastern Dakota Ethnology," *American Anthropologist* 21, no. 2 (April/June 1919): 173.

124. Walker, *Lakota Society*, 33.

125. Price, "Lakotas and Euroamericans," 458.

126. Lindner, "Nomadic Tribe," 693.

127. Levshin, *Opisanie Kirgiz-kazach'ikh*, 364–65; Bacon, *OBOK*, 71.

128. Lindner, "Nomadic Tribe," 701.

129. Kazakhs who could trace descent from some illustrious progenitor, usually directly to Chingis Khan, were called *aq suiek*, or "white bone." Kazakhs unable to trace descent from Chingis Khan were designated as *kara suiek*, or "black bone." Some outside observers conceived of these two "bone" as some sort of aristocratic distinctions, but they were not. Wealth, age, wisdom, and courage were stronger markers of social distinction than bone, although bone could conceivably reinforce someone's natal status. Primogeniture or white bone lineage did not guarantee leadership in Kazakh society.

2

Pre-Nineteenth-Century Expansion

The process of American and Russian expansion and colonization of the northern plains and the Kazakh Steppe is complex and occurs over centuries. The roots and chronology of American and Russian expansion and colonization represents a major difference between the two processes. French and British traders and trappers penetrated the North American continental interior very slowly in the search for the profitable trade that, in some ways, paralleled Russian expansion into Siberia.[1] In both cases, furs and other natural resources initially attracted Euro-Americans and Russians to the continental interiors; but eventually that attraction waned, and the northern plains and the Kazakh Steppe became contested territory that Americans and Russians believed needed their active intervention in order to stop indigenous attacks against American and Russian traders and settlers.

In the sixteenth and seventeenth centuries, Euro-Americans were a trifling presence in the North American continental interior, whereas Russians were already crossing the Ural Mountains into Siberia and penetrating the northern steppe regions. Russia's contacts, trade relations, and diplomacy with the Kazakhs began almost a century before the French even learned about the Sioux. The Sioux only peripherally integrated into the French and British trade networks—certainly not as fully as some other tribes, such as the Iroquois, Huron, or Ottawa. But scholars struggle to understand fully the Sioux world of the seventeenth and eighteenth centuries because it was a world that generally, as Richard White noted, consisted "largely of dim shadows" pieced together and "preserved in fractured memories."[2]

White correctly noted that the "history of the northern and central American Great Plains . . . is far more complicated than the tragic retreat of the Indians in the face of an inexorable white advance. From the perspective of the most northern and central plains tribes, the crucial invasion during this period was not necessarily that of the whites at all. These tribes had few illusions about American whites and the danger they represented, but the Sioux remained their most feared enemy."[3] Despite their focus on their own successes, British, French, and Russian sources reveal that Euro-Americans and Russians expanded into regions that were not empty but were somewhat unstable and contested by numerous challengers. Throughout the seventeenth and eighteenth centuries, the Sioux and the Kazakhs fought against non-Europeans and indigenous rivals for control of the northern plains and the Kazakh Steppe. The Sioux fought against the Chippewa, Cree, Crow, Iowa, Mandan, and others for control of land and resources and the Kazakhs fought against the Bashkirs, Kalmyks, Kirghiz, Bukharans, and Khivans for control of the steppe. The Sioux and the Kazakhs held their territories with martial strength. Moreover, because of their experiences with other indigenous groups, they often did not feel threatened by Euro-Americans or Russians. Both the Sioux and the Kazakhs developed societies that could resist change, but important differences existed. The Sioux were an expanding power in the northern plains from the seventeenth to the nineteenth centuries but the Kazakhs were fighting on multiple sides, and with each other, as the Russians extended their empire into Siberia and the Kazakh Steppe.

The age of what might be called American expansion unquestionably has its roots in the age of European overseas expansion into the North and South American continents, Asia, and Africa in the sixteenth, seventeenth, and eighteenth centuries. America's eventual expansion across the North American continent traces its birth to European overseas imperialism, whereas Russian expansion was, from the start, an exercise in contiguous territorial expansion. That perception gives Russian expansion an organic flavor, a natural reincorporation of lands dominated by 250 years of Mongol barbarity. The age of Russian imperialism commenced with the slow disintegration of the Mongol Empire (often referred to as the Mongol Yoke), the Golden Horde. In the late fifteenth century, the rise of the Muscovite state under Ivan III (1462–1505), or Ivan the Great, continued a process in Russian history often called the "gathering of the lands of Rus."[4] In the process, the Muscovite state morphed from a relatively small principality into what becomes the Russian Empire.

Euro-Americans, on the other hand, understood their expansion precisely for what it was: economic expansion and imperialism that morphed into settler colonialism.[5]

Most scholars agree that in the seventeenth century, the Eastern Sioux (Dakota) were hunter-gatherers living in the lakes and woodlands of Wisconsin and Minnesota. The Sioux likely hunted buffalo at this time as well, but they were not yet the acclaimed horsemen of the nineteenth century. By the mid-seventeenth century, sporadic contacts with French traders and Jesuit missionaries slowly incorporated the Sioux into the lucrative European trade and commercial orbit of the Great Lakes region. External pressures, however, compelled the Sioux to fight against various rivals to preserve their territory. By the eighteenth century, the Sioux started to migrate west into the Minnesota prairies and northern plains. Nonetheless, it remains unclear why the Sioux left; the debate centers on whether the external pressures exerted by the fur trade pushed the Sioux out or, on the other hand, the acquisition of the horse provided the tool to hunt buffalo more efficiently and allowed them to abandon their semisedentary existence.[6]

By the seventeenth century, Kazakhs divided into the Three Hordes and lived in the steppe regions, but they were not the only peoples fighting to control the steppe. Violence and constantly shifting authority and control seemingly epitomized life in the northern steppe during the seventeenth and early eighteenth centuries. Zhanibek and Kerei resisted incursions in the southern steppe region by former Uzbek allies—Kyrgyz, Oirats, and others. Under Zhanibek's son, Kasym Khan, the Kazakhs defeated the Uzbeks and seized control of Tashkent and the Syr Darya region, including the Silk Road town of Otrar, although these military victories did not bring peace or stability to the steppe.[7] Like the Sioux, the Kazakhs underwent change and expansion.

In the seventeenth century, Euro-Americans and Russians sought to facilitate trade with indigenous populations and ensure security along the boundaries and throughout the networks established by Europeans and Russians; however, in order to facilitate that trade, Europeans and Russians used both negotiations and military force to secure and expand the trade. They built trading posts and military fortifications in order to secure the footholds. In addition, Euro-Americans and Russians structured trade relationships through treaties and oaths negotiated with indigenous peoples. Euro-Americans facilitated relations with the native populations by reciprocal relations and gift giving; Russians awarded those who cooperated with benefits such as titles and privileges rather than symbolic reciprocity.[8]

TO 1700

Comparing Sioux and Kazakh history up to the eighteenth century is not exact. Whereas Sioux history seemingly divided between three distinct periods, Kazakh history was less precise, although it roughly corresponded. Nonetheless, they share many common experiences. Euro-American and Sioux relations in the seventeenth century reflect the "push" forces that later compelled many Dakota and Lakota to migrate from their lakes and woodland homes to occupy parts of Minnesota, Iowa, Nebraska, North and South Dakota, and eastern Montana and Wyoming, where the Americans encountered them in the nineteenth century. The first era was the Iroquois Wars (1641–1701), followed by the French era (1720–1761) and the British era (1761–1819).[9] Russian and Kazakh relations in the seventeenth and eighteenth centuries did not easily partition, but Khan Abulkhair's 1732 decision to pledge his allegiance to Russia distinguished the two eras.[10] This division corresponds approximately to the Dzhungarian-Kalmyk Wars (1680s–1740s) and the era of rebellion (1740s–1822).

The first phase that brought the Sioux into the realm of European expansion began by the late sixteenth century, as the French established settlements along North America's eastern shores but struggled to establish a presence in the interior until 1608, when the French founded the colony of Quebec. The first French trading companies were already operating—mainly purchasing furs—but Quebec settlements were small, with only a handful of inhabitants. The French allied with Algonquian tribes that served as essential partners in the fur trade. The British allied with the Iroquois and, for much of the seventeenth century, the Iroquois and French clashed in small-scale attacks followed by retaliations. By the second half of the seventeenth century, French economic interests oriented toward the fur trade, with Montreal quickly becoming the economic center of the trade. The British firmly established their colonies—which stretched across the eastern seaboard—east of the Allegany Mountains. Throughout the sixteenth and early seventeenth centuries, the French designed policies to contain Britain and restrict its expansion to the small eastern towns and settlements. In general, the Sioux did not establish specifically strong trade relations with either individual European power; however, they gravitated toward the various French and British trading networks then operating in the plains and Great Lakes region.

Russia's expansion in the sixteenth century, by comparison, was much more vigorous. The conquest of Kazan in 1552 served Russia's growing trade interests to the east, particularly the assumed riches in central Asia, Persia, and China.[11] In 1573 one of the first Kazakh delegations visited Moscow, some twenty years after the conquest of Kazan and Astrakhan.[12] This delegation's purpose remains somewhat uncertain, but the Russians likely wanted to negotiate with the Kazakhs to use routes through the Kazakh Steppe to expand trade with the central Asian khanates of Bukhara, Khiva, and Kokand and perhaps with China and Persia as well.[13] In the early years, the Kazakhs acted as middlemen in the central Asian trade, but their most important contribution was to provide protection to caravans crossing the steppe. The problem was that the Kazakhs were just as likely to attack a caravan as protect one. An assurance of protection by one Kazakh clan or horde did not guarantee that a different Kazakh clan or horde was obligated to respect its route or safety.

It is unlikely that this delegation was the first contact between Kazakhs and Russians, but it occurred almost a century before known Sioux-European interaction. The earliest mention of the Sioux appears to be in 1641 by two Jesuit missionaries, Isaac Jogues and Charles Raymbault.[14] They did not meet any Sioux. According to the story, they learned from the Chippewa about a people "who lived eighteen days' journey to the west"; but it was another twenty years before a documented meeting occurred between Sioux and French Jesuit representatives.[15] During this period, the Iroquois were a powerful force in the western Great Lakes region, fighting against the Hurons and Ottawas and pushing these weaker tribes into Sioux territories. The Sioux, according to Reuben Gold Thwaites, "were disposed to welcome the newcomers," but "the impolitic fugitives repaid their kind hosts with base treachery, and the [Sioux] turned upon them with fury."[16] War between many Sioux bands and those tribes pushed west by the Iroquois was common in the 1640s and 1650s. According to historian W. J. Eccles, in the 1650s—after the Iroquois "virtually destroyed the Huron nation"—French traders and missionaries started to establish direct trade relations with tribes, such as the Sioux, who previously hunted and then traded with the "Huron middlemen."[17] The Sioux met the French after the Iroquois destroyed the Huron, breaking a trade barrier rather violently.

It was in the epoch of Iroquois Wars that the first record of a French-Sioux meeting occurred. In 1659 or 1660 Pierre Esprit Radisson and Médard Chouart de Grosseilliers likely met with the Sioux.[18] Radisson believed the Sioux bands, likely Dakota, wanted French goods, especially firearms. He wrote that they met in order for the Sioux to "make a sacrifice to the French, being Gods and masters of all things, as of peace, as wars; making the knives, the hatchets, and ye kettles rattle, etc. That they came purposely to put themselves under their protection." He also assumed that the Sioux desperately needed the French goods to survive, noting, "we kept them alive by our merchandises."[19] Radisson and Grosseilliers did not introduce the Sioux to European commerce or merchandise; the Sioux likely traded with other tribes in the area and were familiar with some products before they met the two Frenchmen.[20] In 1665 missionary Claude Allouez met with some Sioux who described their home along the "Messepi" River, the prairies that abounded in all types of game, and "their fields of tobacco."[21] In 1685 Nicolas Perrot built a trading post called Fort St. Antoine along the east shore of Lake Pepin, in Wisconsin, where he established a brief but profitable trade with some Sioux bands.[22]

As these two meetings suggest, the Sioux and French coupled trade to diplomacy, or at least those who met with the Frenchmen did. It seems the Sioux hoped to establish direct trade relations in order to acquire firearms and other merchandise. According to Radisson, the Sioux wanted French "protection," but it was just as likely that the Sioux perceived the French to be potentially powerful allies against their enemies.[23] Unfortunately for Radisson, the French government refused to authorize his trip, and the governor of New France confiscated all his furs and profits. The government in New France wanted to control the trade, much as the Russians sought to monopolize trade in Siberia, but both governments constantly dealt with natives and Frenchmen or Russians who operated outside official channels. These individuals proved to be intrepid traders and explorers and typically penetrated farther into the plains and steppe than the large, cumbersome government-supported expeditions. In many cases, they did not want, nor need, government sanction.

The construction of small posts by French traders was comparable to Russian expansion, although the French expansion differed in that these were individual traders or monopolies and not military or settler posts. The French generally established posts on land that no tribe claimed or only built with the express permission of the tribe.[24] A French post was strictly a commercial site because the French did not typically establish agricultural settlements; however, *coureurs de bois* (runners of the woods) caused the French colonial government considerable anxiety as they adopted Indian customs and language, married Indian women, and settled around these posts.[25] They played an essential role in the French fur trade, which was individually motivated without much military or government assistance.

In the seventeenth century, Euro-American expansion differed significantly from Russian imperial expansion and colonization in the Kazakh Steppe, which, acclaimed nineteenth-century Russian historian Vasilii Kliuchevskii characterized by "jerks and jolts." The Russian government accomplished expansion, he wrote, not by "spreading out, but by changing its lines of advance."[26]

That line of advance was a series of small Cossack posts and forts—the "Trans-Kama Line"—constructed to preserve Russia's territorial gains around the Ural Mountains. Cossacks manned each fort under the command of a *voevoda*, or military governor (who was also the top civil administrator), and the Russian government allotted the Cossacks land adjacent to the fort to farm.[27] Security against Tatar, Bashkir, and other peoples' raids on Russian and Cossack settlements and Russian desires to expand trade pushed the Russian movement eastward. Euro-American expansion into Sioux lands centered on commerce rather than the settler agriculture evident in the Russian advance but was also characterized by jerks and jolts. Interestingly, much as French colonial officials expressed concern that the "coureurs de bois were metamorphosing into *sauvages*, that is, men beyond the control of legitimate authority," Russian officials struggled to understand that Cossack settlers rarely shared interests that coincided or aligned with the empire's interests.[28]

The French and Cossacks who settled near the Sioux or the Kazakhs were not agents of the state sent to conquer the region but rather represented typically "mutualistic and cooperative" relations that transformed the identity of both.[29] The French were merchants or missionaries; they were not serving a conquest agenda. The posts were not zones of imperial subjugation or separation but were, as White argued, the middle-ground places "in between cultures, peoples, and in between empires and the nonstate world of villages."[30] In both cases, the imperial state was unable to regulate fully the interactions between traders-settlers and indigenous populations; their interests did not coincide because of the weakness, or outright absence, of imperial institutions in the distant regions.

The imperial state relied instead on the social and economic networks established by the French and Cossacks to exert, at the very least, its symbolic power, influence, and authority. Later Russian historians depicted the Cossacks as the vanguard and agents of "Russian civilization on the wild Asiatic east" but without the similar expectation expressed by the French traders in this early contact period.[31] When the Cossacks blurred the imperial vision by "intermarriage, interactions, conversions, acculturations, and desertions," that environment was comparable to "borderland communities of interests" in North America, where, as Thomas Biolsi observed, the "middle ground has commonly been a marrying ground" as these posts and places became zones of cultural as well as economic exchange.[32]

Throughout the seventeenth century, while the French busied themselves trying to establish their trading networks and fending off the British and their Iroquois allies, the Russians struggled to maintain their networks in Siberia and the Kazakh Steppe. From the fall of Kazan in 1552 until the ascension of Peter the Great in 1682, the Russian advance was slow and oriented toward increased territorial expansion in Siberia and exploitation and trade in the region's natural resources. Siberia's fur and timber wealth continued to attract Russian interest and compelled its further expansion. In 1558 Anika Stroganov successfully petitioned the tsar to grant him the monopoly rights to develop the western regions of Siberia, which was followed by similar charters bestowed on his two sons in 1574.[33] Shortly thereafter, the Cossack Ermak defeated the Tatar khan of Sibir, Kuchum (who fled south into the Kazakh Steppe).[34] Within a century, Russia crossed the continent, and by the early eighteenth century, explorations of the Aleutians and Alaska began.[35]

To facilitate trade in Siberia and central Asia, Ivan IV's charter instructed the Stroganovs to grant traders from the Kazakhs or Turkestan unfettered travel to trade. The instructions forbid the Stroganovs from imposing a tax or any financial burdens on this trade. The problem was that trade traffic required mutual benefit. With seeming impunity, Kazakhs frequently attacked Russian trade caravans traveling through the steppe, plundered the goods, and often sold Russian survivors in the slave markets in Bukhara. An English emissary to the Russians in the 1550s, Anthony Jenkinson, described how the Kazakhs, "living in the fields without house or towne," dominated the steppe and hindered trade. Consequently, he wrote that the Kazakhs made it "impossible for any Caravan to pass unspoiled, so that 3 years before our being there, no Caravan had gone."[36] By this time, the Kazakhs proved to be a significant barrier to Russian trade and expansion, a process that later played out in the plains when Americans pushed into a region dominated by a powerful indigenous force. Although the chronology differs significantly, both the Americans and the Russians perceived barriers to overcome in the plains and steppe with military force, trade, and colonization.

By the ascension of Peter I (1682–1725, Peter the Great), the Russian government consolidated its authority in western Siberia but found that the frontier along the Kazakh Steppe was fragile and perennially threatened by Kazakh incursions. Under Peter I, Russia's expansion continued eastward, and the regime turned its "gaze to the Kazakh hordes" because the tsar regarded the Kazakhs as potential "partners in trade and political affairs"; but he also considered the Kazakh Steppe a "beach-head for extending its own trade objectives in the east."[37] Russia, however, expanded into a volatile situation in the steppe, and it was decades before Russia fully controlled it. The Kazakhs weakly exercised control over the steppe, and they were constantly fending off rivals who attempted to push the Kazakhs from the prime pastures and water sources. Kazakhs faced serious incursions by the Oirat-Kalmyk hordes in the southeast, along the Ili River valley, and in the northeast, along the Altai region between China, Mongolia, and Kazakh territory.[38] Comparable to the Kazakhs, the Sioux also struggled to fend off rivals in the lakes and woodlands of Minnesota and

Wisconsin. Some western Sioux bands, particularly the Teton, started migrating deeper into the northern plains, and many remained there on a permanent basis.

Throughout the seventeenth and early-eighteenth centuries, the Sioux engaged in intermittent conflict with the Chippewa, Ottawa, Huron, and others. French traders in the late seventeenth century also tried to cement diplomatic ties with the Sioux and other Indian tribes in the Upper Mississippi River region, which meant that trade and alliances, according to White, "became inseparable."[39] The British government's 1670 charter of the Hudson's Bay Company motivated the French to obstruct British efforts, but the British did not yet desire direct competition with the French in the interior. Instead, the British sought profit rather than conquest, as "long as enough furs reached its posts to produce a dividend for its shareholders, the company's servants were content to remain in a 'sleep by the frozen sea.'"[40]

In 1671 the French informed the Wisconsin tribes that they were "the subjects of the great French king across the ocean," although this probably meant very little to the tribes.[41] It took another twenty years before the French government established a formal alliance ceremony that some Sioux bands acknowledged as legitimate. The French wanted to end the intertribal warfare and secure safe passage for their merchants and their native allies. In the 1670s, the Sioux and Chippewa were at war with one another, and that disrupted trade. In 1679 Daniel Greysolon Dulhut (Duluth) negotiated a tenuous peace between the Sioux and Chippewa at Mille Lacs; he also claimed "possession of the Sioux country" in the name of Louis XIV of France.[42]

The economic competition to furnish peltries to the French and British in order to secure European goods likely increased warfare between the Sioux and their rivals, creating new motivations, or as Bruce G. Trigger observed, "new forms" of intertribal warfare that were often more deadly and more economically motivated than before European incursion into the upper Mississippi region.[43] In 1695 the first Sioux delegation, led by Teeoskahtay (or Tioscaté), visited the *Onontio*, the governor of New France, which, according to Louise Phelps Kellogg, "cemented the alliance" between the Sioux and the French.[44]

By most accounts, it seems Teeoskahtay desired guns—something the French were reluctant to trade—but the meeting resulted in the first formal alliance between the French and the Sioux.[45] Interestingly, the Russians were also reluctant to trade guns with the Kazakhs and issued a decree in 1749 that forbid selling Kazakhs "weapons, gun-powder, flint, or lead."[46] The French and British believed that the weapons trade might positively affect the fur trade, but only if natives used the weapons to hunt and trap and not in warfare against traditional enemies—or worse, against their traders. The French and the British never resolved the problem. Frequently and hypocritically, they willingly traded in weapons if it obstructed their enemies' trade rather than benefited their own. Restricting the trade in weapons was something that both the British and French tried but failed to do to limit conflict between the Sioux and their enemies. The British and French wanted unhindered trade, but they also believed that conflict destabilized the region. The Russians also wanted to expand trade and believed that Kazakh hostilities in the steppe needed to cease, but they also failed to obstruct the weapons trade with the Kazakhs.[47] There was no evidence to suggest that trade in weapons increased warfare in the plains and the steppe, but colonizers certainly believed it did.

1700 TO MIDCENTURY

The first half of the eighteenth century marked significant transitions for the Sioux and the Kazakhs. The Sioux—in particular, the Teton—were migrating westward, having abandoned Wisconsin Territory to occupy regions between the Missouri and Mississippi Rivers, territory claimed by France. Moreover, the French presence in the western fur trade greatly weakened after the Treaty of Ryswick (1697) and subsequent wars with Britain. These imperial conflicts involved numerous Indian tribes, but the conflicts between the Sioux and their rivals continued throughout much of the eighteenth century—in part, for territory, and also, as White noted, because "exchange and alliances were so closely linked, no nation could countenance trade, particularly in weapons, with its enemies or its enemies' allies."[48] The Sioux were only one of the dominant tribes in Minnesota in the seventeenth and eighteenth centuries. The Ojibwa were the dominant tribe in the northern forest regions, whereas the Sioux occupied the southern and western "prairie" parts of the state. Other tribes that migrated into the region included the Hurons, Ottawas, Winnebagos, and Crees.[49]

The Sioux, between 1700 and 1750, were an expanding power on the eastern regions of the northern plains. Most scholars believe that they were motivated to move westward to pursue prime buffalo hunting grounds and due to pressures being applied by Cree expansion into Eastern Sioux regions. There is some evidence to suggest that some Sioux already acquired horses and became quite skilled hunters on horseback. According to the journal of Peter Pond, who spent years living among and trading with the Sioux, the band he traveled with possessed large numbers of horses and dogs, and "thay Run down the Buffelow with thare Horses and Kill as Much Meat as thay Please."[50] As the Sioux migrated westward, they displaced other tribes, such as the Arikara, Mandan, Hidatsa, Assiniboine, Iowa, Omaha, and Ponca.[51] By this time, Euro-Americans reported

FIGURE 2.1. Indian family on the move (courtesy of Denver Public Library).

that the Sioux possessed firearms and frequently referred to them as "turbulent trouble-makers."[52] The Sioux and Chippewa seemingly engaged in ceaseless warfare during this era as the Sioux fought to defend prime hunting grounds, which were vital for survival. War parties from both tribes attacked each other relentlessly if they found an enemy on disputed territory; these skirmishes were necessary for economic security rather than to trade with French or British traders.[53] Euro-Americans were not occupying Sioux territory in this era; although they certainly desired to increase trade, the interaction between the Sioux and Europeans remained chiefly economic, not territorial acquisition.

The Kazakhs were dealing with two slightly different territorial incursions. First, the Russians were actively penetrating the Kazakh Steppe in the early eighteenth century. Between 1714 and 1725, Russia expanded trade with the Kazakhs, profitably exchanging raw materials such as hides, wools, and livestock—especially horses and sheep—and Kazakhs wanted Russian manufactured goods such as "iron and metal shovels and axes, trivets, scissors, buckets and barrels, metal bits, kitchen wares, stirrups, and other goods."[54] In 1713 Siberian governor Prince Matvei Gagarin recommended to Peter the Great that the government build a line of forts to defend the empire's interests.[55]

In 1714 the Russians started construction along a military line—eventually called the Irtysh Line—that consisted of a string of towns and small forts. Several fortified towns started popping up along the Kazakh Steppe, including Omsk (1716), Semipalatinsk (1718), Pavlodar (1720), Ilek (1731), Orsk (1735), Orenburg (1743), and Petropavlovsk (1752).[56] The line extended more than 2,500 miles and eventually included more than forty forts and over one hundred smaller posts.⁵⁷ It would be more than a century before any sort of comparable American presence existed in the northern plains. A significant difference was that the Russians forbid Kazakhs from migrating across the Irtysh Line, a restriction ostensibly placed on Russian peasants as well. The French and British posts, linked loosely together, imposed no such restrictions; no boundary prevented French, British, or, later, Americans, from crossing. The tsarist government, on the other hand, generally barred its peasants from crossing the Irtysh Line into the steppe.⁵⁸

By the early eighteenth century, Russians confronted the Kazakhs along the Irtysh Line, but a second territorial threat seriously challenged Kazakh control in the steppe and altered the relationship between the Kazakhs and the Russians. In the 1720s, a period in Kazakh history called the *Aqtaban-shubyryngdy* (the Great Calamity), the Dzhungar-Kalmyk invasion threatened to overrun the Kazakhs. Chokan Valikhanov, a nineteenth-century Kazakh intellectual, wrote, "the first decade of the eighteenth century was a horrible time in the lives of the Kirgiz [Kazakh] people. The Dzhungars, the Volga Kalmyks, the Siberian Cossacks and Bashkirs from all sides thundered, stole cattle and carried off whole families as prisoners."⁵⁹ It was during the era of the Dzhungar-Kalmyk threat that the Russian government exploited the situation and seized nearly 45 million *desiatin* (1 desiatin equals 2.7 acres) of the most "fertile" land and "secured water sources" for settlement by Russian-Cossack peasants.⁶⁰

Here again is an important difference between the Sioux and the Kazakhs throughout the eighteenth century. Most scholars agree that either the Sioux fled their homeland or they deliberately migrated westward to camp closer to vast plains' buffalo herds, their principal food source. In any event, as the Sioux moved westward, they forced migrations by other tribes and, subsequently, fought to hold the territory formerly occupied or bounded by tribes unable to resist their invasion of the northern plains. Unlike the Kazakhs, the Sioux were an expanding power. By the mid-eighteenth century, guarding and occupying the Kazakh Steppe required constant vigilance and defense against external aggressors. The Sioux were equally vigilant to incursions by neighbors but enemies pressed the Kazakhs from all sides: Russia and its allies; the Tatars and Bashkirs, from the west; China, in the east, claimed parts of the steppe; and, from the south, Turkestan khanates, Kirgiz, and Turkmen were pressing from different flanks. Enemies did not encircle the Sioux in quite the same way. Clearly, other tribes tried to push the Sioux from the prime hunting grounds, but Sioux enemies never mustered a comparable military power to succeed. Added to this volatile, tenuous mix, the Dzhungar-Kalmyk threat rivaled Kazakh military power, and the Kazakhs struggled to find allies to defend their lands. What happened next fundamentally altered the relationship between the Russians and the Kazakhs.

In 1730 two missives from Abulkhair, khan of the Little Horde, reached Saint Petersburg, requesting Russian assistance against the Dzhungar-Kalmyk threat— a request the Russians seemed eager to exploit. In 1731 the Russians dispatched a mission to complete negotiations to bring the horde under Russian suzerainty— or that was how the Russians viewed this diplomatic mission. Abulkhair promised "faithful service" to Russia, but there continues to be a debate about his motives.[61] Abulkhair was fighting against the Bashkirs, who were already subject to Russian rule, and the Dzhungar-Kalmyks. Moreover, Abulkhair faced internal opposition from Sultan Kaip for leadership of the Little Horde. The Russian government was well aware of Abulkhair's precarious position and decided to exploit it in order to strengthen the Irtysh Line and advance its trading interests with Bukhara and Khiva.[62]

In taking the oath, Abulkhair claimed to be "Khan of all the Kazakhs," a dubious notion due to the fact that his authority did not extend beyond the Little Horde—a fact that did not seem to alarm the Russians.[63] In fact, it likely served Russia's interests. The problem was that Abulkhair's interests conflicted with Russia's interests and expectations. Abulkhair wanted to enhance his own authority and perhaps receive an "official" title from Russia. What he wanted was assistance against both the internal challenges to his rule and aid against the external Dzhungar-Kalmyk threat rather than incorporation into the Russian Empire.[64] He was not surrendering Little Horde sovereignty, but that was exactly how the Russians interpreted the oath of loyalty.[65]

This was a turning point because from this moment forward, Russia claimed sovereignty over all of the Kazakhs, not just Kazakhs of the Little Horde. In addition, Russia claimed control of the territory—the Kazakh Steppe—and simply annexed it into the empire. Since the 1730s, many Russians claimed that Abulkhair's request represented the unification (*prisoedinenie*) of Kazakhstan to Russia. Nineteenth-century Russian Orientalist Vasilii Grigoriev insisted the "voluntary submission of the numerous Horde of Kirghiz [Kazakh] who had been formerly hostile to us . . . and it was recalled to mind that Peter the Great himself had been of the opinion . . . that 'this Horde, though a nomad and light-thinking people, was yet the key and the gate of all the lands and countries of Asia.'"[66] Historian Geoffrey Wheeler succinctly summarized the consequences this way: "It can be said with a fair degree of certainty that although by 1730 the Russians had formulated no definite plans for the overrunning of the Steppe Region, the fate of the Kazakhs was sealed in the sense that henceforward their future was to be bound up with Russia."[67] The Kazakhs did not cede or sell the land to the Russians, but that mattered little from the Russian perspective. Over the course of the next several decades, many Kazakhs fought vigorously against Russian rule, and others cooperated with the Russian government. Russia eagerly bestowed titles, lands, and salaries on Kazakh khans, sultans, aksakals, and others who embraced Russian expansion and colonization.

This is an important comparative difference, not just in the temporal sense of Russian internal colonization but also in the manner that incorporated the land into the empire. A border-frontier zone between the Russian Empire and the Kazakhs emerged along the Irtysh Line, but the Russians interpreted Abulkhair's oath as not just the allegiance of the Little Horde to the Russian Empire but Kazakhs surrendering their sovereignty to Russian imperial rule. It was, from the Russian perspective, the surrender of Kazakh claims to the land. In comparison, the French might claim parts of Wisconsin for New France or interpret Teeoskatay's visit to Montreal as cementing an alliance between the French and the Sioux, but it was a commercial alliance, not the surrender of political and territorial sovereignty, which is precisely how the Russians interpreted Abulkhair's oath. Comparatively, the French might claim the posts gave them title to the land where they built them, but the original purpose was to exclude the British from the region rather than assert spurious title to the land or deny Indian title.[68] The French did not assume title to all Sioux lands or authority over all Sioux bands. The Russians were not the first external power to claim suzerainty over the Kazakh Steppe, but the numerous pressures in the steppe prevented the Kazakhs from using the vast lands to flee to safety; it was no longer the refuge from external threats. In other words, flight into the steppe no longer provided safety and security for the Kazakhs. For the Sioux, however, the northern plains and Minnesota prairies became the sanctuary from French, British, and, later, American expansion.

Another difference was that the British tended to settle along the eastern seaboard; the French did not occupy large tracts of land in what became the United States. French, British, and Spanish colonies were sufficiently distant from Sioux territories that trade relations remained sporadic. Settlements near the Sioux were small when compared to the Russian presence near or in the northern Kazakh Steppe. According to the Orenburg governor, in 1755 almost 37,000 Cossacks were dispersed along the Irtysh Line, stationed at the various forts and small posts. This does not take into account the number of Russians living well behind the line or engaged in trade.[69] In the colony of New France, in 1698, the population of Quebec was slightly more than 15,000; in 1754, it was roughly 55,000, well away from Sioux territories.[70] In comparison, between 1719 and 1750, the number of French engaged in the western fur trade was small, perhaps from 200 to 600 men.[71] The French were not inclined to leave the colony or settle outside the comforts of Quebec. The Russians, on the other hand, were actively pushing the line of advance that Kliuchevskii described. No such line of advance appeared in the plains until after American independence. It was not until the nineteenth century that the Sioux confronted American pioneers and military power as an escalating source of confusion and conflict.

MIDCENTURY TO 1800

In the second half of the century, the Sioux were an expanding power in the Minnesota prairies and the northern plains, but Sioux relations with the French or British—or, subsequently, the United States—were chiefly economic. Intertribal warfare, however, caused concern among traders and French and British military men, particularly if it disrupted trade. The Seven Years' War—or, as it is often called in the United States, the French and Indian War—was fought between Great Britain and France for imperial dominance; and when it ended in 1763, according to nineteenth-century historian Francis Parkman, it "made England what she is. It crippled the commerce of her rival, ruined France in two continents, and blighted her as a colonial power."[72] The British pursued a different course than the French in their relations with Indians—in particular, many British leaders believed that the French pampered the Indians, gave unwarranted gifts, and followed a "kind of imperialism that civilized men thought they should by right exert over 'savages.' "[73] Consequently, the Sioux cautiously gravitated toward improved relations with the British. It was a different matter altogether in the Kazakh Steppe.

Following Abulkhair's oath in the 1730s, interludes of peace and trade were shattered by periods of internecine conflict and clashes between Russians and Kazakhs. The Russians attempted to reinforce the Irtysh Line with the Cossacks and expand trade with the Turkestan khanates and China. In 1740 Ablai, of the Middle Horde, swore an oath of loyalty to Russia, but that did not give Russia dominance in the steppe, nor did it end the internecine conflict among the Kazakhs.[74] Ablai become the dominant Kazakh political player in the mid- to late eighteenth century but was unable to assert his control over other Kazakh khans, hordes, or clans. By the 1750s, however, Russia and China eliminated the Dzhungar-Kalmyk threat, reached a trade agreement, and temporarily reconciled their imperial differences.

The Russians pursued a different course with the Kazakhs in an effort to protect their settlements and secure trade routes with China and the Turkestan khanates. In 1757 the Russians imposed further restrictions on Kazakhs that forbid any from migrating and camping within ten *versty* (versta, singular form, a unit of distance equal to 1.06 km) of any Russian fort.[75] If any violated this territorial restriction, Russians required the aksakal to make an "oath of peacefulness" to the post commander.[76] By this time, however, many Kazakhs openly resisted Russian control and Russian officials wearied of "coddling" the Kazakhs and detested addressing their demands with "pleasures and tenderness."[77] Russian historian M. A. Terent'ev understood the issue in a respectable imperial approach: the "submission of the Kirgiz [Kazakhs] was quite odd; they paid no taxes nor fulfilled any obligations, but our government courted them only for the honor of being considered the master of the Kirgiz."[78] In both the British and Russian case, the expanding empire asserted authority over territory claimed by the Sioux and the Kazakhs.

The Treaty of Paris (1763) forced the French to cede Canada and the territory east of the Mississippi River to the British and relinquish the Louisiana colony to Spain.[79] No imperial power consulted the Indians affected, nor did the Sioux fully comprehend that the territory they defended against the Chippewa, Crow, Mandan, and Blackfeet was also claimed by Spain. The Sioux did understand, however, that the French lost the war and the British became the new dominant trading partner. The Spanish made little attempt to engage the Sioux through trade, but the Sioux eagerly hoped to acquire more guns and horses from the Europeans.

Following the Seven Years' War, the British restricted all commercial land transactions between individuals and Indians. After 1763 only colonial governments, acting on behalf of the Crown, conducted and sanctioned land purchases between individuals and Indians. The Proclamation of 1763 transformed the colonial land market, but more importantly, transactions were agreements between sovereign nations rather than contracts agreed to between individuals. The British feared that unregulated land purchases unnecessarily increased tensions with the Indians, particularly in the Ohio Valley and trans-Alleghany west. It transformed a formerly private matter into one in which title to the land was conveyed only by treaty. This fact, according to historian Stuart Banner, made it easier to perceive of Indians' claim to the land as less than title to it.[80]

There was also a concern that the uncivilized environment might seduce European settlers into becoming something less civilized. The fear of the "menacing Asiatic character of the plains" in nineteenth-century American thought echoed British concerns about unregulated settlement in the Ohio Valley and trans-Alleghany west.[81] One reason so many Indians fought alongside the French during the Seven Years' War was the widespread fear that the war was only for the British desire to "plunder Indians." The tribes did not want to surrender their relationship or land rights from one European power to another that might dislocate them or, as the British did, claim the land for themselves. The British vowed to retreat from the Ohio Valley region after the war but changed their minds and occupied the various abandoned French forts.[82]

For this comparison, the concern expressed by British parliamentarian and philosopher Edmund Burke in 1775 is too irresistible to ignore. He explained to the House of Commons that it might isolate settlers cut off from all civilizing influences if the British government failed to occupy the newly acquired territory and tried to prevent settlement in the Ohio Valley and trans-Alleghany west. He reasoned, accordingly, and with utilitarian imagery, that eventually the infected and exposed settlers would "become hordes of English Tartars, and, pouring down upon your unfortified frontiers a fierce and irresistible cavalry" to plunder and pillage in characteristic Asiatic fashion.[83] It was a fear often expressed by Russian officials as well—namely, that Cossacks or Russian peasants might become more native than the natives. In other words, the wilderness—the wild untamed land, a land without civilization—influenced the inhabitants' character and behavior and caused them to regress from civilized to barbarian. Therefore, it was necessary to tame the land and bring the inhabitants under the sway of civilization through trade and sedentary agriculture.[84] To settlers and peasants settling on either side of the frontier, there was a blurred line between civilization and native. In imperial capitals, there was a clear and absolute demarcation.

During the 1760s and 1770s, the Russians also debated the future of relations with the Kazakhs, particularly the continued internecine conflict in the steppe and the Kazakhs' failure to protect caravans. In addition, the Russians were reacting to one of the most serious peasant rebellions in Russian history—the Pugachev Revolt (1773–1775)—in which many Kazakhs also participated. Emelian Pugachev was a Cossack from Siberia, a military deserter who objected to Cossacks' increasing acceptance of Saint Petersburg's authority over them. The revolt tapped into growing peasant discontent and attracted peasants, religious dissenters ("Old Believers"), and many non-Russians, including Kazakhs, Bashkirs, Tatars, and Kalmyks. Pugachev claimed to be Catherine the Great's murdered husband—Peter III—and promised freedom from serfdom, taxes, and military service. Catherine dismissed these promises as "castles in the air," but the revolt spread rapidly.[85] One reason that many Kazakhs joined the revolt was because for several years, the Russians limited and then completely restricted access to various pastures near the Irtysh Line and the fertile fields between the Ural and Volga Rivers, commonly referred to as the Inner Side. Kazakhs continued—illegally, from the Russian perspective—to pasture livestock there, crossing the Ural or, in the minds of many Russian officials, trespassing on regulated lands. These tensions between Kazakhs pasturing their livestock on traditional lands and Russian desires to restrict access heightened tensions between colonized and colonizer.

The revolt was violent, marked by looting and the destruction of large estates and factories. The revolt threatened every major town in western Siberia and the steppe.[86] Well-trained government troops, fresh from Russia's war with the Ottoman Empire, eventually defeated Pugachev's rebel forces, and Pugachev's own men turned him over to the government. He was caged, hauled to Moscow, tried, and decapitated, with his various body parts displayed throughout the city.

Kazakhs divided during the rebellion; some clans fought with Pugachev, some against him, and many remained neutral. Some, such as Nurali, khan of the Little Horde, switched sides during the rebellion, fighting first with Pugachev and then with the Russians.[87] After the revolt, in 1801, the Russians rewarded Nurali for his support during the Pugachev Rebellion and allowed his Little Horde followers to cross the Ural River to pasture their herds on the Inner Side. This prompted his rivals in the Little Horde, and some Kazakhs in the Middle Horde, to accuse him of perfidy. These internal Kazakh political tensions exacerbated the internecine conflict in the steppe. As with American Indians, often forced to side with the French or the British during their imperial conflicts in North America, the Pugachev Rebellion forced many Kazakhs to choose. Many, such as Nurali, sided with the Russians in order to accrue greater benefits, whereas others seemingly believed that rejecting Russian expansion was more in their self-interest. Similar to the Kazakhs, the Sioux confronted difficult choices.

Following the British victory in the Seven Years' War, some Santee Dakota attempted to establish diplomatic and trade relations with the British. In 1763 twelve Dakota leaders offered allegiance to Great Britain, but the motivation to do so was probably similar to Abulkhair's oath to the Russians. Many Sioux bands sided with the colonizing power, and others did not. It appeared that some Santee Dakota wanted British trade goods and assistance against their enemies; siding with the British possibly offered the opportunity to reinforce the relationship. In 1774 Captain Arent DePeyster, commander of Mackinac, mediated a dispute between the Santee Dakota and the Ojibwa. Early in the American Revolution, Wabasha, a Santee chief, traveled to Quebec to pledge alliance to the British, thereby becoming "King George's westernmost allies."[88] Some Sioux attempted to negotiate with the Spanish to increase trade. The Sioux did not play a noteworthy role during the American Revolution. Nonetheless, two significant events followed the war that consequently affected the Sioux as well as all Indians in the newly established United States.

Shortly after the war ended, the United States, following British practice, signed treaties with tribes in the Ohio Valley region that procured large territorial cessions.[89] It was a tactic the United States pursued throughout the nineteenth century, including with various Sioux bands. In May 1783 the British evacuated their forts, and Congress directed the secretary of war to advise the various Indian nations that the conflict was over and that the United States wanted peace with the numerous tribes. In September of that year, Congress prohibited settlement on inhabited or claimed Indian lands outside state jurisdiction and banned the purchase or receipt of any Indian lands "without the express authority and direction of Congress." All such acquisitions, either through purchase or cession, became invalid.[90] These treaties, according to White, were "products of American illusions" that "launched the republic into a confrontation" with western Indians.[91] The United States was unable to control immigration from the eastern states into the Ohio Valley, yet these settlers were "at once the strength of the new republic and the greatest threat to it."[92] More than two thousand families moved onto land in Ohio closed to settlement, a problem that also played out in the Kazakh Steppe throughout the nineteenth century. The Russians called illegal settlers *samovol'tsy* (unauthorized), peasants who defied Russian authorities and moved into the Kazakh Steppe to settle on land putatively set aside for the Kazakhs. As in the United States, these Russian settlers were the vanguard of expansion but were doing so illegally. The government decided to move the boundary rather than remove the settlers.

The expanding American republic did not initially confront the Sioux, as the American boundary remained east of the Mississippi River, but subsequent events brought significant changes. Many Sioux bands continued their own westward migration, but the British and Spanish still played a more important role in the Mississippi and Missouri River regions.[93] The British, in particular, tried to block American fur traders from operating there, but the 1780s experienced a revival in the upper Missouri fur trade.[94] In 1787 the United States passed the Northwest Ordinance to govern its newly acquired lands in Ohio. The essential feature of this act was that it outlined how to admit new states to the union, and, importantly for future expansion, it guaranteed equality between a newly created state with the original thirteen states.[95]

In 1790 the "Act to Regulate Trade and Intercourse With the Indian Tribes" stipulated the right of the United States to invalidate any sale of lands by individual Indians. According to the act, "no sale of land made by any Indians, or any nation or tribe of Indians, within the United States, shall be valid to any person or persons, or to any State, whether having the right of pre-emption to such lands or not, unless the same shall be made and duly executed at some public treaty, held under the authority of the United States."[96] The government designed the act to prevent land speculators from taking advantage of Indians, widely called the right of "pre-emption," but, as Banner argued, it was misleading. It was not the right to preempt the purchase of land before someone else, but rather to deny or prevent anyone but the government to purchase land. Section 7 of the act mention that it "shall be in force for the term of two years," but the act remained in effect throughout the nineteenth century and, in fact, is still US law.

In the 1790s, the trader Jean Baptiste Truteau noticed that many Sioux were engaged in hunting beaver and other peltries that they "exchange for merchandise with the other Sioux."[97] Jay's Treaty in 1794 established reciprocal trade privileges for Americans and British Canadians, easing tensions that trade with the Sioux—in particular, among the Yankton and Teton—improved substantially.[98] The close of the eighteenth century witnessed further expansion of the Sioux into the western plains but also set the United States on its own course of westward expansion. Thus, whereas the United States was only establishing the mechanisms to incorporate and colonize new territories that brought American traders and pioneers closer to the Sioux, the Russians encountered stiff Kazakh resistance to their further colonization in the steppe.

In the 1780s and 1790s, relations between Russia and Kazakhs worsened. In the winter of 1782–1783, Srym Batyr crossed the Ural River to pasture on the Inner Side. The Russians attempted to stop him and managed to force him back across the river. Intermittent fighting between Kazakhs and Cossacks, Kazakhs and Russians, and inter-Kazakh spread throughout the steppe. Typical of the fighting was the complaint made to Catherine by one Kazakh aksakal, who claimed that some 1,500 Cossacks attacked his "innocent aul, plundered, looted, and killed 150 people, took fifty-seven prisoners, and ran off with a large number of horses, camels, cattle, and sheep."[99] This is only one example of the complaints Kazakhs made to the Russian government that foreshadowed similar complaints made by the Sioux to the American government; but Kazakhs were also committing deprivations against Russians and Cossacks and against each other. Russia was taking sides in the internecine Kazakh conflict, favoring some against others. This culminated in 1801, with the creation of the Bukei (or Inner) Horde, although it did not end the opposition of many Kazakhs against Russian expansion.

In conclusion, Euro-American and Russian expansion into the lands claimed by the Sioux and the Kazakhs, respectively, followed different paths. Russian expansion started roughly two hundred years before an American presence in the northern plains. Before the nineteenth century, the northern plains and the Kazakh Steppe were in constant flux and constant struggle, and neither the Sioux nor the Kazakhs controlled the lands they claimed except through the exercise of their own military power. Powerful external forces pushed and pulled the Sioux and the Kazakhs to defend the land against various rivals, of which the Russians, Europeans, and, later, Americans, were only one part.

Europeans barely penetrated the eastern shores of North America when the Russians conquered Kazan in 1552. The waves of the Euro-American trajectory into the northern plains is decidedly different than Russia's route to Siberia and the Kazakh Steppe, but it eventually shared a similar pattern of contiguous territorial advances and stages. Russians had already started building a line of forts bordering the Kazakh Steppe, manned by Cossacks, by the time of the first known tentative meeting between a French Jesuit trader and a Sioux in 1659–1660.

From Euro-American and Russian perspectives, it was necessary to support imperial expansion in order to secure economic profit, which required further access and expanded networks. Moreover, the expansion required security and, ultimately, peace and stability in the frontier regions, but when the Euro-Americans and Russians moved closer to the regions inhabited by the Sioux and the Kazakhs, what they encountered was sporadic warfare that was an obstacle to economic and settler expansion. Euro-Americans and Russians sought to end conflict on the northern plains and in the Kazakh Steppe in order to facilitate trade. The Sioux and the Kazakhs engaged in the fur trade sporadically and in some capacity, but neither were principal participants.

By the nineteenth century, Americans and Russians eventually used the conflicts in the northern plains and the Kazakh Steppe to justify their own military presence and territorial expansion, claiming that violations and depredations committed by the Sioux or the Kazakhs demanded a martial response.[100] In the eighteenth century, as Jeremy Adelman and Stephen Aron observed in the North American context, the Sioux and the Kazakhs lived astride frontier regions that became the sites of "intense imperial rivalry and of particularly fluid relations between indigenous peoples and European interlopers."[101]

Throughout the seventeenth and eighteenth centuries, the French and British sought to increase trade with the Sioux, not expand their territory to force the Sioux to surrender their political or territorial sovereignty. In the seventeenth century, Russia played a minor role in the Kazakh Steppe, but following Abulkhair's oath, the threat to Kazakh sovereignty became tangible. In North America, the Sioux control over their territory was threatened, which lessened as the Sioux migrated west, but the French and British threat was not, as it was with Abulkhair's pledge, an attempt to incorporate the Sioux into the French or British Empires in North America. The French and British wanted trading partners; there was not the comparable territorial extension, which was evident in

Russia's territorial expansion, by the French and the British that posed a threat to Sioux sovereignty. The more strident threat, however, as it was in the steppe, to Sioux sovereignty came from the Chippewa or other tribes and not from European imperialism. Russia's expansion was both a commercial and territorial expansion, whereas in the centuries before American independence the French and British expansion was chiefly economic. In both cases, however, commercial expansion instigated intertribal or internecine conflict.[102]

The Sioux and the Kazakhs defended their territory against powerful, non-European rivals, but Euro-Americans and Russians used their economic relations to foster relations with the Sioux and Kazakhs that slowly evolved to serve as levers for territorial expansion throughout the nineteenth century. In a sense, land was central to these agreements and central to the disputes. The Russians apparently never hesitated to annex the land, whereas Europeans in North American pursued two different paths. Generally, they tried to purchase the land from Native Americans, but on some occasions, they too simply annexed it by right of discovery and conquest. What emerged in American and Russian expansionist thinking in the nineteenth century was a moral argument, or civilization versus savagery, that was largely absent in the seventeenth and eighteenth centuries, when trade and security were the principal incentives for expansion that was more indirect than the direct settler internal colonization of the nineteenth century.

NOTES

1. I decided to use the term *Euro-American* merely to represent, in a generic sense, the French, British, and Spanish expansion into North America for the period before American independence. A comparable generic label describes "Russian" imperialism for this period because more often than not, Russian expansion was the result of Cossack colonization and settlement securing for the Russian regime a region rather than the Russian army or Russian peasants. When appropriate, I will identify French, British, Spanish, or Cossacks specifically.

2. Richard White, *The Middle Ground: Indians, Empires, and Republics in the Great Lakes Region, 1650–1815* (Cambridge: Cambridge University Press, 1991), 2. As with so many others, I owe a debt of gratitude to White for piecing together this "fragmented" history into an excellent, coherent whole. The Russian expansion into Siberia and the Kazakh Steppe in the seventeenth and eighteenth centuries was a complex process, and historians are fortunate to have a deep historical record to draw upon to examine the process of trade and expansion in the Kazakh Steppe. Historians, however, lack the same dense historical record to examine the world of the northern plains in the sixteenth and seventeenth century, although a rough sketch emerges based on the periodic travelers' and traders' reports that survive. By the second half of the eighteenth century, the historical record of events in the northern plains, while still sparse, is much broader. Given the paucity of information about the Sioux when compared to the Kazakhs in the sixteenth, seventeenth, and eighteenth centuries, scholars are required to

piece together the history by gleaning bits and pieces of evidence almost exclusively from a handful of French materials, usually by Jesuits or traders who learned about them from other tribes or had brief contact with some bands. Piecing together the histories of Euro-American expansion into the northern plains and Russian expansion into the Kazakh Steppe requires a heavy reliance on Euro-American and Russian sources, but that is unavoidable.

Some of the earliest French visitors wrote about their times with the Lakota and Dakota, who they usually referred to in these written records by the name "Scioux" (or some variant of "Nadoussious," "Nadousse," "Natowessiwak," or "Nadouessioux") and other phonetic renderings. By the late eighteenth century, however, sources start to use terms such as *Teton* or *Lakota*, or *Teton Lakota* or *Teton Sioux*. In other words, references started to be more consistent and reflected what the Teton or Santee, for example, called themselves. There is similar confusion about the Kazakhs in Russian sources. Throughout the eighteenth and nineteenth centuries, the Russians referred to the Kazakhs as "Kirghiz" or "Kirghiz-Kazakhs," sometimes "Kirghiz-Kaisaks," terms used until the 1920s. The people we know today as Kirgiz the Russians called "Kara-Kirgiz" (Black Kirgiz) or "Dikii-Kirgiz" (Wild Kirgiz).

3. Richard White, "The Winning of the West: The Expansion of the Western Sioux in the Eighteenth and Nineteenth Centuries," *Journal of American History* 65, no. 2 (September 1978): 320–21.

4. Andreas Kappeler, *The Russian Empire: A Multiethnic History*, trans. Alfred Clayton (Harlow, UK: Pearson Education, 2001), 18.

5. By the nineteenth century, Russian expansion remained this organic process—a natural gathering of lands—but American expansion presumed a divine mission: Manifest Destiny.

6. See, for example, Gary Clayton Anderson, "Early Dakota Migration and Intertribal War: A Revision," *Western Historical Quarterly* 11, no. 1 (January 1980): 17–36; Colin G. Calloway, "The Inter-tribal Balance of Power on the Great Plains, 1760–1850," *Journal of American Studies* 16, no. 1 (1982): 25–47; White, "Winning of the West"; Anthony R. McGinnis, *Counting Coup and Cutting Horses: Intertribal Warfare on the Northern Plains, 1738–1889* (Lincoln: University of Nebraska Press, 2010); Joseph M. Prince and Richard H. Steckel, "Nutritional Success on the Great Plains: Nineteenth-Century Equestrian Nomads," *Journal of Interdisciplinary History* 33, no. 3 (Winter 2003): 353–84; Mary K. Whelan, "Dakota Indian Economics and the Nineteenth-Century Fur Trade," *Ethnohistory* 40, no. 2 (Spring 1993): 246–76; James H. Howard, "Some Further Thoughts on Eastern Dakota 'Clans,'" *Ethnohistory* 26, no. 2 (Spring 1979): 133–40; Jeffrey Ostler, *The Plains Sioux and U.S. Colonialism from Lewis and Clark to Wounded Knee* (Cambridge: Cambridge University Press, 2004); Doane Robinson, *A History of the Dakota or Sioux Indians*. . . . (Minneapolis: Ross & Haines, 1967).

7. Sandzhar D. Asfendiarov, *Istoriia Kazakhstana (s drevneishikh vremen)* (Almaty: Sanat, 1998 [1935]), 85–100.

8. In the mid-seventeenth century, however, the Russian expansion in Siberia was more comparable to a network and, as James Belich noted, was a "system of interaction similar to that of the French fur trade in North America at the same time." *Replenishing the Earth: The Settler Revolution and the Rise of the Anglo-World, 1783–1939* (Oxford: Oxford University Press, 2009), 38.

9. Guy Gibbon, *The Sioux: The Dakota and Lakota Nations* (Malden, MA: Blackwell, 2003), 48.

10. Abulkhair was khan of the Little Horde.

11. According to Janet Martin, Russian traders long participated in the fur trade, noting, "In the 11–12th centuries sable, ermine and other northern luxury fur had been exported to the oriental world from Bulgar and to the Byzantine Empire from Kiev." Moreover, "The

Golden Horde did, in fact, collect its first taxes from its northern subjects in fur." "The Land of Darkness and the Golden Horde. The Fur Trade under the Mongols XIII–XIVth Centuries," *Cahiers du monde russe et soviétique* 19, no. 4 (October/December 1978): 403–6. According to George V. Lantzeff, "The iasak collected from natives constituted from sixty-five to eighty percent of the total amount of Siberian furs received by the Treasury of the Tsar." "Beginnings of the Siberian Colonial Administration," *Pacific Historical Review* 9, no. 1 (March 1940): 51.

12. A. P. Okladnikov and O. N. Vilkov, "Prisoedinenie zapadnoi Sibiri k Rossii i razvitie ekonomicheskikh sviazei s Kazakhstanom v kontse XVI—pervoi chetverti XVIII v.," *Izvestiia Akademii Nauk Kazakhskoi SSR* (May/June 1982): 21.

13. Turar R. Ryskulov, *Kazakstan* (Moscow, 1927), 22.

14. Father Lelemant, "The Journey of Raymbault and Jogues to the Sault, 1641," in *Early Narratives of the Northwest, 1634–1699*, ed. Louise Phelps Kellogg (New York: Charles Scribner's Sons, 1917), 24; Reuben Gold Thwaites, ed., "Relation of 1642," in *The Jesuit Relations and Allied Documents* (Cleveland, OH: Burrows Brothers, 1898), 23:223–27. Some spellings are "Raumbaut."

15. Robinson, *History of the Dakota or Sioux*, 21.

16. Reuben Gold Thwaites, preface to *Collections of the State Historical Society of Wisconsin*, ed. Reuben Gold Thwaites, vol. 16 (Madison: State Historical Society of Wisconsin, 1908), xiv.

17. W. J. Eccles, "The Fur Trade and Eighteenth-Century Imperialism," *William and Mary Quarterly* 40, no. 3 (July 1983): 342.

18. Louise Phelps Kellogg, "The First Traders in Wisconsin," *Wisconsin Magazine of History* 5, no. 4 (June 1922): 354.

19. Peter Esprit Radisson, *Voyages of Peter Esprit Radisson, Being an Account of his Travels and Experiences among the North American Indians, from 1652 to 1684* (Boston: Prince Society, 1885), 213.

20. Bruce White, "Encounters with Spirits: Ojibwa and Dakota Theories about the French and Their Merchandise," *Ethnohistory* 41, no. 3 (Summer 1994): 381.

21. Allouez quoted in "Of the Mission to the Nadouesiouek," in Phelps, *Early Narratives*, 132; Charles Moore, *The Northwest under Three Flags, 1635–1796* (New York: Harper & Brothers, 1900), 22. In a brief biographical note about Allouez, compiler and historian John Gilmary Shea quoted Allouez's notes from a council with numerous tribes as "those who gathered round that lone cross of the wilderness, with nations from the western sea, Dahcotahs, Assiniboins and Winnebagoes, with their Tartar dialect and thought." See John Gilmary Shea, ed., *Discovery and Exploration of the Mississippi Valley: With the Original Narratives of Marquette, Allouez, Membré, Hennepin, and Anastase Douay*, 2nd ed. (Albany, NY: Joseph McDonough, 1903), 71–72.

22. Louise Phelps Kellogg, "Fort Beauharnois," *Minnesota History* 8, no. 3 (September 1927): 232; Rhoda R. Gilman, "The Fur Trade in the Upper Mississippi Valley, 1630–1850," *Wisconsin Magazine of History* 58, no. 1 (Autumn 1974): 5.

23. One later scholar writes that Radisson "made a treaty" with the Sioux, although he also writes that little was known of his travels among the Sioux, which suggests he did not consult any number of works that reprint "Radisson's travels." See Clarence A. Vandiveer, *The Fur Trade and Early Western Exploration* (Cleveland, OH: Arthur H. Clark, 1929), 89.

24. Eccles, "Fur Trade and Eighteenth-Century Imperialism," 348.

25. Gilman, "Fur Trade in the Upper Mississippi Valley," 6; White, *Middle Ground*, 58.

26. Kliuchevskii quoted in Alexander Kiesewetter, "Klyuchevsky and Russian History," *Slavonic Review* 1, no. 3 (March 1923): 514.

27. Alton S. Donnelly, "The Mobile Steppe Frontier: The Russian Conquest of Colonization of Bashkiria and Kazakhstan to 1850," in *Russian Colonial Expansion to 1917*, ed. Michael Rywkin (London: Mansell, 1988), 193. According to George V. Lantzeff, the Russians developed "a network of forts and blockhouses, generally referred to as *ostrogs*." "Siberian Colonial Administration," 48.

28. White, *Middle Ground*, 58, italics in original.

29. James F. Brooks, *Captives and Cousins: Slavery, Kinship, and Community in the Southwest Borderlands* (Chapel Hill: University of North Carolina Press, 2002), 4

30. White, *Middle Ground*, x.

31. V. K. Kazantsev, "Russkie starozhily v Sibiri i Srednei Azii," in *Aziatskaia Rossiia*, ed. G. V. Glinka (St. Petersburg: Obshchestvenniia pol'za, 1914), 1:179.

32. Thomas M. Barrett, *At the Edge of Empire: The Terek Cossacks and the North Caucasus Frontier, 1700–1860* (Boulder, CO: Westview, 1999), 165–66; Thomas Biolsi, *Deadliest Enemies: Law and Race Relations on and off Rosebud Reservation* (Berkeley: University of California Press, 2007), 5. In a contrary interpretation, historian Dominic Lieven claimed Russia treated the indigenous Siberians with an appalling brutality and the "trade in indigenous women" was almost as profitable as its trade in furs. *Empire: The Russian Empire and Its Rivals* (New Haven, CT: Yale University Press, 2001), 223.

33. For a brief description of the Stroganov family and its spectacular rise to prominence, see W. Bruce Lincoln, *The Conquest of a Continent: Siberia and the Russians* (Ithaca, NY: Cornell University Press, 1994), 34–40.

34. *Istoriia Kazakhskoi SSR s drevneishikh vremen do nashikh dnei v piati tomakh* (Alma-Ata: Nauka, 1979), 2:282.

35. See Ilya Vinkovetsky, *Russian America: An Overseas Colony of a Continental Empire, 1804–1867* (Oxford: Oxford University Press, 2011).

36. Anthony Jenkinson, *Early Voyages and Travels to Russia and Persia by Anthony Jenkinson and Other Englishmen. With Some Account of the First Intercourse of the English with Russia and Central Asia by Way of the Caspian Sea*, ed. E. Delmar Morgan and C. H. Coote (New York: Bert Franklin, 1886), 1:95.

37. V. Ia. Basin and U. A. Umurzakov, "Russko-Kazakhskie torgovye sviazi v period prisoedineniia Kazakhstana k Rossii," *Izvestiia AN KazSSR* (1982): 14.

38. Gavin Hambly, *Central Asia* (New York: Delacorte, 1969), 140–49. Oirat is the name given to several groups of Western Mongols inhabiting the Lake Baikal region. By the fifteenth century, an Oirat confederation expanded westward to establish a region called Dzhungaria, situated on the border between modern-day Kazakhstan and China. Kalmyks are an Oirat tribe that resettled in the Kazakh Steppe region. The Kalmyks eventually submitted to Russian suzerainty in the early eighteenth century.

39. White, *Middle Ground*, 25.

40. Eccles, "Fur Trade and Eighteenth-Century Imperialism," 348.

41. Frank E. Ross, "The Fur Trade of the Western Great Lakes Region," *Minnesota History* 19, no. 3 (September 1938): 275. It is unlikely that any Sioux were included in this ceremony, but it reflects French aspirations to control the fur trade. Moreover, according to Gary Clayton Anderson, early sources seem to confirm the fact that, by the late seventeenth century, the majority of Dakota already migrated west of the Mississippi, so the Sioux that the French dealt with in the 1790s and subsequently were Lakota. See Anderson, "Early Dakota Migration," 22.

42. Ross, "Fur Trade of the Western Great Lakes," 277–84; White, *Middle Ground*, 31–33.

43. Bruce G. Trigger, "The Jesuits and the Fur Trade," *Ethnohistory* 12, no. 1 (Winter 1965): 34

44. Kellogg, "Fort Beauharnois," 233.
45. White, "Encounters with Spirits, 389.
46. I. I. Kraft, *Sbornik uzakonenii o kirgizakh stepnykh oblastei* (Orenburg: Zharinov, 1898), 20, 25.
47. Gilman, "Fur Trade in the Upper Mississippi Valley," 6. King William's War, between France and Britain, however, spilled over into North America and renewed hostilities between the French and the British-backed Iroquois. Less than a year after Teeoskatay's visit to Montreal, the French closed the western trading posts, resulting in a two-decade disruption to the French fur trade.
48. White, *Middle Ground*, 107.
49. Lucius F. Hubbard, James H. Baker, William P. Murray, and Warren Upham, eds., *Minnesota in Three Centuries, 1655–1908* (Mankato: Publishing Society of Minnesota, 1908), 1:93.
50. Peter Pond, "1740–75: Journal of Peter Pond," *Collections of the State Historical Society of Wisconsin*, ed. Reuben Gold Thwaites, vol. 18 (Madison: State Historical Society of Wisconsin, 1908), 353.
51. Calloway, "Inter-tribal Balance of Power," 45.
52. George Hyde, *Red Cloud's Folk: A History of the Oglala Sioux Indians* (1937; Norman: University of Oklahoma Press, 1975), 14.
53. John Ewers, "When Red and White Men Met," *Western Historical Quarterly* 2, no. 2 (April 1971): 142; White, *Middle Ground*, 147.
54. Basin and Umurzakov, "Russko-Kazakhskie," 14.
55. *Istoriia Kazakhskoi SSR s drevneishikh vremen do nashikh dnei v piati tomakh* (Alma-Ata: Nauka, 1979), 3:27. According to W. Bruce Lincoln, Gagarin will later be executed by Peter the Great "for all he had stolen during his term." *Conquest of a Continent*, 151.
56. Glinka, *Aziatskaia Rossiia*, 1:347; I. Strebelsky, "The Frontier in Central Asia," in *Studies in Russian Historical Geography*, ed. James H. Bater and R. A. French (London: Academic Press, 1983), 1:151.
57. George Demko, *The Russian Colonization of Kazakhstan, 1896–1916* (Bloomington: Indiana University Press, 1969): 42.
58. G. N. Potanin, *Materialy dlia istorii Sibiri sobral G. Potanin* (Moscow: Izdanie Imperatorskogo obshchestva istorii i drevnostei Rossiiskikh pri Moskovskom universitete, 1867), 180.
59. Chokan Valikhanov, *Sobranie sochinenii v piati tomakh* (Alma-Ata: Kazakhskoi Sovetskoi Entsiklopedii, 1984–1985), 1:426.
60. G. F. Dakhshleiger, "Iz opyta istorii osedaniia Kazakhskikh kochevykh i polukochevykh khoziaistv (do massovoi kollektivizatsii sel'skogo khoziaistva)," *Sovetskaia etnografiia*, no. 4 (July/August 1966): 4.
61. *Krasnyi arkiv* 5 (78) (Moscow: Tsentral'noe arkivnoe upravlenie, 1936), 188.
62. Martha Brill Olcott, *The Kazakhs*, 2nd ed. (Stanford: Hoover Institution Press, 1995), 31.
63. I. Kraft', "Priniatie kirgizami russkago poddanstva," *Izvestiia Orenburgskago otdela imperatorskago Russkago geograficheskago obshchestva, vypusk' 12-I* (1897): 31.
64. Alan Bodger, "Abulkhair, Khan of the Kazakh Little Horde, and His Oath of Allegiance to Russia of October 1731," *Slavonic and East European Review* 58, no. 1 (January 1980): 57; Alton S. Donnelly, *The Russian Conquest of Bashkiria, 1552–1740* (New Haven, CT: Yale University Press, 1968), 58.
65. D. A. Turashbekova, "Pravovye aspekty voenno-diplomaticheskikh deistvii khana mladshego zhuza Abulkhaira," *Al-Farabi Kazakh National University, KazNU Bulletin, Law Series* No. 3 (67) (2013): 3–7.

66. Vasilii Grigoriev, "The Russian Policy Regarding Central Asia. An Historical Sketch," in *Turkistan: Notes of a Journey in Russian Turkistan, Kokand, Bukhara and Kuldja*, by Eugene Schuyler (New York: Scribner, Armstrong, 1877), 2:403–4.

67. Geoffrey Wheeler, *The Modern History of Soviet Central Asia* (New York: Praeger, 1964), 36.

68. Eccles, "Fur Trade and Eighteenth-Century Imperialism," 349.

69. *Omskogo oblgosarkiva*, f. 366, o. 1, d. 24, l. 2–3; d. 25, l. 6–7. A copy of the documents is in the Institute of History, Archaeology, and Ethnography, Academy of Sciences, Republic of Kazakhstan.

70. *Censuses of Canada, 1608 to 1876* (Ottawa: Maclean, Roger, 1878), 5:166–68.

71. Eccles, "Fur Trade and Eighteenth-Century Imperialism," 355.

72. Francis Parkman, *Montcalm and Wolfe* (Boston: Little, Brown, 1912), 1:4.

73. White, *Middle Ground*, 256.

74. Aleksei I. Levshin, *Opisanie Kirgiz-kazach'ikh, ili Kirgiz-kaisatskikh, ord i stepei* (1832; Almaty: Sanat, 1996), 178.

75. *Kazakhsko-russkie otnosheniia v XVI–XVIII vekakh. Sbornik dokumentov i materialov* (Alma-Ata: Nauka, 1961), 546–48, 661–62.

76. V. V. Vel'iaminov-Zernov, *Istoricheskie izvestiia o Kirgiz-kaisakakh i snosheniiakh Rossii so Srednei Aziei so vremeni konchiny Abulkhair-khana (1748–1765 gg.)* (Ufa: Gub. tip., 1853), 91; A. Sabyrkhanov, "Zemel'naia politika tsarskogo pravitel'stva v mladshem zhuze vo vtoroi polovine XVIII veka," *Izvestiia AN KazSSR, seriia obshchestvennaia*, no. 2 (1968): 42.

77. Ia. V. Basin, "Politika Rossii v mladshem i srednem zhuzakh v kontse 50-kh i v 60-kh godakh XVIII veka," *Izvestiia AN KazSSR, seriia obshchestvennaia*, no. 3 (1968): 45.

78. M. A. Terent'ev, *Istoriia zavoevaniia Srednei Azii* (St. Petersburg: Tipografiia Komorova, 1906), 1:57–58.

79. Fred Anderson, *Crucible of War: The Seven Years' War and the Fate of Empire in British North America, 1754–1766* (New York: Knopf, 2000), 505–6.

80. Stuart Banner, *How the Indians Lost Their Land: Law and Power on the Frontier* (Cambridge, MA: Harvard University Press, 2007), 85–108. Banner notes that the proclamation was an "abysmal failure" that created a black market in land sales from Indians. He quotes Lord Hillsborough, secretary of state for the colonies, who claimed that the proclamation had "so entirely failed in its Object, as to have produced the very Evils to which it was proposed as a Remedy" (104).

81. Henry Nash Smith, *Virgin Land: The American West as Symbol and Myth* (1954; Cambridge, MA: Harvard University Press, 1978), 177.

82. White, *Middle Ground*, 248–52.

83. Burke quoted in Smith, *Virgin Land*, 177.

84. According to Yuri Slezkine, a typical Cossack did not divide the world "into the Christian and non-Christian spheres" and did not regard Kazakh ways as inferior to their own. *Arctic Mirrors: Russia and the Small Peoples of the North* (Ithaca, NY: Cornell University Press), 40.

85. In the 1762 palace coup that brought Catherine to power, her husband, Peter III, who was more Prussian than Russian and quickly made enemies at court, was killed several months later, possibly during a drunken argument with one of Catherine's favorites. Many peasants believed he was deposed and killed because he planned to emancipate the serfs, a sentiment that Pugachev exploited by calling himself Peter III. See Nicholas V. Riasanovsky and Mark D. Steinberg, *A History of Russia*, 8th ed. (New York: Oxford University Press, 2011), 257–59.

86. *Istoriia Kazakhskoi SSR s drevneishikh vremen do nashikh dnei v piati tomakh* (Alma-Ata: Nauka, 1979), 3:94–97; For more about Pugachev and the revolt, see Paul Avrich, *Russian Rebels, 1600–1800* (New York: Schocken Books, 1972), 180–254.

87. See Alan Bodger, *The Kazakhs and the Pugachev Uprising in Russia, 1773–1775* (Bloomington: Research Institute for Inner Asian Studies, Indiana University, 1988).

88. For a brief analysis of Wabasha and Santee Dakota diplomacy during the American Revolution, see Paul L. Stevens, "Wabasha Visits Governor Carleton, 1776: New Light on a Legendary Episode of Dakota-British Diplomacy on the Great Lakes Frontier," *Michigan Historical Review* 16, no. 1 (Spring 1990): 21–48.

89. See US Department of War, *Indian Treaties, and Laws and Regulations Relating to Indian Affairs: To which is Added an Appendix, Containing the Proceedings of the Old Congress, and Other Important State Papers, in Relation to Indian Affairs* (Washington City: Way & Gideon, 1826), 8–10.

90. Francis Paul Prucha, *American Indian Treaties: The History of a Political Anomaly* (Berkeley: University of California Press, 1994), 42.

91. White, *Middle Ground*, 417.

92. Ibid., 418.

93. See Abraham P. Nasatir, "Anglo-Spanish Rivalry on the Upper Missouri," *Mississippi Valley Historical Review* 16, no. 3 (December 1929): 359–82.

94. Ross, "Fur Trade of the Western Great Lakes," 298–99.

95. See *Laws of the Territory of the United States North-West of the Ohio* (Cincinnati: W. Maxwell, 1796), iii–xiii.

96. US Congress, "An Act to Regulate Trade and Intercourse with the Indian Tribes," in *The Debates and Proceedings in the Congress of the United States; with an Appendix Containing Important State Papers and Public Documents and All the Laws of a Public Nature, With a Copious Index* (Washington, DC: Gales & Seaton, 1834), 1:2242–43.

97. Truteau quoted in Abraham P. Nasatir, ed., *Before Lewis and Clark: Documents Illustrating the History of the Missouri, 1785–1804* (1952; Lincoln: Bison Books, 1990), 2:165–67.

98. Gilman, "Fur Trade in the Upper Mississippi Valley," 11.

99. *Materialy po istorii Kazakhskoi SSR (1785–1828)* (Moscow: Akademiia nauk SSSR 1940), 4:137.

100. It is important to note that describing Sioux or Kazakh conflicts does not mean that the entire Sioux or Kazakh nation went to war or that the conflict engulfed the entire Sioux or Kazakh peoples in some life or death struggle. Sources from the seventeenth and eighteenth centuries describe a conflict—for example, between the Sioux and Chippewa or the Kazakhs and the Kalmyks—but they do not distinguish between the Lakota and Dakota or the Great and Middle Horde. It is more important to recognize that Euro-Americans and Russians viewed the conflicts as serious obstacles to trade, and their efforts to mediate to end the conflicts were simply to increase commerce and protect their traders and merchants. The sources very rarely reveal which division or band or which clan or horde was involved. Thus, using the more generic reference to the "Sioux" or the "Kazakhs" is necessary to illustrate Euro-American and Russian perceptions and concerns about the seemingly perpetual conflicts in the plains and steppe.

101. Jeremy Adelman and Stephen Aron, "From Borderlands to Borders: Empires, Nation-States, and the Peoples in Between in North American History," *American Historical Review* 104, no. 3 (June 1999): 817.

102. The intertribal warfare in the seventeenth and eighteenth centuries was the consequence of the "commercialism" introduced by the European fur trade, which, according to Gary Clayton Anderson, became more frequent as "nations on the upper Mississippi fought

over resources." "Early Dakota Migration," 19. The Russians, on the other hand, established a military administration and offered titles and gifts to leaders they believed facilitated Russian commercial expansion in order to "guarantee . . . security and regular delivery of the fur tribute." The result was internecine conflict among the Kazakhs and external pressure by Kalmyks and others. Lantzeff, "Siberian Colonial Administration," 52.

3

Conquest and Martial Resistance

Comparing American and Russian expansion and internal colonization of the Sioux and the Kazakhs naturally leads to a discussion of the martial resistance by the indigenous population against the imperial power. The internal colonizer destroyed native sovereignty as it asserted social, political, and economic authority over the lands and peoples colonized. Scholars, politicians, commentators, and participants in the events have long chronicled the wars, rebellions, uprisings, revolts, battles, and massacres so often associated with the conquest of the Sioux and the Kazakhs that a complete retelling of the Battle of the Little Bighorn or Srym Batyr's rebellion does not necessarily need to be done again. American scholars examined so many facets of the so-called Indian Wars that comparing them to the Kazakh revolts reveals the idiosyncratic nature inherent in each battle, war, revolt, or conflict but does not illuminate a feature, context, or perception not already scrutinized by other scholars.

More importantly for this comparison, it was the process, the perceptions, and the consequences of conquest and colonization rather than an examination of the separate events or episodes that matter. But Sioux and Kazakh efforts to resist reinforced American and Russian perceptions that the nomads must settle and that pioneers and peasants must occupy the land. Sioux and Kazakh opposition bolstered American and Russian views that the natives were naturally uncivilized communities. When examined through the prism of process and consequence rather than the particulars of each confrontation, resistance and suppression became part of the internal colonization. Therefore, this chapter examines the process of military conquest—the comparable objectives, policies, and consequences—that resulted in the eventual suppression of Sioux and Kazakh martial resistance.

DIFFERENT OBJECTIVES

In the first half of the nineteenth century, both the United States and Russia initiated active military and commercial expansionist policies into the northern plains and the Kazakh Steppe. Initially, it was an economic penetration—chiefly by fur trappers and merchants. The expanded military movement often followed economic expansion into those regions in order to secure trade and the movement of goods and people. In the first half of the nineteenth century, pioneer and peasant expansion was a modest, relatively measured movement that accelerated rapidly after 1850. Consequently, the United States and tsarist Russia both demarcated land and subsequently allotted it in ways that restricted independent movement by the Sioux and the Kazakhs. Both the United States and Russia attempted to contain the indigenous populations' access to the land and resources necessary for the Sioux and the Kazakhs to exercise their traditional economic, social, and political sovereignty. Simply put, the colonizer wanted the colonized to stop being nomads.

Through various mechanisms, the United States and Russia managed literally and metaphorically to divide and conquer the Sioux and the Kazakhs. The concept of divide and conquer may not have always guided the policies, or even considered the objective, but that was the practice. By gradually asserting political sovereignty over the Sioux and the Kazakhs before completing their physical subjugation, the United States and Russia ushered in an era of armed resistance. The United States and Russia mistakenly anticipated the exact opposite Sioux and Kazakh reaction. They drew lines on the map and expected the Sioux and the Kazakhs to acknowledge and respect those lines. The Americans and Russians expressed surprise, disappointment, and exasperation when the Sioux and the Kazakhs exhibited independent decision-making and hostility to American and Russian political actions.

Up to the 1820s, the situation in the northern plains and the Kazakh Steppe generally reflected American and Russian expectations of control rather than the reality. The Americans and Russians desired essentially two things: initially, recognition of American and Russian political authority followed by peace among the peoples living there. Acknowledgment by the Sioux and the Kazakhs of the first objective required the colonizer to suppress Sioux and Kazakh political sovereignty and a serious military commitment by the Americans and Russians before the second objective: a safe and secure resettlement for American pioneers and Russian peasants. Peace in the northern plains meant signing numerous treaties with all of the tribes that lived there, including the Sioux, Crow, Blackfeet, Cheyenne, and others. It was a slow, piecemeal process that took several decades to accomplish. The United States used these treaties to force territorial concessions and required the various tribes to settle on reservations in order to prevent conflicts between each other and, more importantly, conflicts with white Americans who were moving through the northern plains or settling on land that tribes claimed as their own. The United States managed to divide and conquer the northern plains from the 1820s to the 1870s.

By aligning with one band or tribe, the United States separated different Indian tribes and bands from one another, a process it followed with the Sioux. In a strict legal sense, treaties signed by one band—for example, a treaty with one band of the Santee—did not obligate the Teton to adhere to its stipulations; however, in practice, the United States often tried to impose its will on the so-called non-treaty Sioux. Band by band, tribe by tribe, the United States was able to isolate and conquer the northern plains and the Sioux. The Russians employed a similar tactic; clan by clan or horde by horde, the Russians were able to divide and conquer the Kazakhs and the Kazakh Steppe. From the American and Russian perspectives, expansion meant security and enhanced trade; the incremental divide and conquer was more the result of American and Russian actions rather than an articulated strategy, but one that worked to isolate and incorporate disaffected and potentially loyal and peaceful Sioux and Kazakhs from the more hostile bands, clans, and hordes. In the Russian case, the government believed it had to end what was, essentially, a Kazakh civil war exacerbated by Russian policies designed to exert imperial control in the Kazakh Steppe from the 1820s to the 1840s. At no time in either case were the Sioux or the Kazakhs able to unite into a single military, economic, or territorial force that—although unlikely given the military and economic superiority of the United States and Russia—might possibly resist a determined, expanding imperial power.

There was, however, a notable difference in the comparison of American and Russian expansion and internal colonization: chronology. While the Americans slowly edged into the plains between 1820 and the 1840s, the Russians were consolidating their control in the Kazakh Steppe. In 1847 the last major rebellion by the Kazakhs against Russian expansion culminated with the death of Kenesary Kasymov, which essentially ended more than a century of sporadic Kazakh resistance to Russian expansion. For the rest of the nineteenth century, the Russian government consolidated its control of the Kazakhs and the steppe, and by 1881 the Russians conquered, annexed, and colonized the central Asian khanates (Bukhara, Khiva, and Kokand). Because of this continued Russian expansion, by the 1890s, Russia and Britain resolved their geopolitical differences and agreed to boundary commissions to establish the southernmost extension of the Russian imperial border on the Persian-Afghan frontier. By comparison, the American conquest of the Sioux and the northern plains occurred much more quickly and later in the century but without the similar imperial, geopolitical dynamics and rivalries in central Asia that frequently erupted between Britain and Russia (the era called "the Great Game").

In the United States, the federal government resolved its northern and southern borders with British Canada and Mexico by 1848.[1] The Spanish and British were still powerful imperial rivals who could be potent impediments to any American expansionist agenda. American expansion and settlement ultimately required defined boundaries and stability. Conversely, it was the absence of defined boundaries and the persistence of instability that propelled Russian expansion into the Kazakh Steppe and central Asia. Thus, in comparison, the United States made certain, although not as a prerequisite, that its imperial rivals, Britain and Spain, agreed on defined, international boundaries before the massive westward movement began in earnest. Russia, on the other hand, used the absence of defined boundaries to justify its expansion and colonization into the Kazakh Steppe and, later, Turkestan.[2]

Therefore, unlike the Russian-Kazakh case, in which the violent resistance to Russian expansion occurred between 1732 and 1847, most scholars argue that Sioux resistance to American expansion starts in 1851, with the signing of the Fort Laramie Treaty, and concludes in 1890 at Wounded Knee. Some scholars claim the resistance ended in 1877–1878, with the death of Crazy Horse. Regardless of which dates are used, Kazakh resistance ends in the first half of the century, whereas the Sioux resistance is a second-half-of-the-century story that accelerated rapidly after the American Civil War. Despite this temporal difference, throughout the nineteenth century, the United States and Russia unquestionably planned, revised, and implemented the economic, political, social, and cultural policies of subjugation.

One other distinction to acknowledge, but far more difficult to evaluate, was that the trade goods that the Americans and Russians desired differed considerably. Trade and settlement, in a sense, differed in these two cases. One reason was that the northern plains initially was the route to someplace else during much of the nineteenth century—meaning that migrants going to the Montana or Colorado goldfields or Oregon were not the vulnerable or rich targets of opportunity for the Sioux. That was not the case in the steppe, as Kazakhs frequently attacked Russian or central Asian caravans throughout the eighteenth or nineteenth centuries. The Sioux facilitated the early nineteenth-century trade, but it was nearly a one-product (fur) trade that attracted the British, French, and Americans. The Kazakhs' trade was more diversified, as they supplied the Russians with wool, meat, livestock, and hides. The Sioux and the Kazakhs desired manufactured products as well as modern weapons, ammunition, and powder—items that the United States and Russia were equally reluctant to trade.

The Russians wanted to tap into the central Asian markets, trading with merchants from China, Persia, and the Ottoman Empire who visited the ancient Silk Road market towns of Bukhara and Samarkand. Because the Americans were not sending large caravans of trade through the northern plains, with the goal of returning with goods from elsewhere, the need to protect the trade differed somewhat. In time, the Russian government built fortified lines that presumably separated Russian territory from the rest of central Asia—particularly Turkestan and the southern Kazakh Steppe. The boundary crept over the territory claimed, or at least used, by the Kazakhs, whereas the United States superficially cloaked Sioux lands within American territorial boundaries, initially moved through it, but American pioneers ultimately came to settle on it. Contiguous expansion and settlement was more common in Russia than the pattern in the United States, although Americans claimed the northern plains before physically incorporating western territories such as California or Oregon. As a consequence, the Americans leapfrogged Sioux territory due to the California gold rush, the Mexican-American War, and the boundary demarcation between British Canada and the United States—all occurring in the 1840s. In Russia, expansion was one small step after another; in the United States, it was one giant leap.

In addition, there was an element to the trade that is ubiquitous in the histories written about the conquest of North America generally that is almost completely absent in similar histories about Russian eastward expansion: the use of liquor to bilk the natives. There is no question among scholars of American history that traders, merchants, and others used alcohol and hard spirits excessively and to the detriment of Indians throughout the eighteenth and nineteenth centuries. The American government worked hard—some may question how hard—to obstruct the trade and prevent alcohol from ever reaching Indians; but it was, by all accounts, a serious issue in which simple prohibitions failed to stop it. Many Indians also tried to stop the trade. Nevertheless, little disagreement exists about the role liquor played in the American expansion and dispossession of Indians from the land; similar evidence was not a part of the Russian experience. There is anecdotal evidence about drunken Russians on the frontier,

FIGURE 3.1. Southern Kazakh Steppe, June 2008 (photo by author).

but they were not part of the conquest and colonization story in the American example.[3]

Another interesting, but somewhat minor, difference is that, unlike the Sioux Wars of the nineteenth century, there are no infamous battles or massacres that one can point to as turning points or seminal moments in the Kazakh resistance to Russian expansion. There was no Grattan Massacre, no Fetterman Massacre, and certainly no equivalent to the Battle of the Little Bighorn in the Russian conquest and colonization of the Kazakhs.[4] There were, however, prolonged "rebellions," as the Russians defined them, led by charismatic, generally enigmatic figures. There were no large-scale, pitched battles; the vast majority of these encounters were relatively small skirmishes or raids.[5] In a sense, that differs little from the well-known violent encounters between the American military and the Sioux, or even American civilians and the Sioux. That does not mean, however, that subsequent scholarship neglected to examine the rebellions. Quite the contrary, it is more likely that Russian children do not know the name or exploits of Ablai Khan or Kenesary Kasymov. Americans, on the other hand, know the names of Sitting Bull or Crazy Horse. The reason—or so it seems—is because there were few occasions during Russia's expansion into the Kazakh Steppe that scholars can identify as major, seminal battles. The Russians always considered these conflicts and skirmishes to be merely rebellions and not wars because after 1732 the Russian government considered the Kazakhs subjects of the empire. Moreover, and perhaps as a consequence, during the

Soviet era, scholars interpreted the rebellions as little more than feudal reactions by khans and sultans who sought to oppress their own people rather than submit to Russian rule.[6]

On the other hand, the United States referred to conflicts with the Sioux as wars. In a practical sense, Red Cloud's War or the Black Hills' War were comparable military events to rebellions by Srym Batyr or Kenesary Kasymov. Red Cloud, Sitting Bull, and Crazy Horse rebelled and resisted American expansion as much as Srym or Kenesary rebelled and resisted Russian expansion.[7] The Americans called them wars, but they differed little from the military efforts the Kazakhs conducted against the Russians. Interestingly, America had its celebrated and tragic Indian Wars in the nineteenth century; Russia had its celebrated and tragic wars in the Caucasus and central Asia but not in the Kazakh Steppe. For the Russians, the major wars or battles that captured the public's attention—comparable to Red Cloud's War or the Battle of the Little Bighorn—occur in the Caucasus against Imam Shamil or, later, against the Turkmen and the tragic Battle of Geok-Tepe. The Russians, however, never defined or described the more than century-long struggle to subjugate the Kazakhs as a war.[8] In the minds of Russian officials, from the moment of Abulkhair's 1732 oath, Kazakhs were subjects of the Russian Empire. In that context, subjects rebelled and surrendered political sovereignty to the emperor, but they did not go to war against the colonizer. Nevertheless, in a comparable sense and in that context, as Robert M. Utley noted, "Every important Indian war since 1870 [was] essentially a war not of concentration but of rebellion—of Indians rebelling against reservations they had already accepted in theory if not in fact."[9]

Thus, to call the resistance a war or a rebellion does not change the simple fact that the Sioux and the Kazakhs fought to prevent the Americans and the Russians from expanding into the plains and the steppe. These wars or rebellions were a response to imperial expansion, territorial loss, and internal colonization. The Russians interpreted Abulkhair's 1732 oath differently than Americans interpreted their government's practice of signing treaties with the Sioux. This may also account for the two different terms—wars or rebellions—used to define Sioux and Kazakh resistance.

CONCEPTS OF SUBMISSION

Following independence, the United States adopted many elements of British economic and political policies in its relations with Indians. It was not until 1789 that article 1, section 8 of the US Constitution assigned and preserved the conduct of Indian relations. According to the Constitution, it gave Congress the power to "regulate Commerce with foreign Nations, and among the several States, and with the Indian Tribes." Treaties throughout the nineteenth century echoed British practice, shaped partially by the Proclamation of 1763—a decree designed to acknowledge Indian rights to land but also to establish the only legal procedure to extinguish that right. Treaties became the principal instrument of Indian-British, and subsequently American-Indian, relations.[10] According to Stuart Banner, after American independence, the treaties represented "strong political pressures to acquire land quickly and cheaply. The result was a dramatic change in the method of obtaining Indian land. The federal government began to dictate to tribes the extent of land they would be allowed to occupy."[11] Until 1871 the United States understood that treaties, in concept and practice, operated between politically sovereign entities; however, most treaties signed between the United States and some Sioux bands were more akin to real estate ventures than transactions between sovereign peoples.

The Russians, on the other hand, never signed treaties with the Kazakhs. Throughout the eighteenth century and into the nineteenth century, the tsarist government administered oaths rather than employed legal documents. The Russians simply annexed the land and claimed sovereignty over the people living there. Whereas the British and, later, Americans took "great pains to establish the legality, morality, and philosophical legitimacy of their possession and occupation of new lands," the Russians, according to Valerie Kivelson, appear "to have not lost a wink of sleep over this issue."[12] Moreover, as Russia lacked a constitution, government-native relations were always the prerogative of the tsar, his or her government, or its official representatives. Once the Russian government administered an oath, it assumed that the people—including Kazakhs, Poles, Georgians, and others—became subjects of the empire. It assumed that they voluntarily surrendered their political sovereignty to the tsar or tsarina. From the Russian perspective, treaties were legal accords agreed to only by coequal sovereigns.

After a subject people surrendered their sovereignty through an agreement sworn to by a khan or some other recognized leader, treaties were superfluous and irrelevant. The treaties in the United States, however, served a somewhat different purpose. The United States ratified 367 Indian treaties, as well as others Congress never ratified, from 1778 to 1868.[13] The vast majority of these treaties forced land concessions; or, to describe it more simply, these treaties created a legal mechanism to get land from Indians but did not affect their sovereignty. In fact, the United States needed sovereign Indian nations so that the federal government could sign treaties beneficial to the government. Initially, treaties between the United States and various tribes did not subvert Indian sovereignty to the American government; however, in Russia, the system of oath-taking was, in the Russian mind, a clear act of submission.

THE TROUBLE WITH FRANCE

Despite these differing concepts of submission to the prerogatives of the colonizer, during the era of early expansion, in the late eighteenth and early nineteenth centuries, the United States and Russia both administered relations with the Sioux and the Kazakhs as military matters. Shortly after establishing the first executive branch departments—which included state, treasury, and war—the US Congress placed management for Indian affairs in the War Department.[14] The Ordinance of 1785 and the Northwest Ordinance of 1787 laid the groundwork for American settlement in these territories. The passage of these acts, according to historian Robert F. Berkhofer Jr., created a "novel colonial system" because these new territories, after achieving statehood, incorporated easily into the federal system as coequals. Ohio, Wisconsin, and Minnesota, for example, were initially territories, as Berkhofer argued, to distinguish American expansion "from the old imperial type."[15] Historian Jeffrey Ostler described the process as a way to establish "new colonies that were organized into territories and then states."[16] The administration of indigenous peoples in the United States started first under the Department of War but was placed later under Interior Department control. The Russians, on the other hand, never doubted that they expanded as an "old imperial type" that colonized newly acquired territory, but territorial administration was always under military control. Civilians and bureaucrats always reported to military governor-generals, a structure that differed markedly from the American administrative process. Throughout the nineteenth century, control of Indian affairs in the United States periodically erupted into heated debate and power struggles between the Interior and War Departments and often marred relations between the two. It was a political and institutional rivalry, often bitter and controversial. Russia did not experience a similar debate. Governance in the provinces was a military matter, although a Russian Department of Internal Affairs existed and administered some native (*inorodtsy* "alien" or "of another people") civil concerns. Different Russian ministries surveyed the land and administered resettlement, but political rule in the steppe was always under military rule. An interesting and parallel element to the process of conquering and eventually colonizing the plains and the steppe originates in the shadow of the Napoleonic Wars, which diverted Russia's attention and eventually ensnared the United States as well.

In the nascent United States, the Napoleonic Wars caused the young republic to vacillate between enthusiasm for the French Revolution and anger at both the French and the British for the impunity with which they violated American neutrality; seized American ships, men, and goods; and generally ignored American protests and sovereignty. As the situation changed in Europe, it proved beneficial for the United States in ways that can never be overstated. The American purchase of the Louisiana Territory from the French in 1803 was, perhaps, the most significant imperial step taken by the United States in its history. It fundamentally altered the United States, creating in one stroke of the pen a country that expanded, almost effortlessly, past the magnificent Mississippi watershed to the Rocky Mountains. Just one year before the sale, Napoleon declared that France must "engage herself not to sell or alienate in any manner the property or enjoyment of Louisiana."[17] The Spanish opposed the sale, which Napoleon simply ignored in his need to raise revenue and divest France of unwanted real estate. But events in Europe, American diplomacy, and Napoleon's mercurial character resulted in such a momentous occasion that historian Henry Adams later euphorically exclaimed that the "annexation of Louisiana was an event so portentous as to defy measurement . . . but as a matter of diplomacy it was unparalleled, because it cost almost nothing."[18]

TOOLS OF SUBJUGATION

The full extent of the Louisiana Territory was unclear; the United States was uncertain of the boundaries and had little knowledge about the people and resources that it just paid $15 million (less than three cents per acre) to own. The course of American and Sioux relations, however, changed significantly after the Louisiana Purchase. Some Americans were already trading with the Sioux prior to the acquisition, but those meetings and trade opportunities were sporadic. In addition, the Louisiana Purchase changed the relationship between the United States and Great Britain in the northern plains. Up to this point, the British still dominated the fur trade, and the Americans were a minor annoyance. The United States controlled Ohio, but American pioneers were aggressively expanding and settling in regions east of the Mississippi River.

President Thomas Jefferson had plans and imperial ambitions to exert American authority in the newly acquired lands, and he quickly, and somewhat quietly, dispatched various expeditions to explore the territory, hopefully to find waterways to the Pacific Ocean and to inform the Indians that they had a new "Great Father" in Washington. The Lewis and Clark Expedition established trade relations with various tribes, including the Sioux. These expeditions commercially benefited the United States and enticed Indian tribes away from the more experienced British traders and merchants. For example, in 1805 Zebulon Pike commanded an expedition to explore the upper Mississippi region, where he met some Dakota at Lake Pepin. Pike's visit with some Santee was far more profitable than Lewis and Clark's encounter with the Teton. Little Crow, Chief of the Mdewakanton Sioux, visited Pike, who was then traveling on to the mouth of the Minnesota River. Pike signed the first treaty between one band of the Sioux and a representative of the United States.[19]

Little Crow agreed to relinquish a nine-mile strip of land on both sides of the Mississippi River, from the mouth of the St. Croix River to the Falls of St. Anthony. The United States agreed to pay $2,000. The land was to be used to construct a military and trading post, but it was not until 1819 that the American government started construction of a fort on the newly purchased land. Consequently, Pike's 1805 treaty apparently opened the door to further land cessions from other Sioux bands after the United States purchased Little Crow's tract. This treaty also represents the instrument by which the United States began to divide and conquer the Sioux, although it differs slightly from the process employed by the Russians against the Kazakhs.

Russia's relations with France were complicated and unsettled. The French Revolution horrified Catherine the Great—as an autocrat, no matter how enlightened, it was disturbing to watch from afar a rabble of peasants and revolutionaries execute a fellow monarch. After 1789 Catherine's relations with France intended to prevent the spread of revolutionary ideology, particularly in the Russian Empire. Ideologies that preached individual liberties, the rights of man, and nationalism were anathema to an autocrat who ruled over a multinational empire. She died in 1796, ending a remarkably complex period in Russian history. Her son, Paul I (1796–1801), was an ignorant sod. His domestic and foreign policies seemingly reflected his unstable mind. An 1801 palace coup ended his erratic reign.

His son, Alexander I, ruled until 1825. From 1801 to 1815, Russia clearly focused its attention on European affairs and the Napoleonic threat. Because of these external issues, Russia's territorial expansion into the Kazakh Steppe was haphazard. Consequently, Alexander's Russia sought merely to consolidate its administrative control in the territories behind and along the Irtysh Line. The Russians focused on expanding trade in the Kazakh Steppe and central Asia, not territorial expansion and colonization. Kazakh clans and hordes continued to fight among themselves for access to pastures and territory, raid Russian caravans, and seize goods and Russian and Cossack peasants to sell as slaves in Bukhara, Kokand, and Khiva. The Kazakh Steppe remained a dangerous place for Russians.

More importantly, the allegedly constant conflict in the steppe convinced many Russian officials that only military conquest there could provide the necessary security and stability for trade.

In 1801 the Russian government manufactured the Bukei Horde, a fanciful Kazakh entity designed to reward some Kazakhs for their good behavior by making the Inner Side pastures available. The Bukei Horde, whom the Russians often called the Inner Horde, permitted Bukei's followers to remain permanently west of the Ural River.[20] It made available millions of acres of lush pastures for Kazakh shepherds, but for the Russians it meant improved security along the Irtysh Line. The Russians allowed Bukei to pasture on the Inner Side, between the Ural and Volga Rivers, separating his factions of the Little Horde from other Little Horde clans. His reward for good relations was that Russia acknowledged him as khan and bestowed gifts and lands, which attracted followers but essentially divided Kazakhs between those considered friendly and loyal and those that the Russian government considered hostile and rebellious. Permitting Bukei to pasture on the Inner Side became a measured device to incorporate clans from the Little Horde into the Russian Empire. Bukei's followers had access to prime grazing land and, equally important, Russian economic and military support and protection from Kazakhs who opposed Bukei.

Some scholars argue that this was part of the Russians' divide and conquer strategy, but it seems more likely that the Russians were able to take advantage of divisions and internecine conflict in order to penetrate the Kazakh Steppe because, more than anything else, the Russians wanted peace and stability rather than expansion simply for expansion's sake. By splitting the Little Horde and privileging some Kazakhs with benefits such as pastures, the Russians unwittingly intensified internecine conflicts among the Kazakh clans and hordes rather than secured a more stable environment to increase trade. During the Napoleonic Wars, the United States expanded exponentially, whereas Russia sought merely to consolidate its earlier territorial gains. Nonetheless, each used the opportunity to divide and conquer, albeit in sporadic and tentative ways.

The Americans and Russians used treaties and oaths to secure, as much as possible, friendly relations and trade. Treaties and oaths also, perhaps unwittingly, created wedges in which to reward friendly Sioux and Kazakhs—especially between various Sioux bands and Kazakh clans—in order to pacify and segregate those Sioux and Kazakhs who opposed further American and Russian expansion. Allowing Bukei and his supporters to access specifically defined land and favoring certain Kazakh clans with benefits divided Kazakhs among the Little Horde clans and forced them to choose between cooperation and opposition. In the American case, the Sioux bands that signed treaties were favored with gifts and annuities. Of course, the consequence for this cooperation was the loss of Sioux and Kazakh lands and, concomitantly, their political sovereignty. In each case, the United States and Russia considered these steps necessary actions in order to promote peaceful relations and, more importantly, secure trade and promote agriculture, civilization, and, eventually, assimilation.

This is evident in the United States in the early nineteenth century as Americans hoped to wrest the fur trade away from the British. In 1806 the War Department appointed an agent, Nicholas Boilvin, to the Sacs, but he also had contacts with some Sioux around Prairie du Chien. One of his tasks was to invigorate trade with the various tribes. By 1808 British traders withdrew from the region, opening the trade for American commercial development. At a council held at Prairie du Chien in 1809, many Dakotas expressed a desire for American merchandise. Boilvin seemed confident that American traders could carry on a profitable trade with the upper Mississippi tribes, but American traders did not cultivate the necessary relationships with the Sioux to exploit fully the commercial opportunities following the British departure.[21] The process in the steppe, however, favored a more rapid divide-and-conquer process because the Russians had the one thing that some Kazakhs desperately needed: rich pastures that lay behind the Russian fortified lines. The Russians managed to penetrate politically rather than economically at first because they controlled certain lands. The Russians also believed that political control facilitated and secured trade. The United States also wanted to facilitate trade, but the Sioux and other Indian tribes still controlled the land. The United States could claim ownership, but ownership did not represent control.

The era of American dominance in the western fur trade follows the war, despite continued efforts by the British to interfere with American ambitions. The Sioux actively participated in the trade throughout the heyday in the 1820s and 1830s. American fur trader Joshua Pilcher claimed, "no Indians ever manifested a greater degree of friendship for the whites in general, or more respect for our government, than the Sioux."[22] Great fur trade scholar Hiram Chittenden noted that the Yanktons "were the least troublesome of all the Sioux tribes and gave the traders comparatively little annoyance." He claimed, however, that the Yanktonai were "treacherous, stealthy, vindictive, and caused a great deal of trouble." He also observed that the Sioux regarded "the approach of the American traders with an unfriendly eye . . . But as time wore on and the traders became firmly established among them, this hostile feeling largely passed away."[23] One reason the Sioux thrived during this period was that the fur trade was changing from beaver and other fine fur to buffalo fur and hides. The Sioux—in particular, bands in the western plains such as the Teton—were more easily able to facilitate this trade due to the extensive buffalo herds that roamed the plains and prairies, profiting economically and militarily.

In July 1815 the Treaty of Portage des Sioux was signed between the United States and various Sioux bands, although absent from the negotiations were two prominent Sioux chiefs, Wabasha and Little Crow. The essential fact of the treaty was that each party desired "perpetual peace and friendship between all citizens of the United States of America" and the Sioux people. In addition, the treaty stipulated that tribes place themselves "under the protection" of the American government and that "Every injury or act of hostility committed by one or either of the contracting parties against the other, shall be mutually forgiven and forgot."[24] Doane Robinson described the "great council" that met to haggle out the terms of the treaty "one of the most notable ever held on the continent." He claimed that, at this time, the Sioux "gave complete submission to the United States government, and since that date, no matter how hostile they may have been in local matters, they have never failed to recognize the sovereignty of the great father at Washington."[25]

It is difficult to understand how or why the Sioux might ever consider that this treaty represented the complete surrender of their sovereignty to the United States; certainly, later Sioux leaders, such as Sitting Bull and Crazy Horse, rejected American domination. This illusion was reminiscent of Russia's beliefs that Abulkhair's 1732 oath made all Kazakhs "subjects" of the Russian Empire. Vasilii Grigoriev recognized the futility of Abulkhair's actions when he wrote that it was merely a trick "by which they hoped to get from us presents and other advantages."[26] The American-Sioux 1815 treaty—or, in the Kazakh case, the 1732 "oath—did not accomplish final submission by the Sioux, as Robinson assumed, but required military defeat; and even then, subjugation was political. More importantly, by the 1820, the US government resolved to extend into the Mississippi and Missouri River valleys and the Russians determined to move deeper into the Kazakh Steppe, where resistance was more strenuous.

CONFLICT WITHIN THE PLAINS AND THE STEPPE

One obstacle, however, that both the United States and Russia had to overcome was conflict in the plains and the steppe. There was a major difference in this regard: conflict in the plains was generally between different Indian tribes, whereas in the steppe it was Kazakh against Kazakh. Although the Sioux rarely, if ever, fought another band—internecine conflict—they were often in conflict with neighboring tribes. By the 1820s, many western Sioux bands lived and migrated in and around the Black Hills. They managed to drive the Kiowa out of the region and laid claim to much of the Missouri River region. The Teton and Yankton/ Yanktonai managed to expel other tribes such as the Ponca, Pawnee, Arikara, Mandan, and Crow from the contested territory and became, as Utley exclaimed, the "monarchs of the northern Plains."[27] Conflict in the plains, however, in the early nineteenth century was the direct result of Sioux, not American, expansion. Americans perceived this intertribal conflict as a serious hindrance to future expansion—a threat to American trappers, traders, and, eventually, settlers. In the Kazakh Steppe, Russian expansion was the reason for the internecine conflict because Russia's divide-and-conquer strategy caused Kazakh clans and hordes to fight each other for access to pastures and trade. In order for Russian economic penetration into the steppe to increase, the Russian government believed that it needed to end the Kazakh internal fighting and restore order.

In 1803 the Russians managed to hold a council at Orenburg, inviting many of the hostile Kazakh leaders, at which they agreed to promote peace, stability, and trade in the steppe. Governor-General Grigorii Volkonskii issued a decree demanding an end to all conflict. He also stated categorically that Russia would withhold all titles, salaries, and privileges in the event the fighting continued. This declaration outwardly produced the desired affect, and the fighting abated for a while. More likely, the growing presence of Khiva in the southern steppe quelled the fighting among the Kazakhs than any demand made by the governor-general. Much as the Dzhungarian threat a century before pushed Abulkhair to seek Russian assistance, the extended threat from Khiva caused some Kazakh khans to move toward improved relations with Russia. In other words, Russian expansion into the steppe, and its accompanied tactics to reward those deemed loyal, further fractured Kazakh society. It increased competition for Russian gifts and, additionally, the desire for Russian protection or support. The one gift, of course, that caused the biggest problem for the Kazakhs was the Russian habit of making certain pastures available to loyal Kazakhs and denying access to those deemed hostile. Land became the imperial wedge used to compel the Kazakhs to submit to Russian expansion.

In the United States, conflicts between tribes ostensibly increased in the plains by the presence of an old enemy that threatened to thwart American claims to the region. In 1819 Secretary of War John Calhoun insisted that the United States exert its influence in Minnesota Territory, fearing that the British were continuing to outmaneuver Americans in the region. Calhoun ordered the army to construct a permanent post in the territory. The fort, initially called Fort St. Anthony—in 1825 it was renamed Fort Snelling—was located at the junction of the Minnesota and Mississippi Rivers on land acquired by Pike in 1805.[28] Just three years before, the US Congress passed a law calculated to oust British fur traders from American territory. This act proposed to supplement the trade and intercourse laws with Indians, which stipulated, "licenses to trade with the Indians within the territorial limits of the United States shall not be granted to any but citizens of the United States."[29]

The line of forts, comparable to the Russian Irtysh Line, became a chain of American military posts—from Fort St. Philip and Fort Jesup in Louisiana, northward to Fort Atkinson in Wisconsin, up to Fort Snelling—and defined, as Utley noted, the "so-called Permanent Indian Frontier." These posts represented American authority in western regions but did very little to exert that influence successfully to suppress the continuing intertribal warfare or exhibit in any real way American power.[30] It was, however, as Utley astutely described it, a "tantalizing abstraction" that ultimately "crumbled" and "collapsed" under the "wheels of wagons bearing gold seekers to the new US possessions on the Pacific."[31]

In the 1820s, the Russians reasserted their power and influence in the Kazakh Steppe in the decade following the Napoleonic Wars. Throughout the 1820s, the Russians constructed a second line of forts and posts chiefly within the territory of the Middle and Great Hordes, running from Kokchetav through Akmolinsk to Sergiopol and Baian-Aul; called the Ilek Line (or Iletskii) that connected the provincial capital, Orenburg, closer to the steppe trade. Cossack *stanitsy* (settlements) were interspersed throughout the Ilek Line, often constructed near the best water sources and wooded regions.[32] According to historian Madhavan Palat, it is only with this new line of forts that Russia entered the steppe "purposefully, politically, administratively, legally, and economically, with the intention of converting it into a colonial appendage, and later, a territory for Russian peasant colonization."[33] The Americans and the Russians used artificially constructed boundaries to limit Sioux and Kazakh mobility and intertribal or internecine conflicts to provide for more stable environments for traders and settlers.

The anticipated goal in both cases was to maintain the peace in the American plains and prairies or in the Kazakh steppe by assigning territory and forcing the Sioux and the Kazakhs to acknowledge American and Russian political control. In the 1820s and 1830s, the Sioux transformed into a "hegemonic power" that successfully warred against sedentary tribes along the Missouri and by the 1830s had forced the Kiowa from the rich Black Hills and forged alliances with other powerful plains tribes, such as the Cheyenne and Arapahos.[34] Moreover, in order to stop continued attacks against American fur traders, in 1823 an American expedition commanded by Col. Henry Leavenworth joined with a number of Teton and Yankton warriors to punish the Arikara for attacking a party of trappers who had come to their village to trade for some horses. Leavenworth hesitated, although the Sioux were ready to attack the Arikara who had garrisoned themselves inside their village. According to George Hyde, the Tetons were disgusted with Leavenworth's timidity and packed up their horses, gathered some corn from Arikara fields, stole eight of Leavenworth's horses as trophies, and departed.[35] It seems these events greatly diminished any fear or concern these Sioux had regarding American military capabilities, perhaps even evoked some contempt among the Sioux. Indeed, it gave them little to fear that the Americans posed a menace to their supremacy in the northern plains.[36]

In 1824 Indian agent Lawrence Taliaferro, at the St. Peter's Agency near Fort Snelling, convinced some Santee to travel to Washington, DC, to meet with American political leaders. While in Washington, Taliaferro convinced Secretary Calhoun to convene a meeting for the following year at Prairie du Chien in order to negotiate treaties with the various Sioux bands under his jurisdiction to end the intertribal warfare that hindered trade. The conference opened in August 1825; the American delegation included Gov. Lewis Cass (Michigan Territory) and Superintendent of Indian Affairs William Clark. The plan they proposed to the Indians who gathered was to draw tribal boundaries that clearly defined hunting lands, which the Americans believed were the root of the conflicts. Creating specific tribal territories dominated American thinking through most treaty-making attempts in the nineteenth century. The American government planned to create inviolable boundaries and segregate tribes from one another and from white Americans. Unfortunately, creating tribal boundaries also required accurate maps, of which there were none.

RESISTANCE: KAZAKHS

At this point, it is necessary to examine Sioux and Kazakh resistance through separate contexts because the chronological differences reflect as well the idiosyncratic distinctions. While the grievances expressed by the Sioux and the Kazakhs reveal many similarities, conflating the resistance into a single comparative prism might inadvertently mask the colonizers' efforts to subjugate the indigenous populations. The Americans and the Russians each wanted the land; they each sought peaceful and stable frontiers and wanted to make room for settlement by pioneers and peasants, but the resistance by the Sioux and the Kazakhs to American and Russian expansion was in direct relation to policies and tactics employed against them. It is to the Kazakhs' resistance that this chapter now turns.

In 1822 the governor-general of Siberia, Mikhail Speransky, issued reforms that fundamentally altered the relationship between the Kazakhs and the Russian Empire, which reflected the Russian government's desire to regulate and demarcate Kazakh mobility. The key element to affect the Kazakhs was the Regulations on the Siberian Kirgiz. Administratively, it segregated Little Horde Kazakhs from the Middle Horde. The Russian government designated Kazakhs from the Little Horde "Orenburg Kirgiz," whereas Middle Horde Kazakhs became "Siberian Kirgiz." Great Horde Kazakhs remained outside this structure until the 1840s, when the government designated them "Semirechie Kirgiz."[37] Under this administrative system, the Russians subdivided Kazakh administrative forms, comparable to the Russian model that appealed to a bureaucrat's sensibilities, which cut across traditional Kazakh sociopolitical structures. The Russians restricted movement between districts, and the regulations dictated that Kazakhs could migrate only within their specifically designated territory. In the event a Kazakh aul wanted to leave the district, the government required Kazakhs to receive special permission from a Russian government official or military officer to do so. As land later opened to Russian and Cossack resettlement, the Russian government further limited permission to cross a restricted district boundary. In this case, it differed from American efforts to impose boundaries on Indian tribes, including the Sioux. The Americans believed explicit and recognized boundaries reduced intertribal conflict, not internecine Sioux conflicts. The Russians, however, desired to limit conflict between Kazakh auls, clans, or hordes that might affect trade and resettlement. Kazakhs from both the Little and Middle Hordes resisted Russian subjugation with a vigor that caught the Russian government by surprise and represented the most serious rebellions against Russian expansion in the nineteenth century. The goal in both the American and Russian cases was the same—reduce conflict that threatened expansion and trade—but the targets differed. In the United States, intertribal warfare required multiple treaties and negotiations with numerous tribes; in Russia, different Kazakh clans and hordes required frequent negotiation and manipulation.

Between 1824 and 1847, four significant, widespread, and intense Kazakh rebellions against Russian colonization kept the Kazakh Steppe in near-constant turmoil. The Russians interpreted the rebellions as little more than mere banditry, led by men who preferred to remain uncivilized and nomadic; but these rebellions were not just against Russian colonization. In each case, the fight was against Kazakh sultans and khans who superficially benefited from Russian colonization—between those who owed an allegiance to Russia and those who did not. It was particularly strident among Kazakhs in the Bukei Horde supported by Russia and Kazakhs in the Little Horde who lost land, pasture, migration privileges, and opposed Russian colonization. In the Middle Horde, the conflict was equally against Russian colonization and Kazakhs not allied to Russia. The conflicts were as much anti-Russian as they were part of a Kazakh civil war.[38]

Following Speransky's 1822 reforms and the Russian government's 1824 decision to abolish the title of khan, Kazakhs in the Little Horde, led by Sultan Kaip-Galii Ishimov, rebelled against Russia. A particularly harsh winter in 1826–1827 prompted Kaip-Galii to pasture on the wrong side of the Ilek Line. The Russian government sent a large force to push the Kazakhs back, but as punishment, the government also seized thousands of heads of livestock, prompting violent protest by the Kazakhs. The government's ham-fisted treatment led to several small, but fierce exchanges between Kaip-Galii's supporters and Russian troops. By 1828 the Russian government arrested and tried more than two hundred Kazakhs, but Kaip-Galii avoided arrest and fled south to Khiva, where the khan there gave him sanctuary. Russia's decision to fortify its military line spawned other rebellions.

The Ilek Line intersected rich pastureland and migratory routes claimed by the Tabyn clan of the Little Horde. In response to the Russian expansion, in 1830 the Tabyn clan leader, Zholaman Tlenchiev, rebelled against the Russians and Kazakhs loyal to Russia. Zholaman and his supporters successfully disrupted caravan trade and harassed Cossacks living along the Ilek Line. In 1830 the Russian Orenburg Frontier Commission reported that on one raid against Zholaman the government seized goods, livestock, and prisoners, but that Zholaman escaped.[39] Zholaman wrote the commission that he wanted the Ilek Line disbanded—something Russia was unwilling to consider. He claimed in the letter that the Kazakhs had abundant lands to graze their herds, but that after the Russians constructed the Ilek Line, they had none.[40] He wrote again to demand that Russia remove the forts. He claimed, "when you return those places, then we will be friends, and if you give them away [to Cossacks], we will be enemies."[41]

At the peak of Zholaman's revolt, and a principal cause for the insurgency, the Russian government allotted roughly 7 million desiatin along the Ural River region for Russian and Cossack peasants.[42] In another request to the governor-general, Zholaman requested permission to pasture between the Ural and Ilek Rivers, but the Russians denied this request, fearing that it might spark a land dispute between Kazakhs and Cossacks who settled there.[43] It was an example of Russian divide-and-conquer tactics in that by designating only specific territories that Kazakhs might use, the government managed to reward some Kazakhs who exhibited good behavior with access to pasturelands and punish those that it deemed antagonistic. Russian punitive attacks and raids against Zholaman's aul and the loss of land and livestock eventually forced him to flee but not surrender, as he allied with Sarzhan Kasymov to fight against the Russians.

Zholaman's decision to ally with Sarzhan reveals the nature of the various rebellions in the steppe between 1824 and 1847. Weakened Kazakh leaders were readily willing on many occasions to join with other Kazakhs of different clans or hordes to oppose Russian expansion. Sarzhan's rebellion grew significantly, in part because so many Kazakhs from different clans or hordes rallied to his banner. In July 1826 one report suggested he had more than one thousand men under arms and that the "thieves" stole livestock and attacked Kazakhs friendly to Russia.[44] Another report indicated that Kazakhs from several volost abandoned their territory, joined Sarzhan, or attempted illegally to cross over to the Inner Side, which created a crisis in the steppe.[45]

The Russian government attempted to negotiate with Sarzhan, but between 1827 and 1830, the situation in the steppe calmed a bit, and from the Russian perspective, it seemed the rebellion had ended and peace, or at least some security, had been restored. The reason had nothing to with Russia; in fact, Sarzhan and his followers had moved south, and he was involved in an armed struggle with Tashkent—one of the wealthiest cities in central Asia, nominally under Kokand's control but desired by Bukhara—to control the southern steppe regions. The Russian governor-general called him the "dangerous enemy" who had "significant influence among the Kirgiz [Kazakhs] of the Middle Horde."[46] Sarzhan continually attacked caravans, raided Kazakh auls loyal to Russia, and in 1835–1836, he attempted to ally with Kokand against the Russians, although Kokand was an inconsistent partner. In the summer of 1836 the Tashkent *Kushbegi* (ruler) feared that Sarzhan's influence among Kazakhs living around his dominion potentially threatened his territorial possessions; his assassins managed to kill the unfortunate Kazakh leader.[47]

Sarzhan's death was not the durable respite that either Russia or Tashkent hoped because his younger brother, Kenesary, quickly assumed command of Sarzhan's forces and inspired the revolt to become an even broader and more serious obstacle to Russian expansion. The Kenesary Kasymov Revolt was the turning point in the steppe, as Russia committed more men and resources to fighting Kenesary than any other previous Kazakh rebellions. One element that made the revolt unique was that at various times it extended to all three hordes, attracting Kazakhs regardless of clan or horde to rally to his cause. Indeed, the revolt was unique because at different times during the revolt, according to its most prominent historian, Ermukhan Bekmakhanov, every clan allied with Kenesary. The problem was that at no time during the revolt did all clans at the same time ally with Kenesary.[48] Despite what might seem to suggest that he marshaled huge numbers to his side, the best estimates are that at the revolt's peak (1844–1845), he could field between two thousand to ten thousand "well-armed horsemen."[49]

In December 1838, Kenesary sent a letter to Tsar Nicholas I (1825–1855) that included four demands Russia must agree to before he would lay down his arms to end the rebellion. In the letter, Kenesary insisted that Russia abandon the Aktau fort and destroy it. He further demanded that Russia "destroy all other establishments in steppe locations" in order to dismantle the Akmolinsk judicial tribunal (*divan*), and "free our imprisoned people."[50] In June 1841, Kenesary wrote to the chairman of the Orenburg Frontier Commission to explain the reasons for his continued hostility to Russian expansion in the steppe. He claimed that in 1825 Ivan Karnachev, with a force of three hundred Russians and one hundred sympathetic Kazakhs, attacked his brother Sarzhan's aul. They "sacked the aul . . . [and] plundered an untold quantity of livestock and property, and slaughtered 64 people; the remainder saved themselves by flight."[51] He cited a number of different atrocities purportedly committed by Russians or Cossacks that demanded defensive, retaliatory acts by Kazakhs. Kenesary described the Russians as "leeches sucking the blood of the Kazakhs."[52]

Most observers at the time, as well as subsequent scholarly accounts, fault Kenesary for the continued internecine struggle in the Kazakh Steppe. Kenesary, according to these interpretations, made a political miscalculation that he could force clans hostile to his resistance to Russian colonization to join him and proclaim their allegiance to him.[53] By 1845, Russia was fully committed to defeating Kenesary and restoring order to the steppe. The constant warfare resulted in lost warriors, lost livestock, and increased hostility among Kazakhs who refused to submit to Kenesary's rule. Kenesary fled south—a tactic Kazakhs often used to escape Russian retaliation—eventually finding temporary sanctuary among the Kirghiz in Semirechie. The problem was, however, that Kokand was fighting Bukhara and attempting to assert control over Semirechie, where Kenesary was camped. The Kirghiz were fighting against Great Horde Kazakhs for the province, and Kenesary, weakened by the flight south, attempted to get the Great Horde Kazakhs to join his cause to resist Russia and oust the Kirghiz nomads from the lush Semirechie pastures. Kenesary started negotiating with the Kirghiz, to end the fight against the Kazakhs and Kokand, but at some point in the negotiations, the Kirghiz decided Kenesary was a liability and took him prisoner. Sometime in April 1847, the Kirghiz executed him, bringing to an ignoble close the last major Kazakh military resistance to Russian expansion into the Kazakh Steppe.[54]

There will be other, relatively minor rebellions in the 1850s among some Great Horde clans resisting Russian expansion into Semirechie, but in 1854 the Russians took the region and established a permanent settlement at Vernyi (present-day Almaty). This opened the metaphorical door to Kokand, Khiva, and Bukhara, but that push was temporarily delayed by the Crimean War (1853–1856) and the subsequent "great reforms" under the "tsar liberator" Alexander II (1855–1881). The greatest of the great reforms was the 1861 peasant emancipation, which liberated Russian peasants from the burdens of serfdom but not from the harsh realities of life in the empire. There were other reforms—judicial, military, and economic—but the reforms also, unintentionally, unleashed a wave of peasant migration to Siberia and the Kazakhs Steppe that challenged the government's ability to manage it, resulting in the further loss of Kazakh economic and social sovereignty.[55]

A consequence of this new attention was a wave of administrative reforms in Siberia and the Kazakh Steppe as well as a renewed imperial effort to conquer the Kokand, Bukhara, and Khiva. In 1867 cash-strapped Russia decided to abandon its colony in Alaska, selling it to the United States for the paltry sum of $7.2 million.[56] Alaska clearly lay outside Russia's imperial vision of itself. In 1864 Russian foreign minister Prince Alexander Gorchakov, issued what many scholars consider the government's clearest justification for the empire's continued expansion into central Asia. He explained for all "civilized States 'which are brought into contact with half-savage, nomad populations, possessing no fixed social organization . . . it always happens that the more civilized state is forced . . . to exercise a certain ascendency over those whom their turbulent and unsettled character make most undesirable neighbors.'" He continued, using language that any ardent American expansionist might appreciate: that the "tribes on the frontier have to be reduced to a state of more or less perfect submission." It was, he claimed, a "peculiarity of Asiatics to respect nothing but visible and palpable force; the moral force of reason and the interests of civilization has as yet no hold upon them."[57]

RESISTANCE: SIOUX

Comparable to Kazakh resistance to Russian expansion and colonization, with its three major rebellions from 1824 to 1847, scholars tend to identify three major Sioux uprisings, or wars, following the so-called 1857 Spirit Lake Massacre. The first comes within five years of the tragedy at Spirit Lake—the 1862 Dakota War—followed by the 1866–1868 Powder River War (Red Cloud's War) and the 1875–1877 Black Hills War (Sitting Bull's War). These three conflicts represent the most serious clashes waged between the Sioux and Americans in the 1860s and 1870s, ending with the vast majority of Sioux forced to settle on government-approved reservations and the near complete loss of Sioux political and economic sovereignty. As with the Kazakh rebellions, the three major Sioux conflicts are a series of battles, skirmishes, and raids that conflate into larger episodes that Americans describe as wars.

Following the 1825 Prairie du Chien treaty, the United States remained a relatively minor player in the northern plains. The south–north line of forts created a somewhat porous boundary that demarcated American territory; Americans expressed a desire to remove all Indians east of the line, which meant, essentially, all Indians east of the Mississippi River. The treaty established not just boundaries between the United States and western tribes but also boundaries between the tribes in the plains, in order to reduce intertribal warfare and stabilize the environment for the lucrative fur trade. By the 1820s, the Sioux—especially the Teton—benefited from westward migration; according to Colin G. Calloway, the strength of the Teton derived from their "ruthless exploitation of a favorable economic position and to reduction of enemy tribes by European diseases."[58]

In 1830 the United States signed another treaty of Prairie du Chien with some Santee bands, Sacs, Fox, Omaha, and others, in which, according to the preamble, the signatories acknowledged the "unfriendly feeling" between them but, more importantly, sought to "provide sources for supplying their wants besides those of hunting, which they are sensible must soon entirely fail them." In essence, in order to survive, they ceded land to the United States and agreed to live within allotted territory and receive annuities to sustain them.[59]

In 1836 and again in 1837, the Yankton ceded lands to the United States, surrendering their claim to almost 2.2 million acres. Despite these significant cessions to the United States in the 1830s and 1840s, these decades witnessed years of continued Sioux territorial expansion. Different Sioux bands forged alliances with Arapahos and Cheyennes, secured the Black Hills from the Kiowa, and, as Richard White argued, the United States moved into a region in which the people did not consider themselves "wards," were not some defenseless people but an overly confident and powerful people that was also expanding.[60] This was partially a clash of nations and partially a clash of civilizations, but it was clearly a clash of expanding powers into a region that both claimed.

In the 1840s, Manifest Destiny became the dominant theme of American expansion westward, and the discovery of gold in California in 1849 accelerated that migration. Relations between the United States and the Sioux during those decades were generally peaceful, but the various peace initiatives of the previous decade began to crumble with the declining fur trade economy. Some Sioux bands, led by Mdewakanton and others in the Minnesota prairies and woodlands, became farmers and grew a variety of crops, such as potatoes and corn. They represented, as Gary Clayton Anderson noted, a Dakota subculture, but it was vulnerable to climate and crop failures.[61] By the end of the 1840s, the

United States confronted a growing crisis on the plains that many Americans believed was necessary to resolve with treaties, removal, and reservations.

Many scholars agree that 1851 was a turning point in US-Sioux relations. The United States signed treaties with the Sioux at Traverse des Sioux in July, at Mendota in August, and at Fort Laramie in September. Representatives of the United States, including Superintendent of Indian Affairs David Mitchell and numerous Indian representatives, which the Americans insisted on identifying as chiefs and head chiefs, from the Sioux, Cheyennes, Crow, Arapahoes, Mandans, Arikaras, Assiniboines, and Gros Ventres negotiated and concluded a treaty near Fort Laramie in Wyoming. Certainly, the Americans wanted the treaty to reestablish peace between the Sioux and their allies with their neighbors in order to stabilize the northern plains and end intertribal conflict. From the American perspective, defined, specific tribal boundaries opened the door for additional American expansion. In the treaty, the United States also gained the right to construct roads and military posts across Indian lands. The tribes agreed not to harass emigrants that used the trails to California and Oregon. For agreeing to the terms, the various tribes expected to receive a substantial annual annuity and, more importantly, the right to hunt on un-ceded lands.[62] In fact, between 1851 and 1858, the Sioux treaties extinguished their title to almost 28 million acres, which they exchanged for annual annuities and a reservation.[63]

These 1851 treaties, as Jill St. Germain noted with subsequent treaties, demanded certain behavior by not just the bands but by all Sioux as individuals.[64] In other words, the burdens to fulfill the treaty obligations had almost no consequence for an American emigrant or pioneer but imposed financial and administrative action on the US government and its representatives (agents and others). The consequence, however, was that if a single Sioux violated an article of the treaties, the American government reserved the right to withhold its obligations to the Sioux. The act of an individual meant that the United States could punish all Sioux people, which it did frequently. Article 8 of the Treaty of Fort Laramie stipulates that the "United States may withhold the whole of a portion of the annuities mentioned . . . from the nation so offending, until, in the opinion of the President of the United States, proper satisfaction shall have been made."[65] In 1857 the Spirit Lake Massacre, sometimes called Inkpaduta's War, refocused American attention on the Minnesota frontier (Minnesota was made a territory in 1849) and what becomes the Sioux problem.

It is difficult to call the Spirit Lake Massacre a rebellion, and even harder to consider it part of the larger Sioux Wars of the 1860s and 1870s. Nonetheless, it was an act of resistance and, more importantly, a signal many Americans interpreted to suggest that the frontier remained a dangerous place that needed final subjugation to complete American control. The only way to do that was to commit military force and either compel the Sioux onto reservations or exterminate them. The United States did not control the frontier. The settlements where the attacks occurred were located on the border between northern Iowa and southern Minnesota, found on the "extreme frontier . . . although on ceded lands, were really in the very heart of the Indian country, and absolutely unprotected and defenseless."[66] The winter of 1856–1857 was a severe one, and the annuities failed to alleviate Sioux suffering in the region. Many Sioux were forced to beg, and someone in Inkpaduta's camp killed a settler's dog (which had bitten one of them), prompting a confrontation with some Americans. Shortly thereafter, Inkpaduta's group attacked and killed thirty-four settlers, moved to the settlement of Springfield near Spirit Lake, and attacked the settlers who were prepared and had found refuge in an impromptu fortification. The attacks killed some settlers and others were taken prisoner, and they caused a panic throughout the territory. The crisis ended almost as quickly as it started. Inkpaduta and his followers fled west, although the Americans captured some of them. The government repeatedly failed to capture the notorious Inkpaduta.[67]

Many scholars, however, argue that the failure to punish Inkpaduta emboldened the Sioux to resist American colonization, but, as Roy W. Meyer writes, it also meant that "hostility towards the Indians increased enormously . . . [and] the danger of a real uprising was intensified because of a shift in the attitudes of both whites and Indians."[68] Five years later, Minnesota erupted again in senseless violence. In August 1862, in the midst of the Civil War, four young Santee murdered five settlers near Acton, Minnesota. It was an arbitrary act of violence that sparked a larger, more violent clash between the Sioux struggling to survive on the reservations and settlers who both feared and distrusted them.[69]

One thing that appears repeatedly in many of the recollections, memoirs, and reports published over the years about the conflict was the clearly expressed fear among many Sioux that the Americans held the entire tribe responsible for the violent acts committed by four young men—that, once the murders occurred, many Sioux leaders reluctantly agreed to join the hostiles rather than try to prove their innocence. The Minnesota Sioux rightfully feared American retribution, and that the American government held all Sioux in the state accountable. It happened before, and many treaties signed between the United States and the Sioux apparently enshrined the very concept.[70] Equally fascinating, of course, was that, during the uprising, a large number of Sioux defended whites against violence, saved their lives, and literally put themselves between white men, women, and children and those who wanted to kill them. There were deep divisions among the Sioux about this conflict, which the conflict manifested and amplified and further fractured the bands.

Roughly two thousand Sioux surrendered to the Americans, but hundreds of others, including Little Crow, fled to the plains. Sibley placed some 400 Sioux on trial for various crimes, including murder and rape, and the government convicted and sentenced to hang 303 of them. The state's newspapers fueled the desire to exterminate or expel all Sioux from the state. "The cruelties perpetrated by the Sioux nation in the last two weeks," one editor wrote, "demand that our government shall treat them for all time as outlaws who have forfeited all rights to property and life."[71] Of course, the failure to conduct proper investigations and hold legitimate trials to determine guilt or innocence, followed by the merciless decision to executive over three hundred Sioux deemed guilty by the military tribunal, smacks more of vengeance than justice. President Abraham Lincoln's intervention saved the lives of most, but the military tribunal still bore the mark of retribution and not jurisdictive integrity. In December 1862, the Justice Department reversed the tribunal's conviction and subsequently hanged 39 Sioux. For the Sioux, according to Angela Cavender Wilson, the 1862 Minnesota-Sioux conflict became "a pivotal point around which many stories within the oral tradition are referenced. Not just because this was a traumatic period in Dakota history, but because this is the event which marks the separation from the homeland."[72]

Between 1862 and 1866, the United States engaged in a number of small battles with the Sioux throughout the Dakota, Wyoming, Nebraska, and Montana Territories. The Sioux and their allies continued to harass and attack travelers along the Bozeman Trail, which led to the Montana goldfields, and kept the army on constant alert. In October 1865, the United States signed treaties with several different Sioux bands at Fort Sully, including the Miniconjou, Lower Brulé, Two Kettle, Blackfeet, Sans Arcs, Hunkpapa, Yanktonai, Upper Yanktonai, and Oglala.[73] The treaties demanded an end to the hostilities and reasserted the US right to construct roads and defend travelers. In June 1866, Col. Henry Carrington met with several Sioux leaders at Fort Laramie to negotiate an end to the crisis, but the Sioux refused to surrender the Powder River region to American forts.

In 1866 the United States built three forts along the trail, ostensibly to protect travelers from Indian depredations. From the American perspective, the articles of the 1851 Fort Laramie Treaty clearly permitted these forts. Several Sioux bands in the Powder River region disagreed. In December 1866, one of the notable defeats for the United States occurred when a young lieutenant—William Fetterman—inadvertently led a force of eighty men into a skillfully executed ambush near Fort Phil Kearny. The Sioux killed Fetterman and all his men. "We must," insisted Gen. William Tecumseh Sherman, "act with vindictive earnestness against the Sioux."[74]

Frustrated by the crisis in the northern plains, the United States, in July 1867, created the Indian Peace Commission, charged by the government to return peace and stability to the region. It consisted of civilians and military men. The commission traveled west to meet with the Sioux to resolve the conflict; they did this eleven times. Typically absent from these meetings, however, were two of the more influential Sioux leaders—Red Cloud and Sitting Bull—both of whom refused to meet with the commissioners. Red Cloud made specific demands—namely, that the United States completely abandon the three forts along the Bozeman Trail and remove all whites from the territory. Only then, Red Cloud made clear, would he meet with the government's representatives. His insistence that the United States abandon the forts strongly echoed similar demands made by Zholaman and Kenesary during the Kazakh rebellions. Unlike the situation in the Kazakh Steppe, however, the United States ultimately agreed to abandon the posts.

Ultimately, the negotiations resulted in the signing of the 1868 Treaty of Fort Laramie. It conceded significant swaths of territory to the Sioux and the Americans agreed to abandon the forts, but it also acknowledged the Black Hills were located on Sioux land; tragically, the government surrendered land to the Sioux that was already reserved for the Ponca.[75] It was a flawed treaty. If the commissioners' goal was to establish a durable peace with the Sioux, this treaty failed miserably. Although Red Cloud never again went to war against the United States, the treaty's provisions were dependent upon the United States fulfilling its obligations explicitly. It did not. That failure, and continued American expansion, pushed the United States and the Sioux toward another military confrontation.

The United States forced many Sioux onto the Great Sioux Reservation, but it quickly became clear that the Sioux interpreted the provisions differently.[76] As a case in point, the Sioux established peace with the United States, but that had no bearing on their relations with other tribes and the intertribal warfare on the northern plains continued much as before.[77] Moreover, pioneers, eager to take advantage of the Homestead Act, continued to pour into the Dakotas, Nebraska, and, to a lesser extent, Montana. The perception of conflict between pioneers and the Sioux kept the American government on edge. Having completed the first transcontinental railway in 1869, a new northern route conceived of a different westbound line that cut through northern Dakota Territory, which required further negotiation with the Sioux to permit its construction. Various

Sioux bands continued to live by the chase and had occasional skirmishes with American soldiers or emigrants, but in 1872–1873, these encounters increased significantly. Sioux often attacked surveying teams of the Northern Pacific Railroad—Jay Cooke's Gamble—planned to go from Duluth, Minnesota, to Seattle, Washington.[78]

Of all the conflicts between the United States and the Sioux in the nineteenth century, none received even close to the same amount of attention from scholars, commentators, or casual observers, as the 1876 conflict. The immediate source of the conflict erupted in 1874, after the US government dispatched an expedition, led by Lt. Col. George Custer, to investigate rumors of gold in the Black Hills, although that was not the mission's explicitly stated purpose. Miners and others frequently violated the 1868 Fort Laramie Treaty and moved into the region well before Custer's expedition. The American government made half-hearted efforts to remove them, but the expedition itself spent almost two months in the Black Hills. Unable, or unwilling, to control its own citizens, who daily violated the treaty's provisions, the United States reached the conclusion that it was necessary to "violate the treaty in order to restore it."[79] By late 1875, more than fifteen thousand miners and others had rushed to the Black Hills to exploit its natural resources.[80] In the end, however, a treaty that American officials pledged would last forever barely lasted six years.

Unlike previous conflicts between the American and the Sioux, in which fault could be attributed to each side, possibly with varying degree of responsibility, the Great Sioux War of 1876 was initiated by the United States for naked conquest and differed not a whit from the British in Africa, the French in Algeria, or the Russians in the Kazakh Steppe. It was the clearest evidence that the United States exercised imperial ambitions that mirrored other nineteenth-century powers. As Ostler observed, President Ulysses S. Grant faced a difficult choice—expansion or honor—and in this situation, he "sacrificed the latter."[81] In late 1875, the American government ordered all Plains' tribes to return to the reservations. In December of that year, Secretary of the Interior Zachariah Chandler ordered the Sioux to return to the reservations by the end of January 1876 or accept the label "hostile." If they failed to return, the government determined to use military force to compel compliance. Despite the enormous victory at the Battle of the Little Bighorn, several Sioux and Cheyenne bands, throughout the fall and winter of 1876–1877, migrated toward various reservations to surrender. The army kept the pressure on the Sioux, and in May 1877, Crazy Horse and his followers surrendered at Red Cloud Agency. The war ended, as Jerome A. Greene noted, with a "whimper." The United States achieved the specific goal of forcing the Sioux onto selected reservations and abandoning their nomadic, buffalo-hunting economic lifeways and opening territory to pioneer settlement.[82] The Sioux Wars were essentially over. The United States militarily and politically subjugated the Sioux. Internal colonization in both the United States and Russia began in earnest.

Throughout the nineteenth century, the Sioux and the Kazakhs opposed different colonizing agendas and policies, but they exhibited similar martial reactions. They each fought against the loss of land and their political sovereignty. In short, specific Sioux and Kazakh conflicts are not the key to this comparison. They were each peculiar to the imperial environment as it existed in the plains and steppe. There was little in common between Red Cloud's War in the northern plains and Kenesary Kasymov's Rebellion in the Kazakh Steppe that this comparison exposes, except that American and Russian expansions triggered the martial reactions with obvious conclusions. Red Cloud and Kenesary resisted the expansions. The conflicts reveal, however, in both cases that indigenous peoples vigorously resisted; but comparing the course of the conflicts does not illuminate as much as comparing the reasons behind the conflicts and, more importantly, the consequences. The United States and Russia determined to settle the nomads and allot the land, effectively ending, or severely restricting, the Sioux and Kazakh nomadic existence.

The benefit of this comparison is that examining motivations to resist through the comparative prism demonstrates that the United States engaged in an expansionist agenda that differed little from the Russian experience. The conflicts produced an overwhelming response and use of force to localized affairs but was clearly motivated by a desire to complete the colonization of land arguably controlled by a native people. These conflicts were rebellions, and they represented military resistance by a people whose political sovereignty the colonizers already determined lacked national unity or national integrity to treat as equals. In that sense, the American expansion west was not a unique colonizing exercise.

The ultimate failure of the martial resistance by the Sioux and the Kazakhs to prevent American and Russian expansion into the plains and the steppe did not mean that all resistance ceased. Resistance took different forms as the Sioux and the Kazakhs continued to resist cultural and social pressures to change and, to the extent possible, maintain their fractured identities into the early twentieth century. What is interesting in this difference of chronological resistance is that Kazakh opposition to Russian expansion began well before Kazakhs experienced intensified Russian settler colonialism, before the massive influx of Russian peasants settling on land designated for Kazakh use in the second half of the nineteenth century. Kazakh hostility seemingly anticipated this settler-colonial expansion, but the conflicts were a twofold reaction to Cossacks settling along the Irtysh Line. The Russian prohibition against Kazakhs migrating to pastures on the Inner Side fully exacerbated Kazakh internal political strife, represented by Abulkhair's 1732 oath and other Kazakh khans and sultans fighting each other for political and economic dominance in the Kazakh Steppe. Sioux resistance, on the other hand, occurred most vigorously after 1851, after treaties signed between some Sioux bands ceded territory to the United States. It was after 1851, and clearly after the American Civil War (although the 1862 Minnesota Uprising was a significant exception), that American expansion and colonization on the northern plains intensified and sparked much broader, more passionate hostility by the Sioux. There was internal disagreement among the Sioux, as well, about how to respond, but it did not result, as it did among the Kazakhs, in an internecine conflict.

For comparison, the construction of the Ilek Line corresponds to the Bozeman Trail forts that Red Cloud and other Sioux opposed so vigorously in the 1860s. The physical presence of the Russians in the steppe—and, later, the Americans in the plains—meant that the visible and tangible reminder these forts represented added considerable anxiety and hostility to American and Russian colonization. That issue, certainly more than whether or not the Americans or the Russians recognized a head chief or a khan, fueled the rebellions. Sioux and Kazakh economic decline was associated with—and, in part, a product of—American and Russian expansion. Consequently, the Sioux and the Kazakhs responded with martial force. One difference, of course, was the duration of the rebellions against American and Russian colonization; but both the United States and Russia determined to crush the military capability of the Sioux and the Kazakhs and make the northern plains and the Kazakh steppe secure for trade and settlement.

The conquest of the Sioux and the Kazakhs was both a military and economic process. As the Americans slowly squeezed the Sioux by territorial limitations, the Sioux also suffered from the loss of the main economic necessity that sustained them in the northern plains: the buffalo. In the Kazakh Steppe, severe winters and the absence of available pasture also diminished Kazakh economic power, and, subsequently, in both cases, the loss of economic autonomy resulted in the ability to resist American and Russian expansion. Without the buffalo, the Sioux needed other sources for food—something the Americans offered but only on reservations, where the American government assumed it was easier to control them. Without pastures, Kazakh livestock suffered, and only by agreeing to Russian demands that restricted migration patterns could the Kazakhs receive the assistance Russia offered. Although confined to districts rather than reservations, the Russians believed they could better control the Kazakhs by imposing territorial limitations. In both cases, restricting movement compelled the Sioux and the Kazakhs into a dependency on the American and Russian governments that completely eroded their political and economic independence.

Here the comparison shares some similarities with the US-Sioux case, but there were differences as well. For example, the Americans and the Russians both stressed the need to identify individuals who could be held accountable, and that were possibly already acknowledged by other Sioux and Kazakhs as chiefs or khans. The problem was that, in principle, these positions in Sioux and Kazakh society were not specifically hereditary titles but rather based on a more culturally ambiguous recognition of the individual's personal skills, courage, wealth, and prestige. This does not mean that hereditary transfers of power from father to son did not occur; instead, Sioux and Kazakh society was fluid enough to allow Sioux or Kazakhs to select their leaders based upon this other criteria. The title was essentially meaningless without followers, but during the eighteenth and nineteenth centuries, the United States and tsarist Russia acknowledged men designated as chief or khan by the colonizer in order to advance expansion. Two such examples were securing Little Crow's signature on an 1805 treaty and Abulkhair's 1732 oath. Both the United States and Russia also employed a couple of common colonizer tactics in the quest to expand. They awarded titles, selected leaders, granted benefits, and attempted to marginalize chiefs or khans who did not acknowledge the colonizer's right to create what Robert K. Thomas called "cooperative marginal people," leaders elevated by the colonizer in order to subvert recognized indigenous authority or leadership.[83] According to Utley, this practice created a "chaos of authority" that plagued American-Sioux relations in the second half of the nineteenth century.[84] "From the outset," Ostler argued, "as the United States tried to established control over the Plains Sioux, the government's relationship with Sioux leaders was structured by a basic contradiction . . . officials were dependent on native leaders, at times going so far as to declare particular leaders 'head chief' of the Sioux nation or one of its subdivisions. On the other hand, the government's goal of assimilation called for the eventual destruction of native political organization."[85] In both cases the United States and Russia destabilized Sioux and Kazakh sociopolitical structures in order to diminish or tear down leaders opposed to expansion and colonization. Therefore, American and Russian government officials typically perceived internal power struggles as evidence of backwardness or traditionalists opposing American or Russian civilization; it was evidence of the cultural, social, and political inferiority of native structures.

Aleksei I. Levshin summarized Russian frustration when he wrote in 1832,

> For over 90 years they [the Kazakhs] have been under Russia's authority, and for 90 years the government has tried to establish amongst them some sort of order, but only now are we starting to see the beginning of success. The reprimands, labor, expenses to establish trading centers, schools and mosques; the construction of homes for some sultans to accustom them to a sedentary life; the creation of the council of khans, tribal jurisdictions and frontier courts, providing salaries for khans and clan officials; supporting the costs of the mullahs and secretaries; permitting them to winter beyond the empire's frontier—all has been in vain. These measures have not advanced the Kirgiz-Kazakhs toward civilization [*obrazovanie*].[86]

Critics of Indian policies echoed this sense of futility in the United States during the 1860s and 1870s, at the height of the Sioux Wars. The fact that Levshin traveled through the Kazakh Steppe during the rebellions in the Little and Middle Hordes characterized his sense that only by imposing a firm order, a powerful military presence, would the Kazakhs be compelled to behave in a manner that advanced Russia's civilizing mission in Asia.

In the United States, similar comments punctuated the concerns of the government, the military, reformers, and observers of American policy. One difference, however, appeared in an 1867 report submitted to Congress that, just as an example, identified failures by the US government to fulfill its treaty obligations and explained the rebellions. In 1972 William Welsh (of the Board of Missions of the Protestant Episcopal Church) repeated the charge against the government.[87] Certainly, Helen Hunt Jackson, in her classic monograph, *A Century of Dishonor*, convicted the United States for its failures, which sparked a new round of reform efforts.[88] In each case—and there are numerous other examples that can be cited—Americans were far more willing to criticize US government policies for the rebellions than Russian observers experiencing similar difficulties in the Kazakh Steppe. In a sense, Jackson and Welsh almost proclaimed that the Sioux were justified (there are just as many observers unwilling to agree with those interpretations), something Russians were unable to concede until the 1890s, when the evidence of impoverishment and utter economic dislocation among the Kazakhs was readily apparent. Only then did some—a small minority to be sure—Russians demand reforms.

What this also suggests is that Americans and Russians typically blurred and linked perceptions and policies during the military conquest of the Sioux and the Kazakhs. American and Russian perceptions also linked the Sioux and Kazakhs to a general imperial expansion—particularly, negative attitudes about Sioux and Kazakh society, culture, and behavior. Perceptions, positive and negative, based typically on clichés, stereotypes, and misunderstanding Sioux and Kazakh sociopolitical and economic structures, animated policies that the Americans and Russians designed to deal with these powerful, seminomadic peoples. It is to perceptions of the Sioux and the Kazakhs that this work will now turn.

NOTES

1. Of course, Americans started moving west before independence, but the discovery of gold in California started a stampede westward; and so, in the 1840s, the United States either fought a war (Mexico) or negotiated a treaty (Britain) that fixed its northern and southern boundaries. While California—or even Texas before the 1840s—might have experienced an influx of Americans, it was only after the boundaries were fixed that the United States and the Sioux started to have a real problem with each other. In Russia, as late as 1864, the government was using the absence of fixed boundaries to justify expansion, and it was only after defeating the Turkmen at Geok Tepe in 1881 that the British determined to use diplomacy to stop Russian expansion.

2. In a sense, what Russia did not have was a powerful imperial rival that opposed Russian expansion into the Kazakh Steppe. British India was a long way away and none too eager to expand territorially into central Asia; the British wanted to dominate trade, not territory. It is conceivable, in an imperialist way of thinking, that had Britain completely abandoned North America after 1783 that the United States would have expanded into Canada without, as in the Russian case, an imperial rival to hinder the movement. The fact that, after 1783, Britain and the United States shared a border was not a condition that Russia faced until the 1870s, when its border with China was fully demarcated. In the 1890s, Britain and Russia finally formalized a recognized border for the Russian Empire, but they surveyed the borders in such a way that Persia and Afghanistan remained as neutral, relatively independent buffers—meaning the British and Russian Empires never shared a border.

3. At first glance, the possible reason might be Islamic prohibitions against its consumption and, therefore, Kazakhs did not drink, but that might be only a part of the answer. For this comparison, however, it is more important simply to identify the exploitation of spirits rather than explore fully why. Answering why is an exercise in speculation due to the lack of evidence from the Russian-Kazakh case.

4. James O. Gump effectively used the Battle of the Little Bighorn and the British defeat at Isandlwana in 1879 to compare American subjugation of the Sioux and the British conquest of the Zulu. See James O. Gump, "The Subjugation of the Zulus and Sioux: A Comparative Study," *Western Historical Quarterly* 19, no. 1 (January 1988): 21–36; James O. Gump, *The Dust Rose Like Smoke: The Subjugation of the Zulu and the Sioux* (Lincoln: University of Nebraska Press, 1996).

5. Referring to them as "small skirmishes" is not meant in any way to diminish the suffering and the terrible loss of life both Kazakhs and Russians experienced because of these rebellions. Russian government reports and the testimony by both Russians and Kazakhs are filled with accounts of fifty killed here or one hundred killed there. It is fair to say that more Kazakhs and Russians died in these rebellions than Sioux or Americans died during the Sioux Wars of the 1860s and 1870s. The difference, in that sense, is that Russians and Kazakhs did not give dramatic names to these battles. Thus, there is no Spirit Lake Massacre or Custer's Last Stand to mark these occasions.

6. For an excellent analysis of changing Soviet interpretations, see Lowell R. Tillett, *The Great Friendship: Soviet Historians and the Non-Russian Nationalities* (Chapel Hill: University of North Carolina Press, 1969).

7. For standard biographies of Sitting Bull, Crazy Horse, and Red Cloud, see Robert M. Utley, *The Lance and the Shield: The Life and Times of Sitting Bull* (New York: Henry Holt, 1993); Robert W. Larson, *Red Cloud: Warrior-Statesman of the Lakota Sioux* (Norman: University of Oklahoma Press, 1997); Kingsley M. Bray, *Crazy Horse: A Lakota Life* (Norman: University of Oklahoma Press, 2006). For two slightly different but interesting interpretations, see Ernie LaPointe, *Sitting Bull: His Life and Legacy* (Layton, UT: Gibbs Smith, 2009); R. Eli Paul, ed., *Autobiography of Red Cloud: War Leader of the Oglalas* (Helena: Montana Historical Society Press, 1997). Since the collapse of the Soviet Union in 1991, the Kazakhs have republished equally good biographies of Srym Batyr and Kenesary. Kazakh historians are very interested in both men and the era. See Mikhail Viatkin, *Batyr Srym* (Almaty: Sanat, 1998 [1947]); Ermukhan Bekmakhanov, *Kazakhstan v 20–40 gody XIX veka* (Almaty: Kazakh Universiteti, 1992 [1947]).

8. Since the collapse of the Soviet Union, the Kazakhs have consistently described the rebellions—particularly the Kenesary Kasymov Rebellion—as wars for "National Liberation." See Steven Sabol, "Kazak Resistance to Russian Colonization: Interpreting the Kenesary Kasymov Revolt, 1837–1847," *Central Asian Survey* 22, nos. 2–3 (June/September 2003): 231–52; Yuriy Malikov, "The Kenesary Kasymov Rebellion (1837–1847): A National-Liberation Movement or 'a Protest of Restoration'?," *Nationalities Papers* 33, no. 4 (December 2005): 569–97.

9. Robert M. Utley, *The Indian Frontier, 1846–1890*, rev. ed. (Albuquerque: University of New Mexico Press, 2003), 196.

10. Jill St. Germain, *Broken Treaties: United States and Canadian Relations with the Lakotas and the Plains Cree, 1868–1885* (Lincoln: University of Nebraska Press, 2009), 5.

11. Stuart Banner, *How the Indians Lost Their Land: Law and Power on the Frontier* (Cambridge, MA: Harvard University Press, 2005), 127.

12. Banner, *How the Indians Lost their Land*, 35; Valerie Kivelson, "Claiming Siberia: Colonial Possession and Property Holding in the Seventeenth and Early Eighteenth Centuries," in *Peopling the Russian Periphery: Borderland Colonization in Eurasian History*, ed. Nicholas B. Breyfogle, Abby Schrader, and Willard Sunderland (London: Routledge, 2007), 21–22.

13. Francis Paul Prucha, *American Indian Treaties: The History of a Political Anomaly* (Berkeley: University of California Press, 1994), 1.

14. This, according to Robert F. Berkhofer Jr., "indicates as much about Congress's conception of native sovereignty as its fear of native warfare." *The White Man's Indian: Images of the American Indian from Columbus to the Present* (New York: Vintage, 1979), 146.

15. Berkhofer, *White Man's Indian*, 141. Berkhofer noted, as well, that the addition to create equal territories that could become states potentially complicated American-Indian relations because it "added new voices in Congress for native cessions and war" (148).

16. Jeffrey Ostler, *The Plains Sioux and U.S. Colonialism from Lewis and Clark to Wounded Knee* (Cambridge: Cambridge University Press, 2004), 2.

17. Napoleon quoted in Henry Adams, *History of the United States of America during the First Administration of Thomas Jefferson* (New York: Charles Scribner's Sons, 1909), 1:400.

18. Adams, *History of the United States of America*, 2:49.

19. During the nineteenth century, several Mdewakanton leaders used the name Little Crow. Gary Clayton Anderson writes that the Little Crow who signed the treaty with Pike was Cetanwakanmani, a leader who brought the Little Crow "dynasty to prominence." *Little Crow: Spokesman for the Sioux* (St. Paul: Minnesota Historical Society Press, 1986), 15. Doane

Robinson writes that Pike made Little Crow "head chief of the Dakotas" and that his name, Cetanwakanmani, means "Who walks pursuing a hawk." According to Robinson, "Little Crow was the name of a dynasty rather than of a man." *A History of the Dakota or Sioux Indians. . . .* (Minneapolis: Ross & Haines, 1967), 109.

20. For a brief history of the Bukei Horde, through the 1860s, and its place in the Russian expansion into the Kazakh Steppe, see M. Ivanin, "Vnutrenniaia ili Bukeevskaia Kirgizskaia Orda," *Epokha*, no. 12 (1864): 1–117.

21. Gary Clayton Anderson, *Kinsmen of Another Kind: Dakota-White Relations in the Upper Mississippi Valley, 1650–1862* (Lincoln: University of Nebraska Press, 1984), 85.

22. Pilcher quoted in Richard White, "The Winning of the West: The Expansion of the Western Sioux in the Eighteenth and Nineteenth Centuries," *Journal of American History* 65, no. 2 (September 1978): 328.

23. Hiram Martin Chittenden, *The American Fur Trade of the Far West: A History of the Pioneer Trading Posts and Early Fur Companies of the Missouri Valley and the Rocky Mountains and of the Overland Commerce with Santa Fe* (New York: Francis P. Harper, 1902), 2:864–66.

24. US Department of War, *Indian Treaties, and Laws and Regulations Relating to Indian Affairs: To which is Added an Appendix, Containing the Proceedings of the Old Congress, and Other Important State Papers, in Relation to Indian Affairs* (Washington City: Way & Gideon, 1826), 276–82.

25. Robinson, *Dakota or Sioux Indians*, 95–96.

26. V. Grigoriev, "The Russian Policy Regarding Central Asia. An Historical Sketch," in *Turkistan: Notes of a Journey in Russian Turkistan, Khokand, Bukhara, and Kuldja*, by Eugene Schuyler (New York: Scribner, Armstrong, 1877), 2:397.

27. Utley, *Indian Frontier*, 9–10.

28. In 1837 a trader and his half-blood Sioux wife—John Baptiste Ferribault and Pelagie Ferribault—claimed that in August 1820, the Sioux made a grant of land—chiefly an island at the rivers' confluence, called Pike's Island—that belonged to her and "her heirs forever." Lawrence Taliaferro, Indian agent at St. Peter's, vigorously disputed the claim, noting that he instructed Colonel Leavenworth that the island was more useful as a military reserve. Several Sioux chiefs were summoned to Fort Snelling in 1838, as witnesses to the transfer in 1820, but as Bad Hail told the government officials, "we did not give away any land, only the privilege to cut wood." This is a case of who had the right to purchase or receive land from Indians. As the commanding officer at Fort Snelling noted in an 1838 opinion, "that, if the Government sanction the practice of the Indians giving their land to individuals, much of the public domain now in the Indian country will be proved to belong to aliens and other transient persons who may pass through Indian country." See "Purchase of Island—Confluence of the St. Peter's and Mississippi Rivers," 26th Cong., 1st sess., House Executive Document 82 (Washington, DC, 1840).

29. Francis Paul Prucha, ed., "Exclusion of British Traders," *Documents of United States Indian Policy*, 3rd ed. (Lincoln: University of Nebraska Press, 2000), 28–29.

30. Roger L. Nichols, "The Canada-US Border and Indigenous Peoples in the Nineteenth Century," *American Review of Canadian Studies* 40, no. 3 (September 2010): 419.

31. Utley, *Indian Frontier*, 35.

32. I. Strebelsky, "The Frontier in Central Asia," in *Russian Historical Geography*, ed. James H. Bater and R. A. French (London: Academic Press, 1983), 1:155.

33. Madhavan K. Palat, "Tsarist Russian Imperialism," *Studies in History* 4, nos. 1–2 (February 1988): 257.

34. Pekka Hämäläinen, "The Rise and Fall of Plains Indian Horse Cultures," *Journal of American History* 90, no. 3 (December 2003): 860.

35. George Hyde, *Red Cloud's Folk: A History of the Oglala Sioux Indians* (1937; Norman: University of Oklahoma Press, 1975), 36–37.

36. Ostler, *Plains Sioux and U.S. Colonialism*, 32.

37. Semirechie, also known in Kazakh as *Zhety Su*, or "Land of the Seven Rivers," was the southeastern province, bordering China, Kokand, and Bukhara.

38. Another element to the rebellions that complicated relations between Russians and Kazakhs, and between Kazakhs in the three hordes, was the expansionist pressure applied by Kokand, Khiva, and Bukhara to control Kazakh territory in the southern Kazakh Steppe. Moreover, Great Britain was disturbed by Russia's expansion into the Kazakh Steppe and feared that Russia's ultimate imperial goal was to keep on going all the way to India. The rebellions in the Kazakh Steppe were only one conflict of many that Russia was fighting. Russia was expanding and fighting in the Caucasus, fought a couple of wars against Persia in the 1810s and 1820s, fought against Ottoman Turkey in the 1820s and 1830s, and was faced with a serious Polish rebellion in 1830. In addition, the British had intelligence, which was clearly in the minds of Delhi's colonial officials, that suggested that Russia was encouraging Afghanistan's ruler to ally with Russia against Britain in India. The "Great Game," as it was called, was part of the "Eastern Question" and the geopolitical backdrop to Russia's expansion, but it pitted the Turkestani khanates against two imperial powers, Russia and Britain. See Peter Hopkirk, *The Great Game: The Struggle for Empire in Central Asia* (New York: Kodansha International, 1992). The two Anglo-Afghan Wars (1839–1841, 1879–1881) were triggered by Britain's desire to replace seemingly hostile Afghan rulers with a ruler that Delhi could manipulate or, at a minimum, be trusted to block Russian expansion. Both wars ended badly for Britain.

39. The Orenburg Frontier Commission was the administrative name for the Russian territorial government administration, headquartered in Orenburg. It would be dissolved in 1844 and replaced by the Orenburg Governor-Generalship. See Martha Brill Olcott, *The Kazakhs*, 2nd ed. (Stanford: Hoover Institution Press, 1995), 61.

40. *TsGA RK*, f. 4, op. 1, d. 1820, ll. 720–721; *Materialy po istorii Kazakhskoi SSR (1775–1828)* (Moscow: Akademiia nauk SSSR, 1940), 449.

41. *TsGA RK*, f. 4, op. 1, d. 1036, l. 141.

42. M. Zh. Abdirov, *Istoriia Kazachestva Kazakhstana* (Almaty, 1994), 55.

43. Zh. Artykbaev, *Kazakhskoe obshchestvo v XIX veke: traditsii i innovatsii* (Karaganda: Poligrafiia, 1993), 272–74.

44. *TsGA RK*, f. 64, op. 1, d. 5, l. 16.

45. *TsGA RK*, f. 64, op. 1, d. 5, 1. 35.

46. *TsGA RK*, f. 64, op. 1, d. 13, ll. 158–59.

47. Ermukhan Bekmakhanov, *Kazakhstan v 20–40 gody XIX veka* (1947; Almaty: Kazakh Universiteti, 1992), 206.

48. Bekmakhanov, *Kazakhstan v 20–40*, 170–73.

49. According to estimates by the Orenburg Frontier Commission, he could field two thousand men. See *TsGA RK*, f. 4, op. 1, d. 4957, l. 11. One of the first historians of the revolt, N. A. Sereda, believed he had up to ten thousand "well-armed horsemen." See N. A. Sereda, *Bunt kirgizskogo sultana Kenesary Kasymova, 1838–1847* (Atyrau: Po zakazu Oblastnogo otniīa fonda kul'tury g. Atyrau Respubliki Kazakhstan, 1992).

50. *TsGA RK*, f. 374, op. 1, d. 25, ll. 15–16.

51. *TsGA RK*, f. 4, op. 1, d. 1996, ll. 3–6. The original was written in the Arabic script commonly used by Kazakhs. It was reprinted in Cyrillic Kazakh in M. K. Kozbaev,

Natsional'no-osvoboditel'naia bor'ba Kazakhskogo naroda pod predvoditel'stvom Kenesary Kasymova (Almaty: Gylym, 1996), 35–37.

52. *TsGA RK*, f. 4, op. 1, d. 2622, 1845g., l. 1059.

53. Later scholarly interpretations describe Kenesary as a solid military leader, but one who was at times politically tactless. See two recent interpretations of the rebellion, Zh. Kasymbaev, *Kenesary Khan* (Almaty, 1992), 171; Kh. Aubakirova, "Uchastie Sibirskogo Kazachestva v podavlenii natsional'no-osvoboditel'nogo dvizheniia Kazakhskogo naroda pod predvoditel'stvom sultanov Sarzhana i Kenesary," (PhD diss., Eurasian University of Astana, 2000), 97. In addition, in English, two recent articles analyze the rebellion's "national-liberation" aspects. See Sabol, "Kazak Resistance to Russian Colonization," 231–52; Malikov, "Kenesary Kasymov Rebellion," 569–97.

54. Bekmakhanov, *Kazakhstan v 20–40*, 313–40.

55. The Russian and, later, Soviet governments continued to struggle with peasant migration well into the twentieth century. As Lewis H. Siegelbaum and Leslie Page Moch explained, "Each iteration of state power—the tsarist, Soviet, and post-Soviet—engendered a variety of *migration regimes*, that is, policies, practices, and infrastructure designed to both foster and limit human movement." *Broad Is My Native Land: Repertoires and Regimes of Migration in Russia's Twentieth Century* (Ithaca, NY: Cornell University Press, 2014), 3, emphasis in original.

56. For a recent examination of Russia's colony in Alaska and its decision to sell, see Ilya Vinkovetsky, *Russian America: An Overseas Colony of a Continental Empire, 1804–1867* (Oxford: Oxford University Press, 2011). For an interesting comparative analysis of Alaska's native population under Russian and American rule, see Sonja Luehrmann, *Alutiiq Villages under Russian and U.S. Rule* (Fairbanks: University of Alaska Press, 2008).

57. A. M. Gorchakov, memorandum, 21 November 1864, in *British Documents on Foreign Affairs: Reports and Papers from the Foreign Office Confidential Print*, ed. D. C. B. Lieven, part 1, series A (Frederick, MD: University Publications of America, 1983), 1:287–88.

58. Colin G. Calloway, "The Inter-tribal Balance of Power on the Great Plains, 1760–1850," *Journal of American Studies* 16, no. 1 (1982): 44.

59. Charles J. Kappler, ed., *Indian Affairs. Laws and Treaties* (Washington, DC: Government Printing Office, 1904), 2:305–6.

60. White, "Winning of the West".

61. Anderson, *Kinsmen of Another Kind*, 144.

62. See Remi Nadeau, *Fort Laramie and the Sioux* (1967; Santa Barbara, CA: Crest, 1997), 66–82; Kappler, *Indian Affairs*, 2:594–96.

63. Utley, *Indian Frontier*, 76. The 1851 commissioner of Indian affairs report, however, claims that the 1851 treaties alone amounted to almost 35 million acres. US Department of the Interior, Office of Indian Affairs, *Report of the Commissioner of Indian Affairs to the Secretary of the Interior*, 32nd Cong., 1st sess., House Executive Document 2 (Washington, DC: Government Printing Office, 1851), 280.

64. St. Germain, *Broken Treaties*, 73.

65. Kappler, *Indian Affairs*, 2:595.

66. Charles E. Flandrau, "The Inkpaduta Massacre of 1857," in *Collections of the Minnesota Historical Society*, vol. 3 (St. Paul: Minnesota Historical Society, 1880), 388.

67. See Roy W. Meyer, *History of the Santee Sioux: United States Indian Policy on Trial* (Lincoln: University of Nebraska Press, 1967), 97–101.

68. Ibid., 101. Thomas Hughes wrote that these "considerations had great weight with Little Crow and his followers, five years later, in deciding on the second and greater massacre."

Thomas Hughes, "Causes and Results of the Inkpaduta Massacre," in *Collections of the Minnesota Historical Society*, vol. 12 (St. Paul: Minnesota Historical Society, 1908), 282.

69. More than a decade before, a missionary wrote a report in which the sentiment revealed the strong possibility that a conflict was already in the making. Referring to the Santee Sioux as the "wild Dakota," the author wrote, "Though there are four stations on the Minnesota River and two on the Mississippi below St. Paul, the prospects of the Dakota mission are not bright. The male portion of the nation with but few exceptions, [has] an inveterate hatred of the Christian religion, and look upon the missionaries as intruders who drink their water and plough their soil, but give nothing in return." See "Miscellaneous: Mission to the Dakotas," *Christian Observer* (September 7, 1850), 144. One history, written almost a century after the conflict, concluded that government maladministration, bad weather and crop failures, alcohol, "fraudulent treaties, insolent traders, swindling fur companies, and dishonest agents" caused the "rebellion." The author also concluded that it needed Sioux leaders, such as Shakopee and Little Crow, who were willing to sacrifice everything and commit the atrocities. See C. M. Oehler, *The Great Sioux Uprising* (1959; New York: Da Capo, 1997), 236–37. Oehler's explanation for the causes differ little from the first book to appear about the conflict—interestingly, in 1863—although that author, Isaac V.D. Heard, also claimed that the Sioux (and all Indians) had a predisposition to violence. See Isaac V.D. Heard, *History of the Sioux War and Massacres of 1862 and 1863* (New York: Harper & Brothers, 1863), 31–51. In retaliation for the 1862 conflict, the Sioux were forced to leave Minnesota. Sibley and his militia made certain that the Sioux were expelled. Throughout 1863 Sibley remained active and did not disband his militia but increased its size and marched north to the Minnesota-Dakota Territory border. Several other skirmishes occurred—first at Big Mound and later near Dead Buffalo Lake. While these engagements were relatively minor affairs, they increased hostile tensions across the northern plains. The US War Department created the Department of the Northwest, under Maj. Gen. John Pope, to subdue the Sioux and force them to retreat westward into Dakota Territory. Another battle, near Killdeer Mountain, in July 1863, revealed the government's intent with this overwhelming military force. The goal was to inflict significant hardship on the Sioux by destroying their food, capturing other supplies, and forcing them, as one historian noted, to "submit to the largesse of the U.S. government." See Bill Yenne, *Indian Wars: The Campaign for the American West* (Yardley, PA: Westholme, 2008), 103.

70. Gary Clayton Anderson and Alan R. Woolworth, eds., *Through Dakota Eyes: Narrative Accounts of the Minnesota Indian War of 1862* (St. Paul: Minnesota Historical Society, 1988), 99.

71. Quoted in Hugh J. Reilly, ed., *Bound to Have Blood: Frontier Newspapers and the Plains Indian Wars* (Lincoln: University of Nebraska Press, 2011), 5.

72. Angela Cavender Wilson, "Walking into the Future: Dakota Oral Tradition and the Shaping of Historical Consciousness," *Oral History Forum/Forum d'histoire orale* 19 (1999): 29.

73. All of the treaties are reprinted in Kappler, *Indian Affairs*, 2:883–908.

74. Quoted in Utley, *Indian Frontier*, 106.

75. According to Joe Starita, "The Lakota had not asked for the Ponca land, didn't need or want it. But what the government later characterized as 'a blunder' now gave the Lakota legal incentive to go after the smaller, weaker, peaceful tribe. So, for eight years, Lakota war parties, mostly Brule, terrorized the besieged Ponca in their villages, destroying their crops, stealing their horses, slaughtering their livestock, killing and scalping the people whenever they could." *"I am a Man": Chief Standing Bear's Journey for Justice* (New York: St. Martin's Griffin, 2008), 34.

76. According to Guy Gibbon, during the Sioux Wars of the 1870s, "less than one-third of all Sioux remained free roaming bison hunters." *The Sioux: The Dakota and Lakota Nations* (Oxford: Blackwell, 2003), 106.

77. St. Germain, *Broken Treaties*, 93; White, "Winning of the West," 341.

78. See M. John Lubetkin, *Jay Cooke's Gamble: The Northern Pacific Railroad, the Sioux, and the Panic of 1873* (Norman: University of Oklahoma Press, 2006).

79. St. Germain, *Broken Treaties*, 252.

80. Howard R. Lamar, *Dakota Territory, 1861–1889: A Study of Frontier Politics* (New Haven, CT: Yale University Press, 1956), 150. It was not just gold that attracted outsiders but other natural resources, especially timber.

81. Ostler, *Plains Sioux and U.S. Colonialism*, 61.

82. Jerome A. Greene, "Out with a Whimper: The Little Missouri Expedition and the Close of the Great Sioux War," *South Dakota History* 35, no. 1 (2005): 1–39. As Greene noted, the war "passed into history with a fizzle instead of a bang" (39).

83. Robert K. Thomas, "Colonialism: Classic and Internal," *New University Thought* 4, no. 4 (1966): 40.

84. Utley, *Indian Frontier*, 228–30.

85. Ostler, *Plains Sioux and U.S. Colonialism*, 194.

86. In the 1832 publication of Levshin's book, *Opisanie Kirgiz-kazach'ikh, ili Kirgiz-kaisatskikh, ord i stepei*, he used the word *obrazovanie*, which usually translates as "education," but not what one simply learns in school. It can mean a cultured, civil, knowledgeable person. In the French translation of his book, *Description des hordes et des Steppes des Kirghiz-Kazaks ou Kirghiz-Kaïssaks*, the word used was *civilisation*. What this illustrates for this comparison is that the ideas, sentiments, and process are essential. Simply because Russians might not have used words such as *savage*, *barbarian*, or some other pejorative to describe the Kazakhs does not mean that the same sentiment or attitude was absent. The key is to detect that sentiment rather than identify a specific word. See Aleksei I. Levshin, *Opisanie Kirgiz-kazach'ikh, ili Kirgiz-kaisatskikh, ord i stepei* (1832; Almaty: Sanat, 1996), 372; Alexis de Levchine, *Description des hordes et des Steppes des Kirghiz-Kazaks ou Kirghiz-Kaïssaks* (Paris: Imprimerie Royale, 1840), 403.

87. See, for example, "Letter of the Secretary of the Interior Communicating, in Compliance with a Resolution of the Senate of the 8th Instant, Information Touching the Origin and Progress of Indian Hostilities on the Frontier," 40th Cong., 1st sess., Senate Executive Document 13 (Washington, DC: Government Printing Office, 1867); William Welsh, *Report of a Visit to the Sioux and Ponca Indians on the Missouri River* (Washington, DC: Government Printing Office, 1872).

88. According to Helen Hunt Jackson, "Had the provisions of these first treaties been fairly and promptly carried out, there would have been living to-day among the citizens of Minnesota thousands of Sioux families, good and prosperous farmers and mechanics, whose civilization would have dated back to the treaty of Prairie du Chien." Russian officials rarely express a similar sentiment before the 1890s. *A Century of Dishonor: A Sketch of the United States Government's Dealing with Some of the Indian Tribes* (New York: Harper & Brothers, 1881), 143.

4

Through the Colonial Looking-Glass

The progression of American and Russian expansion across the continents was conquest based on military might and populations willing to migrate, endure harsh terrains and climates, and settle on the land. The American growth across the plains and the continent did not precisely parallel the Russian advance eastward into the Kazakh Steppe and Siberia, but there were comparable perceptions and attitudes expressed about the land and people being colonized to justify internal colonization. Americans and Russians shared with their European contemporaries the same philosophies, science, ethnologies, and agrarian motivations prevalent in the nineteenth-century imperial vision. These mutually held beliefs shaped the relationships and policies between the colonial frontier and the metropole, between the central government and local administrations, and between colonizer and colonized.

The American and Russian perceptions and attitudes were not, however, mirror images of each other, but Americans and Russians nonetheless held firmly entrenched perceptions and attitudes about the Sioux and Kazakhs. Backwardness and barbarism were like conjoined siblings in the minds of Americans and Russians, whose civilizing missions could elevate the Sioux and Kazakhs sufficiently from their backwardness and barbarism to prevent the seemingly inevitable extinction. When analogized against competing perceptions, attitudes, typologies, and images—particularly American and Russian exceptionalism—the result was denigration and dislocation of the Sioux and Kazakhs.

Internal colonization operated under amalgamated typologies and imagology in the depiction of other peoples, as well as one's own, which fused with American and Russian nationalisms in the latter half of the nineteenth century. According to Margaret Ziolkowski, typologies and imagology was "not transparent but a conventionalized process" that placed value on social constructions and identities.[1] Typology and imagery presented portraits of Sioux and Kazakhs that did not "simply reflect stereotypes—it reinforces or even helps to engender them."[2] Contrasted against concepts of "American" and "Russian," these typologies and imageries reinforced imperial expansion that resulted in the process of internal colonization.

In order to understand this process, it is important to note that the military conquest and subsequent internal colonization of the Sioux and the Kazakhs did not happen in a political, economic, or social vacuum. The United States and Russia eagerly consumed the land and adopted and implemented strategies to assimilate the people but failed consistently to achieve the objective using the policies and programs designed with that purpose in mind. In this regard, the two processes differed considerably despite sharing similar objectives. In the end, however, the consequences for the Sioux and the Kazakhs were comparable. Americanization or Russification, two policies designed to assimilate the Sioux and the Kazakhs, also intentionally destroyed or severely undermined the social bonds that seemed to Americans and Russians as the reason for Sioux and Kazakh backwardness and barbarism.

Therefore, while the process is manifest, that alone does not explain the consequences for the Sioux or the Kazakhs, nor does it necessarily illuminate the perceptions and attitudes voiced by Americans and Russians about expansion, conquest, and internal colonization. It was clear that the seemingly empty spaces of the plains and the steppe attracted pioneers and peasants to that presumably free land, which pushed the United States and tsarist Russia to expend considerable resources and effort to conquer and colonize the regions claimed by the Sioux and the Kazakhs. This chapter examines the American and Russian typologies and imageries of the land and people used to justify and eventually implement expansion and internal colonization.

AMERICAN VERSUS RUSSIAN EXCEPTIONALISM

Throughout the nineteenth century, Americans and Russians created exceptionalist narratives to justify expansion and conquest and to explain the accompanying cultural, social, political, and economic rejuvenation. The United States and Russia both desired to distinguish themselves from European traditions, empires, societies, and cultures. In the American case, the goal was to illustrate that the United States differed from Europe; but the Russians desired to demonstrate their similarities. The American narrative, according to Barbara Bush, imagined "an exceptional republic [destined] to spread the superior American way of life, rooted in democratic republicanism and Protestant religious values."[3] Thomas Jefferson explained in an 1809 letter to James Madison that "we should have such an empire for liberty as she has never surveyed since the creation: & I am persuaded no constitution was ever before so well calculated as ours for extensive empire & self government."[4] It was as optimistic an expression as one could possibly imagine that prophesied an American expansion across the continent. Historian Walter Nugent summarized American ideologically constructed exceptionalism that exuded "progress, national glory, and successful stewardship all rolled into one. White Americans were certain that they had the right and duty to take land because they would make it more productive than native peoples, or Spaniards, or Mexicans, had done."[5]

American exceptionalism situated American expansion as something different from the old European imperialism and colonialism; it was a break with old European social and political edifices. The American vision for the future was optimistic and enlightened; it had a destiny. It was none other than Alexis de Tocqueville, in his classic *Democracy in America*, who envisioned a destiny for the United States that paralleled the destiny of the Russian Empire—only the obstacles and consequences seemed to differ. He explained that the "American struggles against the obstacles that nature opposes to him, the adversaries of the Russian are men. . . . The conquests of the American are therefore gained by the plowshare; those of the Russian by the sword."[6] Much as the expansion west rejuvenated and invigorated American ideals, Russia's expansion east resurrected Russia and moved it beyond the self-loathing sometimes evident in literature.

Russian writer Peter Chaadaev lamented, "From the outset of our existence as a society, we have produced nothing for the common benefit of all mankind; not one useful thought has sprung from the arid soil of our fatherland; not one great truth has emerged from our midst; we have not taken the trouble to invent anything ourselves and, of the invention of others, we have borrowed only empty conceits and useless luxuries."[7] Most Russian intellectuals and government officials did not share Chaadaev's views.[8] According to historian Andrzej Walicki, Chaadaev believed Russia was "forgotten by Providence, a country without past and without future . . . isolated from mankind and playing no part in universal history."[9]

Foreign observers also wondered about the civilizing benefits of Russia's expansion, as Charles Rudy suggested, "the rising sun of progress" casting "its golden beams over the regions of the East. Are these to be intercepted by the clouds which envelop the Russian Empire?"[10] Russia's burden, however, was the deleterious stereotypes that one unyielding but prominent critic of Russian imperialism in Asia—George Curzon, an ardent Russophobe—voiced in expressive but rather misanthropic imagery. He claimed that Russia's expansion into central Asia was a "conquest of Orientals by Orientals, of cognate character by cognate character."[11] It was not, Curzon asserted, European civilization that "marched forth to vanquish barbarian Asia. This is no nineteenth-century crusade of manners or morals; but upon its former footsteps to reclaim its own kith and kin."[12] Nonetheless, Walicki rightly noted that Russian backwardness—and to some extent, its exceptionalism—radiated a "peculiar advantage." Russia "could learn from the experience and use the achievements of Europe, that the intellectual and cultural impact of the West served as a powerful catalyst in the emergence and development of Russian social thought."[13] The diverse intellectual currents in Russia likewise juxtaposed Russia with the United States, often relying on de Tocqueville's descriptions.[14]

In 1837 Russian historian, journalist, and Slavophile Mikhail Pogodin critiqued the United States as a country that "cares solely for profit; to be sure she has grown rich, but she will hardly ever bring forth anything great of national, let alone universal significance."[15] According to historian Abbott Gleason, many Russian intellectuals believed that the Russian Empire and the Russian people represented a "healthy collectivism" and a "peasant socialist utopia" that compared favorably to an America "fated to embody extreme individualism."[16] Slavophile thought was, Walicki argued, rooted in a "retrospective utopia, a yearning for a lost harmony, a Russian variant of conservative romanticism, setting itself in opposition to the institutions and values of modern, capitalist civilization."[17] American and Russian intellectuals and political leaders tended to imagine their empires rooted in the agrarian ideal, although it differed somewhat.

Americans sought to distinguish their social and political institutions from Europe, which de Tocqueville highlighted. Those institutional differences became the basis of American exceptionalism, which intensified the contrast between whites and Indians (as well as blacks, Mexicans, and other minorities) in the American milieu. Russia shouldered a different, but very onerous, exceptionalism. Russian autocracy, serfdom, and economic backwardness persisted in the minds of most Europeans and many Russian intellectuals and statesmen. Europeans often used Orientalist rhetoric to characterize Russian social and political institutions, as Curzon did in his polemic against Russian imperialism in central Asia.

These images of Russia as being equally backward and little more than talented imitators of Europe permeated Russian exceptionalist typologies. In this convoluted calculus, Russians were little more than Oriental Orientalizers. Russian novelist Feodor Dostoevsky, for example, echoed the thinking of many Russian intellectuals who enthusiastically supported Russia's expansion into the Kazakh Steppe and central Asia. He wrote, in "Europe we were hangers-on and slaves, while in Asia we shall be the masters. In Europe we were Tatars, while in Asia we are the Europeans. Our mission, our civilizing mission in Asia will encourage our spirit . . . A new Russia will be created that will restore and resurrect the old one in time and will clearly show her the path to follow."[18] Russia's nineteenth-century imperial expansion into central Asia and the Far East represented Russia's future; it made Russia equal to its European neighbors, who, more often than not, praised Russian mimicry rather than Russian innovation. Russia's autocratic, subservient past and seemingly unlimited present and future firmly grounded its exceptionalism; however, for many, Russian exceptionalism, its contributions to mankind, directly correlated to its eastward expansion.

Thus, American expansion and the pioneer exemplified the new empire of liberty and the rugged individualist, unshackled by the European cultural and social limitations. An 1871 *Handbook for Immigrants to the United States*, produced by the American Social Science Association, explained, "The American is born free, he lives free, and he dies free. His government regards him not as a subject, but as a citizen. His laws treat him as equal with everybody about him . . . The whole spirit of this society is in favor of personal independence."[19] For many Russian intellectuals, unquestionably for Russian Slavophiles, the Russian peasant symbolized and embodied the communal rebirth of the Russian Empire and the Russian nation that European influences unnecessarily corrupted. Historian Hans Kohn, an astute student of Russian history, explained Russia's exceptionalism: "Out of the very consciousness of her backwardness and lack of liberty grew extravagant dreams of Russia as the founder of a new civilization, as the bearer of universal salvation."[20] As part of the rhetorical conquest of the Sioux and the Kazakhs, Americans, Russians, and foreign observers evoked ancient images—what later scholars defined as Orientalism—to justify expansion and to characterize the obligation of civilization and progress on ostensibly backward and barbarian peoples.

COMPARATIVE ORIENTALISTS

Typologies and imagery were essential elements in American and Russia exceptionalist concepts and vital to the perceptions and attitudes that influenced policies. Edward W. Said's influential study, *Orientalism*, defined the term in its most negative connotations—exploitative, dominating, and expropriating—a

European invention to describe the exotic, the unusual, the romanticized but not realistic East.[21] The American West, and the indigenous people who lived there, provided a comparable opportunity for Americans to exoticize the region and the people. Writers expropriated Orientalist rhetoric to explain the geography and the people living beyond the frontier of civilization in terms that readers would associate with difference—not one of us, but something old, exciting, perhaps even dangerous, but also weak and slowly dying. Richard Francaviglia, however, defined it in the American context as "a mind-set that readily imagines or perceives an East when it encounters non-Eastern peoples and places."[22] According to Francaviglia, the Orient fascinated Americans, which created an exotic region and peoples to colonize; the Americans exoticizing the "American landscape worked hand in hand with the Orientalization of people in frontier America."[23] In 1858 William Pidgeon observed, "Traits of ancient nations in the Old World are everywhere seen in the fragments of dilapidated cities, pyramids of stone, and walls of immense length; but here, in North America, is found the wreck of empires . . . older than the beginning of the pyramids, and whose history may only be read in the imperishable relics of tumuli, and such great records."[24] The Orient these writers described, or the images conveyed, was decadent and backward. Although the Orient once had a glorious past, its present and future was rapidly and indisputably vanishing when confronted with modern civilization.

The travelogues, memoirs, histories, literature, and even official reports used terms, languages, and expressions that a reader readily recognized and that needed no explanation. In the 1894 book *Slav and Moslem*, Jane Milliken Napier Brodhead descriptively wrote, "the Steppes of Asia, for so many centuries the scenes of permanent rapine and pillage, have been made safe highways by these noble [Russian] pioneers."[25] The steppe and its nomads axiomatically meant "rapine and pillage." The words *savage* or *barbarian* evoked specific images of the people encountered; lengthy definitions were unnecessary. As Robert F. Berkhofer Jr. noted in the American case, "commentators linked Indians with most of the cultures known previously to Westerners from Old World antiquity: to ancient Greeks, Scythians, Tartars, Spaniards, Hebrews," but Russians understood these concepts as well.[26] In medieval Europe, the term *barbarian* meant "Tartar."[27] Americans embraced the belief that civilization and agriculture were synonymous. The antonym was barbarism, and Americans, Russians, and Europeans readily depicted nomadic peoples to be barbarians and uncivilized. Thus, in the nineteenth century, Americans expropriated some of these ideas and references to describe the American West. "The analogues," to reference Plains tribes such as the Sioux, according to Henry Nash Smith, that appeared most often were "the Bedouins of the Arabian desert [and] the Tartars of the Asiatic steppes."[28]

American readers clearly understood Indians as comparable, and writers framed their analysis, observations, and depictions in expropriated Orientalist images. For example, one description of a possible attack on a wagon train by Indians evoked central Asian imagery without ever mentioning the tribe: "Nothing could be more interesting, than to witness this little caravan surrounded by hordes of the ruthless red Tartars of the desert, brandishing their lances on horseback, and scenting the plunder with panther keenness of instinct."[29] The author even noted that the scene described served to "remind the classical reader of the deportment of the ten thousand amidst the strange and innumerable hordes of barbarians, through which, partly by battle, and partly by policy, they made their way."[30] Every reader understood the context and image: Old World antiquities applied to the American environment. For what other reason would an author refer to "red Tartars"? It was literary typology; America had red Tartars, but so did Russia.

Russians often referred to all Muslims as Tatars—particularly in Siberia and the Kazakh Steppe—failing to distinguish specifically between Tatars and Kazakhs or Tatars and Bashkirs. Russian writers often used terms that a Russian reader interpreted differently although in context might make sense to an American or European. *Kochevnik* (nomad) needed no explanation in the Russian milieu, nor did *musulman* (Muslim), and, therefore, Russian writers rarely used terms such as *savages* or *barbarians* to describe the Kazakhs but instead relied on words that inferred the inferior character of the non-Russian population. The most authoritative four-volume Russian dictionary of the period defined *Tatar* to mean "dishonest, cunning, sly, and crude."[31] There was no need to translate *Tatar*—Americans understood it as well, and many used the term to define Indians, including the Sioux. Russians easily embraced the term as well. Kazakh and Tatar languages were part of the large Turkic language family; Kazakhs and Tatars were both Muslims, but Kazakhs were not members of the Tatar nation. In the United States, similar etymological transfers occurred; a Sioux was an Indian, a savage was a nomad, but not all Indians were Sioux, nomads, or even savage. In the American lexicon, nineteenth-century American colonizers and pioneers simply carried the typologies and imageries westward to graft these Orientalist concepts onto indigenous peoples. If Indians were red Tartars, so too was an Indian sly, savage, crude, and so on; a Sioux shared those characteristics and was a nomad.

Americans, however, had a term to describe Indians that did not penetrate Russian thinking about the Kazakhs. Americans had, or so they believed, their own uncivilized barbarians to observe; and by the mid-eighteenth into the nineteenth century, interest in the "noble savage" of the American West replaced fascination with barbarians in Asia or Africa.[32] According to Roy Harvey Pearce, Americans embraced the image of the Indian as noble savage, a supposed opposition to civilization, in order to justify expansion, colonization, extinction, and assimilation.[33]

The Russians never considered Kazakhs to be noble savages.[34] In America the noble savage was dying; in Russia the noble East was already dead—its history lost and replaced by nomads who had no future because they had no past. Nomads existed within the landscape, but they did not remake it. Nomads were a part of the natural world; they were not able to influence it but merely react to its whims. Nomads could follow a trail; they could not make a road. Nomads left no discernible impression on the world they occupied. A nomad never built a library because he had no need for a book. Observers defined nomads by what they were not, not for what they were. For the Russian poet Alexander Pushkin, as with many of his contemporaries, peoples of the East had no sense of history, which he regarded as necessary for a civilized people. He wrote that a "respect for the past is a characteristic that distinguishes the educated person from the savage; nomadic tribes have neither a history nor a nobility."[35] Thus, using language that evoked images of a distant place or a distant past also meant that the people encountered—Sioux or Kazakh—represented a "natural history, not quite human history. Indians became, in the eyes of Euro-Americans, a people with a past, but without a history."[36] Nomads, such as the Sioux and the Kazakhs, were part of the landscape; and when Americans or Russians entered the plains or the Kazakh Steppe, they perceived "places empty of history, and gave them a beginning and thus meaning."[37]

The noble savage was living history but also primitive and often a disappointment to Americans hoping to catch a glimpse of a member of a dying breed of man. Sarah Raymond Herndon, describing her encounter with some Sioux, noted that they "were the most wretched-looking human creatures I ever saw, nothing majestic, dignified, or noble-looking . . . I fail as yet to recognize 'The noble red man.' They are anything else than dignified; they seem lazy, dirty, obnoxious-looking creatures."[38] It should be noted, however, that by the time Herndon encountered her "creatures," the concept of the noble savage was withering away and being replaced by thoughts that the Sioux, as nomads, were prisoners of their primitive society and environment.

In the course of the nineteenth century, Americans and Russians focused on so-called scientific discoveries to explain the backwardness of the Sioux and the Kazakhs, who became objects for study. Americans and Russians embraced science to justify expansion and colonization as well as to provide seemingly empirical evidence to characterize whole societies as barbaric, backward, uncivilized, ignorant, superstitious, warlike, and untamable. Berkhofer noted that the "effect of physical environment as an explanation of human social and cultural diversity goes back at least to the ancient Greeks, but as a way of analyzing the place of the American Indians among the races of man it was particularly characteristic of Enlightenment thought. An environmental explanation of Indian life originated in Europe, but this approach particularly appealed to thinkers in the newly founded United States."[39] As Sherry L. Smith asked, "Was savagery an inherited state, or did physical environment explain it?"[40] A nineteenth-century traveler to the Kazakh Steppe, Ellsworth Huntington, raised a similar notion of the "primitive" Kazakhs. He wrote that the "Kirghiz [Kazakhs] are so primitive, their manner of life is so simple and so closely bound up with their physical surroundings, and they are so little influenced by outside forces, that they furnish an unusually good example for the study of the influence of environment on human life."[41] Huntington also subjectively asserted, "Everywhere the Kirghiz are lazy, according to Occidental standards."[42]

The disappointment expressed by Herndon and the curiosity conveyed by Huntington reflect two essential perceptions—and one unquestioned assumption—that seemingly merged during the expansion into the plains and steppe: perceptions and attitudes proliferated about the land and people and their relationship to one another. The land was rich, open, untamed, undeveloped, unsettled, and unquestionably an integral part of the expanding state. The people were wild, warlike, in the way, and unquestionably compelled to assimilate or suffer extinction. The land and people both were dangerous, unconquered, untamed, and living in a world outside American and Russian state structures. These perceptions often melded into common attitudes, typologies, stereotypes, and clichés to explain the environment and its inhabitants; they shared similar socio-environmental explanations to describe the failure of the indigenous populations to exploit the land or socially evolve above their barbarism. Americans and Russians assumed that the Sioux and the Kazakhs must assimilate—to which Americans, more than Russians, also accepted the probability of extinction.

Thus, the idea of the noble savage was an exaggerated exoticism that diminished by the time the United States determined to conquer the Sioux, but Americans measured themselves by the images and typologies they constructed and encountered. Russians continually used Europe—its culture, its own civilizing progress—to evaluate their societal growth; it was also a useful barometer easily measured against the peoples of the steppe. The United States and Russia juxtaposed their own societies against the exotic Other, the axiomatic backwardness of those peoples colonized; Americans and Russians both exhibited their own different brand of Orientalism.

ORIENTALISM IN THE AMERICAN WEST AND THE RUSSIAN EAST

Writers and travelers in the United States or Russia provide some of the richest descriptive Orientalist accounts that reflected not only their own perceptions and attitudes; travelogues conveyed to the reader those essential elements of the people or the environment they encountered in a language and utilitarian manner that reinforced attitudes and perceptions about the other. It is also a form of Orientalism that is not often attendant with American expansion and colonization but is typically associated with British, French, and Russian imperialism in South Asia, the Near East, North Africa, and central Asia. It was not always an overtly conveyed juxtaposition but was often surreptitiously concealed within the narrative.

American and Russian perceptions, attitudes, typologies, and imageries were not nineteenth-century fabrications but manufactured over two or three centuries of expansion and reinforced during the nineteenth-century era of conquest. Equally important, Americans and Russians had perceptions of themselves as superior, civilized, and Christian that easily juxtaposed against the people they encountered during expansion, conquest, and colonization. The Americans knew Indians—or at least thought they did—dealt with them, fought against and with them, and perceived them, ultimately, as obstacles to expansion. Just as the wilderness needed to be conquered and tamed, it was understood that so too the people should be governed and disciplined. When Americans encountered the Sioux, they already possessed, in their minds, indisputable facts about their Indianness that made the Sioux obstacles to American expansion. In the world that Americans created during westward expansion, the Sioux were warlike and uncivilized. It was almost axiomatic—supported by new science and reinforced by seemingly weekly reports of attacks and depredations despite evidence of intelligent, articulate, educated Sioux who shared and exhibited all the characteristics of Americanness that Americans wanted, such as faith, frugality, and labor.

Similarly, when Russians encountered the Kazakhs, they possessed attitudes already shaped by a discourse that evolved over centuries, reinforced during the nineteenth century by scholars and government officials, and not quickly abandoned by a newly formed respect or disgust for these incorrigible Turkic nomads. In the nineteenth century, the Russian perspective evolved through an emerging sense of greatness and empire, Christian civilization, and both Americans and Russians regarded nomadic peoples as obstacles to expansion, empire, and civilization. But Russians also equated the Kazakhs with a horrific past—the Mongol Yoke—a memory not easily erased during expansion. It was, instead, partial justification for further expansion, which was always about land and people. As both empires expanded their frontiers, they incorporated new territories and new populations. The land, whether the American West or the Russian East, was fresh; untilled; and a vast, open space just waiting for the right people to exploit its bounty. Many Americans and Russians believed fervently that they were the people chosen to civilize and tame the untapped riches long neglected by the indigenous peoples. In a sense, the Sioux and Kazakhs saw the land as it was; Americans and Russians saw the land for what they wanted it to be.

PLAINS VERSUS STEPPE

The American Great Plains for decades persisted in the public consciousness as the "great American desert," comparable to the "sandy wastes of the deserts or steppes of Siberia rather than to the dead sands of Africa."[43] Zebulon Pike, one of the first Americans to cross it, described it as a desert that might "become as celebrated as the African deserts," although he also believed it could support pastoral livestock rather than intensive agriculture.[44] Sir Arthur Conan Doyle described the plains as preserving "the common characteristics of barrenness, inhospitality, and misery. There are no inhabitants of this land of despair."[45] It was a region that "for many a long year served as a barrier against the advance of civilization."[46]

Russians had no illusions about the steppe; it was arid, dangerous, and absent all signs of civilization. But while it might not possess anything of great value, the steppe was the path to Asia's riches. In the United States, the plains were not always the destination; the plains gave access to the West's riches (California's or Montana's gold). In both cases, the plains and the steppe opened the doors to something better, richer, and settled after Americans and Russians charged through to the other side. Of course, accounts of a journey across the barren Kazakh Steppe mirrored similar fears and dangers expressed by American travelers across the barren plains. One seemingly fatigued writer revealed, "Fourteen weary days were occupied in crossing the steppe; the marches were long, depending on uncertain supplies of grass and water, which sometimes wholly failed them; food for man and beast had to be carried with the party, for not a trace of human habitation is to be met with in these inhospitable wilds."[47] And so, the weary traveler notes the "[a]rid uniformity and silence characterize the steppe. Throughout its entire extent of four hundred and thirty-four miles, one discovers trees in two places only; moreover, everywhere only small prickly shrubs sprouting three feet in height, and but sparingly distributed, so that the eye of an European is unable to support the monotony of this horrible desert."[48] British traveler Fred Burnaby described his venture into the steppe as a place that "underwent an entire change. We had left all traces of civilization behind us, and were regularly upon the steppes."[49] The American Great Plains could be likened to "the dead level extending on either side the Father of Waters . . . like an ocean petrified in the midst of a great storm . . . where, if ever, broken surface and pines, sparse and stunted, bring relief to the eye."[50]

Many travelers compared the plains and steppe to the ocean: "a vast unbroken plain, like that in which we now travelled for nearly one hundred and fifty miles, is little less tiresome to the eye, and fatiguing to the spirit, than the dreary solitude of the ocean."[51] For many observers, the rolling, treeless, and stunted hills prompted the ocean images, with those unending gentle waves. Perhaps it was the horizon, so distant yet always seemingly within reach; mountains with trees become a new but formidable shoreline to attain. Quoting geographer Alexander von Humboldt, another writer notes that the plains and the steppe resemble "the ocean, the steppe fills the mind with the feeling of infinity; and thought, escaping from the visible impressions of space, rises to contemplations of a higher order."[52] A British journalist offered this description of the American plains and prairies: "walk out to the east till all sight and sound of the little village is lost in the distance, and then look round you. There is a huge, undulating ocean of long, rich grass and flowers . . . not a shrub or bush to break the dead level of the distant horizon—nothing to vary the wide-spread sea of verdure."[53] Father Pierre De Smet described his journey across the plains as "a troubled sea that had suddenly calmed. Day after day the scene is unchanged. Like waves, hills succeed valleys interminably . . . In summer it is an ocean of verdure strewn with flowers."[54]

The ocean metaphor was ubiquitous: "that terrestrial ocean well styled 'The Great Plains'" where one sees "that wonderful platitude of the continent . . . As far as the eye can reach—not a house, not a tree, not shrub, except the dwarf sage-brush! It is one rolling sea of light green, often settling into a level as smooth as Holland."[55] Emigrants and traders departed Independence, Missouri, to "embark upon the great prairie ocean" along the Oregon Trail,[56] where they encountered "scenery, though tame, [that] is graceful and pleasing. Here are level plains, too wide for the eye to measure; green undulations, like motionless swells of the ocean."[57] Railroads across the plains and, much later, the steppes and Siberia, became "those palace ships that navigate the great ocean of the plains, ay, and run the breakers of the mighty mountains, dashing through canons and over devious passes."⁵⁸ On the steppe, "Not a tree nor a shrub is to be seen on which the wearied eye can rest. The whole steppe may be compared to the boundless ocean when its wide-spreading waves have become all at once motionless."⁵⁹ Sunsets conjured stirring and romantic visions on the plains, where "out at sea in this green, waveless ocean, the sun goes down upon us. Seldom has such a setting been seen."⁶⁰ Similarly, on the Kazakh Steppe, Charles Rudy observed that its "uninterrupted expanse . . . lends an almost inconceivable splendor to the reddened sky, and the sands, rendered blood-red by the sinking orb, are reflected upon the overhanging sky in innumerable and ever-changing forms."⁶¹

Trees, mountains, trails, and even a solitary cabin or hut morphed into majestic symbols of civilization; the plains and steppe remained barren and strangely wild, backward, and uncivilized. As historian Katya Hokanson explained, "the flatness of the [plains and steppe] indicated a lack of cultural and historical highs and lows—names and places that should have left their mark on history but instead remained uninscribed by culture."⁶² A Russian traveler, Baron von Meyendorf, wrote after crossing the steppe, "I can scarcely give the reader an idea of the joy which I experienced when I found myself once more in a wood; the roaring of the wind through the branches, the quivering of the leaves of the trees, the greenness of the landscape, all this seemed to me as something entirely new, recalled to me the memories of my father-land, and raised in me the most pleasurable sensations. Amongst the deserts and with the nomads one first learns to appreciate the good fortune of being a European."⁶³ Americans had similar thoughts, rediscovering civilization at some point along the overland trails heading west, and writers often used analogies and similarities between the plains and the steppe that appeared frequently in scientific and popular literature. Many writers described the plains or steppe by referring to the other, tapping into preconceived images. One such author described the plains as "solitary as the Steppes of Siberia, crossed only by roaming herds of buffaloes or by Indian warriors on their wild horses, darting swiftly as the wind, and occasionally by the train of the immigrant moving slowly along and disappearing on the horizon like the caravan on the desert."⁶⁴ Referencing Siberia immediately conjured images of distant, remote, desolate, and uninhabited regions of Russia, with its long "arable plains [that] are comparable to our prairies and Argentina's pampas."⁶⁵

American John W. Bookwalter employed a different tactic to describe his journey through the grassland regions of Russian Siberia into the Kazakh Steppe. He described images that he knew his readers would easily understand: to "all Americans who have traveled to the Rocky Mountains through the States of Illinois, Minnesota, Iowa, Kansas, and Nebraska, the country I have come through is easy to describe. To simply say it is exactly like it would constitute a more or less perfect description. Indeed, I have never seen any two things more absolutely similar than are the prairie and plains regions of our country and that vast region lying in southeast Russia."[66] It was easy for most Americans to perceive the region he visited by sketching the analogous impression of a comparable climate and topography. Americans had a fixed perception of the plains that Bookwalter exploited in his description of the steppe; he relied on canonical typologies to conjure specific images. But Bookwalter was also a tourist; his eyes focused on descriptive features of the land and its inhabitants. He was not there to study, merely to describe what he experienced.

Frederick von Hellwald, who echoed Meyendorf's appreciation of trees after weeks on the steppe, argued that "steppes and mountain tracts here also form that fundamental contrast which pervades all conditions of nature and civilization. The lofty mountains with their plenteous supply of water tend to produce food, to impart animation, and advance civilization; whereas the low level steppe causes everything to waste away and become depressed, and thus acts as a hindrance to civilization."[67] Hugo Stumm traveled throughout the steppe and claimed that west of the Urals was Russian civilization, but east was "interminable plains and steppes . . . and, like the nomad Kirghiz-Kaissaks by which they are inhabited, giving a picture of thorough Asiatic wildness and absence of civilization."[68] Nature was, as Mark Cocker noted, "fruitful but she was also wild and threatening, which carried profoundly negative implications for those humans who lived closest to her."[69]

American, Russian, and foreign travelers depicted the Sioux and the Kazakhs, living closest to the wild plains and steppe, as representatives of ancient mankind, observed for what they might explain about mankind's social and cultural evolution. The Americans and the Russians eagerly dispatched scientific expeditions to study the land and the people. In a sense, the conclusions and interpretations merged into one: the barren land created barren peoples—peoples who lacked civilization, modernity, and culture. Not all imagery was negative, however. The plains and the steppe appeared, occasionally, to be a garden, a new Eden, beautiful and welcoming but desperately in need of enterprising pioneers and peasants willing to tame and exploit its bountiful possibilities. That control and exploitation of the land meant taking it from those who stood in the way or neglected nature's gifts.[70] The Sioux and Kazakhs occupied land they failed to exploit; the sentiment was so eloquently expressed by John Quincy Adams in 1802 when he asked, "Shall the liberal bounties of Providence to the race of man be monopolized by one of ten thousand for whom they were created? Shall the exuberant bosom of the common mother, amply adequate to the nourishment of millions, be claimed exclusively by a few hundreds of her offspring?"[71] Similar views appeared countless times in the press, historical works, fiction, and scientific or other published sources.[72]

Foreign travelers to the steppe, however, generally used language and expressions to describe the Kazakhs that illustrated the literal comparison their readers easily recognized and understood. For example, John Foster Fraser visited an aul and described the Kazahks as the "Red Indians of the West Siberian steppes."[73] He noted that the Russians "have conquered them, and pushed them upon the least fertile tracts of land to make room for immigrants. The race is decreasing in number, and will one of these days disappear from the face of the earth altogether."[74] He observed parallels between the fate of Kazakh and Sioux populations in the United States. According to Fraser, Kazakhs "lost their heritage and are soon to be extinct. The touch of civilization means death to them."[75]

The idea of extinction was axiomatic to describe the fate of Indians in the United States; when confronted with the Sioux, Americans were prepared to accept the same fate for them as they acknowledged it for all colonized, uncivilized peoples. According to Pearce, Americans were also of "two minds about the Indian whom they were destroying. They pitied his state but saw it as inevitable; they hoped to bring him to civilization but saw that civilization would kill him."[76] For Fraser and others, echoing Adams, the Kazakhs must civilize or die in order for Russia to exploit "land capable of immense agricultural possibilities, great stretches of prairie waiting for the plough . . . I saw a country that reminded me from the first day to the last . . . of the best parts of western America."[77]

BLINDED BY SCIENCE AND THE IDEA OF PROGRESS

In the nineteenth century, educated Americans and Russians embraced the idea that society progressed through clearly delineated phases, and widely read Enlightenment philosophies reinforced those beliefs. Art, science, and technology progressed society toward civilization, and progress involved all facets of the human condition. Eventually, science seemingly proved the idea of progress, evident in the rapid technological and social advances made throughout the nineteenth century. In his work *History of the Idea of Progress*, historian Robert A. Nisbet noted, "faith in arts and sciences" was "still further intoxicated by confidence in progress as a universal law in mankind's history."[78] Nineteenth-century Americans enthusiastically embraced progress, whereas many Russians, according to historian Sidney B. Fay, were more skeptical.[79] Nonetheless, many revered science and embraced the notion that man could understand the natural world, control it, and bend it to humanity's will.

Educated Americans and Russians believed that the natural world served humanity's progress. Those closer to an untamed, natural world—the nomads—either progressed or succumbed to extinction. By the early nineteenth century, Lord Kames's theoretical four distinct stages of human development were widely influential in both the United States and Russia. The four stages—hunter-gather, herder, farmer, marketer—echoed strongly in the emerging fields of history, philosophy, anthropology, and sociology. American and Russian literary and social Romanticism reflected these concepts in art and literature. Kames claimed, "there is great uniformity in the gradual progress of men from the savage state to the highest civilization: beginning with hunting and fishing, advancing to flocks and herds, and then to agriculture and commerce."[80] Science, evident in the embryonic fields of geology, history, sociology, ethnography, and anthropology, unwittingly perhaps, reinforced perceptions and attitudes during the nineteenth century. These disciplines legitimized American and Russian internal colonial policies and programs. The Sioux and the Kazakhs, the plains and the steppe, were exciting and exquisite repositories and laboratories to examine unspoiled nature and primitive man.

Americans and Russians dispatched numerous expeditions to discover and study the lands and peoples they conquered, which paralleled similar efforts conducted by the British, French, and Germans in Asia, the Middle East, Africa, and South America.[81] Initially in the United States, the military led the majority of these expeditions, of which the Lewis and Clark voyage was but one; but fur trappers also gathered significant information that proved useful to the government. By the 1820s, travelers to the plains published accounts of their adventures that also yielded ostensibly important data on the land and peoples, which further reinforced so-called scientific assessments about civilization's influence on primitive man and the natural landscapes. In Russia, most expeditions in the eighteenth and nineteenth centuries were under the auspices of the military or the Academy of Sciences and, later, the Imperial Geographic Society. Scientific expeditions and military leaders, such as Chokan Valikhanov, Vasili Radlov, and Peter Semenov, expanded the fields of geography, geology, botany, ethnography, and sociology in the Russian Empire.[82]

The United States and Russia dispatched dozens of scientific expeditions into the plains and steppe in order to ascertain the regional natural and human resources, access routes, agricultural suitability, climate, etc. It was also evident that most government-sponsored expeditions were precursors to expansion and conquest. President Jefferson instructed Lewis and Clark not only to map the newly acquired Louisiana Territory, but that the expedition was a "triumph of the American Enlightenment . . . [that] would combine scientific, commercial, and agricultural concerns with geographical discovery and nation-building."[83] He insisted that the explorers identify the various tribes along their route, negotiate with them, and inform them that there was a new "Great Father" to advise and protect them. They were to learn all they could about the more powerful tribes, including the Sioux, who inhabited the lands along their route to the Pacific Ocean. Other intrepid explorers followed Lewis and Clark on dozens of similar expeditions, including Zebulon Pike, Stephen Long, Ferdinand Hayden, and even George Custer, on his infamous exploration of the Black Hills in 1873. Beginning in the 1730s and throughout the nineteenth century, Russia dispatched numerous diplomatic and scientific missions to the steppe. In the process, these missions gathered detailed information about the Kazakhs and the land, its resources and commercial opportunities. Herein is one of the major differences between how the United States mapped its interior and learned about its inhabitants compared with Russia's methods.

Throughout the eighteenth century, Americans used natives as guides and translators, something Russia did as well (chiefly Tatars). In the nineteenth century, however, Russia employed Kazakhs to explore and map the steppes and to penetrate deeper into central Asia. The difference rests on the length of contact and incorporation. Russia claimed sovereignty over the Kazakh Steppe beginning in 1732, and, following the defeat of Kenesary Kasymov in 1847, Russian domination over the steppe and the Kazakhs was generally unchallenged. The United States, on the other hand, was a relative newcomer to the northern plains, purchasing the region in 1803 from France in the Louisiana Purchase. It took the United States another four decades to exert a serious presence there. Well before the American government actively supported formal education for Sioux, the Russian government opened schools in the steppe designed to assimilate Kazakhs into the empire. The Russians wanted to use Russified Kazakhs to explore and negotiate with steppe and central Asian inhabitants.

In 1847 the Russian government's *Omsk kadetskii korpus* (Omsk Corps of Cadets) opened and graduated many Kazakhs for duty in the army as translators, guides, and scribes. One of its first students was Chokan Valikhanov (1835–1865), regarded by many scholars as the "first modern scholar and intellectual of his people."[84] He became a close friend of novelist Dostoevsky (after his exile to the steppe due to his "revolutionary" activities), who later encouraged the young Kazakh to be "the first of your people to interpret for Russia the steppe, its significance, and your people in their relation to Russia."[85]

Valikhanov's own scientific career started soon after his appointment to the steppe military staff. In 1858 he undertook the difficult mission to Kashgar, which was his most significant adventure as well as the one that earned him widespread acclaim. This was a part of the Great Game with Great Britain for influence and control of central Asia.[86] The Russian Geographical Society published accounts of his expedition that were subsequently reproduced in German and English works.[87] As the editors of the English translation noted in the introduction, "Although an officer in the Russian service and a man of good education, he is the son of a Kirghiz Sultan and a native of the Steppes. He is consequently well acquainted with the language and customs of the people of Central Asia, and could go amongst them without exciting the least suspicion of being connected with Russia."[88] After Valikhanov's triumphant return, the government assigned him to the War Ministry and, later, to the Asiatic Department of the Ministry of Foreign Affairs in Saint Petersburg. While living in the capital he enjoyed the life of a young army officer, but tuberculosis compelled him to return to the Kazakh Steppe in a futile attempt to recover his health.[89]

Valikhanov represented the fully assimilated Kazakh—educated, civilized, and espousing views that conformed to Russia's agenda; he thoroughly criticized Islamic fanaticism and urged Kazakhs to embrace Russian civilization. He was a remarkable figure—a statue of him still stands in front of the Republic of Kazakhstan's Academy of Sciences building—transcending opposite cultures (nomad versus sedentary, Turk versus Slav, Muslim versus Christian). The American government did not create comparable educational opportunities for the Sioux or most natives, although it later used education to accelerate assimilation. Clearly, there were Indians who emerged in the nineteenth century—most notably, Ely Parker (Seneca), but he was the exception. Americans certainly did not create an opportunity for a Sioux that resembled Valikhanov's extraordinary expedition. But clearly, Valikhanov was the exception, and his accomplishments did little, if anything, to influence positively the conventional perceptions and attitudes about Kazakhs. By the 1890s, there were certainly some Sioux who exemplified the American ideals of assimilation, such as Charles A. Eastman (*Ohíye S'a*, "Wins Often") and Gertrude Bonin (*Zitkala-Sa*, "Red Bird"), but they too remained exceptions, as long as the vast majority of Sioux remained confined on the reservations.[90] Opportunities for Indians, including Sioux, and for Kazakhs existed in the United States and in tsarist Russia, but they were generally rare and did little to alter base typologies. Predictable stereotypes and clichés were firmly entrenched; although individuals emerged to complicate the typologies and perceptions, their individual successes—exceptional though they might be—could not shake apart the more universally accepted imagery and attitudes that the Sioux and Kazakhs were backward, inferior peoples in desperate need of American or Russian civilizing benefits.

FIGURE 4.1. Charles A. Eastman, 1913 (courtesy of National Anthropological Archives, Smithsonian Institution).

Eastman or Valikhanov, however, represented an idealized version of a civilized Sioux or Kazakh, and Americans and Russians promoted both men as examples of a Sioux or Kazakh successfully elevated from barbarism to civilization because they embraced American or Russian culture. Nevertheless, while the nineteenth-century literature is replete with negative characterizations of the Sioux and the Kazakhs, there were some positive examples as well. For example, Sioux men were "grand-looking men, the warriors, well-made, powerful, and lithe, grave and courteous, dignified, solemn, and majestic."[91] They might be "extremely symmetrical of form, well knit, agile, and easy in their movements."[92]

FIGURE 4.2. Carlisle Indian Industrial School students (courtesy of Denver Public Library).

The Kazakh was "Mongol-Turkic," his "face was flat and wide ... [with] narrow black eyes, small mouth," and rarely any "facial hair."[93] His body might be "thick, compact, stout," of "varying height," and "strong, when he sits on a horse, so powerfully, it would be difficult to dislodge him."[94] Individuals could be positively described, such as Meyendorf's meeting with Kazakh sultan Harun Ghazl, "the most distinguished head of the Kirghizzes": he had "a healthy complexion, large, good-looking eyes, and a pleasant as well as earnest expression; we could easily perceive that he was an exceedingly intelligent person."[95] These physical characteristics are relatively neutral commentaries—quite generalized—but physical appearance was not an attribute of Sioux or Kazakh decline. For these and other observers, the cultural, social, economic, and political conditions established the decline narrative that influenced subsequent American and Russian policies. As Smith noted in the American case, but which was wholly applicable to the Russian one as well, these observers were not "ethnologists or anthropologists in the twentieth-century mold; they did not transcend their own values and worldviews and assumptions about savagery and civilization to meet tribes on their own terms."[96]

Writers, government officials, and settlers often depicted the Sioux and Kazakhs as childlike, lazy, and prone to rapaciousness. The governor of Orenburg,

FIGURE 4.3. Sioux men (courtesy of Denver Public Library).

D. V. Volkov, wrote Catherine II that Kazakhs were not innate barbarians but rather were immature and lacked proper morals and manners; they were like infants.[97] The negative perceptions reinforced simplistic stereotypes, such as Sioux being profligate, "unable or unwilling to save enough food for winter, consuming enormous amounts of food at feasts one week then starving the next."[98] A Kazakh "can go for two days without eating . . . but on the first opportunity that offers itself he will eat enough for three persons."[99] While Sioux and Kazakh men were lazy gluttons, the women did all the work. Women did "most of the cultivating" and were enslaved by their husbands; "women do all of the work."[100] The treatment of women reflected the uncivilized state of the Sioux and the Kazakhs because "[c]ivilized people pampered women; savage people enslaved them."[101] Americans and Russians identified these various cultural markers to dehumanize the Sioux and the Kazakhs, to treat them as less than individuals with personalities and sensibilities that might require more than simple stereotyping. Dehumanizing the Sioux and Kazakhs absolved the colonizers of guilt and responsibility as they implemented policies that dislocated them from their land, eroding further Sioux and Kazakh social and political institutions.

A certain Sioux and Kazakh behavior that often flummoxed Americans and Russians was the value the Sioux attached to raiding and horse stealing and the value Kazakhs committed to the practice called *barymta* (that which is due me), believed by the Russians as little more than theft and comparable to American reactions to the Sioux.[102] In the minds of both Americans and Russians, these practices epitomized Sioux and Kazakh backwardness, even more than their ostensible mistreatment of women. The simplest reason contrived by Americans and Russians for these two seemingly pointless practices was that the Sioux and Kazakhs were congenital and incorrigible thieves. It was a far more complex cultural and social explanation, but the Americans and the Russians generally failed to look beyond preconceived notions and, instead, relied on well-established typologies.

Scholars identified the role that raiding and horse stealing had for Sioux men, but it was never just simple thievery. Anthony R. McGinnis concluded that the "prestige that came from the risk taken in stealing the horses" equaled the "glory" associated with the "risk of counting coup in battle."[103] Americans often complained about the practice, considered it one of many reasons for unrelenting conflict on the plains, viewed it as motivation for persistent depredations committed against pioneers crossing the plains, and demanded it stop in the numerous treaties they negotiated with the Sioux. The practice also disturbed American sensibilities, conflicted with American perceptions of law and respect for property, and was a source for sustained misunderstanding between Americans and Sioux. According to Agent N. S. Porter on the Fort Peck Indian Reservation, stealing horses caused him "more trouble than any other one thing . . . Where a horse belonging to a white man is found in the possession of the Indians I have no difficulty in getting him; but horses stolen from other Indians they do not like to give up, as they claim it is one of their customs to steal from one another, and the more horses an Indian steals the great Indian he is considered among his tribe."[104] The Kazakhs also frustrated the Russians with a practice that from the colonizers' perspective was simple larceny, but to the Kazakhs it had far more complex social and cultural meaning. The Russians could only see value in the property taken during a barymta, but they were unable to see value in the act or its important cultural or social symbolism. In the Kazakh case, Russian officials understood barymta permitted a claimant to press a grievance; as Aleksei I. Levshin noted, the claimant should not take more than the contested value during a raid.[105] Historian Virginia Martin described barymta as a means to avenge "insult and upholding personal and clan honor."[106] Even if an American or Russian understood the practice, it still represented a defect in native character, native society, and the cultural attachment to something considered fundamentally uncivilized.

What happened on the frontier of expansion affected and influenced attitudes and policies in the metropole, which more often than not seemed to be playing catch up with boundaries—both the arbitrarily erected physical and political boundaries and the less tangible but equally powerful cultural and social boundaries that distinguished Sioux from American and Kazakh from Russian. The American and Russian governments instituted policies designed to control their indigenous populations, but each also had to manage the expansion and resettlement of millions of pioneers and peasants in the newly conquered territories. In order to facilitate that transfer of land and its resources, the United States and tsarist Russia developed policies that were based on specific need, such as removal and reservations—or, in the Russian case, districts—and were often based on fragile and faulty perceptions of the Sioux and Kazakhs as backward, uncivilized peoples. Essentially, Americans and Russians dehumanized the Sioux and Kazakh symbolically and physically; Americans and Russians Orientalized the Sioux and Kazakhs as subjects to study and a people to assimilate or eliminate. Americans and Russians also Orientalized the places conquered and resolved to remove the land from Sioux and Kazakh control. This process of conquest and internal colonization subsequently deprived sovereignty in the name of civilization. For Americans and Russians, the Orient as an imagined place easily applied to the lands and peoples they encountered. Russia had a real Orient on its frontier, but there was also the imagined one that was backward, decadent, and required Russian civilization. The United States had the West—Orientalized in the imagination—but it too required the American civilizing influence.

The Americans had a wonderful means to express this sense of entitlement, expansion, and empire: Manifest Destiny—a term coined in the 1840s to explain and, more importantly, justify westward expansion. The Russians, on the other hand, never devised a useful singular term, but they certainly debated their role in Asia and just as eagerly embraced rhetorical justifications about Russia's expansion, empire, and destiny. Consequently, in the United States after the Civil War, railroads; municipalities; and local, state, and the federal government all promoted expansion and settlement, rapidly accelerating the process and increasing the potential for conflict between pioneer and Sioux. Promotional materials and state instutitions are also rich resources to detect perceptions and attitudes. The Russian government, however, officially resisted peasant resettlement until the 1880s, when the government started to enact numerous laws designed to assist peasants who wanted to migrate east. This difference also reflected the pattern of expansion and settlement, but it also complicates the historian's effort to decipher perceptions and attitudes among Russians regarding the Kazakhs or imperial expansion and colonization.

The United States ardently encouraged pioneers to go west, but the Russian government did not. The Russian government, essentially, tried to plug a hole in the dike with a finger. Russian peasants went east anyway, defying authorities, and settled on land claimed and used by Kazakhs. Conflict ensued, but by the 1880s—as in the United States and the conflict between pioneers and the Sioux—violence against Russian peasants or Kazakh nomads diminished significantly. Moreover, in both cases, the violence was never as ubiquitous as reported. There are numerous examples of friendship and cooperation between pioneers and Sioux and between peasants and Kazakhs. However, when violence did occur, it was vicious and widely reported, especially in the American case. Americans and Russians usually attributed the violence to Sioux and Kazakh martial characters, their purportedly ingrained warlike traits. American and Russian retaliation was usually disproportionate to the first act of violence, regardless of who committed it, and used to justify further conquest and colonization. What this meant was that both the United States and Russia struggled to fulfill their obligations to the Sioux and the Kazakhs, but try they did. Ultimately, confining the Sioux and the Kazakhs to limited spaces was the solution reached by both colonizing states while giving liberally to the pioneers and peasants that very land the Sioux and Kazakhs claimed as their own and necessary for their survival.

The American government encouraged westward settlement but struggled throughout the century to uphold its treaty obligations to keep pioneers off land accorded to Native Americans. The Russian government, however, discouraged peasant migration, but land shortages in the European regions of the empire pushed many peasants eastward; landed nobility in the Russian Empire did not want to lose its unfree labor (serfs) to the east. The Russian government hesitated to allow authorized peasant resettlement in the Kazakh Steppe, even after the 1861 peasant emancipation, but finally conceded to what seemed the inevitable fact of peasant migration with legislation designed to assist it. The American government chose a somewhat different course. Both situations led ultimately to the loss of political and individual sovereignty for the Sioux and the Kazakhs—the subject of the next chapter, which examines the policies that shaped internal colonization.

NOTES

1. Margaret Ziolkowski, *Alien Visions: The Chechens and the Navajos in Russian and American Literature* (Newark: University of Delaware Press, 2005), 25.

2. Ibid.

3. Barbara Bush, *Imperialism and Postcolonialism* (Harlow, UK: Pearson Longman, 2006), 24.

4. J. Jefferson Looney, ed., *The Papers of Thomas Jefferson*, vol. 1, *4 March 1809 to 15 November 1809* (Princeton, NJ: Princeton University Press, 2004), 168–70. Many years earlier, in 1780, during the struggle for independence from Great Britain, Jefferson confided to George Rogers Clark that "in the event of peace on terms which have been contemplated by some powers we shall form to the American union a barrier against the dangerous extension of the British Province of Canada and add to the Empire of liberty an extensive and fertile Country thereby converting dangerous Enemies into valuable friends." See Julian P. Boyd, ed., *The Papers of Thomas Jefferson*, vol. 4, *1 October 1780–24 February 1781* (Princeton, NJ: Princeton University Press, 1951), 233–38.

5. Walter Nugent, *Habits of Empire: A History of American Expansion* (New York: Knopf, 2008), 234.

6. He continues, noting that the "Anglo-American relies upon personal interest to accomplish his ends, and gives free scope to the unguided strength and common sense of the people; the Russian centres all the authority of society in a single arm. The principal instrument of the former is freedom; of the latter, servitude." Alexis de Tocqueville, *Democracy in America*, trans. Henry Reeve (New York: Century Co., 1898), 1:559.

7. Peter Chaadaev, "Letters on the Philosophy of History," in *Russian Intellectual History: An Anthology*, ed. Marc Raeff (New York: Harcourt, Brace & World, 1966), 167.

8. Richard Tempest, "Madman or Criminal: Government Attitudes to Petr Chaadaev in 1836," *Slavic Review* 43 (Summer 1984): 281–87.

9. Andrzej Walicki, "Russian Social Thought: An Introduction to the Intellectual History of Nineteenth-Century Russia," *Russian Review* 36 (January 1977): 7. The author also noted that Chaadaev's commentary "aroused extreme indignation in official circles and among conservative and nationalistic Russians. The government declared Chaadaev mad and put him under medial surveillance, *Teleskop* [the periodical that published the "Philosophical Letter"] closed and its editor . . . banished" (7). See also Yuri Glazov, "Chaadaev and Russia's Destiny," *Studies in Soviet Thought* 32, no. 4 (November 1986): 281–301.

10. Charles Rudy, "Despotic Russia, Part II, Adventures in the Steppes of Russian Asia and the Frosty Caucasus," *Reformed Quarterly Review* (July 1880): 355.

11. George N. Curzon, *Russia in Central Asia in 1889 and the Anglo-Russia Question*, 2nd ed. (London: Longmans, Green, 1889), 392.

12. Ibid.

13. Walicki, "Russian Social Thought," 1.

14. See, for example, David Hecht, *Russian Radicals Look to America, 1825–1894* (Cambridge, MA: Harvard University Press, 1947).

15. Pogodin quoted in Hans Kohn, ed. *The Mind of Modern Russia: Historical and Political Thought of Russia's Great Age* (New Brunswick, NJ: Rutgers University Press, 1955), 67. For more about Slavophilism and its origins and influence in nineteenth-century Russia, see Susanna Rabow-Edling, *Slavophile Thought and the Politics of Cultural Nationalism* (Albany: State University of New York Press, 2006).

16. Abbott Gleason, "Republic of Humbug: The Russian Nativist Critique of the United States, 1830–1930," *American Quarterly* 44 (March 1992): 10. According to Gleason, Russian "radicals of the post-Emancipation period [1861] began developing their own version of Russian exceptionalism—the belief that Russia had an extraordinary destiny, which would consist in the development of a new and equitable socialist civilization, based on the spontaneous, if untutored, socialism of the Russian peasant" (10).

17. Walicki, "Russian Social Thought," 10. See also Susan Layton, "The Search for the Primitive in Russian Literature: From Tolstoy to Pasternak," *Dialectical Anthropology* 4, no. 3 (October 1979): 179–203.

18. Dostoevsky quoted and translated in Robert Geraci, "Genocidal Impulses and Fantasies in Imperial Russia," in *Empire, Colony, Genocide: Conquest, Occupation, and Subaltern Resistance in World History*, ed. A. Dirk Moses (New York, Oxford: Berghahn, 2010), 361.

19. American Social Science Association, *Handbook for Immigrants to the United States* (New York: Hurd & Houghton, 1871), 45.

20. Hans Kohn, "Dostoevsky's Nationalism," *Journal of the History of Ideas* 6, no. 4 (October 1945): 389.

21. Edward W. Said, *Orientalism* (New York: Vintage, 1979).

22. Richard V. Francaviglia, *Go East Young Man: Imagining the American West as the Orient* (Logan: Utah State University Press, 2011), 8.

23. Francaviglia, *Go East Young Man*, 15. See also Holly Edwards, ed., *Noble Dreams, Wicked Pleasures: Orientalism in America, 1879–1930* (Princeton, NJ: Princeton University Press, 2000); Dorsey Rodney Kleitz, "Orientalism and the American Romantic Imagination: The Middle East in the Works of Irving, Poe, Emerson, and Melville" (PhD diss., University of New Hampshire, 1986).

24. William Pidgeon, *Traditions of De-Coo-Dah and antiquarian researches: Comprising extensive explorations, surveys, and excavations of the wonderful and mysterious earthen remains of the mound-builders in America. . . .* (New York: Horace Thayer, 1858), 15.

25. Jane Milliken Napier Brodhead, *Slav and Moslem: Historical Sketches* (Aiken, SC: Aiken, 1894), 147.

26. Robert F. Berkhofer Jr., *The White Man's Indian: Images of the American Indian from Columbus to the Present* (New York: Vintage, 1979), 35.

27. W. R. Jones, "The Image of the Barbarian in Medieval Europe," *Comparative Studies in Society and History* 13, no. 4 (October 1971): 398.

28. Henry Nash Smith, *Virgin Land: The American West as Symbol and Myth* (1954; Cambridge, MA: Harvard University Press, 1978), 176–77.

29. Timothy Flint, ed., "The Personal Narrative of James O. Pattie of Kentucky," in *Early Western Travels, 1748–1846*, ed. Reuben Gold Thwaites (Cleveland, OH: Arthur H. Clark, 1905), 18:330.

30. Ibid.

31. Vladimir Dal', *Tolkovyi slovar' zhivogo velikorusskogo iazyka v 4 tomakh* (Moscow: Russkii iazyk, 1991), 4:392.

32. See E. H. P. Baudet, *Paradise on Earth: Some Thoughts on European Images of Non-European Man*, trans. Elizabeth Wentholt (New Haven, CT: Yale University Press, 1965).

33. See Roy Harvey Pearce, *The Savages of America: A Study of the Indian and the Idea of Civilization*, rev. ed. (Baltimore: Johns Hopkins Press, 1965), 136–68. Alden T. Vaughan writes, "Hints of the Indian as a noble savage had appeared in the earliest decades of European contact with America, but the concept did not reach major stature until the middle of the eighteenth century in Europe and the early nineteenth century in America. Largely as a reaction against what they considered the corruptions of their own societies, European *philosophes* sought models of the natural simplicity and order from which 'civilized' society supposedly had fallen in its insatiable quest for property and power." "From White Man to Redskin: Changing Anglo-American Perceptions of the American Indian," *American Historical Review* 87, no. 4 (October 1982): 950, emphasis in original.

34. Nineteenth-century Russian romantic literature certainly embraced the noble savage concept but situated the archetype in the Caucasus rather than in central Asia. See Susan Layton, *Nineteenth-Century Russian Mythologies of Caucasian Savagery* (Bloomington: Indiana University Press, 1997); Harsha Ram, *The Imperial Sublime: A Russian Poetics of Empire* (Madison: University of Wisconsin Press, 2006).

35. Alexander Pushkin, "Nabroski stat'i o russkoi literature," *Polnoe Sobranie sochinenii* (Moscow: Akademiia nauk SSSR, 1937), 11:184.

36. Steven Conn, *History's Shadow: Native Americans and Historical Consciousness in the Nineteenth Century* (Chicago: University of Chicago Press, 2004), 21.

37. Kate Brown, "Gridded Lives: Why Kazakhstan and Montana Are Nearly the Same Place," *American Historical Review* 106, no. 1 (February 2001): 28.

38. Sarah Raymond Herndon, *Days on the Road: Crossing the Plains in 1865* (New York: Burr Printing House, 1902), 105–6. Herndon experienced what Mark Cocker called "a kind of post-coital disappointment. Ideas like the 'noble savage' then supplied the sharp edge to a deepening cynicism." *Rivers of Blood, Rivers of Gold: Europe's Conquest of Indigenous Peoples* (New York: Grove, 1998), 12.

39. Berkhofer, *White Man's Indian*, 38.

40. Sherry L. Smith, *The View from Officers' Row: Army Perceptions of Western Indians* (Tucson: University of Arizona Press, 1990), 20.

41. Ellsworth Huntington, "The Mountains and Kibitikas of Tian Shan," *Bulletin of the American Geographical Society* 37, no. 9 (1905): 515.

42. Ibid., 526–27.

43. Richard H. Dillon, "Stephen Long's Great American Desert," *Proceedings of the American Philosophical Society* 111, no. 2 (April 1967): 102.

44. Pike quoted in Ralph C. Morris, "The Notion of a Great American Desert East of the Rockies," *Mississippi Valley Historical Review* 13, no. 2 (September 1926): 191–92. See also Robert G. Athearn, "The Great Plains in Historical Perspective," *Montana The Magazine of Western History* 8, no. 1 (Winter 1958): 13–29.

45. Arthur Conan Doyle, *Tales of Sherlock Holmes: Detective Stories*, Three Owls ed. (New York: W. R. Caldwell, 1920), 69.

46. Ibid.

47. H. C. Rawlinson, "Observations on two Memoirs recently published by M. Veniukof on the Pamir Region and the Bolor Country in Central Asia," *Proceedings of the Royal Geographical Society of London* 10, no. 4 (1865–1866): 150.

48. Baron von Meyendorf, *A Journey from Orenburg to Bokhara in the Year 1820*, trans. E. F. Chapman (Calcutta: Foreign Department Press, 1870), 5.

49. Fred Burnaby, *A Ride to Khiva: Travels and Adventures in Central Asia* (New York: Harper & Brothers, 1876), 134.

50. Lavinia S. Goodwin, "Our Country and its Resources: The Great Plains," *Phrenological Journal and Science of Health* (April 1877): 254.

51. Edwin James, "Account of an Expedition from Pittsburgh to the Rocky Mountains performed in the years 1819, 1820," in *Early Western Travels*, ed. Reuben Gold Thwaites (Cleveland, OH: Arthur H. Clark, 1905), 15:232.

52. "Aspects of Nature: Steppes and Deserts," *Western Journal of Agriculture, Manufactures, Mechanic Arts, Internal Improvement, Commerce, and General Literature* (August 1850): 286. See also William MacGillivray, *The Travels and Researches of Alexander von Humboldt: Being a Condensed Narrative of his Journeys in the Equinoctial Regions of America, and in Asiatic Russia; Together with Analyses of His More Important Investigations* (New York: J. & J. Harper, 1835).

53. "A Prairie," *Friends' Review; a Religious, Literary and Miscellaneous Journal*, January 5, 1861, 285.

54. Quoted in Father E. Laveille, S.J., *The Life of Father De Smet, S.J.: Apostle of the Rocky Mountains, 1801–1873*, trans. Marian Lindsay (New York: P. J. Kennedy & Sons, 1915), 341.

55. Theodore L. Cuyler, "Across the Great Plains," *New York Evangelist*, July 5, 1877, 1. Another writer described the plains, "which stretch unbroken to the Rocky Mountains. The country was flat like Holland, but far from be dull." See R. L. Stevenson, "Across the Plains: Leaves from the Notebook of an Emigrant Between New York and San Francisco," *Littell's Living Age*, August 4, 1883, 309.

56. "Prairie Caravans—Trade in the Far West," *Niles' National Register*, September 26, 1846, 52.

57. Francis Parkman, "The Oregon Trail," *The Knickerbocker; Or, New-York Monthly Magazine*, May 1847, 396.

58. "From Lawrence to Cheyenne," *Ladies' Repository: A Monthly Periodical, Devoted to Literature, Arts, and Religion*, January 1870, 42.

59. Frederick von Hellwald, *The Russians in Central Asia: A Critical Examination down to the Present Time of the Geography and History of Central Asia*, trans. Theodore Wirgman (London: Henry S. King, 1874), 48–49.

60. "On the Pacific Trail: Nebraska. Great Plains. A Sunset. Excelsior," *Zion's Herald*, June 25, 1868, 306.

61. Rudy, "Despotic Russia," 331.

62. Katya Hokanson, *Writing at Russia's Border* (Toronto: University of Toronto Press, 2008), 6.

63. Meyendorf, *Orenburg to Bokhara*, 17.

64. "Our New Territories," *New York Evangelist*, April 2, 1863, 1.

65. Samuel P. Orth, *The Imperial Impulse: Background Studies of Belgium, England, France, Germany, Russia* (New York: Century Co., 1916), 208.

66. John W. Bookwalter, *Siberia and Central Asia* (Springfield, OH, 1899), 18–19.

67. Hellwald, *Russians in Central Asia*, 57.

68. Hugo Stumm, *Russia in Central Asia: Historical Sketch of Russia's Progress in the East up to 1873, and of the Incidents which Led to the Campaign against Khiva; with a Description of the Military Districts of the Caucasus, Orenburg, and Turkestan*, trans. J. W. Ozanne and Captain H. Sachs (London: Harrison & Sons, 1885), 188.

69. Cocker, *Rivers of Blood*, 13.

70. Historian Ben Kiernan argued, "Genocidal conquers legitimize their territorial expansion by racial superiority or glorious antiquity at the same time as they claim a unique capacity to put the conquered lands into productive agricultural use." *Blood and Soil: A World History of Genocide and Extermination from Sparta to Darfur* (New Haven, CT: Yale University Press, 2007), 29.

71. Adams quoted in Cyrus Thomas, "Introduction to Indian Land Cessions in the United States," ed. J. W. Powell, Edward William Nelson, and Charles C. Royce, *Eighteenth Annual Report of the Bureau of American Ethnology to the Secretary of the Smithsonian Institution, 1896–97* (Washington, DC: Government Printing Office, 1899), 536.

72. Mayne Reid remarked in *The Scalp Hunters*, "No handful of men have the right to hold from the great body of mankind a valuable portion of the earth's surface, without using it." Reid quoted in Ray Allen Billington, *Land of Savagery, Land of Promise: The European Image of the American Frontier in the Nineteenth Century* (New York: W. W. Norton, 1981), 142. The character Elisha Peabody, in *The Big Sky*, quips, "When a country which might support so many actually supports so few, then by thunder, the inhabitants have not made good use of the natural possibilities. That failure surely is justification for invasion, peaceful if possible, forceful if necessary, by people who can and will capitalize on opportunity." A. B. Guthrie Jr., *The Big Sky* (New York: William Sloane, 1947), 278.

73. John Foster Fraser, *The Real Siberia: Together with an Account of a Dash Through Manchuria* (London: Cassell, 1904), 40.

74. Ibid., 41.

75. Ibid., 42.

76. Pearce, *Savages of America*, 64.

77. Fraser, *Real Siberia*, vii–viii.

78. Robert A. Nisbet, *History of the Idea of Progress* (New York: Basic Books, 1980), 129.

79. See Sidney B. Fay, "The Idea of Progress," *American Historical Review* 52, no. 2 (January 1947): 239–40; Bertram D. Wolfe, "Backwardness and Industrialization in Russian History and Thought," *Slavic Review* 26, no. 2 (June 1967): 177–203; J. B. Bury, *The Idea of Progress: An Inquiry into Its Origin and Growth* (London: Macmillan, 1920); Arnold Burgen, Peter McLaughlin, and Jürgen Mittelstrass, eds., *The Idea of Progress* (Berlin: de Gruyter, 1997). Many Russian intellectuals remained unconvinced about Russia's destiny and progress; see an excellent analysis in Valerii Kuvakin, ed., *A History of Russian Philosophy: From the Tenth Through the Twentieth Centuries*, 2 vols. (Buffalo, NY: Prometheus, 1994).

80. Henry Home (Lord Kames), *Sketches of the History of Man*, 3rd ed. (Dublin: James Williams, 1779), 2:92. See also Mark Pluciennik, "The Invention of Hunter-Gatherers in Seventeenth-Century Europe," *Archaeological Dialogues* 9, no. 2 (December 2002): 98–118; A. I. Abramov, "Reflections on Russia's Destiny in the Philosophical Work of Russian Romanticism," *Russian Studies in Philosophy* 35, no. 3 (1996): 6–18.

81. See, for example, James Clifford, *Routes: Travel and Translation in the Late Twentieth Century* (Cambridge, MA: Harvard University Press, 1997); Patrick Petitjean, Catherine Jami, and Anne Marie Moulin, eds., *Science and Empires: Historical Studies about Scientific Development and European Expansion* (Boston: Kluwer Academic, 1992); Lewis Pyenson, "Why Science May Serve Political Ends: Cultural Imperialism and the Mission to Civilize," *Berichte zur Wissenschaftsgeschichte* 13, no. 2 (1990): 69–81; Lucile H. Brockway, "Science and Colonial Expansion: The Role of the British Royal Botanic Gardens," *American Ethnologist* 6, no. 3 (1979): 449–65; Americus Featherman, *Thoughts and Reflections on Modern Society: With an Introduction on the Gradual Social Evolution of Primitive Man* (London: Kegan Paul, Trench, Trübner, 1894); Charles Bucke and William P. Page, *On the Beauties, Harmonies,*

and Sublimities of Nature: With Occasional Remarks on the Laws, Customs, Manners, and Opinions of Various Nations (New York: Harper & Bros., 1841); Elizabeth Hallam and Brian V. Street, eds., *Cultural Encounters: Representing "Otherness"* (New York: Routledge, 2000).

82. Radlov, V. V., *Iz Sibiri: Strantsy dnevnika.* (1893; Moscow: Nauka, 1989); Francine Hirsch, *Empire of Nations: Ethnographic Knowledge and the Making of the Soviet Union* (Ithaca, NY: Cornell University Press, 2005).

83. Stephen E. Ambrose, *Undaunted Courage: Meriwether Lewis, Thomas Jefferson, and the Opening of the American West* (New York: Touchstone, 1996), 81.

84. Kermit E. McKenzie, "Chokan Valikhanov: Kazakh Princeling and Scholar," *Central Asian Survey* 8, no. 3 (1989): 2.

85. Chokan Valikhanov, *Sobranie sochinenii v piati tomakh* (Alma-Ata, 1985), 5:176–79. This is the only surviving letter from Dostoevsky to Valikhanov, and he declares his deep love and admiration, writing, "I have never been attracted to someone, not even my brother, as I am to you." He admonishes the young man to "write more often [and] I will always answer you" (176). Included in this volume was a photograph from 1859, in Semipalatinsk, of Valikhanov and Dostoevsky. In addition, these five volumes contain many of the drawings and watercolors created by Valikhanov while on some of his various scientific expeditions to Semirechie, Issik Kul, Kuldja, and Kashgar.

86. For an enjoyable examination of this interesting diplomatic struggle, see Peter Hopkirk, *The Great Game: The Struggle for Empire in Central Asia* (New York: Kodansha International, 1992).

87. Some of Valikhanov's works appeared in *The Russians in Central Asia: Their Occupation of the Kirghiz Steppe and the line of the Syr-Daria: Their Political Relations with Khiva, Bokhara, and Kokan: Also Descriptions of Chinese Turkestan and Dzungaria*, trans. John Michell and Robert Michell (London: Edward Stanford, 1865).

88. Michell and Michell quoted in ibid., iv.

89. Many believed that the climate, as well as *kymyz*, a favorite beverage of the Kazaks derived from fermented mare's milk, might cure his condition. Indeed, drinking kymyz was a common method to treat tuberculosis in nineteenth-century Russia.

90. Charles A. Eastman (1858–1939), Santee Sioux, was born in Minnesota but fled with his grandmother during the Dakota War of 1862. Fifteen years later, he reunited with his Christian Sioux father and was given the Christian name Charles A. Eastman. He graduated from Dartmouth College, attended Boston University, and earned a medical degree. He joined the Bureau of Indian Affairs (BIA) and served at the Pine Ridge Reservation in South Dakota, where he treated survivors of the 1890 Wounded Knee Massacre. His American wife, Elaine Goodman, encouraged him to write; he eventually published numerous books and stories about his Sioux life, becoming one of the first authentic Sioux voices for an American reading public. In 1902 he published his memoir, *Indian Boyhood*. He helped found the Boy Scouts and became politically active in Indian affairs, being one of the cofounders of the Society of American Indians.

Gertrude Bonin (1876–1938) was born on the Yankton Indian Reservation in South Dakota. She went to school in Indiana as part of the off-reservation education policy used by the BIA. She later wrote about this experience in numerous articles and short stories. She attended Earlham College in Indiana; although she did not graduate, she took a job teaching music at the Carlisle Indian Industrial School in Pennsylvania, leaving after several years, in 1901. She wrote many books and stories that garnered considerable attention among the American public. She also became politically active in the early twentieth century, working with the Society of American Indians, the American Indian Defense Association and other groups.

See Charles A. Eastman, *Indian Boyhood* (New York: McClure, Phillips, 1902); Charles A. Eastman, *From the Deep Woods to Civilization: Chapters in the Autobiography of an Indian* (Boston: Little, Brown, 1916); Zitkala-Sa, *Indians of North America* (Washington, DC: Hayworth, 1921); Zitkala Sa, *Dreams and Thunder: Stories, Poems, and The Sun Dance Opera*, ed. P. Jane Hafen (Lincoln: University of Nebraska Press, 2001).

91. "Perils of the overland Route to California," *Graham's American Monthly Magazine of Literature, Art, and Fashion*, February 1857, 114.

92. Officer of the US Army, "Occidental Reminiscences: Farther West; or, Rough Notes Dragoon . . . ," *Spirit of the Times; A Chronicle of the Turf, Agriculture, Field Sports, Literature and the Stage*, May 30, 1846, 163.

93. Aleksei I. Levshin, *Opisanie Kirgiz-kazach'ikh, ili Kirgiz-kaisatskikh, ord i stepei* (1832; Almaty: Sanat, 1996), 301.

94. I. G. Andreev, *Opisanie Srednei ordy Kirgiz-kaisakov* (1785; Almaty: Ghylym, 1998), 63–64.

95. Meyendorf, *Orenburg to Bokhara*, 6.

96. Smith, *View from Officers' Row*, 41.

97. *Kazakhsko-russkie otnosheniia v XVI-XVIII veka* (Alma-Ata: Nauka, 1961), 653; *Istoriia Kazakhstana c drevneishikh vremen do nashikh dnei v piati tomakh* (Almaty: Atamura, 2000), 3:209.

98. Mary K. Whelan, "Dakota Indian Economics and the Nineteenth-Century Fur Trade," *Ethnohistory* 40, no. 2 (Spring 1993): 259.

99. Rudy, "Despotic Russia," 333.

100. Robert H. Lowie, *Indians of the Plains* (1954; Lincoln: University of Nebraska Press, 1982), 19; "An American in Turkistan," *Scribner's Monthly*, December 1876, 217.

101. Smith, *View from Officers' Row*, 57.

102. Kazakhs committed barymta to extract justice or vengeance; it formed part of *adat* (Kazakh customary law).

103. Anthony R. McGinnis, *Counting Coup and Cutting Horses: Intertribal Warfare on the Northern Plains, 1738–1889* (Lincoln: University of Nebraska Press, 2010), 66; Anthony R. McGinnis, "Intertribal Conflict on the Northern Plains and Its Suppression, 1738–889," *Journal of the West* 18 (April 1979): 49–60; Richard White, "The Winning of the West: The Expansion of the Western Sioux in the Eighteenth and Nineteenth Centuries," *Journal of American History* 65, no. 2 (September 1978), 319–43; Jeannette Mirsky, "The Dakota," in *Cooperation and Competition among Primitive Peoples*, ed. Margaret Mead (1937, Boston: Beacon, 1961), 382–427.

104. N. S. Porter, "Fort Peck Indian Agency, Poplar River, Montana, August 12, 1880," US Department of the Interior, Office of Indian Affairs, *Annual Report of the Commissioner of Indian Affairs to the Secretary of the Interior for the Year 1880* (Washington, DC: Government Printing Office, 1880), 113–14.

105. Levshin, *Opisanie Kirgiz-kazach'ikh*, 370. See also *Materialy po Kazakhskomu obychnomu pravu* (1948; Almaty: Zhalyn Baspasy, 1998). This work has numerous references to barymta, attempting to contextualize it within Kazakh customary law.

106. Virginia Martin, "Barïmta: Nomadic Custom, Imperial Crime," in *Russia's Orient: Imperial Borderlands and Peoples, 1700–1917*, ed. Daniel R. Brower and Edward J. Lazzerini (Bloomington: Indiana University Press, 1997), 251.

5

Internal Colonization

Throughout the nineteenth century, American and Russian politicians, intellectuals, and others typically concluded that American and Russian continental expansion was territorial consolidation, unification, or some sort of destiny. That expansion also included indigenous populations that possessed, in the colonizers' view, inferior social, cultural, economic, and political norms: they were allegedly uncivilized and claimed more land than necessary for their needs and survival. In addition, the United States and Russia each perceived themselves within exceptionalist representations and discourses, often expressed differently from concomitant European overseas expansion and imperialism.[1] Yet, American and Russian internal colonization was "as dependent on colonial relations of dominance as were any of Europe's external incursions."[2]

Both the Americans and the Russians perceived internal colonization as a process that differed from European imperialism and colonization in Asia and Africa, which they both claimed to reject but clearly paralleled and mimicked. Interestingly, the American government rarely used the term *colonization* to describe its expansion or policies. In the regions that experienced internal colonization, the term was referenced occasionally to force Indians onto reservations, but Americans never called them colonies. For example, in 1853, the *Friend*, a Quaker publication, debated the concept, noting that "[i]t has been suggested that it would be good policy to colonize these people along the rich bottoms with which those wild regions are interspersed, giving them lands to be held in individual right as long as actually occupied. The suggestion is worthy of consideration."³ In 1865 Army captain James L. Fisk urged the commissioner of Indian affairs and the American government "towards colonizing all the tribes of Indians who now roam over the territorial domain between Minnesota and Iowa and the Rocky mountains."⁴ He claimed, "the policy of colonizing them on a common and restricted reservation of sufficient dimensions and resources for their subsistence will . . . prove a direct and immediate relief and benefit to both the government and the Indians."⁵ Americans used the term to describe the territorial restrictions to be imposed on the Indians—the allotment of land for their specific and designated use—but colonization was not a reference to designate where Americans could settle.

The Russians often used the term *colonization*, but it was not until the 1880s that the government described parts of Siberia and Turkestan as colonies; beforehand, Russians interpreted expansion as integration and unification, similar to American perceptions of Manifest Destiny. Nonetheless, during the nineteenth-century expansion, the Russians looked to other European empires to model their own internal colonial policies—particularly the British in India and the French in Algeria.⁶ Some Russian officials and intellectuals also looked to the United States and its administration of internally colonized regions and people. Many Russians studied the importance of the American transcontinental railroad when constructing the Trans-Siberian Railway in the 1890s, and they also debated the utility of the American 1862 Homestead Act as a model for their peasant resettlement policies in Siberia, the Kazakh Steppe, and Turkestan. Interestingly, Russia was not the only European empire to study American expansion and colonization. After 1870 Germans also studied the American example, as they equated it to nineteenth-century European expansion and colonization in Asia and Africa. According to historian Jens-Uwe Guettel, many Germans "increasingly identified American expansion and racial policies as models that colonizers could replicate elsewhere in the world" and which linked the "American frontier to other areas colonized by Europeans."⁷

Internal colonization, and its attending ambition to nurture civilization, therefore, meant subverting—perhaps even destroying—Sioux and Kazakh social, cultural, political, and economic structures. The multiple American and Russian policies and programs were not, however, temporal mirrors of each other but did reflect comparable colonial ideologies and philosophies. Equally important, the policies, programs, ideologies, and philosophies reflected the sense of territorial unification and incorporation of uninhabited and unused land. The Americans and Russians asserted that the nomadic Sioux and Kazakhs claimed more land than was reasonable for a backward, uncivilized people. Internal colonization was, therefore, comparable to settler colonialism in other contexts and included a set of policies, programs, and strategies designed to incorporate the land and socially and culturally integrate the people into the colonizing state structures and institutions.[8]

ADMINISTERING THE LANDS

In the nineteenth century, Americans and Russians shared a civilizing philosophy and imperial ideology with other European imperial powers. Unlike their European counterparts, however, neither the United States nor Russia established ministries or departments to deal with internal colonization. In other words, neither created a colonial office comparable to the British, the Dutch, or the French to deal with colonized people. For example, the British created a colonial office inside its War Department in 1801; it later became its own department.[9] The Dutch established a colonial ministry in 1806. The French created something similar in the 1890s, known as the Ministry of Overseas France, but it did not administer Algeria. The French considered Algeria a province, not a colony and directed it under the auspices of the Ministry of the Interior.[10] Other nineteenth-century European empires organized the alchemy of internal colonization differently than the United States and Russia. Although the United States and Russia both created components of centralized, organizational administrations that implemented various policies and programs, they did not create a colonial ministry.

In 1824 the United States established the Bureau of Indian Affairs (BIA), initially under the Department of War but later transferred in 1849 to the Department of the Interior, which was also the central department to manage the increasingly expanded federal lands and resources in the American West.[11] The BIA was as close to a colonial office as the United States ever had during the nineteenth century, certainly until the Spanish-American War brought the Philippines and Hawaii into the American fold. The Russians pursued a slightly different path to govern their colonized lands and peoples. The Ministry of State Domains (established in 1837) managed the land. A governor-general within the Department of War, however, administered the people. According to Willard Sunderland, in a recent analysis, the "various peoples of the [Russian] empire tended to be administered according to their location, religion, occupation, or some combination of these criteria, and they often fell at once under several administrative structures. But no central organ existed to administer colonial people defined as a group."[12]

It appears that the main reason the Americans and the Russians never established colonial ministries was because the land and peoples were internal to the international boundaries. The United States and Russia incorporated and integrated contiguous territory. Another reason, perhaps, was that the United States and Russia each expected the internally colonized people eventually to amalgamate under the same governing structures that existed for the state's other citizens or subjects. Essentially, at some point in the future, natives might enjoy whatever rights and privileges accorded to Americans or Russians. Settler colonization, the American and Russian form of internal colonization, required the state to intervene militarily, politically, and economically and typically emphasized recreating the colonizing society's social, political, and economic characteristics in the new territory.

The United States and Russia did create geographic societies, similar to their European counterparts, initially chartered to investigate the new lands and peoples being discovered in Asia, Africa, and the Americas—the Russian Imperial Geographic Society (RGO) in 1845 and the American Geographical Society in 1851. Throughout the nineteenth century, Europeans dispatched scholars around the world, but the RGO focused its considerable energies chiefly on Russia's territories in the Caucasus, central Asia, and Siberia. American scholars set off around the world as well, but they also recognized that their unexplored continent preserved its own incredible geography and indigenous populations. In a sense, the United States and Russia possessed internal, undiscovered lands and peoples that equaled whatever the Europeans might discover in recently colonized places.

At the core of American expansion into the plains and Russian expansion into the steppe, and all the internal colonization policies implemented by the United States and Russia, land was the indispensable stimulus: its control, its redistribution, and its use. As Patrick Wolfe correctly noted, "Whatever settlers may say—and they generally have a lot to say—the primary motive for elimination is not race (or religion, ethnicity, grade of civilization, etc.) but access to territory. Territoriality is settler colonialism's specific, irreducible element."[13] Throughout the nineteenth century, the United States and Russia pushed rapidly across a defensive frontier boundary, behind which they possessed an immediate base of power that could and did operate at long distances from the dominant metropole, authority, populations, and resources. They established military posts in order to protect trade in the borderlands and later created settlements that permanently situated Americans and Russians in the plains and the steppe. Crossing the artificially imposed boundaries, American pioneers and Russia peasants engaged in settler internal colonization. By the 1820s, the Americans were still barely a presence west of the Mississippi River; Russia, on the other hand, was more fully prepared to extend its reach further into the steppe regions south into Turkestan.

In both the American and Russian cases, resituating the frontier boundary around and over the colonized people physically integrated the land and indigenous people into the territorial contours of the colonizing state. It was, as anthropologist Deborah Bird Rose argued, a situation in which to be in the way of settler colonization, all the indigenous population had to do was stay home.[14] Put another way, what constituted places where the Sioux and Kazakhs could live on the frontier was possible only as long as the frontier remained stagnant, immobile: "Indian homelands were only possible on the frontier; and as the frontier moved, so did the homelands."[15] Early twentieth-century traveler George Frederick Wright observed the comparable ideologies at work in the plains and the steppe. He wrote, the "result is the same ... the pioneers [Russian peasants] who are far beyond the reach of the central government became a law unto themselves ... their dealing with the native races of Siberia can be easily enough equaled in that of the frontiersmen of the United States, who have by similar means gradually wrested the continent of America from the improvident hands of the Red Indian."[16] The nomadic Sioux and Kazakhs used the land extensively rather than intensively. Therefore, Sioux and Kazakh claims to the land meant it was also their most important commodity. In Russian minds, the Kazakhs failed to exploit the land to its agrarian potential. Expelling the Kazakhs from pastures opened the land for intensive agricultural exploitation by Russian peasants rather than extensive livestock production by potentially marauding nomads.

In 1822 Mikhail Speransky, the governor-general of Siberia, proposed a series of reforms—essentially, administrative regulations—which demarcated specific territories for Kazakhs in the steppe.[17] The new regulations also imposed stronger civil administrative codes on the Kazakhs in order to integrate the nomads further into tighter union with the Russian Empire. The goal was to advance Russian trade, culture, and control throughout the steppe.[18] The new organizational pattern also resembled the Russian peasant system, appealing to a Russian administrator's native sensibilities. Indeed, the Russians expropriated almost 7 million *desiatin* (1 desiatin equals roughly 2.7 acres) of land in the Ural River region for exclusive use by Russian peasants.[19] Speransky's reforms left Kazakh social and cultural norms generally unaffected; converting Kazakhs to Christianity was not part of the alchemy of Russian internal colonization and certainly not a part of Speransky's objectives. What Speransky's reforms revealed, as well, was that the internal colonization of the Kazakhs was an ad hoc reorganization designed to deal with only the steppe region. It was not part of a larger set of organizational restructuring that characterized a singular Russian colonial or settler policy or program to incorporate the Kazakhs into the empire.

By the time of Speransky's reforms in the Kazakh Steppe, the Americans were only beginning to formulate policies and programs to integrate the land and the people internally colonized. Americans, however, generally confined relations with the Sioux at that time to trade; land was not the issue in the West that it was in the East. The federal government assumed control of economic intercourse with all Indian tribes, and in 1806 Congress created the superintendent of Indian Trade; all Indian affairs were under his supervision. Trade between the United States and Indians, including the Sioux, was organized chiefly through treaty relations. Nevertheless, treaties also served as a different mechanism to integrate Indians than the Russian method, which they never predicated on treaties and the notion of mutual sovereignty between signatories.

In both American and Russian cases, the colonizer determined to manage what land the indigenous population could use and, more importantly, how much land was necessary for survival. Unlike the United States, which controlled economic relations with Indians—particularly the marketplace for land—the Russians did not directly interfere with economic exchanges. One significant difference that influenced the character of the policies devised was the role that the Sioux and the Kazakhs played in the colonizers' general economy. Put simply, as the fur trade declined by the 1840s, the Sioux hunting nomadism produced nothing valued by the Americans; whereas the Kazakhs' pastoral nomadism generated large numbers of sheep, hides, and wool that Russians sought at annual markets throughout the steppe.[20] In addition, Kazakhs were required to pay an annual *kibitka* tax (kibitka is the Russian word for *yurt*)—usually only about one ruble, which increased to four rubles by the end of the century. The Americans never extracted a comparable revenue stream from the Sioux; instead, treaties obligated the American government to compensate tribes for the land cecession. The Russians did not compensate the Kazakhs. The United States used annuities and allotted land to regulate Sioux behavior, or at least behavior it considered consistent with civilization. The Russians never followed that path; instead, the Russians simply removed land on which the Kazakhs could migrate, thereby forcing Kazakhs to settle on the least favorable tracts of land to adopt farming.

THE ALCHEMY OF SETTLER COLONIZATION AND ALLOTMENT

Throughout the nineteenth century, the United States and Russia allotted land for a specific use. Land was allotted for resettlement by either pioneers or peasants and different tracts were set aside for the Sioux and the Kazakhs. The American treaty system did not employ the concept of colonized land or people. Treaties, instead, established the framework whereby Indians ceded land to the Americans. Russia merely annexed the land, which it did in 1824 when it announced formal annexation of the Kazakh Steppe. The American treaty system and land cessation was complicated further by a new policy—removal—which was, according to Francis Paul Prucha, "the culmination of a movement that had been gradually gaining momentum in government circles for nearly three decades."[21] It did not affect the Sioux directly, but it fashioned a legal relationship between all Indians and the American government. In 1831 the US Supreme Court decision in *Cherokee Nation v. Georgia* acknowledged the "distinct political society" that ultimately placed all Indians in a legal ambiguity called "domestic dependent nations." As such, the Sioux and all Indians became "wards" under the guardianship of the United States. The American government claimed Indian land "independent of their [Indian] will, which must take effect in point of possession when their right of possession ceases."[22] Those Indians relocated, or removed, from their territories east of the Mississippi subsequently, and forcibly, resettled on communally reserved lands in what Americans generously called Indian Territory, in present-day Oklahoma.

Indian removal was the result of conquest, treaties, legislation, and legal action. In the 1830s, removal forced some eastern Indian tribes onto reservations, but the Sioux continued to migrate freely on the plains. Although not called allotment, the affect meant setting aside specific land for a specific people. More importantly, it established the idea of using reservations to set aside land only for Indians to use. Conversely, the Russians similarly segregated land, but that segregated land was for Russian peasants to use rather than for the Kazakhs, more in common with other European colonial environments in Asia and Africa. The Russian colonizer initially segregated itself apart from the native population on land the natives could not use. In the United States, the government segregated native populations, quickly enclosed by colonial settlements, on land apart from the colonizer.

The Russians prohibited Kazakhs to migrate or pasture their livestock on or near steppe land reserved for Russian settlement; it was removal without treaties or obligations. The Russian goal was to integrate, economically and administratively, the Kazakhs, to manage their movement and open land for further Russian internal colonization. As such, Kazakhs were restricted to specific districts (volost); special permission was required from a Russian official for Kazakhs to move from one district to another. The persistent Kazakh resistance to Russian internal colonization in the 1820s did not impede Russian expansion and peasant resettlement in the steppe. In time, however, the Russians created land funds designated for agriculture and settlement but not held in reserve only for Russian peasants. The Russian government eventually permitted Kazakhs to accept allotted sections of land in order to abandon nomadism and take up agriculture.

To manage this allotment process in 1837 the Russian government created the Siberian Survey to direct and identify lands in the steppe most suitable for Russian colonization. It operated based on fifteen desiatin per adult male being the norm necessary for peasant settlement and agriculture.[23] Beginning in 1843, the government permitted Russian peasants from regions in European Russia considered "exceptionally short of land" to migrate and resettle in Siberia and the Kazakh Steppe.[24] As will be recalled, in 1847 the Kenesary Kasymov rebellion ended, and by 1850 the Russian government halted Cossack colonization in the steppe region because the original purpose—namely, the defensive mission—was outdated.

By the late 1840s, the discovery of gold in the Far West triggered a massive migration that certainly aggravated the situation in the northern plains between the American government and the indigenous populations. According to Jeffrey Ostler, in 1841 less than 100 emigrants crossed the plains, but in 1849 that number exceeded more than 25,000.[25] The Sioux complained about the increased traffic, claiming that the thousands of migrants competed with them for resources, especially timber, water, and game. This competition seemingly elevated the possibility of conflict between American pioneers and the Sioux for those limited resources. The widespread belief, however, that Indians constantly harassed and attacked emigrants was, as subsequent research revealed, the perception rather than the reality. Between 1840 and 1860, more whites killed Indians than Indians killed whites.[26] Certainly, confrontations occurred, but not to the extent that the American public believed. Nonetheless, the United States took steps to administer Indian affairs and protect emigrants traveling west. The removal policy no longer worked.

In 1849 Congress created the Department of the Interior and moved the Bureau of Indian Affairs from the War Department into this new executive-branch department. The BIA appointed agents, paid annuities, distributed supplies, and administered relations with Indians. In 1850 the commissioner of Indian affairs, Luke Lea, proposed to establish reservations for the Plains tribes. The proposal included definite boundaries in order to protect tribes from trespassing whites on native lands, usually in violation of many previous treaties, and to restrict native lands and open territory to American settlements. The American government envisioned individual reservations for the

FIGURE 5.1. Kazakhs on the move (courtesy of Central State Archives, Republic of Kazakhstan).

many different tribes to assist them as they adopted civilized behavior and agriculture.

Commissioner Lea ardently supported the reservation idea; he argued that the Sioux, Chippewa, and other tribes, given their "remoteness and scattered condition, it is difficult to exercise any effective restraint over them."[27] In addition, he claimed that the constant intertribal warfare was "revolting to humanity" because it fostered "that insatiable passion for war, which, in combination with love of the chase, is the prominent characteristic feature of our wilder tribes, and presents a formidable obstacle in the way of their civilization and improvement."[28] Therefore, he urged reservations for the Sioux and other Plains tribes so that they may be "placed in positions where they can be controlled, and finally compelled by stern necessity to resort to agricultural labor or starve."[29] For the first time, beginning in the late 1840s, the Sioux became an essential factor to consider as American government policy changed.

Subsequent treaties with the Sioux reflected Lea's attitude that a "portion of this country must soon pass *sub judice*; opening, by the extinction of the Indian title, a new theatre for the great drama of western civilization."[30] American pioneers and Russian peasants were, as geographer Rodolphe De Koninck suggested, the "territorial spearhead of the state" in a process he referred to as the "territorial compromise."[31] It was the "gathering of the pieces that comprise them [the state] and the colonization of their borderlands have relied at least partially on the peasantry, or on a process of peasantization."[32] In Russia, the government built a fortified line that Kazakhs could not cross, but that did not stop Russian peasants, which compelled Russian government officials to extend their authority into contested territory in order to protect their interests. In the minds of many Americans and Russians, military forts, posts, and settler communities were a "protest against barbarism," but often along the border or frontier the government, in the guise of the military, seemed a step behind the settler pioneer or peasant.[33]

To ensure that Americans traveling through the plains were safe, the American government determined to extend its military reach deeper into the northern plains and built a series of forts and posts. In 1851 and again in 1858, the American government signed treaties at Fort Laramie comprising most Plains tribes, including a significant number of Sioux bands. The 1851 treaty established tribal territories throughout the plains. According to Robert M. Utley, the government created these tribal territories to diminish intertribal warfare on the plains and reduce the chance of fateful encounters between warring tribes and emigrants. These tribal territories were not technically reservations but rather set the foundation for their future creation.[34] Some Sioux bands relinquished title to more than 25 million acres in exchange for annuities and, ultimately, a reservation along the Minnesota River.[35] The problem, from the American perspective, was that many Sioux remained outside of American control; many Sioux bands remained generally sovereign and not obligated to the treaty restrictions.

The American government determined to prevent attacks by the Sioux against emigrants and, to the extent possible, avert violations of the treaties' provisions by Americans pioneers and emigrants. Those Sioux that signed treaties with the American government typically agreed to submit violators to American justice. The treaties obligated many Sioux to "agree and bind themselves to make restitution or satisfaction for any wrongs committed . . . by any band or individual of their people, on the people of the United States, whilst lawfully residing in or passing through their respective territories."[36] The consequence, however, was that if a single Sioux violated an article of the treaties, the American government reserved the right to withhold its obligations to the Sioux.

The treaties were a mechanism of control, one that the American government frequently and increasingly exercised during the next several decades. Any hostile act by an individual Sioux meant the United States reserved the right to punish all Sioux, which it did habitually. For example, article 8 of the 1851 Fort Laramie treaty stipulated that the "United States may withhold the whole of a portion of the annuities mentioned . . . from the nation so offending, until, in the opinion of the President of the United States, proper satisfaction shall have been made."[37] The treaties did nothing to limit Americans from crossing the plains or violating Sioux rights. While the American government ostensibly designed treaties to prevent violations by either an American or a Sioux, the Sioux could only appeal to the Bureau of Indian Affairs to hear their grievances. Resolution rarely favored the Sioux, but it was a different situation for the Kazakhs.

The Speransky reforms created courts systems in the steppe, purportedly designed and tasked to resolve disputes between farmer and nomad, native and Russian. In the event that a Kazakh alleged a Russian peasant committed a crime or violated the law, the regulations permitted Kazakhs to mediate the case in a Russian court. The reforms, however, did not compel Russians to attend native Kazakh courts, which used Kazakh customary law (*adat*), but a Russian could bring a case against a Kazakh in the Russian court.[38] Despite Russian attempts to create judicial institutions that legally integrated Kazakhs to resolve disputes, the system generally failed or benefited Russian peasants at the expense of Kazakh rights. One of Kenesary Kasymov's constant complaints to Russian officials was that Russian peasants settled on Kazakh land, and the Russian government and its courts ignored the situation. Russian resettlements continued unabated to partition the Kazakh Steppe. Similarly, one Sioux chief at the 1851 Fort Laramie negotiations echoed Kenesary's concerns when he declared, "You have split my land and I don't like it."[39] Resettlement by Americans in the plains and Russians in the steppe altered the respective regions' demographics, a process that accelerated in the 1850s.

Population shifts evident in the United States and Russia compelled the American and Russian governments to establish frameworks to accommodate that resettlement and reorganization. American pioneers and Russian peasants moved and settled on the plains and the steppe, a process that clearly resembled colonies in other contexts. The scholar Jürgen Osterhammel referred to this particular type of "socio-political organization" and "system of domination" as border colonization, a case in which the boundary was pushed into a wilderness that was contiguous to the recognized boundaries of the expanding state.[40] In the American case, internal colonization occurred at the same time as the military conquest. Similar growth happened in the plains territories, Colorado, Montana Territory, the Dakotas, and Texas.

Russian settler colonization was different and did not initially transgress the Russian military conquest and its frontier. Nonetheless, once the Russians established a boundary that prohibited Kazakhs to cross, Russian peasant settlers—legal and illegal—quickly followed to occupy the land in general proximity to those regulated areas. In 1854 the Russians founded the city of Vernyi (present-day Almaty) in Semirechie, which gave the Russians the geographic base necessary to expand deeper into Turkestan. Within a decade, the Russians occupied Tashkent; and by the 1870s, the khanates—Khiva, Bukhara, and Kokand—fell under Russian rule. The Russians did not initially attempt to open Turkestan to Russian peasant resettlement; in fact, the Russian government closed Semirechie and Turkestan colonization for a couple of decades. Instead, the Russians focused their attention on trying to manage the settlement process in the Kazakh Steppe, which many observers believed was chaotic and out of control.

Russia's problem was that the government tried to restrict peasant movement within the empire, which became more difficult following the 1861 serf emancipation. In the United States, the government prohibited settlers from occupying land set aside for Indian reservations, but the restrictions did not pose an obstacle to migration before or after the Homestead Act. In Russia, the government restricted peasant migration by numerous edicts and regulations, but peasants still managed to find their way to the Kazakh Steppe. Indeed, within a couple decades after the emancipation, Russian officials estimated that more than 70 percent of Russian emigrants to Siberia and the steppe settled there illegally.[41] It was not difficult to understand the surge of pioneer and peasant resettlement in the plains and steppe: accessible land. In the United States, 160 free acres was too attractive for pioneers to ignore. After the serf emancipation, the average peasant holding in European Russia was only 3.5 desiatin, but a Russian peasant could occupy at least 15 desiatin (roughly 40 acres) in the Kazakh Steppe, according to resettlement rules enacted decades earlier.[42] A later Soviet source claimed that more than 75 percent of peasants indicated that land shortages in European Russia was the reason to migrate east to find available allotments.[43]

According to economic historian Maurice Dobb, the empire's wheat yield in European Russia was between eight to ten bushels per acre, which ranked below Serbia and Italy, and only about half as much as Austria-Hungary.[44] The average cultivated area was little more than 1 desiatin, which failed to increase significantly following the 1861 emancipation. Moreover, as the Russian population grew significantly between 1861 and 1897 (the year of the first Russian All-Empire census), arable land became scarcer.[45] European Russia's population density, excluding Poland, was almost twice that of the United States, whereas the total amount of cultivated land was no more than 25 percent.[46] Siberia and the Kazakh Steppe captivated the Russian government's attention as an obvious answer to the agrarian problem in European Russia, but the government failed to devise mechanisms to control migration and resettlement.

In the 1850s and 1860s, the United States and tsarist Russia tried to develop mechanisms to demarcate the land for pioneers and peasants as well as for the

Sioux and the Kazakhs. The American and Russian governments reserved land for their emigrants to claim and farm, but they also designated land ostensibly reserved only for the nomadic Sioux and Kazakhs to use. Pioneers and peasants often ignored the artificially applied boundaries. The 1860s was a watershed decade, in many respects, for American and Russian internal colonization of the plains and the steppe.

THE EARLY STAGES OF ALLOTMENT

In 1862 the US Congress passed the Homestead Act, considered by some scholars one of the most important legislative acts in American history, although it was not the only land policy at work in the plains or the American West.[47] The homestead idea, deeply grounded in the Jeffersonian ideal of the yeoman farmer, seemingly reignited during the free-soil and antislavery debates tearing the country apart in the 1840s and 1850s.[48] The act, according to historian Richard Slotkin, was also "part of a large social improvement program designed finally to purge American society of those nagging disorders that plagued it. The perennial 'Indian question' would now be justly resolved by dividing Indian lands into Homestead-type allotments and having the Indian integrated with civilized society in the sanctified status of yeoman farmer."[49] The Homestead Act opened land in the West for individuals to file permits to acquire a 160-acre allotment; farmers were required to occupy the land for five years and improve the land. The Russians, who considered it a possible example to follow to promote more organized resettlement in Siberia and the Kazakh Steppe, studied its success extensively.[50]

Although the Russian government never enacted a comparable homestead law, Russian statutes and regulations designed to manage the resettlement process included similar elements, such as financial incentives to improve the land on allotments and inducements to construct permanent dwellings or other buildings. One Russian agronomist, writing many years after the Homestead Act's passage, noted that it helped the United States to "create prosperous [*tsvetiushchiia*] provinces on their own uninhabited lands in a very short time," and he seemed to lament the fact that Russia failed to follow the American example.[51]

In 1865 the United States and Russia established commissions to investigate their respective policies and administration of native affairs. The US Congress created the Doolittle Commission, chaired by Sen. James R. Doolittle, to investigate failures of American policies and recommend reforms to resolve the Indian problem, especially in the plains. In the United States, the discovery of gold in Montana, the 1862 Sioux rebellion in Minnesota, and the Homestead Act created a combustible mix of circumstances that accelerated the process of confining the Sioux to reservations.

Also in 1865, the Russian government formed the Steppe Commission, which it instructed to investigate conditions in the steppe and propose new regulations for its administration. The commission spent two years traveling around the Kazakh Steppe, in Semirechie, and in Turkestan. The Doolittle Commission also spent two years investigating and issued a report in 1867; its work received added impetus due to the increased violence along the Bozeman Trail and the 1866 Fetterman Massacre.

Although the Doolittle Commission's report highlighted the failures of American policy, it produced little legislatively to stem the violence. It was, as one scholar noted, an aptly named commission.[52] As Prucha observed, the report's most significant contribution was that it stimulated eastern Christian reformers to demand changes to American government policy toward natives.[53] In Russia, the Steppe Commission did not investigate policy failures; rather, it considered what policies to enact in order to yield a more efficient colonial administration. Its report did not highlight mistreatment of the Kazakhs or insist upon equitable land distribution. It did not deviate from its instructions to demand any substantial reforms; it proposed only organizational and administrative restructuring.

The Russian Steppe Commission produced a significant administrative regulation, which the Russian government enacted in 1868, known as the Provisional Statute on the Administration of the Turgai, Akmolinsk, Uralsk, and Semipalatinsk Oblasts.[54] Intended to be a temporary (until 1871) reorganization, it remained in effect until 1917. The provisional statute essentially created two *guberniia*, one for the steppe and the other for Turkestan.[55] The statute subdivided the steppe into four *oblasti*, highlighted in its title. It further reduced native leadership, and, additionally, the Russian government unified the civil and military authority in the region under the command of a governor-general.[56] The commission concluded, as well, that the Kazakhs were unprepared to adopt an agrarian life because the steppe was unsuited to extensive agriculture—except for settlers with agricultural experience, such as Russian peasants.[57] American diplomat Eugene Schuyler visited the steppe and Turkestan shortly after the regulation went into effect. He concluded, "the gulf between the conquerors and the conquered has been widened and deepened through defects inherent in methods of government subsequently developed, as well as through the faults of the administrators."[58]

The 1868 statute recommended nothing in the way of assistance for Kazakhs dislocated by increased Russian peasant resettlement in the steppe; the government also became the final arbiter to resolve land disputes not just between

Russian peasants and Kazakhs but among Kazakhs themselves. This established, more firmly, the allotment of specific territory for agriculture and livestock, between sedentary Russian peasants and nomadic Kazakhs. According to historian Peter Holquist, "Russia was unique among colonial powers in establishing 'norms for meeting the land needs of natives'" but nonetheless confirmed "a clear preference for sedentary over nomadic life."[59] Although not called reservations by the Russians, the effect was the same. Kazakhs could only use designated territories within a specifically assigned district in a particular province.

Russia implemented policies that historian Matthew G. Hannah observed, in the American case, emphasized "[s]patial fixation and restriction [that] were of central importance to the plan for civilization."[60] The Russian government severely curtailed Kazakh migration and prohibited movement from one district to another without official permission. The American government exhibited similar restrictive bureaucratic hurdles after it consigned Sioux to specific reservations. For example, in September 1886, No Flesh, a Sioux assigned to the Pine Ridge Reservation in South Dakota Territory, requested permission to go with a small party to visit friends who lived on the Rosebud Agency. The acting agent, Capt. James Bell, wrote to BIA commissioner John D.C. Atkins to request permission to let No Flesh go. Atkins replied, "I have to say that while it is against the policy of the Government to permit Indians to leave their reservation for the purpose of visiting Indians upon other reservations, I cannot see that any harm could result . . . provided that such visits are made at the proper time and will not interfere with the work of the visiting Indians or the friends whom they may visit."[61] Atkins reminded Bell that it was the "object of the Government to encourage all Indians to become self-supporting by means of agriculture or other employment and the practice of visiting to and fro should be discouraged."[62]

Atkins concluded the message to Bell by explaining that these sorts of decisions should remain at the agent's discretion. What Atkins's missive reveals was the truly intrusive nature of American internal colonization. The Russians, however, imposed restrictions chiefly to prevent conflict between different migrating Kazakh auls that might fight to use specific pastures or between Kazakhs and Russians. Thus, the Russian regulations restricted Kazakhs to a specific uezd, the Russian government entertained Kazakh requests to pasture livestock in a different district. It was highly unlikely that a Russian official ever even considered it necessary to ask if a Kazakh could travel to visit friends or relatives who happened to live in a different uezd. The Russians restricted the Kazakh Steppe land to specific uses; the Americans restrictions were more socially, culturally, and personally pervasive.

The Homestead Act and the Russian provisional statute further threw open the doors to American pioneers and Russian peasants to resettle in the plains and the steppe. While different in conception, they were similar in consequence. American pioneers benefited far more from the new circumstances than did Russian peasants, generally because the Russian government continued to monitor closely all peasant migration and resettlement in the steppe. The Russian government also maintained rigid restrictions on rural populations in European Russia. Nonetheless, illegal emigration to the steppe continued, and local Russian officials often just ignored the problem. The Russian officials in Saint Petersburg were aware that Russian peasants settled illegally in the steppe, but officials in the capital and the steppe tended to ignore the problem because the peasants served the state's interests by fortifying Russia's demographic position along the frontier. For example, in Turgai Oblast, from 1875 to 1882, the area under settlement by Russian peasants grew from 17,000 to 44,000 desiatin.[63] The peasants were the spearhead of Russian internal colonization.

Before the provisional statute, Kazakhs had relatively free movement in the steppe south of the Russian line. After 1868 the Russian government more closely regulated Kazakh migrations. It was comparable to what happened to the Sioux following the 1851 Treaty of Fort Laramie. At that time, the American government and some Sioux bands agreed to tribal boundaries and reinforced and reorganized in 1868 after the American government established new territorial limitations to demarcate the Great Sioux Reservation. By the 1870s, however, the Black Hills, initially located on the reservation and reserved for the Sioux, became a source of tension after the Custer expedition reported discovering large quantities of gold there. The American government proved unable—even unwilling—to prevent American pioneers from pouring into the Black Hills, in violation of the 1868 treaty. This pattern happened repeatedly; the Americans and Russians imposed territorial margins and defined the boundaries between colonizers and colonized but watched, unmoved but not uninterested, as pioneers and peasants defied the government's authority to breach the margins. Internal colonization in the steppe and the plains accelerated after 1868 in both the United States and the Russian Empire.

ALLOTMENT

By the end of the 1860s, both the United States and Russia reevaluated internal colonization, its administration, and, to a lesser extent, the mechanisms to manage resettlement of pioneers and peasants and the native populations on colonized land. The United States already embarked upon a policy of using treaties to secure the Sioux on reservations; Russia started allotting land generally designated for Russian peasants (i.e., sedentary) and Kazakhs (i.e., nomads). There were other events that pushed the United States toward its own reforms in Indian affairs. The 1868 Fort Laramie treaty ended Red Cloud's War and helped initiate President Ulysses S. Grant's so-called Peace Policy to reform American Indian administration and policy. Another issue that bothered many Americans was the treaty system, which many considered fundamentally inconsistent with the goal of assimilation and the unique position granted Indians by annuities and treaty responsibilities imposed on the American government.

In 1868 Grant's reform agenda—the Peace Policy—included a program that was probably inconceivable to Russian administrators in the Kazakh Steppe. The Grant administration subscribed to the idea that the BIA was rife with corruption, graft, and irregularities that completely mishandled relations with Indians since its inception in 1824; that it was largely responsible for antagonizing the various tribes, which led to conflict; and that it stole land and goods from Indians with impunity. Russia's colonial structures were not immune to similar allegations; many Russian officials also noted significant corruption that accompanied Russian administration and resettlement in the Kazakh Steppe—what one critical observer described as "nothing but a long and nasty anecdote" that was replete in "thefts and embezzlement" of state funds, "impenetrable stupidity," and "brutality and wastefulness" in the government's policies.[64]

The solution to these problems in the United States, and one long advocated by many reform-minded Americans, was to appoint Christian leaders as agents, teachers, and matrons on the reservations and to positions of authority throughout the BIA. Russian officials never considered using Russian Orthodox leaders to serve as administrators in the steppe. Nevertheless, the United States followed that course exactly, and in early 1869, Congress established an independent institution—the Board of Indian Commissioners (BIC)—charged with oversight responsibilities of the BIA and government treatment of Indians. It issued annual reports every year well into the twentieth century.

Within three years of its inception, BIC members proclaimed success but noted there was still work to do. According to the third annual report in 1872,

> of the warlike tribes of the Sioux of Dakota, Montana, and Wyoming, hunting peacefully for buffalo without occasioning any serious alarm among the thousands of white settlers whose cabins skirt the borders on both sides of these plains, shows clearly ... the efforts of the friends of peace in establishing confidence between the white people and the Indians. We contrast this picture with that presented by the same tribe, when, five years ago, in

consequence of our Government's bad faith in violating its treaties with them, they were engaged in a war made memorable by the so-called Fort Kearney massacre . . . and in the course of which many settlers on the frontier lost their lives, and so many hundreds of others were compelled to abandon their cabins and flee to the larger towns for safety.[65]

Grant never completely suspended his belief that BIA ought to transfer from the Interior Department to the War Department. Nonetheless, he agreed with Gen. William T. Sherman that all Indians must settle on their respective reservations and, more importantly, it should be a "double process of *peace* within their reservation and war *without*."[66]

By the mid-1870s, Grant's Peace Policy reforms also included replacing all Indian agents with Quakers, Protestants, Catholics, and, in some cases, Army officers on the many reservations. The goal was to eliminate the corruption that American reformers insisted was one of the major reasons for continued conflict with the Sioux and other Indians. In 1871 the United States unilaterally abandon treaty making with all Indian tribes, which meant that relations with the Sioux became a domestic relationship rather than one under the guise of "foreign relations."[67] The decision stipulated, "hereafter no Indian nation or tribe within the territory of the United States shall be acknowledged or recognized as an independent nation, tribe, or power with whom the United States may contract by treaty."[68] No longer were relations dictated by diplomacy; instead, the relationship was based on social policy, and American social policies demanded assimilation. Despite these steps, the "political anomaly" that treaty making created for reformers was not resolved as long as the Sioux lived communally on reservations.[69]

It was a transitional phase of American Indian federal policy that had no comparison in Russian policy, particularly reforming to manage the Russian Empire's minority nationalities. Reform groups in the United States spearheaded the reforms; oversaw government appropriations, education, and the distribution of annuities; and rigidly adhered to a Christian, civilizing, and coercive character and agenda. Many reform-minded organizations, led by men such as Herbert Welsh and organizations such as the Women's National Indian Association and the Indian Rights Association, eventually coalesced in 1883 with the first meeting of the Lake Mohonk Conference of the Friends of the Indian. These reformers generally lacked official status but connected informally to the Board of Indian Commissioners.[70] All of these individuals and groups, inspired by their Christian faith, seemed driven by a simple ideology: they knew how to help the Indian better than the Indian knew himself. In order to save the Indian, he must stop being an Indian. In the case of the Sioux, they must adopt American civilization, embrace Christianity, and learn to read and write English and labor. Well-known nineteenth-century American educator Richard H. Pratt succinctly described this ideology as "kill the Indian in him, and save the man."[71] It was the clearest articulation of the American policies and justifications behind internal colonization, which meant Americans wanted the Sioux to abandon completely Sioux culture, language, and spiritual attachments to become Americans. The Russian government did not subject Kazakhs to similar coercive pressures; the Orthodox Church did not involve itself intrusively in the spiritual affairs of the Kazakhs until the early twentieth century. Christian reform movements did not influence Russian policies in the steppe. The Russians did not want to make the Kazakhs become Russians; they merely wanted the Kazakhs to be less like Kazakhs. Essentially, the Kazakhs could keep their language, traditions, and even religion; but the Russians just wanted them to stop being nomads. Once settled, Russians expected Kazakhs to learn civilization and, in time, adopt the culture, language, and religion of the empire.

In both cases, however, governments determined that the best way to achieve their objective was land allotment. It was, essentially, land redistribution. Both governments allotted natives specific parcels of land to settle and farm and redistributed the surplus— significantly more than the native allotment—to American pioneers and Russian peasants. The American and Russian governments implemented allotment differently; however, both regarded allotment as the surest way to settle the Sioux and the Kazakhs. The intended consequence made land available to those who might best exploit its bounty, but, more importantly, it eroded the communal bonds that ostensibly kept the Sioux and the Kazakhs uncivilized.[72] The American government considered a variety of solutions, but the means chosen was the 1887 General Allotment Act, or Dawes Act, which "mandated a fundamental change in Indian-White relations."[73] Commissioner Atkins clearly articulated the act's intent: "It is the earnest desire of the Government that the Indians give up their nomadic habits; settle upon land in severalty; go to work and earn a living; educate their children and become intelligent, respected and worthy citizens."[74] Many well-intentioned supporters of the act believed it appropriately encouraged Indians to be more amenable to white settlement and to adopt agriculture permanently. Writing many years after the act's passage, Commissioner of Indian Affairs Francis E. Leupp wrote that most Americans regarded the reservations as "a system whose evils it requires the larger part of the energy of recent Indian administration to remedy," but also that each was somehow "a princely domain."[75] It assumed, one advocate claimed, to elevate the barbarian because civilization "follows the improved arts of agriculture as vegetation follows the genial sunshine and the shower, and that those races who are in ignorance of agriculture are also ignorant of almost everything else."[76]

The agrarian life produced, presumably, industrious, productive farmers who settled on large tracts and were rapidly assimilated into civilized society. Atkins endorsed the reforms because the "benign policy on the part of the Government toward the Indian race, dictated by a love of humanity, one in which both political parties have fortunately and exceptionally agreed, is a proud national distinction." Nevertheless, he cautioned critics and supporters of allotment to be patient. He noted, "Character, habits, and antecedents can not be changed by an enactment. The distance between barbarism and civilization is too long to be passed over speedily."[77] Most historians concluded, however, that the Dawes Act, in effect until 1934, was a dismal failure.

According to the act, the head of each family was eligible to receive a 160-acre tract of land; single individuals over the age of eighteen received an additional 80 acres and children under eighteen received 40 acres. On reservations with land suitable only for livestock, the allotment doubled. Allotment was compulsory; the government assigned land to individuals who refused allotment within four years. Allotments were technically twenty-five-year trusts, during which time the individual could not sell nor lease the land. The government granted title after twenty-five years, but all reservation land not allotted was available for sale, with the proceeds held in trust by the government. Initially, the Sioux had the right to approve all sales of surplus land, but in 1903 the courts determined that approval was unnecessary. Therefore, the Sioux ultimately had no say in the disposition of their land; neither tribe nor individual could reject allotment—the government simply imposed the legislation.

In 1889 Commissioner of Indian Affairs T. J. Morgan identified eight "simple, well-defined, and strongly-cherished convictions" to guide his administration, including that the "reservation system belongs to a 'vanishing state of things' and must soon cease to exist." All Indians, he argued, must be absorbed "into our national life, not as Indians, but as American citizens." Morgan wanted Indians to adjust accordingly to destroy tribal relations, "peacefully if they will, forcibly if they must."[78] He understood the difficulties, however, writing in 1890 that the "natural conservatism of the Indians, which leads them to cling with tenacity to their superstitions and inherited practices, adds to the difficulty of inducing them to abandon their own and accept the white man's ways."[79] Allotment proceeded slowly, but another principal blow to the Great Sioux Reservation was President Benjamin Harrison's 1890 proclamation that broke the reservation into several smaller reserves, granted rights-of-way to railroads, and made land available to homesteaders.[80]

Throughout the 1890s, reservation agents reported "progress" toward allotment's completion, but they also noted that opposition remained. In 1894 the Pine Ridge Reservation agent reported that roughly 90 percent of the Sioux there opposed the plan.[81] In 1897 Sen. Richard F. Pettigrew, chairman of the Senate Committee of Indian Affairs, interviewed a delegation of four Oglala Sioux from Pine Ridge as they visited Washington. He asked them directly if any selected their allotments; all four said no. The reason was not solely an objection to the law but rather, they claimed, because the land was incapable of supporting large-scale agriculture; it was, however, suitable to raising livestock. Red Cloud, one of the delegates and well-known to American officials for his role in the conflict along the Bozeman Trail in the 1860s, explained to Pettigrew that his people knew the land well, but that it was unsuitable for agriculture. "We can not," he said, "raise anything on it . . . we do not want it."[82] Pettigrew asked about cattle, and Red Cloud turned the discussion to American desires for the Sioux to be self-supporting people, telling the senator that "if we try to depend on tilling the land we have no returns for it; there is no way of making ourselves self-supporting when the Government lets us alone."[83] The delegates submitted a petition to the committee, which rejected allotment and claimed "that by following stock raising we will in time become civilized, enlightened, thrifty, self-governing, and independent citizens."[84]

It was, essentially, a plea to allow the Sioux to use the land as they saw fit, not allot the land in parcels too small to support livestock because they could only be self-supporting through livestock, not agriculture. Allotment, according to Red Cloud and the other delegates, kept the Sioux on Pine Ridge wards of the government, contrary to the law's elementary purpose. It could be too that Red Cloud simply failed to convince Pettigrew that the land was unproductive; dry farming in the plains had a large number of adherents, and there was unquestionably a belief that the "rain followed the plow."[85]

Even if that was the case, it is also doubtful that the Sioux had the knowledge, seed, or implements to farm successfully in the northern plains without adequate water resources.[86] In a sense, the Sioux delegation's comments echoed Zebulon Pike, who considered the plains suitable for livestock but not agriculture.[87] In fact, the Sioux complaints matched what various reservation agents were telling different commissioners of Indian affairs for decades; but after 1887 the government was determined to settle the Sioux onto individual allotments and make them farmers.[88]

The Kazakhs noted similar difficulties with forced sedentarization on the steppe.[89] Russian geographers often debated the feasibility of intensive agriculture in the Kazakh Steppe; many argued that it was suitable only for livestock,

FIGURE 5.2. Pine Ridge Reservation, August 2008 (photo by author).

which required extensive allotments to be profitable and effective. Of course, the Russian government was compelled to accelerate migration to the Kazakh Steppe, especially following the disastrous 1891–1892 famine in European Russia.[90]

The idea of virgin untilled land, even land that specialists understood was arid and not suitable to intensive agriculture, led to mass corruption and further impoverished Kazakhs and robbed them of land. Alikhan Bokeikhanov, a Russian-trained Kazakh agronomist, joined an expedition to the steppe—the so-called Shcherbina Expedition—and observed that Kazakhs in many districts averaged only about 6 desiatin of land, not the 15 desiatin promised following the 1896 Russian statute to allot land in the steppe.[91] Moreover, Kazakhs who agreed to settle and become farmers received more land than those who persisted with livestock nomadism.[92] Gen. Aleksei Kuropatkin, governor-general of Turkestan, after touring recently colonized lands in Semirechie, noted, "Particularly inadmissible to me is the giving . . . of 180,000 desiatin of pasture land to various individuals including 10,000 desiatin to Porotikov, police chief of the city of Vernyi . . . Turning the Kirgiz to a sedentary life we parceled out to them only plough lands while the pasture lands—180,000 desiatin—we gave to speculators, not to the Kirgiz."[93]

In the Russian case, allotment policies implemented in the Kazakh Steppe were not enacted to break apart reservations or necessarily designed to erode Kazakh society, but the consequences impoverished Kazakhs and, even if unwittingly, forced them to abandon their nomadic life and settle on land utterly insufficient to raising livestock.[94] Kazakhs were compelled to take menial jobs, usually as laborers or hired field-workers, simply to survive. Kazakh sociopolitical structures collapsed as a result.

Beginning in the 1880s, the Russian government enacted several new laws that drastically altered the steppe's demographics and worsened economic conditions for the Kazakhs. The movement of samovol'tsy (voluntary, or unauthorized) peasants dominated the second half of the nineteenth century. The government failed to control this movement, which increased conflict and tensions for land, as the samovol'tsy generally occupied land allotted for Kazakhs. Initially, the government rhetorically discouraged samovol'tsy from occupying Kazakh lands but did very little to prevent it.[95] The samovol'tsy were no different from Americans who defied American laws that prohibited squatters from settling on Indian reservations. Similar to the Russian situation, as Patricia Nelson Limerick noted in the American case, "Squatters defied the boundaries of Indian Territory and then were aggrieved to find themselves harassed and attacked by Indians."[96] Russian courts generally decided in favor of Russian peasants when land disputes were presented, forcing Kazakhs to migrate or settle elsewhere.

The number of peasants seeking new lives in the steppe overwhelmed Russian officials. These officials also recognized the potential for conflicts in the steppe between impoverished Kazakhs and Russian peasants. They decided the best remedy was, similar to the American case, to prohibit Russians from settling on allotted Kazakh lands. In 1883 the Russian government once again announced a ban against resettlement in the steppe oblasts.[97] Even with the prohibitions, the government was unable to regulate the movement of Russian peasants into the steppe; the prohibitions proved ineffective.[98] The Russian government decided to reevaluate how much land Kazakhs needed and how much land to make available to Russian peasants. The illegal migrants were, according to one local Russian official, "unable to be patient" and tended to settle in places that lacked "supervision" (nabliudenie), occupying the land "without proper permission."[99] One official complained that at the rate the Russian peasants were flooding into the steppe, they were on the verge of "completely covering the steppe with Russian settlements."[100] Indeed, according to historian Geroid T. Robinson, "among the peasants west of the Urals," the land to the east was "regarded as a kind of Utopia."[101]

In 1888 Russian officials observed significant increases the number of indigent Kazakhs. One report noted, "in order not to die from starvation, they [poor Kazakhs] take work as seasonal laborers at local markets and factories, and live as farm hirelings doing agricultural work for other Kazakhs. Contact with

Russians has taught them how to cultivate fields and small gardens. The number of these beggars already numbers in the thousands."[102] In 1889 the Russian government established the Resettlement Act, which permitted peasants to migrate legally and settle on lands that the Russian Interior Ministry deemed excessive—namely, on lands that the government believed were unnecessary for Kazakh nomads. Often these were communal lands, shared by Kazakhs from the same clan or horde. Moreover, given that Russian laws that restricted Kazakhs to specific districts disrupted Kazakh migration patterns, the land assigned to Kazakhs was often not suitable for livestock.

This combination of rules severely weakened the Kazakh nomadic economy and sociopolitical structures. To encourage Russian peasants to settle on steppe lands and to make tangible improvement to them (permanent buildings and year-round occupation), Russian peasants were granted tax exemptions and provided some assistance to construct new residences. The 1889 act, according to a Kazakh scholar, threw the door to the steppe wide open once again; but even under the new act, local officials were not able to manage effectively the resettlement process. Russian peasants tended to settle where they wanted, not on land the government assigned to them.[103]

In addition, beginning with the 1889 statute, the Russian government designated certain lands excess, or superfluous (*izlishnii*), for nomadic use and placed such land under the jurisdiction of the Ministry of Agriculture and State Property. Consequently, peasant holdings often exceeded the 15 desiatin normally allotted by the government for settlement. This was a Russian version of the Homestead Act, but it was still a rather chaotic environment. In 1896 the Russian Interior Ministry established a special Resettlement Administration (*Pereselencheskoe Upravlenie*), which assumed certain duties formerly handled by the ministry's "land section" (*Zemskii otdel*). This new administrative structure managed and promoted the practice of "scouting" (*khodachestvo*) to survey the best land for Russian peasants to occupy.[104] One French visitor commented that the "scouts" were little more than thieves sanctioned by the state to seize land from the natives.[105] In the zest to identify "surplus lands," in a somewhat comical turn, an overzealous official—a certain Mazurenko—inadvertently incorporated some Chinese territory in the tracts he categorized as surplus and fit for settlement.[106] In order to organize peasant resettlement with better empirical evidence, the Russian government dispatched several scientific expeditions to the steppe to determine what lands were best suited for resettlement. In one case, a Russian government expedition surveyed roughly 36 million desiatin in the steppe reserved for Kazakhs, but it concluded that it was more than double the amount necessary for them to survive.[107]

Russia's Resettlement Administration established regulations to manage allotments but often ignored its own rules, which forced many Kazakhs to resettle on hilltops, mountainsides, and deserts in order to survive.[108] One Kazakh described his allotment as "worthless" because Russians allotted the best land to peasants or wealthy Kazakhs. He lacked provisions and fodder for his livestock, which was "falling into extreme impoverishment."[109] Another Kazakh claimed that he was not granted his full 15 desiatin allotment of "suitable land" (*udobnoi zemli*) guaranteed by law, which caused his family to live in absolute poverty.[110] The government provided inadequate training and support to Kazakhs forced to take up the sedentary, agrarian life.[111] A similar situation existed in the United States. Stories of corruption and unscrupulous Americans taking advantage of Indians—not just the Sioux—were almost axiomatic. Helen Hunt Jackson's 1881 classic, *A Century of Dishonor*, was not the first to highlight this fact, but it certainly seemed to galvanize reformers to demand drastic changes to the American treatment of Indians.[112] One of the principal means devised to reform Indian affairs was allotment—the very thing many Sioux opposed. It did not matter.

In the United States, Sen. Charles Dawes of Massachusetts, the architect of allotment, seemed to echo similar concerns when he spoke for the Sioux a couple of years after the act's passage. He observed that Indians had "no homes, no horses, no hoes, no seeds, and had they had ploughs, they would not know how to use them."[113] The United States and Russia desired to expand agriculture because each believed that the agrarian, sedentary life was markedly superior to nomadism. Both governments allotted land to force the Sioux and the Kazakhs to accept small allotments to farm, even though both governments also recognized that the Sioux and the Kazakhs were not experienced farmers. Perhaps the most unusual explanation for the Kazakh land shortage—not one that seems to be used in the United States—came from well-known Russian Orientalist Vasilii Grigoriev, who attributed the Kazakh problems in the steppe not to Russian colonization or because Russian peasants occupied the best land. Grigoriev claimed that before Russian expansion into the steppe, Kazakhs were in a constant state of internecine warfare. As a consequence, this barbaric warfare kept the Kazakh population small relative to the available land. Russian colonization brought order, peace, and stability to the steppe; the Kazakh population thereby increased, and they "began to live in peace and multiply their numbers. This development resulted in land shortages."[114]

The expanding American and Russian colonizers allotted the land in specific ways, using specific categories; but both governments also had to deal with pioneers and peasants who transgressed against the allotted boundaries. There were, in both cases, severe consequences for the Sioux and the Kazakhs following the intensified allotment efforts evident in the American Dawes Act and the Russian 1889 and 1896 statutes. Historian Richard White summarized the Dawes Act this way: "The policy of allotment in severalty was as draconian a case of social reform forced on an outside group—most Indians were not yet citizens—and with as disastrous consequences as anything in American history. It was done in the name of capitalist progress, democracy, Christianity."[115] According to Emily Greenwald, it was an effort to "atomize Indians, to break down their economic and social bonds by dispersing them onto individually owned parcels of land."[116] By 1907 about 3,000 of the 6,700 Pine Ridge Sioux eligible for allotment had made their selections. The impetus for future allotments, according to George E. Hyde, Red Cloud's biographer, was that the United States had effectively destroyed the Sioux sociopolitical structures by compelling them to take land.[117] The Dawes Act made more than 9 million acres available through allotment to American settlers, essentially dismantling the Sioux reservations. In fact, according to Wolfe, in total land redistribution, "in the half-century from 1881, the total acreage held by Indians in the United States fell by two thirds, from just over 155 million acres to just over 52 million."[118] Rather than assimilating the Sioux, allotment and forced sedentarization created deep social, cultural, and economic crises on the various Sioux reservations well into the twentieth century. In the Kazakh Steppe, as David Moon described Russian efforts, "Hand-in-hand with Russian conquest, peasant settlement, loss of land, and sedentarization came attempts to undermine the local culture as the Russian state began to move away from its earlier policy of accommodation with local elites."[119]

The United States and Russia imposed their culture on the Sioux and the Kazakhs; they compelled social and political accommodation and demanded assimilation into the dominant society by insisting that the Sioux and the Kazakhs accept allotments in order to become part of the agrarian ideal. The colonizer used schools and education to teach assimilation, the social and cultural behaviors Americans and Russians deemed essential for settled, civilized, and productive members of society. Education was the tool to destroy the barriers that kept the Sioux and the Kazakhs primitive peoples; it was the instrument to create social, cultural, and political uniformity. It is to that process that this study now moves.

NOTES

1. Richard White argued, "Western expansion was about empire, as much as the American people and many historians would like to treat it as a purely domestic development. . . . [And] the creation of an overseas empire in 1898 was not 'unthinking or accidental.' It had

precedents in continental expansion, which was just as conscious." "The American West and American Empire," in *Manifest Destinies and Indigenous Peoples*, ed. David Maybury-Lewis, Theodore Macdonald, and Biorn Maybury-Lewis (Cambridge, MA: Harvard University Press, 2009), 218–19.

2. Ann Laura Stoler, "Intimidations of Empire: Predicaments of the Tactile and Unseen," in *Haunted by Empire: Geographies of Intimacy in North American History*, ed. Ann Laura Stoler (Durham, NC: Duke University Press, 2006), 12.

3. "Report of the Indian Department," *Friend. A Religious and Literary Journal*, January 22, 1853, 150–51.

4. US Department of the Interior, Office of Indian Affairs, "Report of Captain James L. Fisk to W. P. Dole, Commissioner of Indian Affairs," in *Report of the Commissioner of Indian Affairs for the Year 1865* (Washington, DC: Government Printing Office, 1865), 413–14 (hereafter *Annual Report*, year).

5. Ibid.

6. According to Robert P. Geraci, "Russian statesmen often used Russians' putative empathy with other peoples as a justification for imperialism . . . This view described the Russian Empire as a justifiable philanthropic undertaking in contrast to the other European empires that were supposedly illegitimate, coercive, and exploitative. The capacity for ventriloquism, then, was especially important in Asia, where it turned out that the ulterior motive was not the appreciation of non-Russian cultures but a mission to spread *Russian* culture." "Genocidal Impulses and Fantasies in Imperial Russia," in *Empire, Colony, Genocide: Conquest, Occupation, and Subaltern Resistance in World History*, ed. A. Dirk Moses (New York, Oxford: Berghahn, 2010), 361, emphasis in original.

7. Jens-Uwe Guettel, *German Expansionism, Imperial Liberalism, and the United States, 1776–1945* (Cambridge: Cambridge University Press, 2012), 82–88. See also Carroll P. Kakel, *The American West and the Nazi East: A Comparative and Interpretive Perspective* (New York: Palgrave Macmillan, 2011).

8. According to Patrick Wolfe, "settler colonialism is an inclusive, land-centered project that coordinates a comprehensive range of agencies, from the metropolitan centre to the frontier encampment, with a view to eliminating Indigenous societies." "Settler Colonialism and the Elimination of the Native," *Journal of Genocide Research* 8, no. 4 (December 2006): 393.

9. See, for example, Henry Lindsay Hall, *The Colonial Office: A History* (London: Longmans, Green, 1937); Brian L. Blakeley, *The Colonial Office, 1868–1892* (Durham, NC: Duke University Press, 1972).

10. See, for example, Raymond F. Betts, *Tricouleur: The French Overseas Empire* (New York: Gordon & Cremonesi, 1978); Robert Aldrich, *Greater France: A History of French Overseas Expansion* (New York: St. Martin's, 1996); Frederick Quinn, *The French Overseas Empire* (Westport, CT: Praeger, 2000). For a recent examination of French imperialism in Algeria, see Patricia M.E. Lorcin, ed. *Algeria and France, 1800–2000: Identity, Memory, Nostalgia* (Syracuse, NY: Syracuse University Press, 2006). On the collapse of the French ministry, see James I. Lewis, "The French Colonial Service and the Issues of Reform, 1944–8," *Contemporary European History* 4, no. 2 (July 1995): 153–88.

11. According to Robert M. Utley, "The Indian Bureau had two major purposes: to extinguish Indian land titles and to grapple with the vexing problem of what to do with the people whose title had been extinguished." *The Indian Frontier, 1846–1890*, rev. ed. (Albuquerque: University of New Mexico Press, 2003), 38.

12. Willard Sunderland, "The Ministry of Asiatic Russia: The Colonial Office That Never Was But Might Have Been," *Slavic Review* 69, no. 1 (Spring 2010): 135.

13. Wolfe, "Settler Colonialism," 388.

14. See Deborah Bird Rose, *Hidden Histories: Black Stories from Victoria River Downs, Humbert River and Wave Hill Stations* (Canberra: Aboriginal Studies Press, 1991).

15. J. Edward Chamberlin, "Homeland and Frontier," in Maybury-Lewis, Macdonald, and Maybury-Lewis, *Manifest Destinies and Indigenous Peoples*, 194.

16. George Fredrick Wright, *Asiatic Russia* (New York: McClure, Phillips, 1902), 1:150. Wright did not distinguish between Siberia and the Kazakh Steppe.

17. See "Ustav o Sibirskikh Kirgizakh," *Polnoe sobranie zakonov Rossiiskoi Imperii, povieleniem gosudaria Imperatora Nikolaia Pavlovicha Sostavlennoe. Seriia 1, t. 38, No. 29127* (St. Petersburg: Gosudarstvennaiia tipografiia, 1830).

18. Speransky's reforms targeted not only Kazakhs but Buriats and other Siberian peoples as well.

19. M. Zh. Abdirov, *Istoriia Kazachestva Kazakhstana* (Almaty: Izdatel'stvo Kazakhstan, 1994), 55.

20. According to I. Strebelsky, "Moreover, the garrisons emerged as trading posts where grain was sold to the Kazakh nomads in exchange for sheep, horses, hides, and wool." "The Frontier in Central Asia," in *Studies in Russian Historical Geography*, ed. James A. Bater and R. A. French (London: Academic Press, 1983), 1:152.

21. Francis Paul Prucha, *The Great Father: The United States Government and the American Indians* (Lincoln: University of Nebraska Press, 1984), 1:183.

22. Francis Paul Prucha, ed., "Cherokee Nation v. Georgia," in *Documents of United States Indian Policy*, 3rd ed. (Lincoln: University of Nebraska Press, 2000), 57–59.

23. Donald W. Treadgold, *The Great Siberian Migration: Government and Peasant in Resettlement from Emancipation to the First World War* (Princeton, NJ: Princeton University Press, 1957), 29.

24. Treadgold, *Siberian Migration*, 29.

25. Jeffrey Ostler, *The Plains Sioux and U.S. Colonialism from Lewis and Clark to Wounded Knee* (Cambridge: Cambridge University Press, 2004), 32–34.

26. Michael L. Tate, "From Cooperation to Conflict: Sioux Relations with the Overland Emigrants, 1845–1865," *Overland Journal* 18, no. 4 (Winter 2000–2001): 18. According to Tate, Indians killed only 362 emigrants, whereas during the same period, emigrants killed 426 Indians. These statistics reflect all overland trails, not just the Bozeman, Platte, or other routes that crossed Sioux territory.

27. *Report of the Commissioner of Indian Affairs to the Secretary of the Interior*, 31st Cong., 2d sess., House Executive Document 1 (Washington, DC: Government Printing Office, 1850), 35.

28. Ibid.

29. Ibid.

30. Ibid., 77.

31. Rodolphe De Koninck, "The Peasantry as the Territorial Spearhead of the State in Southeast Asia: The Case of Vietnam," *Sojourn: Journal of Social Issues in Southeast Asia* 11, no. 2 (October 1996): 231–32.

32. Ibid. De Koninck argues that the "same process has been active in the colonization not only of large areas of the so-called New Countries, such as the United States, Canada, or Australia—notwithstanding the larger degree of 'freedom' enjoyed by many of the pioneers in these New Countries—but also of the frontier, buffer, or marginal lands of the old empires. Thus, with the eastward expansion of Russia, particularly throughout the eighteenth and nineteenth centuries, that of Chinese settlers into Manchuria during the nineteenth century, or

of Japanese settlers on the island of Hokkaido, starting in 1868 and continuing well into the twentieth century, and involving soldier-settlers" (232).

33. Selah Merrill, "Central Asia," *New Englander* 34 (New Haven, CT: W. L. Kingsley, 1875), 22.

34. Utley, *Indian Frontier*, 60.

35. Marouf Hasian Jr., "Cultural Amnesia and Legal Rhetoric: Remembering the 1862 United States-Dakota War and the Need for Military Commissions," *American Indian Culture and Research Journal* 27, no. 1 (2003): 95; Utley, *Indian Frontier*, 76.

36. Charles J. Kappler, ed., *Indian Affairs: Laws and Treaties* (Washington, DC: Government Printing Office, 1904), 2:594. See article 4.

37. Ibid., 595.

38. See Virginia Martin, *Law and Custom in the Steppe: The Kazakhs of the Middle Horde and Russian Colonialism in the Nineteenth Century* (Richmond, UK: Curzon, 2001). For a recent interesting analysis of the ancient roots of Kazakh customary law, see Elmira Teleuova, "From History of Nomadic Customary Law," *Sensus Historiae* 7, no. 2 (2012): 169–80.

39. Quoted in Robert A. Trennert Jr., *Alternative to Extinction: Federal Indian Policy and the Beginnings of the Reservation System, 1846–51* (Philadelphia: Temple University Press, 1975), 190.

40. Jürgen Osterhammel, *Colonialism: A Theoretical Overview* (Kingston: Ian Randle, 1997), 4.

41. L. F. Skliarov, *Pereselenie i zemleustroistvo v Sibiri v gody stolypinskoi agrarnoi reform* (Leningrad: Leningradskogo universiteta, 1962), 61–68. See also J. William Leasure and Robert A. Lewis, "Internal Migration in Russia in the Late Nineteenth Century," *Slavic Review* 27, no. 3 (September 1968): 382; George J. Demko, *The Russian Colonization of Kazakhstan, 1896–1916* (Bloomington: Indiana University Press, 1969), 59.

42. Leasure and Lewis, "Internal Migration," 381.

43. I. L. Iamzin and V. P. Voshchinin, *Uchenie o kolonizatsii i pereseleniiakh* (Moscow: Gos. izd-vo, 1926), 39.

44. Maurice Dobb, *Soviet Economic Development since 1917* (1948; New York: International Publishers, 1968), 39.

45. Ibid., 54.

46. Ibid., 39.

47. See, for example, Harold M. Hyman, *American Singularity: The 1787 Northwest Ordinance, the 1862 Homestead and Morrill Acts, and the 1944 G.I. Bill* (Athens: University of Georgia Press, 1986); Paul W. Gates, *The Jeffersonian Dream: Studies in the History of American Land Policy and Development* (Albuquerque: University of New Mexico Press, 1996). According to Gates, the act was "intended to reward him [the pioneer] for his courageous move to the frontier by giving him land, the value of which he and his community would create." See "The Homestead Act: Free Land Policy in Operation, 1862–1935," in *Land Use Policy and Problems in the United States*, ed. Howard W. Ottoson (Lincoln: University of Nebraska Press, 1963), 28. Gates, however, was also a critic of the act, arguing that it did not end land speculation but, instead, the "existence of the Pre-emption Law and its later variations, the Desert Land Act, the Timber Culture Act, the Timber and Stone Act, the land grants to railroads and states, the cash sale system, the Indian land policy, the acts granting land warrants to ex-soldiers or their heirs, and the Agricultural College Act of 1862, which granted millions of acres of land scrip to Eastern states, tended to make it practically as easy for speculators to engross huge areas of land after 1862 as before." "The Homestead Law in an Incongruous Land System," *American Historical Review* 41, no. 4 (July 1936): 656.

48. See Henry Nash Smith, *Virgin Land: The American West as Symbol and Myth* (1954; Cambridge, MA: Harvard University Press, 1978): 165–73.

49. Richard Slotkin, *The Fatal Environment: The Myth of the Frontier in the Age of Industrialization, 1800–1890* (New York: HarperPerennial, 1994), 284–85.

50. S. K. Kann, "Opyt zheleznodorozhnogo stroitel'stva v Amerike i proektirovanie Transsiba," in *Zarubeshnye ekonmicheskie i kul'turnye svaizi Sibiri (XVIII-XX vv.): Sbornik nauchnykh trudov*, ed. L. M. Gorzhushkin (Novosibirsk: Rossiiskaia Akademiia nauk, Sibirskoe otdel, 1995), 128.

51. V. K. Kol', "Amerikanskaia gomstednaia sistema nadeleniia pereselentsev' zemleiu, kak sredstvo uspeshnoi kolonizatsii i ekonomicheskago razvitiia russkikh' okrain,'" *Voprosy Kolonizatsii*, no. 10 (1912): 1.

52. Michael Pau Simon, "Indigenous Peoples in Developed Fragment Societies: A Comparative Analysis of Internal Colonialism in the United States, Canada, and Northern Ireland" (PhD diss., University of Arizona, 1986), 216.

53. Francis Paul Prucha, *American Indian Policy in Crisis: Christian Reformers and the Indian, 1865–1900* (Norman: University of Oklahoma Press, 1976), 14–16; Harry Kelsey, "The Doolittle Report of 1867: Its Preparation and Shortcomings," *Arizona and the West* 17 (Summer 1975): 107–20. See also *Condition of the Indian Tribes: Report of the Joint Special Committee, Appointed under Joint Resolution of March 3, 1865, with an Appendix*, 39th Cong., 2d sess., Senate Report 156 Serial Set 1279. (Washington, DC: Government Printing Office, 1867).

54. "O preobrazovanii upravleniia Kirgizskimi stepiami Orenburgskago i Sibirskago vedomstve i Ural'skim i Sibirskim kazachimi voiskami," *Polnoe sobranie zakonov Rossiiskoi Imperii, povieleniem gosudaria Imperatora Nikolaia Pavlovicha Sostavlennoe. Seriia 2, t. 43, No. 46380* (St. Petersburg: Gosudarstvennaiia tipografiia, 1873).

55. This statute did not happen in a vacuum but was one of dozens of such reforms following Russia's defeat in the Crimean War, the best known being the 1861 peasant emancipation. It was two decades of sweeping institutional reforms—in a sense, a revolution from above—that affected the Russian Empire's military, judiciary, administration, industry and agriculture, and transportation. See Ben Eklof, John Bushnell, and Larissa Zakharova, eds., *Russia's Great Reforms, 1855–1881* (Bloomington: Indiana University Press, 1994); W. Bruce Lincoln, *The Great Reforms: Autocracy, Bureaucracy, and the Politics of Change in Imperial Russia* (DeKalb: Northern Illinois University Press, 1990).

56. Richard A. Pierce, *Russian Central Asia, 1867–1917: A Study in Colonial Rule* (Berkeley, University of California Press), 66; Martha Brill Olcott, *The Kazakhs*, 2nd ed. (Stanford, CA: Hoover Institution Press, 1987), 78. According to these scholars, twenty years passed before the Russian government appointed a governor-general.

57. B. Suleimenov, *Agrarnyi vopros v Kazakhstane poslednei treti XIX-nachala XX v. (1867–1907 gg.)* (Alma-Ata: Akademii nauk KSSR, 1963): 33–47.

58. Eugene Schuyler, *Turkistan: Notes of a Journey in Russian Turkistan, Khokand, Bukhara, and Kuldja* (New York: Scribner, Armstrong, 1877), 2:233. A Russian administrator agreed, noting in the first decade of the twentieth century, Kazakhs continued to practice "primitive agriculture." See Alexandre Ivanovitch Woeikof, "Les Les ressources agricoles de l'Asia Russe," *Annales de Géographie* 18, no. 100 (1909): 369–70.

59. Peter Holquist, "'In Accord with State Interests and the People's Wishes': The Technocratic Ideology of Imperial Russia's Resettlement Administration," *Slavic Review* 69, no. 1 (Spring 2010): 163. Holquist cites D. Fleksor, *Pereselencheskoe Delo v 1908 goda* (St. Petersburg: Pereselenskoe upravlenie, 1908), 28.

60. Matthew G. Hannah, "Space and Social Control in the Administration of the Oglala Lakota ("Sioux"), 1871–1879," *Journal of Historical Geography* 19, no. 4 (1993): 414.

61. "Letter From Office of Indian Affairs Commissioner Atkins to Capt. James M. Bell," September 25, 1886, box 8, Records of the Bureau of Indian Affairs, Pine Ridge Agency, Pine Ridge, South Dakota, Record Group 75, National Archives and Records Administration at Kansas City (hereafter NAKC).

62. "Letter From Office of Indian Affairs Commissioner Atkins to Capt. James M. Bell," NAKC.

63. A. A. Kaufman, *Pereselenie i kolonizatsiia* (St. Petersburg: Biblioteka Obshchestvennoi Pol'zy, 1905), 331.

64. Quoted in Anna Rochester, *Lenin on the Agrarian Question* (New York: International Publishers, 1942), 76–77. The 1822 Speransky reforms also included Kazakh leaders to help administer the steppe provinces, and, as one Russian official described it, Kazakhs were equally susceptible to the administrative corruption as Russian government authorities. He alleged, "The eagerness to become *volost* head . . . can be explained by, on the one hand, a quite significant salary, and, on the other, control over tax collection for the entire county, at a time when unlawful misappropriations, tardy remission of money to the Treasury, and even concealment of the money were possible. Besides, the head of the *volost* . . . could impose fines up to 3 rubles. The control of his activities with regard to such amounts was totally impossible, especially given the nomadic life style of the population." Quoted in Nadira A. Abdurakhimova, "The Colonial System of Power in Turkistan," *International Journal of Middle East Studies* 34, no. 2 (May 2002): 247.

65. US Board of Indian Commissioners, *Third Annual Report of the Board of Indian Commissioners to the President of the United States* (Washington, DC: Government Printing Office, 1871), 3, emphasis in original.

66. Sherman quoted in Clyde A. Milner II, *With Good Intentions: Quaker Work among the Pawnees, Otos, and Omahas in the 1870s* (Lincoln: University of Nebraska Press, 1982), 2.

67. Cathleen D. Cahill, *Federal Fathers and Mothers: A Social History of the United States Indian Service, 1869–1933* (Chapel Hill: University of North Carolina Press, 2011), 17.

68. Quoted in Jill St. Germain, *Broken Treaties: United States and Canadian Relations with the Lakotas and the Plains Cree, 1868–1885* (Lincoln: University of Nebraska Press, 2009), 79.

69. For an excellent analysis of the decision to abandon treaty making, see chapter 12, "The End of Treaty Making," in Francis Paul Prucha, *American Indian Treaties: The History of a Political Anomaly* (Berkeley: University of California Press, 1994), 289–310.

70. Prucha, *American Indian Policy*, 132–68.

71. Richard H. Pratt, "The Advantages of Mingling Indians with Whites," in *Americanizing the American Indians: Writings by the "Friends of the Indian," 1880–1900*, ed. Francis Paul Prucha (Cambridge, MA: Harvard University Press, 1973), 260.

72. Prucha, *Americanizing the American Indians*, 8. According to Prucha, the racial element was a mitigating factor due to the recent influx of eastern and southern European immigrants into the United States.

73. Leonard A. Carlson, *Indians, Bureaucrats, and Land: The Dawes Act and the Decline of Indian Farming* (Westport, CT: Greenwood, 1981), 3.

74. "Letter From BIA Commissioner Atkins to Agent, Pine Ridge Agency," February 2, 1887, box 8, NAKC.

75. Francis E. Leupp, "Indian Lands: Their Administration with Reference to Present and Future Use," *Annals of the American Academy of Political and Social Science* 33, no. 3 (May 1909): 137.

76. *Annual Report*, 1885, 3.

77. *Annual Report*, 1887, 4.

78. Wilcomb E. Washburn, *The American Indian and the United States: A Documentary History* (New York: Random House, 1973), vol. 4: 424–25.

79. Washburn, *American Indian*, 437.

80. See Kappler, *Indian Affairs*, 1:943–45.

81. Sister Mary Antonio Johnston, *Federal Relations with the Great Sioux Indians of South Dakota, 1887–1933, with Particular Reference to Land Policy under the Dawes Act* (Washington, DC: Catholic University of America Press, 1948), 93.

82. *Statements of the delegation of Oglalla Sioux before the Chairman of the Committee on Indian Affairs, United States Senate, April 29 and 30, 1897, relative to affairs at the Pine Ridge Agency, S. Dak.* May 4, 1897, 55th Cong., 1st sess., Senate Document 61 (Washington, DC: Government Printing Office, 1897), 10.

83. Ibid.

84. Eli Seavey Ricker and Richard E. Jensen, eds. *Voices of the American West.* Vol 1: *The Indian Interviews of Eli S. Ricker, 1903–1919* (Lincoln: University of Nebraska Press, 2005), 353.

85. See, for example, Peter A. Russell, "The Far-from-Dry Debates: Dry Farming on the Canadian Prairies and the American Great Plains," *Agricultural History* 81, no. 4 (Fall 2007): 493–521. Writing in 1923, geographer O. E. Baker described the very regions where the various Sioux reservations remained: "the deficiency in moisture is so discouraging to crop production that farmers are compelled to place their principal dependence upon pasture and live stock, that is, where the value of the pasturage exceeds the value of the crops." "The Agriculture of the Great Plains Region," *Annals of the Association of American Geographers* 13, no. 3 (September 1923): 114.

86. In a 1906 source, *Michigan Farmer*, the author of one article claimed the right type of seed was necessary for dry farming to work. The author claimed that the "steppes of Russian and the arid plains of Turkestan have been drawn upon to furnish our seed supply and these when raised under conditions here have given an abundant harvest." This Russian wheat seed base was "grown for years on the steppes of Russia on a rainfall of less than 10 inches. Brought into this country by the Department of Agriculture, the first crop was harvested in 1901." See H. F. Palmer, "Dry Farming as Developed in the West," *Michigan Farmer* 50 (July 21, 1906), 33. See also Gary D. Libecap and Zeynep Kocabiyik Hansen, "'Rain Follows the Plow' and Dry-farming Doctrine: The Climate Information Problem and Homestead Failure in the Upper Great Plains, 1890–1925," *Journal of Economic History* 62, no. 1 (March 2002): 86–120.

87. Ralph C. Morris, "The Notion of a Great American Desert East of the Rockies," *Mississippi Valley Historical Review* 13, no. 2 (September 1926): 191–92. See also Robert G. Athearn, "The Great Plains in Historical Perspective," *Montana The Magazine of Western History* 8, no. 1 (Winter 1958): 13–29.

88. See Thomas R. Wessel, "Agent of Acculturation: Farming on the Northern Plains Reservations, 1880–1910," *Agricultural History* 60, no. 2 (Spring 1986): 233–45.

89. Interestingly, poor Kazakhs also complained about rich Kazakhs taking larger allotments than permitted by law. In March 1889, one petition sent to the Russian government by some poor Kazakhs claimed that a certain wealthy Kazakh, Begali Batyrbekov, several years ago "started to crowd in on our land," pasturing his herds on their best fields, which hurt their ability to pasture their own herds or raised fodder because "this place in not good to grow hay." *TsGA RK*, f. 78, o. 2, d. 2920, l. 3–4; d. 3018, l. 5–6.

90. See James Y. Simms Jr., "The Crop Failure of 1891: Soil Exhaustion, Technological Backwardness, and Russia's 'Agrarian Crisis,'" *Slavic Review* 41, no. 2 (Summer 1982): 236–50.

91. In Uralsk, in the northwest portion of the oblast, by the mid-1890s, the majority of the Kazakh population was forced to abandon nomadism and livestock raising and settle, but their plots were small, usually only between 4.4 and 6.0 desiatin per household. A. A. Kaufman, *K voprosu o kolonizatsii Ural'skoi oblasti* (St. Petersburg: Tipografiia V.O. Kirshbauma, 1903), 22.

92. Alikhan Bokeikhanov, "Kirgizy," in *Formy natsional'nago dvizheniia v sovremennykh gosudarstvakh. Avstro-vengriia. Rossiia. Germaniia*, ed. A. I. Kastelianskii (St. Petersburg: Obshchestvennaia pol'za, 1910), 580; P. P. Rumianztsev, *Kirgizskii narod v proshlom i nastoiashchem* (St. Petersburg, 1910), 37; S. Sundetov, "K voprosu ob osedanii Kazakhov v nachale XX veka," *Izvestiia Akademii Nauk Kazakhskoi SSR, seriia istorii, arkheologii i etnografii*, no. 3 (1961): 69–70.

93. A. Kuropatkin, 'Vosstanie 1916 g. v Srednei Azii,' *Krasnyi arkhiv* 3, no. 34 (1929): 65.

94. Some Kazakhs started raising cattle on the small allotments rather than sheep and horses; they engaged in subsistence farming and produced some dairy products in summer and meat in winter. *TsGA RK*, f. 25, o. 1, d. 3755, l. 13–14.

95. Treadgold, *Siberian Migration*, 30.

96. Patricia Nelson Limerick, *The Legacy of Conquest: The Unbroken Past of the American West* (New York: W. W. Norton, 1987), 42.

97. A. B. Tursunbaev, *Iz istorii krest'ianskogo pereseleniia v Kazakhstan* (Alma-Ata: Akademiia nauk SSSR, 1950), 24.

98. Nikolai V. Alekseenko, *Naselenie dorevoliutsionnogo Kazakhstana (chislennost', razmeshchenie, sostav, 1870–1914 gg.)* (Alma-Ata: Nauka, 1981): 46–47, 77–78. From 1870 to 1897, the number of non-Kazakhs living in Akmolinsk oblast increased from 70,036 to 217,843. In Uralsk, the number grew from 101,712 to 184,948. Semipalatinsk experienced comparable growth, from 48,437 to 80,026.

99. *TsGA RK*, f. 25, o. 1, d. 1446, l. 22.

100. *TsGA RK*, f. 25, o. 1, d. 1502, l. 7.

101. On the imagining of Siberia, see Geroid T. Robinson, *Rural Russia Under the Old Regime: A History of the Landlord-Peasant World and a Prologue to the Peasant Revolution of 1917* (Berkeley: University of California Press, 1969), 251.

102. *TsGA RK*, f. 64, o. 1, d. 125, l. 44.

103. K. S. Aldazhumanov, M. Kh. Asylbekov, Zh. K. Kasymbaev, M. K. Kozybaev, eds., *Istoriia Kazakhstana (c drevneishikh vremen do nashikh dnei). V piati tomakh* (Almaty: Atamura, 2000), 3:427.

104. Treadgold, *Siberian Migration*, 120–21.

105. Ervin de Palosi, "Question de la Terre dans la zone des steppes: L'etat des proprieties chez les Kirghizes," *Turan* (October 1918): 478.

106. Edward Dennis Sokol, *The Revolt of 1916 in Russian Central Asia* (Baltimore: Johns Hopkins University Press), 37.

107. Glinka, G. V., ed. *Aziatskaia Rossiia* (1914; St. Petersburg, Obshchestvenniia pol'za, 1974), 1:542–43.

108. O. A. Vaganov, "Zemelnaia politika tsarskogo pravitelstva v Kazakhstane," *Istoricheskie zapiski*, no. 31 (1950): 71–73.

109. *TsGA RK*, f. 25, o. 1, d. 3281, l. 56.

110. *TsGA RK*, f. 15, o. 1, d. 231, l. 24–25.

111. According to this 1909 Orenburg Revenue Department report, local Russian officials indicated that many impoverished Kazakhs found work as manual laborers, often as "farmhands, shepherds, mowers, ploughmen, unskilled laborers, guards, sentries; hiring themselves out to [wealthy] Kazakhs and settlers [Russians] . . . earning usually only 60 to 115 rubles per

year; the number of such people . . . must be rather significant, since almost every prosperous home of Kazakhs and settlers has Kazakh laborers." *TsGA RK*, f. 25, o. 1, d. 1549, l. 57.

112. Helen Hunt Jackson, *A Century of Dishonor: A Sketch of the United States Government's Dealings with Some of the Indian Tribes* (New York: Harper & Brothers, 1881).

113. *Hearings on H. R. 7902 before the House Committee on Indian Affairs*, part 9, 73rd Cong., 2nd sess. (1934), 468.

114. Grigoriev quoted in Yuriy Anatolyevich Malikov, "Formation of a Borderland Culture: Myths and Realities of Cossack-Kazakh Relations in Northern Kazakhstan in the Eighteenth and Nineteenth Centuries" (PhD diss., University of California, Santa Barbara, 2006), 16.

115. Richard White, "American West and American Empire," 218.

116. Emily Greenwald, *Reconfiguring the Reservation: The Nez Perces, Jicarilla Apaches, and the Dawes Act* (Albuquerque: University of New Mexico Press, 2002), 2. The commissioner of Indian affairs emphasized this view when he stressed that Indians "must abandon tribal relations; they must give up their superstitions; they must forsake their savage habits and learn the arts of civilization; they must learn to labor, and must learn to rear their families as white people do." See *Annual Report*, 1885, v.

117. George E. Hyde, *Red Cloud's Folk: A History of the Oglala Sioux Indians* (1937; Norman: University of Oklahoma Press, 1975), 315.

118. Patrick Wolfe, "Settler Colonialism," 400.

119. David Moon, "Peasant Migration and the Settlement of Russia's Frontiers, 1550–1897," *Historical Journal* 40, no. 4 (December 1997): 884.

6

Assimilation and Identity

The United States and Russia pursued different strategies during internal colonization to force the Sioux and the Kazakhs to abandon the nomadic life for a sedentary, agrarian one. Central to the various policies and programs advanced by the two countries was the belief that the Sioux and the Kazakhs could be civilized and, ultimately, assimilated and integrated into the broad American and Russian social, economic, political, and cultural milieu. The ideological differences did not completely mask the consequences; however, the differences influenced policy and altered the trajectory of internal colonization in the plains and the steppe. In particular, differences in technological advances (chiefly railroads and communication), missionary activities, the use of treaties (examined in previous chapters), and governance existed between internal colonization in the United States when compared to Russia.

THE RAILROAD DIFFERENCE

Historian J. Russell Smith observed, "Gunpowder and the railway reduced the grassland *man* to impotence."[1] As both the United States and Russia expanded railroad capacity throughout their empires, the tracks paved the way for deeper and more concentrated penetration into the colonized territories. The subject of railroad and empires has attracted significant popular and scholarly attention over the decades. Unquestionably, Russian imperial expansion began well before the process started in the United States, but the development of railroads occurred much earlier and more rapidly in the United States than in Russia.[2] Historian Eric Hobsbawm called railroads a "revolutionary transformation" that "[t]ransformed the speed of movement . . . and introduced the notion of a gigantic, nation-wide, complex and exact interlocking routine symbolized by the railway timetable. It revealed the possibilities of technical progress as nothing else had done, because it was both more advanced than most other forms of technical activity and omnipresent."[3]

In the United States, railroads were "quite consciously . . . agents of state," and, as historian Richard White noted, "Just as Manifest Destiny made the expansion of the United States synonymous with the expansion of republican freedom, Christianity, and civilization itself, so the railroads made their expansion an expansion of civilization."[4] Railroads became the symbol of progress and civilization, and "technology, railways, the telegraph and weapons were used to control and order colonial societies."[5] An 1874 *New York Times* editorial enthusiastically insisted that railroads "pierced the jealously-guarded country of the red man; and in its wake will follow the turbulent and aggressive current which he has never been able to withstand."[6]

By 1850 the United States had roughly three times more rail miles than Prussia—a leading European railway builder—a figure that swelled during the next decade.[7] In 1869, after decades of sectional political debate, the transcontinental railroad connected the eastern United States to the West coast. According to James Belich, in "1875, the top five nations in terms of rail miles per capita were the United States (with 1,922 miles of rail per million people), New Zealand (1,350), Canada (1,159), Australia (998), and Britain (527). European Russian had 185 miles of rail per million people, Brazil 72, and India 34."[8] Only by the 1890s did railroads play a comparable role in Russia's imperial expansion, similar to that which occurred in the United States. The Russian government, including the Imperial Geographical Society, considered the Trans-Siberian Railway that linked Moscow to the Pacific Ocean an agent of the state to bring "Christian love and enlightenment into dark Asia."[9] The Russians equated construction of the Trans-Siberian Railway to the American Union Pacific (1869) and the Canadian Pacific Railway (1885). American and Canadian railroads represented models to follow for Russia's industrialization, territorial consolidation, and economic integration. Some Russians hoped to emulate the American example.[10] The American transcontinental lines moved people and commerce, but those railroads also transported the military and, more importantly, pioneers, tourists, and entrepreneurs to the plains. Railways in Siberia and central Asia eased transportation for peasants, foreign visitors, government administrators, and soldiers to the Kazakh Steppe, Siberia, and the Russian Far East.

Railroad travel in both the United States and Russia encouraged pioneers and peasants to resettle in recently opened lands—particularly in the United States, where "the western railroads loosed a flood of stationery, postcards, calendars, timetables, guidebooks, and advertisements" on the public to promote rail travel and commerce.[11] In the United States, railroads were often joint ventures between government and private interests. Russian railroads, however, were almost exclusively state enterprises. Nonetheless, by the 1890s, the Russian government recognized the necessity of promoting railroads among the peasant population in order to encourage migration and resettlement in the steppe and Siberia. According to historian Willard Sunderland, "as the scale of resettlement increased, state publishing houses (usually under the auspices of the Resettlement Administration or the Siberian Railway Committee) started churning out a wide array of settler-oriented materials, including settlement manuals on different settlement regions (*putevoditeli*), itineraries (*marshruty*), maps, and a variety of informational pamphlets."[12] A 1900 promotional *Guide to the Great Siberian Railway*, published by the Russian Ministry of Ways of Communication, claimed "emigration as a factor in Russian history had always tended to secure Russian dominion and Russian culture, and would serve as a stronghold of orthodoxy and Russian law" as the primary rationale to construct the Trans-Siberian Railway.[13] In order to facilitate peasant resettlement, the Russian government reduced the cost of train travel so that a family of five could travel together for the price of a child's third-class ticket.[14]

By 1904 the Trans-Siberian Railway linked Moscow to the Pacific Ocean, and within one year it connected the Kazakh Steppe, Turkestan, and Tashkent (via the Tashkent-Orenburg Railway) more fully into the Russian Empire.[15] Railroads strengthened the American and Russian grasp on internally colonized lands; as a leading American railroad figure suggested, the "[r]ailroad line through Indian territory [is] a Fortress as well as a highway."[16] However, railroads defended the territorial gains made rather than introduced new ideas into the expansionist agenda. Railroads supplemented American internal colonization, but they also followed missionaries, settlers, miners, and others in concert with internal colonization. Railroads in the United States did not mark the path to internal colonization; they merely smoothed the way. In Russia, railroads created a new and easier path for peasants and opened different opportunities. In a sense, railroads in the western United States followed the flood of travelers and settlers; in the Kazakh Steppe, organized peasant resettlement accompanied the railroads. In both cases, railroads accelerated internal colonization, but they did not introduce it. This was most evident in the demographic changes in the plains and the steppe.

Population shifts in the United States and Russia compelled the American and Russian governments to establish frameworks to accommodate pioneers and peasants moving and settling on the plains and the steppe. American and Russian structures, resettlement, and reorganization clearly resembled colonies in other contexts. It was a particular type of sociopolitical organization and system of domination, which scholar Jürgen Osterhammel referred to as "border colonization." Osterhammel argued that border colonization occurred when the expanding state's recognized boundaries extended into and exceeded a contiguous wilderness area.[17] In the American expansion, border colonization occurred at the same time, and in some cases before, the military conquest. For example, in the two decades before the 1862 Sioux rebellion in Minnesota, the neighboring territory of Wisconsin experienced a tenfold increase in Americans settling there, while in the 1850s, Minnesota expanded twenty-eightfold.[18] Similar growth happened in the plains territories, Colorado, Montana Territory, the Dakotas, and Texas.

Russian peasant resettlement in the Kazakh Steppe was much slower, and peasants tended to settle close to the Irtysh Line or Russian fortifications. Peasant resettlement rarely exhibited border colonization. The Russian government tried to retain a firm grip on peasant movements, particular prior to the 1861 serf emancipation. Those peasants permitted to migrate tended to settle in northern steppe regions. In the southern steppe regions, peasants settled much more slowly. According to one Russian survey, peasants frequently settled as "villages" rather than on individual allotments, mimicking the pattern of life they left behind. After the serf emancipation, the Russian government attempted to manage peasant migration and demarcate specific lands available to resettlement in the steppe. Between 1874 and 1892, the number of settlements in the Syr Darya province almost tripled.[19] Akmolinsk, opened longer to resettlement than any other Kazakh Steppe province, also experienced significant growth in the 1890s. The objective, as one source claimed, was to "drive the Kirgiz people out . . . to ensure the life and property of the Russian settlers and restrain the impertinent Kirgiz."[20] After completing the Trans-Siberian Railway in 1904, the Russian government lost control of the situation. Around Semipalatinsk, between 1907 and 1910, the number of resettled peasant families grew from 1,000 to 11,500.[21] Indeed, between 1896 and 1916, more than 2 million Russian peasants settled in the steppe.[22] These demographic changes, driven by comparable pioneer and peasant demands for land, were still somewhat different, particularly the role the railroads played facilitating the movement.

THE MISSIONARY DIFFERENCE

One other difference between American and Russian internal colonization of the Sioux and the Kazakhs was the role played by missionaries. The internal colonization and ideological differences between the United States and Russia, as Roger L. Nichols observed, set the Americans "on a course using the church, the plow, and the school as the central means of incorporating tribal people into the general society."[23] In 1819 the US Congress appropriated ten thousand dollars for Indian affairs, ostensibly to save the Indian from extinction and to promote civilization among the various tribes in the East and throughout the Mississippi Valley regions.[24] Civilizing and Christianizing Indians in the United States was long a practice among various Christian sects but declined in the first decades of independence.

Civilizing and Christianizing in the American case was an imperial ideology nonetheless, an ideology that emphasized assimilation and generally ignored native customs and beliefs during internal colonization. In the 1820s, several groups in the United States, including the American Board of Commissioners for Foreign Missions, dispatched missionaries to work among the various tribes, particularly in the West. From this point forward, civilization and Christianity were "inextricably mixed" in American internal colonization.[25] The Russians followed a slightly different imperial ideology, more similar to British imperialism in India, in which the government focused on legal codes and civil institutions to orchestrate its internal colonization.[26] As such, one Russian observer claimed that "Russian governance gave Central Asia the two most valuable gifts of civilization—security of life and security for property—two things that were not known there previously, and the absence of which made normal life there impossible."[27] The difference between American and Russian approaches to coupling the civilizing agenda with missionary efforts is not difficult to understand: the Kazakhs were Muslims.

Catherine the Great's 1773 "Edict of Toleration of All Faiths," which suspended nearly all Christian proselytizing among the empire's Muslim populations, determined Russia's policies throughout much of the nineteenth century. As such, the edict's proponents expected to integrate Muslim subjects using less compulsory measures—such as forced conversions to Orthodoxy—because "to forbid, or not to allow them to profess *different Modes* of religion, would greatly endanger the Peace and Security of its Citizens."[28] Thus, for almost a century, the Russian government and the Orthodox Church ignored active missionary work among the Kazakh population.[29] In the Kazakh Steppe, parish priests rather than missionaries operated the Orthodox missions. Those priests were often more busy with the job of ministering to Russian peasants in the towns and villages than bothering to convert Muslim Kazakhs to Christianity.[30]

Catherine's edict did not completely discourage the Russian Orthodox Church from proselytizing among the Kazakhs, or even among pagan peoples in Siberia; rather, the government did not actively promote it.[31] In fact, the Russian government and the Orthodox Church tolerated other non-Christian religions throughout the first half of the nineteenth century, including Judaism and Buddhism.[32] Nineteenth-century Russian historian Nikolai Karamzin comparatively claimed that Russia chose not to disturb the "consciences of the vanquished" but determined to enlighten its non-Christians "in the Divine Faith simply by setting them a better example, without recourse to the violence and villainy to which other devotees of Christianity resorted in Europe and America."[33] Russia maintained a civilizing mission throughout much of the nineteenth century that was administrative and integrative rather than religious. The Russians often used the term *grazhdanstvennost'* to describe the integration, but it is not a simple translation. It denotes a form of civil order and civil society—perhaps citizenship, but not assimilation.[34]

The Russian government discouraged missionary work among the Kazakhs because it held a very different perspective toward Islam.[35] From the moment Europeans transplanted themselves in North America, converting the natives to Christianity was axiomatic. As Mark Cocker noted, possibly that first meeting in 1492 fundamentally altered Europeans' intellectual conceptions of human history, as "half the world was obliged to embrace its other half in an instant revolution of the imagination."[36] Steven Conn argued that the very existence of Native Americans made Europeans ask some 'basic" questions, such as "who and where" did these people come from? These questions vexed Americans as well and "lay at the heart of the way several intellectual genres" developed in the United States long into the nineteenth century.[37]

That is not to suggest that when Europeans arrived in the Americas that they were completely ignorant of other peoples—quite the contrary. Europeans knew about Asians, Africans, Muslims, and peoples living beyond (and within) Europe's borders, but that did not prevent Europeans from asking fundamental questions about the world and where Indians fit within that worldview. Americans ultimately identified Indians as a different race, not an identity based solely upon a creed or geography. As such, American Christian missionaries actively worked to convert them throughout much of the nineteenth century. Moreover, many Christian missionaries in Asia, Africa, and elsewhere tended to respect the existence of Islam, although they considered it a flawed and ignorant creed; in the United States, missionaries regarded native religion as unrealistic and paganism. As the frontier moved west, missionary objectives remained the same; only the tactics changed.

The Russians, on the other hand, never troubled to answer such elementary questions. The people the Russians encountered in the Kazakh Steppe and Asia were a known people; they were, of course, misunderstood, stereotyped, and classified but were not a people that challenged the Russians' fundamental biblical or classical understanding of the world and its history. The Russians typically grouped the new subjects as *inozemtsy* (of another land) and later categorized the Kazakhs as *inorodtsy* ("alien" or "of another people"). Both of these terms suggest the extra-territoriality of the annexed people, their non-Russian ethnicity. But in the nineteenth century, Kazakhs were also referred to as *inoverets* (of a different faith), bestowed by the conventions of the day as a religious marker to identify non-Russians (i.e., non-Orthodox). The terms had legal and informal connotations and usages; Kazakhs were "non-assimilable, radically different subjects of the tsarist realm," and the term reflected the degree of civilized development.[38] According to John W. Slocum, assimilation was deemed improbable for inorodtsy; they were people identified by distinct social, cultural, and religious characteristics "whose purportedly 'low level of civilization' placed them in need of a special relationship of trusteeship to the Russian state."[39] Kazakhs and others occupied a different social space in the empire because, as Aleksander Gradovskii noted in 1875, "the inorodtsy population . . . was always ready to rise up against the authority of the Muscovite government."[40] Thus, Russian government policy was designed to "neutralize that threat" in order to integrate rather than assimilate the Kazakhs.[41]

There were many nineteenth-century critics of Catherine's policy—particularly among Russian officials working in the steppe regions—but the edict persisted roughly until the 1870s.[42] Consequently, the Russian Orthodox Church did not concern itself with the Kazakhs' civilization or their spiritual well-being; however, in the United States, Christianity and the civilizing mission went hand-in-hand throughout the nineteenth century. Among the Americans and other European imperial powers, according to Ryan Dunch, Christian missionaries "came to their fields convinced of the intellectual, moral, and spiritual superiority of what they thought of, not as their 'culture,' but as 'Civilization.'"[43]

In 1824 the American Society for Promoting the Civilization and General Improvement of the Indian Tribes Within the United States published its first report, in which it insisted that the "work of civilizing the Indians, is a common obligation of the whole nation, and it is the duty of all to engage in it."[44] Americans also believed the mere proximity to American civilization and good Christian practices transformed Indians. As historian Robert F. Berkhofer Jr.

noted, because for missionaries "the superiority of the American Way of Life appeared self-evident to them, they thought that Indians would see it in their immediate self-interest to adopt the habits and beliefs of the (good) White American after a brief demonstration."[45]

Thus, American missionaries worked more overtly to introduce Indians to Christianity as part of the civilizing mission compared to their Russian counterparts in the Kazakh Steppe or among Muslims in central Asia. American missionaries believed that exposure to Christianity compelled Indians to abandon their heathen, pagan ways and become civilized agriculturists. Missionaries assumed success because such "work, doubtless, is that of raising *half a million* of fellow beings, inhabitants of our country, and original proprietors of its soil, from a state of ignorance, heathenism and wretchedness, to the possession of innumerable blessings, which result from Civilization and Christianity."[46] Stephen R. Riggs, nineteenth-century missionary to the Sioux, pronounced that "a civilization in which Christianity has no place cannot be other than a refined barbarism, and consequently . . . the gospel of Christ should be regarded as the great civilizer of nations."[47] Riggs's views found echoes in most imperial, missionary environments, including the Great Britain House of Commons's 1837 Select Committee on Aborigines, which asserted, "True civilization and Christianity are inseparable: the former had never been found, but as a fruit of the latter."[48] The Russian government did not share that philosophy through much of the nineteenth century. Interestingly, though, both the United States and Russia emphasized civilization and Christianity through education, with fascinating ideological parallels.

INTERNAL COLONIZATION, EDUCATION, AND UNINTENDED CONSEQUENCES

The chief mechanism to emasculate indigenous cultures and affect internal colonization was education. Despite sharing seemingly comparable objectives, the subsequent consequences were not so very different. The United States designed Indian education to civilize and Christianize the native population; Russia designed education to make the natives instruments of the empire in order to teach the skills necessary to serve imperial needs as scribes, translators, and guides. Learning Russian was part of that objective, structured to integrate Kazakhs rather than assimilate them. Americans wanted the Indians to learn skills too, but chiefly to learn English, how to farm, learn a trade, develop a vocational skill, or learn to labor. By the mid-nineteenth century, Americans also inextricably coupled these ostensibly tangible goals to an overt but amorphous desire to civilize. The Russians, on the other hand, only linked education and civilization together by the late nineteenth century. Moreover, the American policies assumed a standardized, somewhat inflexible, universal approach to education. The Russians more quickly recognized that the cultural and linguistic differences among the empire's many nationalities required a more malleable approach to education in the various regions.[49]

Even before independence, in 1775 the American Continental Congress appropriated five hundred dollars to educate "Indian youth at Dartmouth College."[50] In 1818 the American government determined to expand its support for Indian education. The US Congress expressed some admiration for what other European imperial powers accomplished in their efforts to educate natives and justified supporting missionary efforts among its own indigenous populations, noting,

> Great exertions have of late years been made by individuals and missionary societies in Europe and America: schools have been established by those humane and benevolent societies in the Indies, amongst the Hindoos and Hottentots, and notwithstanding that superstition, bigotry, and ignorance have shrowded [sic] those people in darkness for ages, thousands of them have already yielded to instruction.
>
> The government has no such difficulties to encounter: no bibles nor books to translate into foreign or other languages: only establish some English schools: the experiment may be tried at a very small expense. The committee believe that increasing the number of trading posts, and establishing schools on, or near our frontiers for the education of Indian children, would be attended with beneficial effects, both to the United States and the Indian tribes, and the best possible means of securing the friendship of those nations in amity with us, and in time to bring the hostile tribes to see that their true interest lies in peace and not in war.[51]

While the American government provided some limited support for children of eastern Indians to attend schools, the efforts to bring civilization to the Indians in these early years was sporadic and limited. Nonetheless, these labors foreshadowed attempts later in the nineteenth century to civilize the Sioux. Most schools in the 1820s and 1830s were small missionary institutions, often opened with the government's blessing. In addition, most treaties signed between Americans and Indians included some provision for schools. Coupled with the goal of educating Indians was civilizing and Christianizing them; the federal government generally provided financial support and encouragement but was not yet giving material support, such as buildings or teachers. The Bureau of Indian Affairs was not yet in the education business on the reservations, but that changed after the Civil War.

In Russia, education initially played a more instrumentalist role and was used to integrate some natives into the government's administrative structures and institutions rather than assimilate indigenous peoples.[52] In 1847 the Russians opened the *Omsk kadetskii korpus* (Omsk Corps of Cadets), which graduated many Kazakhs, including Chokan Valikhanov, for duty in the army as translators, guides, and scribes. In addition, the Russians established many Russian-native schools (*Russko-tuzemny shkoly*), which taught Russian and Kazakh children; instruction was almost always in Russian, but these schools were not compulsory. In central Asia, however, the Russian-native schools competed with *mektep* (native schools with Tatar teachers, not Russians) for students, although attendance was generally small.[53] Some Kazakh children attended mektep, but the curriculum in the mektep was generally Koranic recitation and catechism, calligraphy, and Islamic texts. By the 1850s, wealthy Kazakhs regularly enrolled their sons in Russian schools, with graduates often taking positions in the steppe bureaucracy as clerks and scribes. Despite Catherine the Great's 1773 edict banning Orthodox proselytizing among Muslims, by the second half of the nineteenth century, the Russian educational agenda included efforts to convert Kazakhs to Russian Orthodoxy.

In the 1860s, Russian education of Kazakhs followed the so-called Il'minskii system, which emphasized the sciences, math, history, and geography but was taught in native vernaculars. Named for Nikolai Il'minskii, a professor of Turkic Languages at the Kazan Theological Academy and Kazan University, the goal was to limit the spread of Islam, particularly among Kazakhs (the Russians understood that Kazakhs were Muslim but believed its tenets were weakly possessed precisely because Kazakhs were nomads).[54] Il'minskii believed native vernacular education better transmitted Russian civilization and Orthodoxy; Il'minski schools also taught Russian but as a subject, not the instructional language.

Il'minskii emphasized that native language education facilitated the transmission of Russian imperial ideas and ideology. Teaching in the vernacular reinforced loyalty to the empire and, ultimately, lead natives, including Kazakhs, to adopt Russian culture and habits.[55] It was a tool to integrate and possibly convert Kazakhs and other national minorities to Orthodoxy.[56] The Russian minister of education, D. A. Tolstoi, wrote to the tsar, "To enlighten the natives, to draw them closer to Russia and to the Russian spirit, constitutes in my opinion a goal of highest political importance."[57] This method differed little from American missionaries who opened schools among the Sioux and on reservations.

Stephen Riggs preached and taught using the Sioux vernacular; he compiled one of the first vocabularies, translated the Bible into Dakota, and spent some forty years among the Sioux as a missionary, educator, and ethnologist.[58] Brothers Samuel and Gideon Pond joined Riggs in efforts to civilize, Christianize, and educate the Sioux. Like Riggs, they relied on the native language to conduct their work.[59] After 1868 the government funded schools, regardless if they were on or off reservations or run by missionaries, but the office of the commissioner of Indian affairs reemphasized the prohibition against teaching in the vernacular.[60]

In Russia, similar debates raged. Il'minskii's critics claimed that the 1864 statute on primary schools mandated instruction only in the Russian language, and they insisted that it accelerated Russification, the Russian version of assimilation: "assimilation of language assimilates also the nationality."[61] In the end, however, Il'minskii won the debate, and in 1870 education minister Tolstoi adopted measures for the education of natives, which required native teachers to be fluent in Russian or Russians who knew the native tongue.[62] Similar to the work of Riggs and the Pond brothers with the Dakota, Kazakh dictionaries, grammar books, and educational material appeared in the Kazakh language, which in the 1860s did not have its own script. The Russians created one using a phonetic-based Cyrillic; however, later Kazakh intellectuals debated the use of Cyrillic or Arabic, with most choosing the modified Arabic script. But it is in education that the assimilation policies adopted by the Americans and the Russians diverge. The Russian government permitted Kazakhs to organize, open, and teach in their own schools; teach in the vernacular; and educate young Kazakhs in primary topics such as history, geography, mathematics, and the sciences. Kazakhs created the curriculum, recruited the students, and used education to try to protect and preserve Kazakh culture in the face of increased Russification.[63]

Thus, in the second half of the nineteenth century, in their own way, American and Russian compulsory education attempted to impose cultural conformity through education and Christianity. It was one thing to force sedentarization and the agrarian life through allotment but quite another to accelerate assimilation through education. In 1875 the commissioner of Indian affairs, John Q. Smith, conjoined education and civilization for all Indians because "they should be recognized and treated for what they are, an ignorant and helpless people, who have a large moral claim upon the United States."[64] Americans owed Indians, Smith insisted, "a debt which cannot be discharged by gifts of blankets and bacon, or any routine official care for their protection or relief."[65] These "trifles" meant nothing compared to the gift of "civilization—which every consideration of humanity requires that we should give them."[66]

216 ASSIMILATION AND IDENTITY

FIGURE 6.1. Ibrahim Altynsarin, *center*, and students (courtesy of Central State Archives, Republic of Kazakhstan, 2-27605).

American and Russian internal colonization clearly manifested over native language issues, but it was a more pernicious feature of American internal colonization than the Russian case. In fact, the US government clearly regarded the persistence of native tongues as one of the more powerful obstacles to assimilation. In 1877 Commissioner of Indian Affairs Ezra A. Hayt advised the government to establish a "rule making it compulsory upon all Indian children between the ages of six and fourteen years to attend schools, and requiring English alone to be spoken and taught therein."[67]

In the United States, education was the blunt tool of assimilation. BIA administrators, teachers, and missionaries all played a prominent role; they imposed American culture, social norms, and civic behavior and strongly privileged English-language education over native languages, culture, and social customs. Schooling and education were not novel concepts for the Sioux. Missionaries had operated among them for several years, but in 1879 the American government funded the first off-reservation boarding school, started by Richard H. Pratt, in Carlisle, Pennsylvania. Only a handful had opened by the time of the Dawes Act, but the government, following the allotment principles established in the act, opened even more boarding schools, including Hampton Institute in Virginia and Haskell Institute in Kansas. By 1898 there were twenty-five such schools, with a couple more completed by 1909. The annual report from the commissioner of Indian affairs that year claimed that the "Indian Service is primarily educational . . . The first division of the Indian Office is therefore naturally called the Education Division."[68] Interestingly, these schools eventually employed a large number of native teachers—more than 20 percent of the total (549 from a force of 2,355).[69]

American education fundamentally rejected the concept of the native. The American government sought to destroy what made native languages, in particular, so inimical to American internal colonization ideology. In 1887 Commissioner of Indian Affairs J. D. C. Atkins reported that it was necessary to wean natives away from their mother tongues in order to instill English, claiming that if it was "good enough for a white man and a black man, [it] ought to be good enough for the red man."[70] To the critics of this policy who claimed "it was a cruel blow to the sacred rights of the Indians," the commissioner rhetorically asked,

> Is it cruelty to the Indian to force him to give up his scalping-knife and tomahawk? Is it cruelty to force him to abandon the vicious and barbarous sun dance, where he lacerates his flesh, and dances and tortures himself even unto death? Is it cruelty to the Indian to force him to have his daughters educated and married under the laws of the land, instead of selling them at a tender age for a stipulated price into concubinage to gratify the brutal lusts of ignorance and barbarism?[71]

As one BIA administrator explained it to Pine Ridge Reservation agent D. Gallagher, "The education of Indians in the vernacular is not only no use to them, but is detrimental to their education and civilization."[72] Many reformers objected to this provision, particularly because it seemed to prohibit the use of bibles published in native languages. In 1888 the commissioner of Indian affairs, John H. Oberly, a former superintendent of Indian schools and a committed Indian school reformer, clarified the policy.[73] He wrote in the annual report that "it may be well to state that it is not the intention of the Indian Bureau to prohibit the reading of the Bible by any Indian in any language, or by anybody to any Indian in any language or in any Indian vernacular, anywhere, at any time."[74] The Russian debate about the use of the vernacular was not as heated, divisive, or invasive. The Russian government did not prevent Kazakhs from speaking the mother tongue; the government wanted, at a minimum, for Kazakhs to be bilingual, in order to serve the empire.[75]

As a consequence, Russian education policies in the steppe allowed Kazakhs to become active participants in education rather than simply recipients of the colonizers' language and culture. Education in the Muslim world had a deep and rich tradition, but by the 1880s, many Kazakhs educated in Russian schools embraced a "new method" (*jadid*) to protect Kazakh culture by improving it. They wanted to control secular instruction, modeled on the Russian schools, but infuse it with cultural reform and literacy. From the Russian perspective—initially, at least—if these reforms created better translators, scribes, guides, and subjects, government officials did not object because the curriculum did not appear to conflict with Russian efforts to educate Kazakhs. The Kazakhs managed to adopt elements of Il'minskii's system but resist, in particular, its Christianizing agenda. In a comparable context, some Sioux managed to perform what historian Thomas G. Andrews called a "tight rope" between accommodation and assimilation. Andrews examined the work of Clarence Three Stars, a Sioux teacher at the Pine Ridge day school, who believed that English language and literacy was the best mechanism to "recast" assimilation as a "tool of Oglala survival."[76] Literacy became the instrument of survival.

The American and Russian schools, however, graduated a generation of intellectuals who became spokesmen for the native culture—translators of Sioux and Kazakh culture to the colonizing power rather than mere representations of it. They could adopt all facets of the dominant society in dress, language, work, and carriage but could also defend the native culture and language. Americanization and Russification fostered a generation of Sioux and Kazakh intellectuals—men and women who could navigate more successfully between the two cultures than previous generations. They were, as Edward J. Lazzerini noted among other native colonized peoples, "partial insiders who knew how to turn the dominant discourse against itself," subsequently adopting a variety of methods to protect the indigenous culture."[77] They aspired to use the dominant culture to their advantage via education and economic advancement, to defend their own culture against the further intrusion of another. Sociologist Karl Mannheim wrote, "in every society there are those social groups whose special task it is to provide an interpretation of the world for that society."[78] But, equally important, Sioux and Kazakh intellectuals interpreted their respective culture for the colonizer more effectively; the colonizer was comfortable because the intellectuals also seemed to exemplify the positive civilizing policies implemented by allotment and education. These Sioux and Kazakh intellectuals epitomized civilization.

This unintended consequence of American and Russian education policies gave the Sioux and the Kazakhs an audience; literacy gave Sioux and Kazakh intellectuals access to an unfiltered, albeit English or Russian, voice. It was the language of the colonizer, but the playing field shifted. Literacy gave the Sioux and the Kazakhs power, some authority over their own history and culture, and allowed them to reach beyond the world of "the Indian problem" or the "nationalities question" to present a different perspective and even, to some extent, a different agenda. Attending schools designed to assimilate them changed the conversation, and Sioux and Kazakh intellectuals became active participants in that dialogue. Armed with the periodical press, they reflected the changes in their society by using methods that mimicked comparable situations in other colonized societies; they could reform their culture by "adjusting it to the requirements of progress while at the same time maintaining its distinctive identity."[79] Sioux and Kazakh intellectuals were able to reimagine their communities because, according to Benedict Anderson, "their vanguard role" derived from their multilingual literacy—or, rather, their literacy and multilingualism. Anderson argued that multilingualism gave native intellectuals valuable access to "modern Western culture in the broadest sense, and, in particular, to the models of nationalism, nation-ness, and nation-state produced elsewhere in the course of the nineteenth century."[80]

In the United States, Sioux intellectuals such as Charles Eastman used the periodical press to defend and highlight the value of native languages, cultures, and traditions. In many Indian boarding schools, administrators and teachers allowed students to publish material that seemed to strengthen assimilationist policies, but students also used the new forums to defend and define their native identities. Among Kazakh intellectuals, such as Akhmet Baitursynov, there was a genealogic line between colonial education and the intellectuals' capacity to turn the "dominant discourse against itself." Eastman and Baitursynov became active leaders in the early twentieth-century sociopolitical movements the Society of American Indians (SAI) and Alash Orda (The Horde of Alash), which claimed to represent the interests of their people against the cultural, social, economic, and political internal colonization that enveloped the Sioux and the Kazakhs over the course of the nineteenth century.[81] They wrote for American and Russian audiences, but they also successfully crossed the social and cultural divide to criticize government policies without threatening the social or political order. They were prolific writers; each advocated learning the colonizer's language and insisted that education was critical for the survival of their people; but they also demanded that the governments desist with allotment and internal colonization.

Sioux and Kazakh intellectuals spawned a renaissance of Sioux and Kazakh literature in the early twentieth century, and they helped to influence renewed examinations of internal colonization and altered American and Russian policies. Allotment, in both the American and Russian cases, was simply the process to organize and stabilize land resettlement. In the American case, it is typically associated with the 1887 Dawes Act; however, in a sense, the Americans allotted land well before that legislation but called it something different, such as removal or reservations. By removing Indians to reservations, Americans were allotting land for one group of people to use and denying it to another. In the Russian case, allotment started the moment the tsar's forces moved into the steppe and established the line of west–east forts manned by Cossack garrisons and Russian peasants. The Russians excluded Kazakhs from using those allotments to pasture their livestock and often denied them permission to migrate to the other side of the line. In other words, that policy effectively removed Kazakhs by forcing them to pasture their herds away from Russian military establishments and peasant settlements. The policy deprived them access to land they had claimed and enjoyed for generations. It was not, as in the American case, a literal and physical removal from one territory to another; but the result was the same.

Sioux and Kazakhs lived with what historian Beth LaDow called the "strange duality" in which the Sioux and other Indians were physically segregated from the dominant American society yet were expected to assimilate culturally.[82] The Kazakhs lived with that same strange duality, categorized as inorodtsy—subjects without benefit—and expected to integrate and imitate Russian peasant sedentary agriculturalists. These two contradictory concepts, apparently sociopolitical handmaidens to civilization, permeated and influenced American and Russian alchemies of internal colonization.

A NEW CENTURY, DIFFERENT SOLUTIONS?

As the nineteenth century closed, the United States faced a crisis of identity, as did the Russian Empire in the early twentieth century. In the United States, many politicians, journalists, and others questioned if America was an empire comparable to Britain and France. The defeat of the Spanish in Cuba and the Philippines triggered an impassioned debate about the meaning and course of American expansion into these recently acquired overseas lands. For some Americans, however, this was not a new or necessary debate. Instead, the terms of the debate resonated clearly with the country's earlier expansion across the continent. Writing in 1900, former journalist, soldier, and senator from Kansas, William A. Peffer, asked rhetorically, "Is our Philippine policy anti-American?" Not in essence, he claimed, because except for those few periods when the American army was engaged against Mexico, the Confederate states, or Spain, "the army was used almost entirely for the Indian service, and stationed in the Indian country along the frontier."[83] As such, he insisted, expansion and "Americanism . . . has consistently exhibited itself in the policy followed by this country . . . which are comparable to the Philippine situation at the present day. If it amounts to imperialism, then, indeed, are we a nation of imperialists without division."[84] America had overseas colonies; it had, or so it seemed, imperial ambitions. This argument was echoed decades later by Richard White, who noted, "Western expansion was about empire, as much as the American people and many historians would like to treat it as a purely domestic development.... [And] the creation of an overseas empire in 1898 was not 'unthinking or accidental.' It had precedents in continental expansion, which was just as conscious."[85] Contiguous expansion, for most Americans, was destiny and natural, but it was also imperial and colonization. Russia and its contemporaries, on the other hand, clearly considered it a continental empire, but no such debate occurred in the halls of government, among military men, or among Russian peasants migrating to the steppe. Russia was an empire, but the regime divested itself of overseas colonies in 1867 when it determined that Alaska was not worth the cost to maintain the overseas imperial grip. Russia's identity crisis, however, was not the result of its continued imperial expansion but rather by its sudden termination.

Japan's defeat of Russia in 1904–1905 exacerbated Russia's internal economic and social fragility and sparked a revolution at home. It was a chastening defeat; an Asian power turned the tide against European economic and military hegemony. If that was not humbling enough, widespread peasant and labor unrest quickly spread and sailors in the Black Sea fleet rebelled, forcing the government to abandon many of its culturally and socially repressive, crucifying policies and return its colonial affairs to what one scholar called its "traditional pattern of flexible pragmatism."[86] The concessions wrested from Tsar Nicholas II resulted in unprecedented reforms. The tsar consented to parliamentary (Duma) elections, permitted political parties to organize, eased censorship, and granted freedoms of movement, the press, and assembly. Russia generally abandoned its policies of forced assimilation in order to pacify nationalist and anticolonial movements inspired by Japan's example. One policy that the Russian government failed to reform was peasant resettlement in the steppe and Siberia. Finally unencumbered by official restrictions, peasant migration rapidly accelerated after 1905 and overwhelmed local officials. As with many other minority peoples in the Russian Empire, Kazakh intellectuals organized to petition the government for relief from the increased economic deterioration caused by peasants occupying land previously reserved for Kazakh nomads. Included in the petition was the demand that the government suspend all allotment and resettlement activities in the Kazakh Steppe.

In 1906 six Kazakhs, including Alikhan Bokeikhanov, were elected to serve in the First Duma; considered far too liberal for the conservative tsar, Nicholas

FIGURE 6.2. *From left:* Akhmet Baitursynov, Alikhan Bokeikhanov, and Mirzhakip Dulatov (courtesy of Central State Archives, Republic of Kazakhstan, 2-95119).

II quickly dissolved it, and new elections were held. The tsar also managed to impose new legislation that greatly reduced national minority participation in all ensuing Duma elections. Nonetheless, Kazakhs, as was the case for many minorities in the empire, fully and actively participated for the first time in the empire's political process. They were not alone. Kazakh intellectuals subsequently organized the Alash Orda, and in 1913 it started publishing a newspaper, *Kazak*. Edited by Akhmet Baitursynov, *Kazak* appeared regularly until 1918, when it succumbed to wartime shortages and the ravages of revolution and civil war. These men were not revolutionaries. In fact, during World War I, Alash Orda actively supported the Russian government's efforts, but it vigorously debated what role Kazakhs ought to play and how the people could best contribute. That was all for naught, however, because in June 1916, the government announced plans to conscript Muslims to serve, which sparked widespread revolts throughout central Asia and the steppe regions.[87] Alash proclaimed Kazakh independence from Russia in December 1917, but, caught between opposing Bolshevik Reds on the one side and Whites (anti-Bolsheviks) on the other, independence was short-lived. By 1923 the Bolshevik government reincorporated Kazakhs into the newly formed Soviet Union—a novel social, cultural, and political experiment that played out for the Kazakhs under Soviet rule, an examination of which is beyond the scope of this work.[88]

In the early twentieth century, despite debates about America's overseas imperial ambitions, allotment continued uninterrupted on the majority of Indian reservations. In 1906 the federal government amended the Dawes Act with the Burke Act. The purpose of the Burke Act was to adjust the twenty-five-year trust period established for Indians granted citizenship and enfranchised. The government established Competency Commissions to evaluate so-called qualified Indians, thereby making Indians unrestricted landowners with the right to lease or sell land without government interference.[89] The act merely accelerated allotment and Indian economic and social dislocation. By the 1910s, Sioux intellectuals such as Charles Eastman also participated in the modestly successful Society of American Indians. Formed in 1911, and similar to Alash Orda, the SAI advocated for increased work and education opportunities and debated the need for greater political, cultural, and economic sovereignty. In 1913 the SAI started to publish the *Quarterly Journal of the Society of American Indians*, which represented the principal organ to disseminate its agenda. The SAI held annual conferences and became the leading voice for reform in Indian affairs.

When the United States entered the First World War, many SAI leaders responded enthusiastically to the country's military need in an essay. They instructed the journal's readers that the United States "has upheld the principles of human liberty, political equality and universal justice and she has invited to her hospitable shores the millions of the world who needed a land of opportunity and has schooled them in those principles." The essay concluded with the challenge, "Already we hear the tread of feet that once wore moccasins; already the red men are enlisting. Let this, then, be a personal question, '*Have you done your share?*'"[90] The SAI was rarely in accord with the American government or the War Department, but on this occasion, the organization never wavered in its support. By the 1920s, the SAI splintered into factions, rent by internal rivalries, but its support for Indian enlistment, service, and domestic contributions (e.g., Liberty Loans and the Red Cross) positively influenced politicians and others to enact necessary reforms, including full citizenship for Indians in 1924.

Two years later, in 1926, Secretary of the Interior Hubert Work sanctioned an independent study to determine the effectiveness of American government policies on behalf of Indian since 1887 and the Dawes Act. The so-called Meriam Report signified the clearest statement of current economic, social, and cultural conditions for Indians, noting that Indians had not "adjusted to the economic and social system of the dominant white society."[91] As historian Margaret Szasz noted, "In the four decades since the passage of the Dawes Act, Indians had become more and more dependent on the Indian Bureau. Ironically, this was the very antithesis of the theoretical aim of Federal Indian Policy."[92]

At the heart of the debates in the United States and the Soviet Union during the 1920s was the issue of self-determination. The concept of self-determination became current in the late eighteenth century, but US president Woodrow Wilson popularized the idea during the First World War. Vladimir Lenin also embraced the concept but for different reasons. Like Lenin, Wilson and his supporters held a liberal worldview in which self-determination represented self-government, nationality, and the nation-state.[93] Neither Wilson nor Lenin defined self-determination within their own country's boundaries as independence or decolonization. According to Rupert Emerson, the "intermingling" of minorities with the "dominant majority people" determined that "no form of self-determination, short of mass migration, can be invoked to satisfy such demands as the minority community may make for recognition of its separate identity and its human rights."[94] Lenin's Soviet Union was the first to try self-determination, as understood then, in a multinational state.

Implementing the ill-defined self-determination program among the Kazakhs, however, was complex and burdened by lingering tensions between Russian settlers and Kazakh nomads. The Soviet Union's self-determination policies promoted forms of nationhood (language, culture), created national territories, and established what historian Terry Martin called an "Affirmative Action Empire."[95] The Soviet government formed commissions to investigate Russian and Kazakh grievances and the Agricultural Commissariat ultimately concluded that protection for Russian agriculture, not "backward" Kazakh nomadism, was paramount. At the 1927 Communist Party Congress, Kazakh leaders claimed that the "Kazakh people interpret autonomy above all else as the right to decide independently questions of land."[96] Kazakh resistance to collectivization decimated livestock and resulted in a famine that claimed nearly 25 percent of the Kazakh population.[97] The Soviets began the "socialist offensive," ostensibly a class war against the "kulaks" (in the Kazakh case, wealthy nomads who possessed large herds). By 1931 Stalin proclaimed that the Soviet Union finally defeated "backwardness" and had become an industrialized, modern socialist society.[98]

In the United States, self-determination took a different path. Similar to Kazakh intellectuals' complaints about Russification, American reformers and the leaders of the SAI demanded an end to the Dawes Act and the restoration of social, cultural, and economic sovereignty. The Meriam Report seemed to sanction the reform agenda. The assimilation policies, reformers claimed, did nothing to elevate Indians but further impoverished them. Reformers such as John Collier hoped to rebuild tribal structures severely fractured during allotment, restore tribal lands, reconstitute tribal self-governance, and preserve or resurrect indigenous culture and languages. In 1934 Congress passed the Indian Reorganization Act (IRA). Staunchly advocated by Collier, President Franklin Roosevelt's newly appointed commissioner of Indian affairs, many American reformers considered this bill to be a vast improvement in Indian-American relations.

Also known as the Wheeler-Howard Act, its sponsor, Sen. Burton Wheeler of Montana, subsequently considered the bill a failure. He wrote in his autobiography,

"I must confess that there is one bill I was not proud of having enacted . . . it was not a good bill."[99] Roosevelt, however, supported the bill because it granted to "Indian people" the opportunity to "take an active and responsible part in the solution to their own problems."[100] Upon its passage, a jubilant Collier wrote, "Whether that date [June 18, 1934—the date Roosevelt signed the law] shall be known hereafter as the Independence Day of Indian history will be determined by the Indians themselves." But, he exclaimed, "The Allotment law—the agony and ruin of the Indians—has been repealed."[101] One supporter of the legislation, Elizabeth Green, compared the IRA with the "changes" evident for the "racial minorities once under the dominion of the Russian Tsars" and a "complete reorientation of Indian administrative policy" once thought "impossible."[102] She also claimed that the most "salient feature of the new legislation is its land policy. The immediate effect . . . was to halt permanently the policy . . . of individual allotment of the tribal lands, previously owned communally."[103]

In the end, most scholars consider Collier's reform efforts a failure. There are several reasons for this, but Collier himself cited the unwillingness of Congress to appropriate sufficient resources to carry out the program, a consistent complaint since the nineteenth century.[104] In the end, the IRA did not implement self-determination or the full cultural revival Collier sought. In fact, in 1937 Senator Wheeler even introduced legislation to repeal it, though it remained in place until the 1950s.[105] It failed for one simple reason: the American government, despite claims to the contrary, legislation, and well-intentioned proposals, was unable or unwilling to relinquish control of Indian affairs. By the late 1930s, the United States and Soviet Russia diverged significantly in their approach to self-determination. Both governments applied a form of "local federalism," as suggested by Polish scholar Oskar Halecki, in which this form of self-determination "can give satisfaction to the claims of smaller groups or of factions of nationalities, without disorganizing the state to which they belong, by inconsiderate changes of frontier."[106] In a sense, one more reform equaled one more failure. Clearly, for both the Sioux and the Kazakhs, self-determination represented a more rhetorical rather than practical exercise.

US and Soviet government authorities continued to direct and intervene in Sioux and Kazakh political, social, and economic processes. According to anthropologist Thomas Biolsi, the "supervisory power could be invoked by the OIA [Office of Indian Affairs] (and occasionally was) to insure that council actions conformed to such standards as the tribal constitutions, OIA policy, and the democratic ideals of the OIA reformers."[107] The Indian Office "engineered" political consent and cooperation from the Sioux (as well among other Indian tribes) in order to manage "tribal council operations . . . of self-government to the Sioux under the IRA."[108] In Kazakhstan, the Soviet federal system did not assume any devolution of centralized political power, but the policy prior to 1928 was to promote Kazakh national forms—specifically, language and culture. The policies that Collier instituted in the United States, albeit embryonic, were nonetheless self-determination. They shared with Soviet efforts the goal to dismantle forced assimilation or integration (Americanization or Russification) with policies designed to foster respect for and defense of indigenous culture, language, traditions, and arts. In the 1920s and 1930s, government officials in the United States and the Soviet Union deployed similar rhetoric to reform and restructure mechanisms to assimilate the indigenous populations; both governments had Sioux and Kazakh supporters in this effort. The governments allied with these reformers to attach greater emphasis to cultural self-determination of indigenous populations rather than political self-determination that superseded demands for political autonomy, even independence and absolute sovereignty.

Despite this invigorated political and social activism, neither the SAI nor Alash Orda fully affected the change they sought. The SAI was, according to historian Hazel W. Hertzberg, "a town meeting of educated English-speaking Indians rather than a representative confederation of tribes."[109] Sir Olaf Caroe dismissed Alash Orda as an organization that was "never much more than a committee which held congresses and issued manifestos."[110] These rather unsympathetic assessments ignored the cultural, social, literary, and political contributions made by the SAI and Alash. The SAI was the first Indian-led organization that demanded a "voice in federal Indian policy" and "respect for Indians as citizens." It established the foundation for the "next wave of reform during the New Deal."[111] Alash Orda was comparable to the SAI. Alash was an unprecedented voice for Kazakh grievances, a voice that unraveled during the Russian Civil War. In the 1920s, Soviet policies briefly resurrected that Kazakh voice, but the Stalinist terror recklessly and violently silenced it during the chaotic 1930s. The SAI and Alash managed to give voice to those who had none to those willing to listen; the legacy was not just town meetings, conferences, or manifestos. The SAI and Alash managed to preserve and promote the culture, languages, and rich traditions previously deemed primitive and destined to perish with the "touch of civilization."

NOTES

1. J. Russell Smith, "Grassland and Farmland as Factors in the Cyclical Development of Eurasian History," *Annals of the Association of American Geographers* 33, no. 3 (September 1943): 160, emphasis in original.

2. See Daniel R. Headrick, *The Tools of Empire: Technology and European Imperialism in the Nineteenth Century* (New York: Oxford University Press, 1981); Richard Mowbray

Haywood, *The Beginnings of Railway Development in Russia in the Reign of Nicholas I, 1835–1842* (Durham, NC: Duke University Press, 1969); Steven G. Marks, *Road to Power: The Trans-Siberian Railroad and the Colonization of Asian Russia, 1850–1917* (Ithaca, NY: Cornell University Press, 1991).

    3. Eric Hobsbawm, *Industry and Empire: The Birth of the Industrial Revolution* (New York: New Press, 1999), 88. Hobsbawm also writes that "the railways collectively constituted the most massive effort of public building as yet undertaken by man . . . Probably the only other by-product of modern technology, the net of telegraph-lines on their endless succession of wooden poles, about three or four times as great in length as the world's railway system, was more universally known." *The Age of Empire, 1875–1914* (New York: Vintage, 1989), 27.

    4. Richard White, "The American West and American Empire," in *Manifest Destinies and Indigenous Peoples*, ed. David Maybury-Lewis, Theodore Macdonald, and Biorn Maybury-Lewis (Cambridge, MA: Harvard University Press, 2009), 206–7.

    5. Barbara Bush, *Imperialism and Postcolonialism* (Harlow, UK: Pearson Longman, 2006), 84.

    6. "Oklahoma," *New York Times* (May 19, 1874) editorial republished in *Editorializing "The Indian Problem": The "New York Times" on Native Americans, 1860–1900*, ed. Robert Hays (Carbondale: Southern Illinois University Press, 1997), 330.

    7. Steven W. Usselman, *Regulating Railroad Innovation: Business, Technology, and Politics in America, 1840–1920* (Cambridge: Cambridge University Press, 2002), 34.

    8. James Belich, *Replenishing the Earth: The Settler Revolution and the Rise of the Anglo-World, 1783–1939* (Oxford: Oxford University Press, 2009), 108.

    9. K. N. Pos'et, "Prekrashchenie ssylki v Sibiri," *Russkaia starina*, no. 99 (July 1899): 168.

    10. See, for example, Stephen E. Ambrose, *Nothing Like It in the World: The Men Who Built the Transcontinental Railroad, 1863–1869* (New York: Simon & Schuster, 2000); William Carey McKee and Georgeen Klassen, *Trail of Iron: The CPR and the Birth of the West, 1880–1930* (Vancouver: Glenbow-Alberta Institute, 1983); Pierre Berton, *The Impossible Railway: The Building of the Canadian Pacific* (New York: Knopf, 1972).

    11. Alfred Runte, "Promoting the Golden West: Advertising and the Railroad," *California History* 70, no. 1 (Spring 1991): 63. See also Earl S. Pomeroy, *In Search of the Golden West: The Tourist in Western America* (New York: Knopf, 1957).

    12. Willard Sunderland, "Peasant Pioneering: Russian Peasant Settlers Describe Colonization and the Eastern Frontier, 1880s–1910s," *Journal of Social History* 34, no. 4 (Summer 2001): 897.

    13. A. I. Dmitriev-Mámonov and A. F. Zdziárski, eds., *Guide to the Great Siberian Railway* (St. Petersburg: Ministry of Ways of Communication, 1900), 72.

    14. George Demko, *The Russian Colonization of Kazakhstan, 1896–1916* (Bloomington: Indiana University Press, 1969), 58–60. In 1900 one ruble was equal to approximately fifty cents.

    15. See M. Kh. Asylbekov, "Nekotorye voprosy istorii stroitel'stva Orenburgsko-Tashkentskoi zheleznoi dorogi," *Izvestiia Akademii Nauk Kazakhskoi SSR, seriia istorii, arkheologii i etnografii*, no. 2 (1962): 44–61; Maurice, Dobb, *Soviet Economic Development since 1917* (1948; New York: International Publishers, 1968), 35.

    16. Grenville Dodge quoted in White, "American West and American Empire," 206–7.

    17. Jürgen Osterhammel, *Colonialism: A Theoretical Overview* (Kingston: Ian Randle, 1997), 4.

    18. Belich, *Replenishing the Earth*, 230. In retaliation for the 1862 conflict, the government forced the Sioux to leave Minnesota. Sibley and his militia made certain to expel the

Sioux. Sibley remained active throughout 1863 and did not disband his militia but increased its size and marched north to the Minnesota-Dakota Territory border. Several other skirmishes occurred—first at Big Mound and, later, near Dead Buffalo Lake. While these engagements were relatively minor affairs, they increased hostile tensions across the northern plains. The US War Department created the Department of the Northwest, under Maj. Gen. John Pope, to subdue the Sioux and force them to retreat westward into Dakota Territory. Another battle, near Killdeer Mountain in July 1863, revealed the government's intent with this overwhelming military force. The goal was to inflict significant hardship on the Sioux by destroying their food, capturing other supplies, and forcing them, as one historian noted, to "submit to the largesse of the U.S. government." See Bill Yenne, *Indian Wars: The Campaign for the American West* (Yardley, PA: Westholme, 2008), 103.

19. K. K. Palen, *Pereselencheskoe delo v Turkestane* (St. Petersburg: Senatskaia tipografia, 1910), 177–78.

20. *TsGA RK*, f. 15, o. 1, d. 331, l. 22–23.

21. Ibid., 17–18.

22. See Demko, *Russian Colonization of Kazakhstan*.

23. Roger L. Nichols, "The Canada-US Border and Indigenous Peoples in the Nineteenth Century," *American Review of Canadian Studies* 40, no. 3 (September 2010): 421.

24. Quoted in Robert F. Berkhofer Jr., *The White Man's Indian: Images of the American Indian from Columbus to the Present* (New York: Vintage, 1979), 149. See also Carol L. Higham, *Noble, Wretched, and Redeemable: Protestant Missionaries to the Indians in Canada and the United States, 1820–1900* (Albuquerque: University of New Mexico Press, 2000).

25. Francis Paul Prucha, *The Great Father: The United States Government and the American Indians* (Lincoln: University of Nebraska Press, 1984), 1:145. See also Robert F. Berkhofer Jr., *Salvation and the Savage: An Analysis of Protestant Missions and American Indian Response, 1787–1862* (Lexington: University of Kentucky Press, 1965).

26. For an analysis of the creation of contemporaneous imperial ideologies, see Thomas R. Metcalf, *Ideologies of the Raj* (Cambridge: Cambridge University Press, 1994). According to Kenneth Pomeranz, civilizing natives according to some concept of civilization has been around as long as there have been empires. He noted, "Some tried hard to 'civilize' their subjects. For instance, a civilizing agenda has been part of Chinese imperial statecraft for more than two thousand years." "Empire and 'Civilizing' Missions, Past and Present," *Daedalus* 134, no. 2 (Spring 2005): 35. As Barbara Bush noted, "French imperialism was 'an affirmation of universalist republicanism' and civilization, a mission to spread French language, culture, and 'genius' in order to achieve political and cultural assimilation of the colonized." *Imperialism and Postcolonialism*, 24.

27. I. L′vov, "Zavoevanie Turkestana," *Russkii Vestnik*, no. 7 (1868): 173.

28. W. F. Reddaway, ed., *Documents of Catherine the Great: The Correspondence with Voltaire and the Instruction of 1767 in the English Text of 1768* (Cambridge: Cambridge University Press, 1931), 289, emphasis in original.

29. According to Frank T. McCarthy, it was only "during Peter's time do we find mention of Orthodox priests travelling among the native peoples, attempting to convert them." "The Kazan' Missionary Congress," *Cahiers du monde russe et soviétique* 14 (July/September 1973): 311. Historian George V. Lantzeff interpreted the Russian civilizing mission differently, arguing, "Political leaders in Moscow realized that the compulsory introduction of Christianity might antagonize the natives. Consequently the government instructed its local officials and clergy never to use any coercion in converting the natives. Christianity had to prevail 'through

love and not through cruelty.' Noninterference in matters of religion was pursued in spite of some advantages which might have been gained by the Christianization of natives. Baptized men, alienated from their kinsmen by the change of religion, might be enlisted to strengthen the Russian garrisons, while the baptized women could relieve the shortage of women in Siberia by providing wives for the Russian colonists." "Beginnings of the Siberian Colonial Administration," *Pacific Historical Review* 9, no. 1 (March 1940): 51.

30. Fanny E. Bryan, "Organization and Work of Missionaries in the Middle-Volga in the Second Half of the Nineteenth Century," *Islam and Christian-Muslim Relations* 6 (1995): 173–86.

31. According to Alan W. Fisher, "Rather than immediately Russifying the Muslims, Catherine wished only to bring them more completely under Russian administration, to regulate their leadership, and to insure the stability and passivity of this leadership." "Enlightened Despotism and Islam Under Catherine II," *Slavic Review* 27, no. 4 (December 1968): 552. According to Alexander Morrison, "The enlightened absolutist state under Catherine the Great espoused a policy of toleration of Islam, creating a muftiate and Muslim religious assembly at Ufa, and cooperating with the Tatar and Bashkir mullahs whom they considered to be a civilizing influence upon the Kazakh Inner Horde." "Russian Rule in Turkestan and the Example of British India, c. 1860–1917," *Slavonic and East European Review* 84, no. 4 (October 2006): 694–95.

32. Simply because the Russian government tolerated different religious faiths does not mean that discrimination evaporated. The government forced Jews into small enclaves and exiled Old Believers to Siberia. According to one foreign visitor, the Orthodox Church found other, more insidious, means to convert Kazakhs to Christianity: "The most ingenious methods are adopted to bring converts into the bosom of the Orthodox Church—for instance, when a Mussulman parent presents his child for registration under some Mussulman name, the officer, instead of registering the name given, substitutes for it some Christian name, and at a later period the father finds to his horror that his child is a member of the Orthodox Russian Church." There is no way to know if this was a widespread practice or merely a rumor, but the author certainly was convinced it happened. See Charles Rudy, "Despotic Russia, Part II, Adventures in the Steppes of Russian Asia and the Frosty Caucasus," *Reformed Quarterly Review* (July 1880): 353.

33. Karamzin quoted in Seymour Becker, "The Muslim East in Nineteenth-Century Russian Popular Historiography," *Central Asian Survey* 5, nos. 3–4 (1986): 35.

34. For the meaning of grazhdanstvennost' in the nineteenth century, see Vladimir Dal', *Tolkovyi slovar' zhivogo velikorusskogo iazyka v 4 tomakh* (Moscow: Russkii iazyk, 1989), 1:390. See also Marcus Wheeler, *Oxford Russian-English Dictionary* (Oxford: Clarendon, 1972).

35. For an excellent analysis of late nineteenth-century Russian government efforts to manage the empire's Muslim population, see Elena I. Campbell, *The Muslim Question and Russian Imperial Governance* (Bloomington: Indiana University Press, 2015).

36. Mark Cocker, *Rivers of Blood, Rivers of Gold: Europe's Conquest of Indigenous Peoples* (New York: Grove, 1998), 7.

37. Steven Conn, *History's Shadow: Native Americans and Historical Consciousness in the Nineteenth Century* (Chicago: University of Chicago Press, 2004), 5.

38. John W. Slocum, "Who, and When, Were the Inorodtsy? The Evolution of the Category of 'Aliens' in Imperial Russia," *Russian Review* 57, no. 2 (April 1998): 175.

39. Ibid., 184.

40. Gradovskii quoted in Ibid., 185.

41. Ibid.

42. See, for example, Iuliia Aleksandrovna Lysenko, "Missionarskaia deiatel'nost' Russkoi pravoslavnoi tserkvi v Kazakhstane (vtoraia polovine XIX-nachalo XX v.)" (PhD diss., Altai State University, Barnaul, 2011).

43. Ryan Dunch, "Beyond Cultural Imperialism: Cultural Theory, Christian Missions, and Global Modernity," *History and Theory* 41, no. 3 (October 2002): 310.

44. American Society for Promoting the Civilization and General Improvement of the Indian Tribes within the United States, *First Annual Report of the American Society for Promoting the Civilization and General Improvement of the Indian Tribes in the United States. . . .* (New Haven, CT: S. Converse, 1824), 15.

45. Berkhofer, *White Man's Indian*, 150; C. L. Higham, "Saviors and Scientists: North American Protestant Missionaries and the Development of Anthropology," *Pacific Historical Review* 72, no. 4 (November 2003): 535. Interestingly, this belief that more progressive, enlightened settlers can be used to raise up backward peoples is still used to justify internal colonization today. There is no evidence from other internally colonized societies that uplifting a backward people simply by proximity to the resettlement of advanced people in the midst of cultural, economically inferiors worked. Grant Evans identified this process in Vietnam, quoting from Vietnamese anthropologists, who observed that the government's efforts to resettle Vietnamese peasants in the country's central highlands would fill in the "time gap" because the "highland people who, it is believed, failed to evolve." He quotes a Vietnamese government official who claimed, "People of a lower civilization follow those of a higher civilization." "Internal Colonialism in the Central Highlands of Vietnam," *Sojourn: Social Issues in Southeast Asia* 7, no. 2 (August 1992): 291.

46. *First Annual Report*, 16, emphasis in original.

47. Stephen R. Riggs, "Thoughts on Civilizing and Christianizing the Dakota Indians," *Independent* (October 10, 1850).

48. Cited in Peter d'Errico, "Native Americans in America: A Theoretical and Historical Overview," *Wicazo Sa Review* 14, no. 1 (Spring 1999): 19.

49. See, for example, E. K. Sysoeva, "Education Policy in Russia from the 1860s Through the 1890s," *Russian Education & Society* 39 (1997): 62–76; Mariia Viktorovna Sturova, "Obrazovatel'naia sreda na territorii Akmolinskoi i Semipalatinskskoi oblastei (50–80-e gg. XIX v.)," *Izvestiia Altaiskogo Gosudarstvennogo Universiteta* 2, no. 4 (80) (2013): 98–102; Vladimir Aleksandrovich Ermolov, "Osobennosti sistemy obrazovaniia v natsional'niykh shkolakh Rossiiskoi imperii: musul'manskie i evreiskie shkoly," *Obshchestvo. Sreda. Razvitie (Terra Humana)* 4 (2009): 100–109.

50. Alice C. Fletcher, "Indian Education and Civilization," in *Bureau of Education, Special Report, 1888* (Washington, DC: Government Printing Office, 1888), 161.

51. *Report of the Committee to which was referred so much of the President's message, as relates to Indian affairs, accompanied with a bill for establishing trading houses with the Indian tribes. . . .* , 15th Cong., 1st sess., House Document 59. Serial Set 7. (January 22, 1818), 3.

52. S. V. Gorbunova, "Zarozhdenie Russkogo obrazovaniia sredi Kazakhov: shkola pri Orenburgskoi pogranichnoi komissii," in *Kul'tura, Nauka, Obrazovanie: Problemy i Perspekivy, Materialy II vserossiiskoi nauchno-prakticheskoi konferentsii, g. Nizhnevartovsk, 8 Fevralia 2013 goda, Chast' I, Istoriia idei i istoriia obshchestva problemy vseobshchei istorii*, ed. A. V. Korichko (Nizhnevartovsk: Izdatel'stvo Nizhnevartovskogo gosudarstvenogo universiteta, 2013), 31–33.

53. Sturova, "Obrazovatel'naia sreda na territorii Akmolinskoi," 98–102.

54. The best biographical examination of Il'minskii in English remains Isabelle Kreindler, "Educational Policies toward the Eastern Nationalities in Tsarist Russia: A Study of Il'minskii's System" (PhD diss., Columbia University, 1969).

55. See S. Chicherin, *O iazykie prepodavaniia v shkolakh dlia vostochnykh inorodtsev* (St. Petersburg: Tipografiia V. Ia. Mil'shteina, 1910); Wayne Dowler, "The Politics of Language in Non-Russian Elementary Schools in the Eastern Empire, 1865–1914," *Russian Review* 54, no. 4 (October 1995): 516–38. A Kazakh educator, Ibrahim Altynsarin, became a leading proponent of the Il'minskii system in the steppe, and today many Kazakhs consider him one of the Kazakh nation's first modern intellectuals. See Grigorii Grigor'evich Kosach, "Ibragim Altynsarin: chelovek v potoke vremeni," *Vestnik Evrazii* 1–2 (1998): 110–31; Isabelle Kreindler, "Ibrahim Altynsarin, Nikolai Il'minskii and the Kazakh National Awakening," *Central Asian Survey* 2, no. 3 (1983), 99–116; Gulnar Kendirbaeva, "'We are Children of Alash . . .' The Kazakh Intelligentsia at the Beginning of the 20th Century in Search of National Identity and Prospects of the Cultural Survival of the Kazakh People," *Central Asian Survey* 18, no. 1 (March 1999): 5–36.

56. Mustafa Özgür Tuna, "Gaspirali v. Il'minskii: Two Identity Projects for the Muslims of the Russian Empire," *Nationalities Papers* 30, no. 2 (2002): 265–89.

57. Tolstoi quoted in Kreindler, "Educational Policies," 79.

58. See Franklin Edgerton, "Notes on Early American Work in Linguistics," *Proceedings of the American Philosophical Society* 87, no. 1 (July 1943): 31.

59. See Theodore C. Blegen, "The Pond Brothers," *Minnesota History* 15 (September 1934): 273–81.

60. For more about education policies and practices in the United States, see, for example, Scott Riney, *The Rapid City Indian School, 1898–1933* (Norman: University of Oklahoma Press, 1999); Karl Markus Kreis, *Lakotas, Black Robes, and Holy Women: German Reports from the Indian Missions in South Dakota, 1886–1900*, trans. from German by Corinna Dally-Starna (Lincoln: University of Nebraska Press, 2007); David Wallace Adams, *Education for Extinction; American Indians and the Boarding School Experience, 1875–1928* (Lawrence: University Press of Kansas, 1995); Clyde Ellis, *To Change Them Forever: Indian Education at the Rainy Mountain Boarding School, 1893–1920* (Norman: University of Oklahoma Press, 1996); Jacqueline Fear-Segal, *White Man's Club: Schools, Race, and the Struggle of Indian Acculturation* (Lincoln: University of Nebraska Press, 2007); Hayes Peter Mauro, *The Art of Americanization at the Carlisle Indian School* (Albuquerque: University of New Mexico Press, 2011); John Wunder, ed., *Native American Cultural and Religious Freedoms* (New York: Garland, 1999).

61. Quoted in Kreindler, "Educational Policies," 80.

62. The 1870 regulation appeared in *Sbornik Postanovlenii Ministerstva Narodnogo Prosveshcheniia* (St. Petersburg: Ministerstvo Narodnogo Prosveshcheniia, 1871), 4:1555–56.

63. For a contemporary overview of Russian policies, see S. V. Rozhdestvensii, ed., *Istoricheskii obzor deiatel'nosti Ministerstva Narodnogo Proveshcheniia, 1802–1902* (St. Petersburg: Ministerstvo Narodnogo Prosveshcheniia, 1902).

64. US Department of the Interior, Office of Indian Affairs, *Report of the Commissioner of Indian Affairs for the Year 1875* (Washington, DC: Government Printing Office, 1875), 1:526 (hereafter *Annual Report*, year).

65. Ibid.

66. Ibid.

67. *Annual Report*, 1877, 3.

68. *Annual Report*, 1909, 1–2. According to the report, there were 27 non-reservation boarding schools, 82 reservation boarding schools, 194 day schools, 43 mission boarding

schools, 8 mission day schools, and 18 so-called contract schools. In addition, Indians attended nine public schools in the United States. According to Cathleen D. Cahill, the Catholic Church, "which had not played a role in Reconstruction education programs . . . [enjoyed] . . . extraordinary success in capturing federal money for Indian contract schools. In 1886, for example, it received more than half of all federal contract-school dollars, and by 1890 its share had risen to 63 percent." *Federal Fathers and Mothers: A Social History of the United States Indian Service, 1869–1933* (Chapel Hill: University of North Carolina Press, 2011), 43.

69. *Annual Report*, 1909, 153.

70. *Annual Report*, 1887, 23.

71. Ibid., 23–24.

72. "Letter from Commissioner of Indian Affairs to Pine Ridge Agent Hugh D. Gallagher," July 16, 1887, box 8, Records of the Bureau of Indian Affairs, Pine Ridge Agency, Pine Ridge, South Dakota, Record Group 75, National Archives and Records Administration at Kansas City.

73. For a brief biographical sketch, see Floyd O'Neil, "John H. Oberly, 1888–89," in *The Commissioners of Indian Affairs, 1824–1977*, ed. Robert M. Kvasnicka and Herman J. Viola (Lincoln: University of Nebraska Press, 1979), 189–91.

74. The report also included the numbers of employees at schools run by the Bureau, totaling 894 people, 137 being Indians. Of the 241 teachers, the report did not describe even one as a "teacher"; the majority of Indians were listed in menial jobs such as "Assistant matrons," "Assistant seamstresses," "Assistant cooks," and "Assistant laundresses." *Annual Report*, 1888, xvii.

75. See, for example, Wayne Dowler, *Classroom and Empire: The Politics of Schooling Russia's Eastern Nationalities, 1860–1917* (Montreal: McGill-Queen's University Press, 2001).

76. Thomas G. Andrews, "Turning the Tables on Assimilation: Oglala Lakotas and the Pine Ridge Day Schools, 1889–1920s," *Western Historical Quarterly* 33, no. 4 (Winter 2002): 422–25.

77. Edward J. Lazzerini, "Defining the Orient: A Nineteenth Century of Russo-Tatar Polemic over Identity and Cultural Representation," in *Russia's Orient: Imperial Borderlands and Peoples, 1700–1917*, ed. Daniel R. Brower and Edward J. Lazzerini (Bloomington: Indiana University Press, 1997), 40.

78. Karl Mannheim, *Ideology and Utopia: An Introduction of the Sociology of Knowledge* (New York: Harcourt Brace, 1936), 10.

79. Ayşe Kadioğlu, "The Paradox of Turkish Nationalism and the Construction of Official Identity," *Middle Eastern Studies* 32, no. 2 (1996): 14.

80. Benedict Anderson, *Imagined Communities: Reflections on the Origin and Spread of Nationalism*, rev. ed. (London: Verso, 1991): 116.

81. The Society of American Indians was a pan-Indian movement; it held annual conferences and published its own periodical. Alash Orda was the Kazakh faction that split from a broader Pan-Turkic, Muslim oriented sociopolitical movement that emerged shortly after the 1905 Russian Revolution. It too held numerous meetings, but, more importantly, it started publishing a newspaper—*Kazak*—also in 1913.

82. Beth LaDow, *The Medicine Line: Life and Death on a North American Borderland* (New York: Routledge, 2002), 181.

83. William A. Peffer, "Imperialism America's Historic Policy," *North American Review* 171 (August 1900): 256–57.

84. Ibid.

85. White, "American West and American Empire," 218–19.

86. Andreas Kappeler, *The Russian Empire: A Multiethnic History*, trans. Alfred Clayton (New York: Pearson Education, 2001), 334.

87. The best work in English about the revolt remains Edward Sokol, *The Revolt of 1916 in Russian Central Asia* (Baltimore: Johns Hopkins Press, 1954). Sokol, however, resorted to traditional interpretations of nomadic society by claiming that it was "understandable that when the nomads were directly affected, as in 1916, they reacted in a vigorous return to their *ancestral tradition of violence and raiding warfare*" (69) (emphasis added). See also TsGA RK, f. 554, o. 2, d. 225, l. 6. According to this archival source, the majority of Kazakhs who revolted were impoverished, whereas "those standing with the government are the privileged class, the rich."

88. In 1924 the Soviet Union delimitated boundaries into ethno-national units, including the Kazakh Soviet Socialist Republic (KazSSR). It also introduced a new nationalities policy, *korenizatsiia* (nativization), designed to give nationalities a greater voice in the various republics. Stalinism eviscerated this form of autonomy, which quickly evaporated in the 1930s. The government accused Bokeikhanov and Baitursynov of nationalism and executed them both. Rehabilitation came only in 1989. The political system remained in place until the Soviet Union's collapse in 1991, and Kazakhstan became the independent Republic of Kazakhstan.

89. See, for example, Janet A. McDonnell, *The Dispossession of the American Indian, 1887–1934* (Bloomington: Indiana University Press, 1991); Russel Lawrence Barsh, "Progressive-Era Bureaucrats and the Unity of Twentieth-Century Indian Policy, *American Indian Quarterly* 15, no. 1 (Winter 1991): 1–17; Leonard A. Carlson, "Federal Policy and Indian Land: Economic Interests and the Sale of Indian Allotments, 1900–1934," *Agricultural History* 57 (January 1983): 33–45.

90. "America Needs Men," *American Indian Magazine* 5 (January–March 1917): 5, emphasis in original.

91. Lewis Meriam et al., *The Problem of Indian Administration: Report of a Survey made at the request of Honorable Hubert Work, Secretary of the Interior, and Submitted to him, February 21, 1928* (Baltimore: Johns Hopkins Press, 1928), 3.

92. Margaret Szasz, "Indian Reform in a Decade of Prosperity," *Montana The Magazine of Western History* 20, no. 1 (Winter 1970): 21.

93. Michla Pomerance, "The United States and Self Determination: Perspectives on the Wilsonian Conception," *American Journal of International Law* 70, no. 1 (January 1976): 2.

94. Rupert Emerson, "Self-Determination," *American Journal of International Law* 65, no. 3 (1971): 472.

95. See Terry Martin, *The Affirmative Action Empire: Nations and Nationalism in the Soviet Union, 1923–1939* (Ithaca, NY: Cornell University Press, 2001).

96. *S'ezdy sovetov RSFSR i avtonomnykh respublik RSFSR*, vol. 1 (Moscow, 1959), 718.

97. For a memoir of this tragic time, see Mukhamet Shayakhmetov, *The Silent Steppe: The Memoir of a Kazakh Nomad Under Stalin*, trans. Jan Butler (New York: Overlook/Rookery, 2006).

98. Joseph Stalin, *Sochineniia* (Moscow: Gospolitizdat, 1946–1951), 13:306–9.

99. Burton K. Wheeler with Paul F. Healy, *Yankee from the West: The Candid, Turbulent Life Story of the Yankee-Born U.S. Senator from Montana* (New York: Doubleday, 1962), 314–15.

100. President Roosevelt's letter to the bill's sponsors in H.R. Rep. No. 1804, 73rd Cong., 2d sess., at 8 (1934).

101. Office of Indian Affairs, *Indians at Work* 1 (Washington, DC: Office of Indian Affairs, March 1, 1934), 1.

102. Elizabeth Green, "Indian Minorities Under the American New Deal," *Pacific Affairs* 8, no. 4 (December 1935): 420.

103. Ibid., 424–25.

104. John Collier, *From Every Zenith: A Memoir; and Some Essays on Life and Thought* (Denver: Sage, 1963), 190–91; John Collier, *Indians of the Americas: The Long Hope* (New York: W. W. Norton, 1947), 169; D'Arcy McNickle and Harold E. Fey, *Indians and Other Americans: Two Ways of Life Meet* (New York: Harper & Brothers, 1959), 116–17.

105. For an excellent analysis of this period as it relates to the Sioux, see Akim D. Reinhardt, *Ruling Pine Ridge: Oglala Lakota Politics from the IRA to Wounded Knee* (Lubbock: Texas Tech University Press, 2007). See esp. chaps. 2–4.

106. See Oskar Halecki, "The Problem of Self-Determination," *Proceedings of the American Philosophical Society* 87, no. 2 (August 1943): 194–98.

107. Thomas Biolsi, "The IRA and the Politics of Acculturation: The Sioux Case," *American Anthropologist* 87, no. 3 (1985): 657.

108. Ibid., 658.

109. Hazel W. Hertzberg, *The Search for an American Indian Identity: Modern Pan-Indian Movements* (Syracuse, NY: Syracuse University Press, 1971), 96.

110. Olaf Caroe, *Soviet Empire: The Turks of Central Asia and Stalinism* (New York: St. Martin's, 1967), 104.

111. Patricia Lee Furnish, "'Aboriginally Yours': The Society of American Indians and U.S. Citizenship" (PhD diss., University of Oklahoma, 2005), 172.

Conclusion

American and Russian internal colonization of the plains and the steppe were phases in a broader national history of expansion. The contiguous expansion occupied different rostra of nineteenth-century European imperialism and colonialism, but the processes of American and Russian expansion and internal colonization illustrate a common set of assumptions and expectations about the land and the indigenous peoples being incorporated also exhibited by contemporary European empires. The American expansionist ideology engendered by its European ancestors—chiefly Britain—amalgamated Lockean liberalism rooted in a philosophy that emphasized private property, individualism, civil liberties, hard work, and contracts. It evolved to coalesce into a purposeful, almost messianic sense of divine mission to conquer the North American continent and to civilize and Americanize the natives. Initially, Russian expansion had no such mission; it was driven by trade and security. By the late nineteenth century, however, Russia's mission evolved to unveil a comparable civilizing agenda designed to integrate non-Russians into an imperial, but not national, framework and identity.[1]

By the second half of the nineteenth century, the US government insisted that the Sioux completely assimilate in language, dress, and work—a process euphemistically described as Americanism. During the same period, the Russian government simply desired loyal subjects faithful to the empire; it did not want to turn Kazakhs into Russians. It was desirable for Kazakhs to adopt the Russian language, culture, and religion but not required. The Russians wanted the Kazakhs to integrate, not assimilate; however, Russia also wanted Kazakh land, increased trade, and enhanced security, which the Kazakh Steppe supplied in abundance. These imperial colonizing traits manifested in numerous other colonial contexts, such as the British in India and Africa and the French in Algeria.[2] In that sense, the United States and Russia mimicked their imperial contemporaries. As with other empires, the United States and Russia depicted the Other—the people on the frontier—as the savage or barbarian. The Roman Empire, as historian Bernhard Maier observed, viewed the Celts from the perspective of a "military adversary" that "goes hand in hand with unconcealed propagandist intent, which places disproportionately strong emphasis on the wild and warlike aspect."[3] The American, Russian, British, and other nineteenth-century European empires used comparable prisms to observe, conquer, and colonize. Americans and Russians did not concoct the prisms, typologies, and images to view their colonized peoples. Instead, they merely inherited the caricatures and fashioned them to suit their nineteenth-century sensibilities.

Americans and Russians characterized the Sioux and the Kazakhs as locked in a time capsule of sorts, capable of civilized behavior but separated from the society and culture the colonizers expected them to imitate. The Sioux settled on reservations, attended government-sanctioned schools to learn English and a trade, and were expected to adopt Christianity. The Russian government forced most Kazakhs to settle; school was expected for only some to serve the empire; and conversion to Christianity was anticipated by the Russians as only a tool to combat their increased fear of an aroused Islam.[4]

What made the United States and tsarist Russia different from their European counterparts was obvious: the contiguous nature of the empires and internal colonization. The civilizing mission was internal rather than external, but it shared comparable objectives. By the start of the twentieth century, the United States and Russia erected the primary mechanisms to fulfill internal colonization of the Sioux and the Kazakhs. Allotment and education posed the twin pillars to civilize them. By the 1890s, the Sioux and the Kazakhs resisted, not with guns and rebellion, but in print and adaptation. Sioux and Kazakh intellectuals—educated to assimilate or integrate—adapted, adopted, and challenged American and Russian civilizing ideologies. This was contrary to many contemporary expectations, expressed by nineteenth-century sociologist John S. MacKenzie, who observed,

> When a people is conquered and subjected to another, it ceases to be a society, except in so far as it retains a spiritual life of its own apart from that of its

conquerors. Yet it does not become an integral part of the victorious people's life, until it is able to appropriate to itself the spirit of that life. So long as the citizens of the conquered state are merely in the condition of atoms externally fitted into a system to which they do not naturally belong, they cannot be regarded as parts of the society at all. They are slaves: they are instruments of a civilization of which they do not partake. Certainly no more melancholy fate can befall a nation than that it should be subjected to another whose life is not large enough to absorb its own.[5]

The British and French constructed civilizing ideologies to elevate and sustain external imperial identities, which the colonizer designed to civilize the colonized people of the empire. For the British and the French, this process was empire building; but due to the contiguous expansion of the United States and Russia, the process was both an empire and, differently from other nineteenth-century empires, simultaneously a state-building process. Americans accepted state-building—they considered expansion across the continent to be an organic process—but many Americans rejected the idea that continental expansion was also imperialism. Russia's expansion was equally organic but unabashedly imperial. The lands and peoples were subjects of the tsar, the societies that remained barbarous and backward. Consequently, Americans and Russians considered the Sioux and the Kazakhs to be expendable exteriors to the dominant society and the state. Russia embraced the imperial concept, but the United States rhetorically rejected it.

These imperial civilizing justifications, adopted not just by overseas empires such as Britain and France but the United States and Russia as well, exacerbated tensions between colonized and colonizer. As scholars have noted, the imperial colonizing goal to elevate a people from savagery to civilization also incubated the justification for its own imperial destruction.[6] For the United States and Russia, however, the imperial ideology was as much about civilizing the indigenous populations as it was civilizing wilderness. The state uniformly assimilated the land but not the people. The people did not disappear—civilization did not exterminate them—but they adapted and survived. Nonetheless, the perception persisted well into the twentieth century that the indigenous peoples caught in American and Russian continental expansions seemingly evaporated in the onslaught of internal colonization. In a 1962 essay titled "Colonialism," historian A. P. Thornton argued that indigenous populations that resisted "expansion of empire overland have . . . been expunged both from the map and the historical conscience—and this is true of the Red Indians of North America as to the Turkomans of Central Asia."[7]

Though Thornton's observation was not a specific reference to the Sioux or the Kazakhs, the point is relevant to this comparison because it conveys the perception rather than the reality: the intrinsic notion that the United States and tsarist Russia exterminated the colonized indigenous peoples, the languages and cultures lost. Moreover, Thornton echoed nineteenth-century expectations of the one inevitable outcome of continental expansion: that the "touch of civilization" always overwhelmed indigenous peoples.[8] Instead, in the early twentieth century, many well-educated Sioux and Kazakhs adapted and organized social movements that used print — newspapers, magazines, and journals — to validate their languages and cultures. These intellectuals emerged as spokesmen for their people at the very moment the United States and Russia confronted two very different crises of identity that followed America's victory in the Spanish-American War and Russia's defeat by the Japanese and the 1905 Russian Revolution.

THE COMPARATIVE PERSPECTIVE

One of the most inherently comparative statements anyone can make about the United States or Russia is that they were, or are, exceptional. The United States and Russia expanded across continents; internally colonized indigenous peoples who lived there; incorporated those peoples into the political entity; allotted lands; and exercised political, social, and cultural control over those peoples with education, language, and religion to integrate, assimilate, or separate them from the dominant colonizing society. The United States and Russia exhibited all of the traits typically associated with nineteenth-century European imperialism in Africa and Asia; the only difference was contiguous expansion as opposed to overseas expansion. The processes might have differed; the consequences for the Sioux and the Kazakhs did not.

The comparative perspective reveals much about empires — their construction, their methods of conquest and administration, their typologies and perceptions, and their uniqueness and similarities. The United States and Russia were not exceptional; they were not unique empires. That does not mean, however, that these two empires did not develop idiosyncratic processes or share commonalities with one other. The Americans and the Russians used allotment and education to accomplish the same thing — compliant subjects of the empire — but the way the colonizers' allotted land and the manner in which the American and Russian governments educated Sioux and Kazakh children was different.

The United States and Russia paralleled, though not precisely, each other in their continental expansion and internal colonization. They developed policies and processes based on many common assumptions, expectations, ideologies, typologies, and consequences for those internally colonized. The United States and tsarist Russia were, as historians Ann Laura Stoler and Carole McGranahan noted, "quintessential" empires, "consummate producers of excepted populations, excepted spaces, and their own exception from international and domestic laws."[9] And yet, in the United States, the debate about American exceptionalism continues. In Russia, the Soviets rejected the idea of Russia's imperial exceptionalism and replaced it with a new Soviet ideology, founding mythologies, and typologies to create a new Soviet exceptionalism. These exceptionalist arguments, whether American, Russian, or Soviet, often, as historian Mary Nolan argued, "promote their own silences and omissions" that mask "the complex nature of American society and its similarities with the interconnections to other nations."[10] The collapse of the Soviet Union ended its exceptionalist claims, forcing reinterpretations of the past—both tsarist and Soviet—in Russia, Kazakhstan, Ukraine, and Georgia. Frederick Jackson Turner's frontier thesis still animates debates among American scholars.

Comparative history ought to illuminate something about the subjects being compared that might not be clear and evident when examined in isolation because, as historians Frederick Cooper, George M. Fredrickson, and James T. Campbell argued, "Comparison suggests the multiple possibilities, pathways, and dead ends that exist within a broader history. A global, interactive approach to history needs comparison, and comparison needs interactive and global analysis."[11] The United States and tsarist Russia in the nineteenth century expanded their empires comparable to other European overseas imperial and colonial processes. Travelers to the American plains and the Kazakh Steppe saw the similarities—not just the geographic similarities but the consequences of expansion and internal colonization. In the nineteenth century, as David M. Wrobel argued in *Global West, American Frontier*, travelers "often placed the West in a broader, comparative global context, viewing it as one developing frontier among many and considering the United States as a colonizing power (like its European progenitors)."[12]

A common feature of empires was the ability of the colonizing society—in this case, Americans and Russians—to express a self-perception that justified expansion and colonization. The United States clearly did so through Manifest Destiny throughout the nineteenth century. Manifest Destiny was a concept rooted in the belief that the United States was a Christian nation that providence selected to expand across the continent, save the Indian from extinction, spread the agrarian ideal, and exploit the bounty that was heretofore neglected and wasted by a race incapable of progressing without the guidance and firm hand of a benevolent American people. The Russians' self-perception stemmed from a belief that the racism evident in American or British empire building was a malignant sort; many Russians believed that they possessed a unique ability to absorb alien peoples into the empire. They believed the conflict and opposition they encountered in the Kazakh Steppe, the Caucasus, and Turkestan was not a response to Russian expansion, but that it derived from an Islamic fanaticism—a social and cultural backwardness that repressed the peoples the empire colonized. Americans and Russians believed they had a Christian duty to save the Sioux and the Kazakhs from the very fabrics of their social, cultural, economic, and political structures that kept them living a nomadic and barbaric life.

The problem with both self-perceptions was that each served a single master: both demanded the land from the people already living and using that land. It was American and Russian self-delusion that failed to recognize that the Sioux and the Kazakhs fought for the land, not just for the ostensibly barbaric culture, society, and economies. The Sioux and the Kazakhs fought for the land that sustained the nomadic life, which existed in juxtaposition to the agrarian perfection Americans and Russians believed was necessary to survive. Americans and Russians believed the agrarian ideal was an essential process to elevate the Sioux and the Kazakhs above the nomadic barbarism they seemingly inhabited. The conflict emerged because the Sioux and the Kazakhs simply gave the land a different value—one that was economic, of course, but one intrinsically connected to their culture, society, and way of life. Moreover, Sioux and Kazakh societies were not stagnant, which contrasted with American and Russian perceptions. Sioux and Kazakh societies and cultures were always in transition, adapting new technologies and strategies to cope with the internal and external pressures that challenged their way of life.

Students of Russian and Soviet imperialism can be, by the same token, seduced by the uniqueness or exceptionalist view, based upon perceptions of tsarist autocracy or Soviet/Stalinist brutality. Moreover, when students of rich Russian history compare its imperial designs and extraordinary geographic expansion, the comparison is usually internal to the empire itself. For example, one might compare central Asia and the Caucasus, or Finland and Poland; even within central Asia itself the comparison might be between the steppe and Turkestan, or a sedentary-nomadic dichotomy. Rarely have students of Russian imperialism ventured outside, except, as Adeeb Khalid noted, to compare Russia with the British Empire. Yet, even an astute scholar like Khalid fell into the "uniqueness" trap when he wrote, "Colonial conquest transformed colonized societies, but colonial empires seldom used state power to transform societies, cultures, or individuals in the way attempted by the Soviet state."[13] But that is precisely what the United States did to the Sioux, and certainly what tsarist Russia wanted to do to the Kazakhs, in the nineteenth century.

This study chiefly focused upon American and Russian central government policies—particularly in the United States, where the Sioux depended upon the federal government rather than individual states. That should not suggest, however, that the states played no role, but that policy typically emanated in Washington and was implemented on reservations or other federal lands by federal employees working for federal institutions. In contrast, in the Russian Empire, the central government in Saint Petersburg developed policies to operate in the various provinces and governor-generalships in Siberia, Turkestan, and the Kazakh Steppe. Russian government officials—in particular, the governor-generals—had far more latitude to execute policies as they saw fit. American governors had no authority to adjust or implement policies on reservations in their states. So Russia, the autocratic and despotic regime, manifested less oversight in local affairs in nationality questions than did Washington, the decentralized and democratic icon, with the "Indian Question." This was, in part, due to constitutional authority in the United States to deal with Indians being vested in the federal government, not in the states; in Russia, no such structure existed. The tsar ruled, the tsar appointed, and the tsar governed; but the tsar relied on thousands of government officials to follow his decrees and that created a highly malleable environment for policy interpretation for those on the ground in the Kazakh Steppe.

American and Russian colonization of the northern Great Plains and the Kazakh Steppe situates comfortably within the framework of nineteenth-century global imperial-colonial expansion. American and Russian colonization of contiguous territories compares well with the mainstream of the analogous phenomenon in Africa and Asia. As with British, French, or Belgian imperialism, the perceptions of uninhabited or underutilized land, backward peoples, or untapped resources justified the need to expand and colonize. The colonizers intended to bring agriculture and develop the resources that fueled and financed their industry. In addition, the imperial powers reconfigured the mission from one of economics to culture and society to elevate the seemingly backward peoples from their barbarism. Imperialism and colonialism was also, ultimately, about people: those who colonized with a self-conceptualized civilizing agenda and those who were the target of that expansion and subsequent colonization.

The process of incorporating the Sioux and the Kazakhs into the expanding country's territorial and political structures was a comparable divide-and-conquer method. The Americans and the Russians used treaties and oaths to get bands or clans to cede land, swear loyalty, or surrender their political and economic sovereignty. The United States and Russia recognized the political—perhaps national—sovereignty of the Sioux and the Kazakhs, but they never signed treaties or swore oaths with a single representative who legitimately spoke for, or had the right to speak for, the entire community. The Sioux and the Kazakhs did not have national leaders and did not have governance mechanisms to represent all Sioux or all Kazakhs; they did not have comparable political systems capable of behaving like a nation-state, nor did they necessarily want that structure. Each treaty or oath taken by one or a few Sioux or Kazakhs did not represent all Sioux or all Kazakhs. The US and Russian governments understood this fact but typically faulted the backward sociopolitical structures of the Sioux and the Kazakhs rather than acknowledge the tactic and policies of divide and conquer. The United States signed treaties with bands and the Russians accepted oaths from clan or even horde khans, but there was never an occasion when Sioux chiefs or Kazakh khans could legitimately claim to represent the nation.

The benefit of this comparison is that examining the internal colonization of the Sioux and the Kazakhs through the comparative prism demonstrates that the United States engaged in an expansionist agenda that differed little from the Russian experience. The internal colonization produced an overwhelming response and use of force to localized affairs, but it was clearly motivated by a desire to complete the colonization of land that was arguably controlled by a native people. Internal colonization provoked resistance and conflict, and these conflicts represented military resistance by a people whose political sovereignty the colonizers already determined lacked national unity or a national integrity to be treated as equals. In that sense, the American expansion west was not a unique colonizing exercise somehow separated from other nineteenth-century European colonizations. And yet, American and Russian perceptions of their continental expansions still maintain a powerful influence on their respective national imaginations.

NOTES

1. As historian Robert J. Kerner described it in 1948, the "Russian people have been and still are a nation in movement. They used their unique river system to reach the seas . . . colonization in one river basin after the other and an advance eastward from one river system over easy portages to the next were the chief characteristics of the Russian movement of exploration and acquisition from the Urals to the Pacific." "The Russian Eastward Movement: Some Observations on Its Historical Significance," *Pacific Historical Review* 17, no. 2 (May 1948): 135–36.

2. See, for example, David Prochaska, *Making Algeria French: Colonialism in Bône, 1870–1920* (Cambridge: Cambridge University Press, 1990); Catherine Hall, *Civilising Subjects: Metropole and Colony in the English Imagination, 1830–1867* (Chicago: University

of Chicago Press, 2002); Julie Evans, Patricia Grimshaw, and David Phillips, *Equal Subjects, Unequal Rights: Indigenous People in British Settler Colonies, 1830–1910* (Manchester: Manchester University Press, 2003); Saliha Belmessous, *Assimilation and Empire: Uniformity in French and British Colonies, 1541–1954* (Oxford: Oxford University Press, 2013).

3. Bernhard Maier, *The Celts: A History from Earliest Times to the Present*, trans. Kevin Windle (Edinburgh: Edinburgh University Press, 2003), 96.

4. By the 1890s, the Russian government started to fear the Pan-Islamic rhetoric that seemed to be coming from central Asia. The laws granting religious freedoms following the 1905 revolution heightened those fears. The Orthodox Church determined to accelerate conversion to Orthodoxy because, it was feared, that the hearts of the empire's Muslims lay with Turkey, not with Russia. Critics charged that the government's policy of allowing Tatar mullahs to operate among the Kazakhs actually worked against government interests, turning the Kazakhs from nominal Muslims into fanatical ones. Islam was no longer a means to civilize the Kazakhs; it was an enemy within the empire that must be eliminated. See Frank T. McCarthy, "The Kazan' Missionary Congress," *Cahiers du monde russe et soviétique* 14, no. 3 (July/September 1973), 308–32.

5. John S. MacKenzie, *An Introduction to Social Philosophy* (New York: Macmillan and Co., 1895), 172–73. MacKenzie further argued, "In so far as there is growth in such a case, it is still a growth from within. The conquering society must be able to absorb the conquered one into itself; otherwise the latter cannot be regarded as forming a real part of it at all, but at most as an instrument of its life, like cattle and trees. And similar remarks may be made of those who in any other way drop out of touch with the life of their people. In so far as they cease to be a part of the system to which they belong, and become only instruments of its advancement or impediments in its way. Such facts illustrate rather the disintegration than the growth of society" (173).

6. Ann Laura Stoler and Frederick Cooper, "Between Metropole and Colony: Rethinking a Research Agenda," in *Tensions of Empire: Colonial Cultures in a Bourgeois World*, ed. Frederick Cooper and Ann Laura Stoler (Berkeley: University of California Press, 1997), 1–56.

7. A. P. Thornton, "Colonialism," *International Journal* 17, no. 4 (Autumn 1962): 344–45.

8. John Foster Fraser, *The Real Siberia: Together with an Account of a Dash Through Manchuria* (London: Cassell, 1904), 42.

9. Ann Laura Stoler and Carole McGranahan, "Introduction: Reconfiguring Imperial Terrains," in *Imperial Formations*, ed. Ann Laura Stoler, Carole McGranahan, and Peter C. Purdue (Santa Fe, School for Advanced Research Press, 2007), 11.

10. Mary Nolan, "Against Exceptionalisms," review of *American Exceptionalism: A Double-Edged Sword*, by Seymour Martin Lipset, *American Historical Review* 102, no. 3 (June 1997): 773–74.

11. Frederick Cooper, George M. Fredrickson, and James T. Campbell, "Race, Ideology, and the Perils of Comparative History," *American Historical Review* 101, no. 4 (October 1996): 1135.

12. David M. Wrobel, *Global West, American Frontier: Travel, Empire, and Exceptionalism from Manifest Destiny to the Great Depression* (Albuquerque: University of New Mexico Press, 2013), 22.

13. Adeeb Khalid, "Backwardness and the Quest for Civilization: Early Soviet Central Asia in Comparative Perspective," *Slavic Review* 65, no. 2 (Summer 2006): 233.

Bibliography

PRIMARY SOURCES

Archives

Tsentral'nyi gosudarstvennyi arkiv, Respublika Kazakhstana (Central State Archive). Almaty, Kazakhstan.

Omskogo oblgosarkiva (Omsk Oblast Archive). Omsk, Russia.

National Archives and Records Administration. Record Group 75. Records of the Bureau of Indian Affairs, Pine Ridge Agency, Pine Ridge, South Dakota, National Archives at Kansas City.

Published

Abdairaeiymov, S., ed. *Golod v Kazakhskoi Stepi: pisma trevogi i boli*. Almaty: Kazakh Universiteti, 1991.

Abramof, N., and John Michell. "Semipalatinsk." *Journal of the Royal Geographical Society of London* 32 (1862): 555–59. http://dx.doi.org/10.2307/1798423.

American Society for Promoting the Civilization and General Improvement of the Indian Tribes within the United States. *First Annual Report of the American Society for Promoting the Civilization and General Improvement of the Indian Tribes in the United States. . . .* New Haven, CT: S. Converse, 1824.

Andreev, I. G. *Opisanie Srednei ordy Kirgiz-kaisakov*. 1785. Almaty: Ghylym, 1998.

Anderson, Gary Clayton, and Alan R. Woolworth, eds. *Through Dakota Eyes: Narrative Accounts of the Minnesota Indian War of 1862*. St. Paul: Minnesota Historical Society Press, 1988.

Atkinson, Thomas Witlam. *Oriental and Western Siberia: A Narrative of Seven Years' Explorations and Adventures in Siberia, Mongolia, the Kirghis Steppes, Chinese Tartary, and a Part of Central Asia*. New York: Harper & Bros, 1858.
Bokeikhanov, Alikkhan. "Istoricheskie sud'by Kirgizskogo kraia i kul'turnye ego uspekhi." In *Rossiia: Polnoe geograficheshoe opisanie nashego otechestva*. Vol. 17, edited by V. P. Semenov-Tian-Shanskii, 156–76. St. Petersburg: Izd. A.F. Devriena, 1903.
Bokeikhanov, Alikkhan. "Pereselencheskie nadely v Akmolinskoi oblasti." *Sibirskie voprosy*, nos. 27–28 (1908): 4–21.
Bokeikhanov, Alikhan. *Shygharmalar*. Almaty, 1994.
Bookwalter, John W. *Siberia and Central Asia*. Springfield, OH, 1899.
Boyd, Julian P., ed. *The Papers of Thomas Jefferson*. Vol. 4, *1 October 1780–24 February 1781*. Princeton, NJ: Princeton University Press, 1951.
Bronevskii, S. B. "O Kirgiz'-Kaisakakh' Srednei Ordy'." *Otechestvennyi zapiski* (1830): 375–450.
Burnaby, Fred. *A Ride to Khiva: Travels and Adventures in Central Asia*. New York: Harper & Brothers, 1876.
Catlin, George. *North American Indians*. 1841. Edited by Peter Matthiessen. New York: Penguin, 2004.
Censuses of Canada, 1608 to 1876. 5 vols. Ottawa: Maclean, Roger, 1878.
Chicherin, S. *O iazyke prepodavaniia v shkolakh dlia vostochnykh inorodtsev*. St. Petersburg: Tipografiia V. Ia. Mil'shteina, 1910.
Custine, Astolphe, Marquis de. *The Empire of the Czar; or, Observations on the Social, Political, and Religious State and Prospects of Russia, made during a Journey through that Empire*. Translated from French. 3 vols. London: Longman, Brown, Green, & Longmans, 1843.
Denig, Edwin Thompson. *Five Indian Tribes of the Upper Missouri: Sioux, Arickaras, Assiniboines, Crees, Crows*. Edited by John C. Ewers. Norman: University Oklahoma Press, 1961.
de Staël, Madame. *Ten Years' Exile; or, Memoirs of That Interesting Period of the Life of the Baroness de Staël-Holstein, Written by Herself, during the Years 1810, 1811, 1812, and 1813, and Now First Published from the Original Manuscript, by Her Son*. Translated from French. London: Treuttel & Würtz, Jun. & Richter, 1821.
Dmitriev-Mámonov, A. I., and A. F. Zdziárski, eds. *Guide to the Great Siberian Railway*. St. Petersburg: Ministry of Ways of Communication, 1900.
Eastman, Charles A. *Indian Boyhood*. New York: McClure, Phillips, 1902.
Eastman, Charles A. *From the Deep Woods to Civilization: Chapters in the Autobiography of an Indian*. Boston: Little, Brown, 1916.
Eastman, Charles A. *Indian Heroes and Great Chieftains*. New York: Quill Pen Classics, 2008.
Elias, Ney, ed. *The Tarikh-i-Rashidi of Mirza Muhammad Haidar, Dughlát: A History of the Moghuls of Central Asia*. Translated by E. Denison Ross. Reprint ed. Patna: Academica Asiatica, 1973.
Eliseev, Efrem. *Zapiski Missionera Bukonskago Stana Kirgizskoi Missii za 1892–1899 gg*. St. Petersburg: Tip. Spb. akts. obshch. diela v Rossii E. Evdokimov, 1900.
Fletcher, Alice C. "Indian Education and Civilization." In *Bureau of Education, Special Report, 1888*. Washington, DC: Government Printing Office, 1888.
Flint, Timothy. "The Personal Narrative of James O. Pattie of Kentucky." In *Early Western Travels, 1748–1846*. 1833. Vol. 18, edited by Reuben Gold Thwaites. Cleveland, OH: Arthur H. Clark, 1905.

Fraser, John Foster. *The Real Siberia: Together with an Account of a Dash Through Manchuria*. London: Cassell, 1904.
Glinka, G. V., ed. *Aziatskaia Rossiia*. 1914. 2 vols. St. Petersburg: Obshchestvenniia pol'za, 1974.
Grudzinska Gross, Irena. *The Scar of Revolution: Custine, Tocqueville, and the Romantic Imagination*. Berkeley: University of California Press, 1991.
Hafen, LeRoy R., and Ann W. Hafen, eds. *Relations with the Indians of the Plains, 1857–1861: A Documentary Account of the Military Campaigns, and Negotiations of Indian Agents—with Reports and Journals of P. G. Love, R. M. Peck, J. E. B. Stuart, S. D. Sturgis, and Other Official Papers*. Glendale, CA: Arthur H. Clark, 1959.
Hafen, LeRoy R., and Ann W. Hafen, eds. *Powder River Campaigns and Sawyers Expedition of 1865: A Documentary Account Comprising Official Reports, Diaries, Contemporary Newspaper Accounts, and Personal Narratives*. Glendale, CA: Arthur H. Clark, 1961.
Heard, Isaac V. D. *History of the Sioux War and Massacres of 1862 and 1863*. New York: Harper & Brothers, 1863.
Hennepin, Louis. *A New Discovery of a Vast Country in America*. . . . Vol. 2, edited by Reuben Gold Thwaites. Chicago: A. C. McClurg, 1903.
Herndon, Sarah Raymond. *Days on the Road: Crossing the Plains in 1865*. New York: Burr Printing House, 1902.
Huntington, Ellsworth. "The Mountains and Kibitkas of Tian Shan." *Bulletin of the American Geographical Society* 37, no. 9 (1905): 513–30. http://dx.doi.org/10.2307/198402.
Il'minskii, Nikolai I. *O perevode pravoslavnykh khristianskikh knig na inorodcheskie iazyky*. Kazan: n.p., 1875.
Ivanin, M. "Vnutrenniaia ili Bukeevskaia Orda." *Epokha*, no. 12 (1864): 1–117.
James, Edwin. "Account of an Expedition from Pittsburgh to the Rocky Mountains performed in the years 1819, 1820." In *Early Western Travels*. Vol. 15, edited by Reuben Gold Thwaites. Cleveland, OH: Arthur H. Clark, 1905.
Jenkinson, Anthony. *Early Voyages and Travels to Russia and Persia by Anthony Jenkinson and Other Englishmen. With Some Account of the First Intercourse of the English with Russia and Central Asia by Way of the Caspian Sea*. Vol. 1, edited by E. Delmar Morgan and C. H. Coote. New York: Bert Franklin, 1886.
Kappler, Charles J., ed. *Indian Affairs: Laws and Treaties*. Vols. 1 and 2. Washington, DC: Government Printing Office, 1904.
Kastelianskii, A. I., ed. *Formy natsional'nago dvizheniia v sovremennykh gosudarstvakh. Avstro-vengriia. Rossiia. Germaniia*. St. Petersburg: Obshchestvennaia pol'za, 1910.
Kaufman, A. A. *K voprosu o kolonizatsii Ural'skoi oblasti: otchet' chlena uchenago komiteta M.Z. i G.I.* St. Petersburg: Tipografiia V.O. Kirshbauma, 1903.
Kaufman, A. A. *Pereselenie i kolonizatsiia*. St. Petersburg: Biblioteka Obshchestvennoi Pol'zy, 1905.
Kazakhsko-russkie otnosheniia v XVI-XVIII vekakh. Sbornik dokumentov i materialov. Alma-Ata: Nauka, 1961.
Kazakhsko-russkie otnosheniia v XVIII-XIX veka. Sbornik dokumentov i materialov. Alma-Ata: Nauka, 1964.
Kazantsev, Ilia. *Opisanie Kirgiz-Kaisak*. St. Petersburg: Obshchestvenniia pol'za, 1867.
Kostenko, L. F. *Sredniaia Aziia i vodvorenie v nei russkoi grazhdanstvennosti*. Saint Petersburg: Tip. V. Bezobrazova, 1871.
Kozybaev, M. K., ed. *Nasil'stvennaia kollektivizatsiia i golod v Kazakhstane 1931–1933gg. Sbornik dokumentov i materialov*. Almaty: XXI Vek, 1998.

Kozybaev, M. K. *Natsional'no-osvoboditel'naia bor'ba Kazakhskogo naroda pod predvoditel'stvom Kenesary Kasymova*. Almaty: Gylym, 1996.
Kraft, I. I. *Sbornik uzakonenii o kirgizakh stepnykh oblastei*. Orenburg: Zharinov, 1898.
Kraft, I. I. *Turgaiskii oblastnoi arkhiv': Opisanie arkhivnykh' dokumentov' s 1731 g. po 1782 g., otnosiashchikhsia k upravleniia Kirgizami*. St. Petersburg: A. P. Lopukhina, 1901.
Krasnyi arkiv 5 (78). Moscow: Tsentral'noe arkivnoe upravlenie, 1936.
Kuropatkin, A. "Vosstanie 1916 g. v Srednei Azii," *Krasnyi arkiv* 3 (34) Moscow: Tsentral'noe arkhivnoe upravlenie (1929): 39–94.
Kuznetsov, V., ed. *Kirgizskoe khoziaistvo v Akmolinskoi oblasti tom 1–5*. St. Petersburg: Pereselencheskoe upravlenie, 1909–1910.
Laws of the Territory of the United States North-West of the Ohio. Cincinnati: W. Maxwell, 1796.
Lelemant, Father. "The Journey of Raymbault and Jogues to the Sault, 1641." In *Early Narratives of the Northwest, 1634–1699*, edited by Louise Phelps Kellogg, 17–26. New York: Charles Scribner's Sons, 1917.
Leupp, Francis E. "Indian Lands: Their Administration with Reference to Present and Future Use." *Annals of the American Academy of Political and Social Science* 33, no. 3 (May 1909): 136–46. http://dx.doi.org/10.1177/000271620903300311.
de Levchine, Alexis. *Description des hordes et des Steppes des Kirghiz-Kazaks ou Kirghiz-Kaissaks*. Paris: Imprimerie Royale, 1840.
Levshin, Aleksei I. *Opisanie Kirgiz-kazach'ikh, ili Kirgiz-kaisatskikh, ord i stepei*. 1832. Almaty: Sanat, 1996.
Lieven, D. C. B., ed. *British Documents on Foreign Affairs: Reports and Papers from the Foreign Office Confidential Print*. Vol. 1, part 1, series A. Frederick, MD: University Publications of America, 1983.
Looney, J. Jefferson, ed. *The Papers of Thomas Jefferson*. Vol. 1, *4 March 1809 to 15 November 1809*. Princeton, NJ: Princeton University Press, 2004.
Lounsbery, Anne. *Thin Culture, High Art: Gogol, Hawthorne, and Authorship in Nineteenth-Century Russia and America*. Cambridge, MA: Harvard University Press, 2007.
Lyall, Robert. *The Character of the Russians, a Detailed History of Moscow*. London: T. Cadell, 1823.
Materialy po istorii Kazakhskoi SSR (1785–1828). Vol. 4. Moscow, Leningrad: Akademiia nauk SSSR, 1940.
MacGillivray, William. *The Travels and Researches of Alexander von Humboldt: Being a Condensed Narrative of his Journeys in the Equinoctial Regions of America, and in Asiatic Russia; Together with Analyses of His More Important Investigations*. New York: J. & J. Harper, 1835.
Materialy po Kazakhskomu obychnomu pravu. Almaty: Zhalyn Baspasy, 1998.
McGee, W. J. "The Siouan Indians: A Preliminary Sketch." In *Fifteenth Annual Report of the Bureau of Ethnology to the Secretary of the Smithsonian Institution, 1893–1894*, by J. W. Powell, 153–204. Washington, DC: Government Printing Office 1897.
von Meyendorf, Baron. *A Journey from Orenburg to Bokhara in the Year 1820*. Translated by E. F. Chapman. Calcutta: Foreign Department Press, 1870.
Murchison, Roderick Impey. "A Few Observations on the Ural Mountains, to Accompany a New Map of a Southern Portion of that Chain." *Journal of the Royal Geographical Society of London* 13 (1843): 269–78. http://dx.doi.org/10.2307/1798151.
Nicollet, Joseph N. *Joseph N. Nicollet on the Plains and Prairies: The Expeditions of 1838–39 With Journals, Letters, and Notes on the Dakota Indians*. Edited and translated by

Edmund C. Bray and Martha Coleman Bray. St. Paul: Minnesota Historical Society Press, 1976.
Palen, K. K. *Pereselencheskoe delo v Turkestane*. St. Petersburg: Senatskaia tipografia, 1910.
Pallas, P. S. *Travels Through the Southern Provinces of the Russian Empire in the Years 1793 and 1794*. 2nd ed. London: John Stockdale, 1812.
Polnoe sobranie zakonov Rossiiskoi Imperii, povieleniem gosudaria Imperatora Nikolaia Pavlovicha Sostavlennoe. Seriia. St. Petersburg: Gosudarstvennaiia tipografiia, 1830–1916.
Pond, Samuel W. *Dakota Life in the Upper Midwest*. 1908. St. Paul: Minnesota Historical Society, 1986.
Powell, J. W., Edward William Nelson, and Charles C. Royce, eds. *Eighteenth Annual Report of the Bureau of American Ethnology to the Secretary of the Smithsonian Institution, 1896–97*. Washington, DC: Government Printing Office, 1899.
Prucha, Francis Paul, ed. *Americanizing the American Indians: Writings by the "Friends of the Indian," 1880–1900*. Cambridge, MA: Harvard University Press, 1973. http://dx.doi.org/10.4159/harvard.9780674435056.
Prucha, Francis Paul, ed. *Documents of United States Indian Policy*. 3rd ed. Lincoln: University of Nebraska Press, 2000.
"Purchase of Island—Confluence of the St. Peter's and Mississippi Rivers." 26th Cong., 1st sess., House Executive Document 82 (Washington, DC, 1840).
Qudaiberdiuly, Shakarim. *Turik, Qyrghyz-Qazaq ham khandar shezheresi*. 1911. Almaty: Qazaqstan i Sana, 1991.
Radisson, Peter Esprit. *Voyages of Peter Esprit Radisson, Being an Account of his Travels and Experiences among the North American Indians, from 1652 to 1684*. Boston: Prince Society, 1885.
"Radisson's Account of his Third Journey, 1658–1660 [1654–1656?]." In *Early Narratives of the Northwest, 1634–1699*, edited by Louise Phelps Kellogg, 27–66. New York: Charles Scribner's Sons, 1917.
Radloff, W. "Die Hausthiere der Kirgisen." *Zeitschrift fur Ethnologie* 3 (1871): 285–313.
Radlov, V. V. *Iz Sibiri: Strantsy dnevnika*. 1893. Moscow: Nauka, 1989.
Radlov, V. V. *Opyt' slovaria tiurkskikh' narechii*. Vol. 2. St. Petersburg: Akademii nauk, 1899.
Reddaway, W. F., ed. *Documents of Catherine the Great: The Correspondence with Voltaire and the Instruction of 1767 in the English Text of 1768*. Cambridge: Cambridge University Press, 1931.
Report of the Committee to which was referred so much of the President's message, as relates to Indian affairs, accompanied with a bill for establishing trading houses with the Indian tribes. . . . 15th Cong., 1st sess. House Document 59. Serial Set 7. (January 22, 1818).
Condition of the Indian Tribes: Report of the Joint Special Committee, Appointed under Joint Resolution of March 3, 1865, with an Appendix. 39th Cong., 2d sess. Senate Report 156. Serial Set 1279. Washington, DC: Government Printing Office, 1867.
Ricker, Eli Seavey, and Richard E. Jensen, eds. *Voices of the American West*. Vol. 1: *The Indian Interviews of Eli S. Ricker, 1903–1919*. Lincoln: University of Nebraska Press, 2005.
Ricker, Eli Seavey, and Richard E. Jensen, eds. *Voices of the American West*. Vol. 2: *The Settler and Soldier Interviews of Eli S. Ricker, 1903–1919*. Lincoln: University of Nebraska Press, 2005.
Riggs, Stephen R. *Contributions to North American Ethnology*. Vol. 9, *Dakota Grammar, Texts and Ethnography*. Edited by James Owen Dorsey. Washington, DC: Government Printing Office, 1893.

Rudy, Charles. "Despotic Russia, Part II, Adventures in the Steppes of Russian Asia and the Frosty Caucasus." *Reformed Quarterly Review* (July 1880): 325–55.

Rumiantsev, P. P. *Kirgizskii narod v proshlem i nastoiashchem*. St. Petersburg, 1910.

Rychkov, N. P. *Dnevnye zapiski puteshestviia kapitana Nikolaiia Rychkova v Kirgiz-Kaisatskoi stepi v 1771 godu*. St. Petersburg: Pri Imperatorskoi akademii nauk, 1772.

Sbornik Dokumentov i Statei po Voprosu ob obrazovanii inorodtsev. St. Petersburg: V Tipografii Tovarishchestva Obshchestvennaia Pol'za, 1869.

Sbornik Postanovlenii Ministerstva Narodnogo Prosveshcheniia. Vol. 4:1555–1556. St. Petersburg: Ministerstvo Narodnogo Prosveshcheniia, 1871.

Schuyler, Eugene. *Turkistan: Notes of a Journey in Russian Turkistan, Khokand, Bukhara, and Kuldja*. 2 vols. New York: Scribner, Armstrong, 1877.

Sedel'nikov, Timofei Ivanovich. *Bor'ba zemliu v Kirgizskoi stepi (Kirgizskii zemel'nyi vopros' i kolonizatsionnaia politika pravitel'stva)*. Astana: Altyn Kitap, 2007.

Serena, Carla. *Seule dans les steppes: Épisodes de mon voyage aux pays des Kalmoucks et des Kirghiz*. Paris: G. Charpentier, 1883.

Shea, John Gilmary, ed. *Discovery and Exploration of the Mississippi Valley: With the Original Narratives of Marquette, Allouez, Membré, Hennepin, and Anastase Douay*. 2nd ed. Albany, NY: Joseph McDonough, 1903.

Sponville, Anatole Jaunez. "Chez les Kirghis." *Bulletin de la societe de geographie* 9 (May 1865): 438–75.

Taylor, Joseph Henry. *Sketches of Frontier and Indian Life on the Upper Missouri and Great Plains*. 3rd ed. Bismarck, ND: published by author, 1897.

Thwaites, Reuben Gold, ed. *The Jesuit Relations and Allied Documents*. Vol. 23. Cleveland, OH: Burrows Brothers, 1898.

Thwaites, Reuben Gold. Preface to *Collections of the State Historical Society of Wisconsin*. Vol. 16, edited by Reuben Gold Thwaites, xi–xvii. Madison: State Historical Society of Wisconsin, 1902.

de Tocqueville, Alexis. *Democracy in America*. Vol. 1, translated by Henry Reeve. New York: Century Co., 1898.

Tynyshpaev, M. *Materialy k istorii kirgiz-kazakskogo naroda. (Chitany v Turkestanskom Otdele Russkogo Geograficheskogo Obshchestva v 1924 i 1925 gg.)*. Tashkent: Vost. Otd. Kirgizsk. Gos. Izd., 1925.

Statements of a delegation of Oglala Sioux before the chairman of the Committee on Indian Affairs, United States Senate, April 29 and 30, 1897, relative to affairs at the Pine Ridge Agency, S. Dak. May 4, 1897. 55th Cong., 1st sess., Senate Document 61. Serial Set 3561. Washington, DC: Government Printing Office, 1897.

US Board of Indian Commissioners, *Third Annual Report of the Board of Indian Commissioners to the President of the United States*. Washington, DC: Government Printing Office, 1871.

US Department of War. *Indian Treaties, and Laws and Regulations Relating to Indian Affairs: To which is Added an Appendix, Containing the Proceedings of the Old Congress, and Other Important State Papers, in Relation to Indian Affairs*. Washington City: Way & Gideon, 1826.

Ushakov, V. A. *Kirgiz-kaisak povest'*. St. Petersburg: Tip. N. Stepanova pri Imperatorskom teatrie, 1830.

Valikhanov, Chokan. *Izbrannye proizvedeniia*. Alma-Ata: Kazakhskoe izd-vo khudozh. lit-ry, 1958.

Valikhanov, Chokan. *Sobranie sochinenii v piati tomakh*. Alma-Ata: Kazakhskoi Sovetskoi Entsiklopedii, 1984–1985.
Valikhanof et al. *The Russians in Central Asia: Their Occupation of the Kirghiz Steppe and the line of the Syr-Daria: Their Political Relations with Khiva, Bokhara, and Kokan: Also Descriptions of Chinese Turkestan and Dzungaria*. Translated by John Michell and Robert Michell. London: Edward Stanford, 1865.
Vambery, Arminius. *Travels in Central Asia*. New York: J. Murray, 1865.
Verwyst, Chrysostom. "On the Mission of the Nadouessiouek (Sioux)." In *Missionary Labors of Fathers Marquette, Menard and Allouez, in the Lake Superior Region*. Milwaukee: Hoffman Brothers, 1886.
Walker, F. A. "The Indian Question." *North American Review* 116 (April 1873): 329–88.
Washburn, Wilcomb E., ed. *The American Indian and the United States: A Documentary History*. 4 vols. New York: Random House, 1973.
Welsh, William. *Report of a Visit to the Sioux and Ponca Indians on the Missouri River*. Washington, DC: Government Printing Office, 1872.
Zitkala-Sa. *Indians of North America*. Washington, DC: Hayworth, 1921.
Zitkala-Sa. *Dreams and Thunder: Stories, Poems, and The Sun Dance Opera*, edited by P. Jane Hafen. Lincoln: University of Nebraska Press, 2001.

SECONDARY SOURCES

Abdirajymova, A. S., S. Rosa Zharkynbayeva, and Karlygash Bizhigitova. "The Image of the Kazakh Women in the Works of Russian Authors in the Context of Imperial Policy in the Steppes (The End of the XVIII-Beginning of XX Century)." *Procedia: Social and Behavioral Sciences* 140 (August 22, 2014): 671–76. http://dx.doi.org/10.1016/j.sbspro.2014.04.491.
Abdirov, M. Zh. *Istoriia Kazachestva Kazakhstana*. Almaty: Izdatel'stvo Kazakhstan, 1994.
Abdirov, M. Zh. *Zavoevanie Kazakhstana tsarskoi Rossiei*. Astana: Elorda, 2000.
Abdurakhimova, Nadira A. "The Colonial System of Power in Turkistan." *International Journal of Middle East Studies* 34, no. 2 (May 2002): 239–62.
Abramov, A. I. "Reflections on Russia's Destiny in the Philosophical Work of Russian Romanticism." *Russian Studies in Philosophy* 35, no. 3 (1996): 6–18. http://dx.doi.org/10.2753/RSP1061-196735036.
Abylkhozhin, Zhulduzbek B., Manash K. Kozybaev, and Makash B. Tatimov. "Kazakhstanskaia Tragediia." *Voprosy istorii*, no. 7 (1989): 53–71.
Adams, David Wallace. *Education for Extinction; American Indians and the Boarding School Experience, 1875–1928*. Lawrence: University Press of Kansas, 1995.
Adams, Henry. *History of the United States of America during the First Administration of Thomas Jefferson*. Vols. 1–2. New York: Charles Scribner's Sons, 1909.
Adas, Michael. "From Settler Colony to Global Hegemon: Integrating the Exceptionalist Narrative of the American Experience into World History." *American Historical Review* 106, no. 5 (December 2001): 1692–720. http://dx.doi.org/10.2307/2692743.
Adelman, Jeremy, and Stephen Aron. "From Borderlands to Borders: Empires, Nation-States, and the Peoples in Between in North American History." *American Historical Review* 104, no. 3 (June 1999): 814–41. http://dx.doi.org/10.2307/2650990.
Akkoshkarov, E. *Iz istorii kazakhov*. Almaty: Zhalyn, 1997.

Albers, Patricia, and Beatrice Medicine, eds. *The Hidden Half: Studies of Plains Indian Women*. Lanham, MD: University Press of America, 1983.

Aldazhumanov, K. S., M. Kh. Asylbekov, Zh. K. Kasymbaev, and M. K. Kozybaev, eds. *Istoriia Kazakhstana (c drevneishikh vremen do nashikh dnei): V piati tomakh*. Vol. 3. Almaty: Atamura, 2000.

Aldrich, Robert. *Greater France: A History of French Overseas Expansion*. New York: St. Martin's, 1996. http://dx.doi.org/10.1007/978-1-349-24729-5.

Altstadt, Audrey L. "Nationality Education Policy in the Russian Empire and the Soviet Union." *Journal Institute of Muslim Minority Affairs* 10, no. 2 (1989): 450–63. http://dx.doi.org/10.1080/13602008908716132.

Alekseenko, Nikolai V. *Naselenie dorevoliutsionnogo Kazakhstana (chislennost', razmeshchenie, sostav, 1870–1914 gg.)*. Alma-Ata: Nauka, 1981.

Allworth, Edward, ed. *Soviet Nationality Problems*. New York: Columbia University Press, 1971.

Ambrose, Stephen E. *Undaunted Courage: Meriwether Lewis, Thomas Jefferson, and the Opening of the American West*. New York: Touchstone, 1996.

Ambrose, Stephen E. *Nothing Like It in the World: The Men Who Built the Transcontinental Railroad, 1863–1869*. New York: Simon & Schuster, 2000.

"America Needs Men." *The American Indian Magazine* 5 (January–March 1917): 5.

American Social Science Association. *Handbook for Immigrants to the United States*. New York: Hurd & Houghton, 1871.

Anderson, Benedict. *Imagined Communities: Reflections on the Origin and Spread of Nationalism*. Rev. ed. London: Verso, 1991.

Anderson, Fred. *Crucible of War: The Seven Years' War and the Fate of Empire in British North America, 1754–1766*. New York: Knopf, 2000.

Anderson, Gary Clayton. "Early Dakota Migration and Intertribal War: A Revision." *Western Historical Quarterly* 11, no. 1 (January 1980): 17–36. http://dx.doi.org/10.2307/967942.

Anderson, Gary Clayton. *Kinsmen of Another Kind: Dakota-White Relations in the Upper Mississippi Valley, 1650–1862*. Lincoln: University of Nebraska Press, 1984.

Anderson, Gary Clayton. *Little Crow: Spokesman for the Sioux*. St. Paul: Minnesota Historical Society Press, 1986.

Anderson, Gary Clayton. *The Conquest of Texas: Ethnic Cleansing in the Promised Land, 1820–1875*. Norman: University of Oklahoma Press, 2005.

Anderson, Gary Clayton. *Ethnic Cleansing and the Indian: The Crime that Should Haunt America*. Norman: University of Oklahoma Press, 2014.

Andrews, Thomas G. "Turning the Tables on Assimilation: Oglala Lakotas and the Pine Ridge Day Schools, 1889–1920s." *Western Historical Quarterly* 33, no. 4 (Winter 2002): 407–30. http://dx.doi.org/10.2307/4144766.

Armstrong, John. *Nations before Nationalism*. Chapel Hill: University of North Carolina Press, 1982.

Aron, Stephen. "Lessons in Conquest: Towards a Greater Western History." *Pacific Historical Review* 63, no. 2 (May 1994): 125–47. http://dx.doi.org/10.2307/3640863.

Asfendiarov, Sandzhar D. *Istoriia Kazakhstana (s drevneishikh vremen)*. 1935. Almaty: Sanat, 1998.

Asylbekov, M. Kh. "Nekotorye voprosy istorii stroitel'stva Orenburgsko-Tashkentskoi zheleznoi dorogi." *Izvestiia Akademii Nauk Kazakhskoi SSR, seriia istorii, arkheologii i etnografii*, no. 2 (1962): 44–61.

Artykbaev, Zhambyl. *Kazakhskoe obshchestvov XIX veke: traditsii i innovatsii*. Karaganda: Poligrafiia, 1993.
Athearn, Robert G. "The Great Plains in Historical Perspective." *Montana The Magazine of Western History* 8, no. 1 (Winter 1958): 13–29.
Austin, Paul M. "Petr Kudrjašev: Russia's First Romantic Ethnographer." *Studies in Romanticism* 15, no. 1 (Winter 1976): 81–96. http://dx.doi.org/10.2307/25599998.
Avrich, Paul. *Russian Rebels, 1600–1800*. New York: Schocken Books, 1972.
Bacon, Elizabeth E. "Types of Pastoral Nomadism in Central and Southwest Asia." *Southwestern Journal of Anthropology* 10, no. 1 (Spring 1954): 44–68. http://dx.doi.org/10.1086/soutjanth.10.1.3629075.
Bacon, Elizabeth E. *OBOK: A Study of Social Structure in Eurasia*. New York: Wenner-Gren Foundation for Anthropological Research, 1958.
Bacon, Elizabeth E. *Central Asians under Russian Rule: A Study in Culture Change*. Ithaca: Cornell University Press, 1966.
Bailey, Thomas A. "America's Emergence as a World Power: The Myth and the Verity." *Pacific Historical Review* 30, no. 1 (February 1961): 1–16. http://dx.doi.org/10.2307/3636327.
Baker, A. R. H., and M. Billinge, eds. *Period and Place: Research Methods in Historical Geography*. Cambridge: Cambridge University Press, 1982.
Baker, O. E. "The Agriculture of the Great Plains Region." *Annals of the Association of American Geographers* 13, no. 3 (September 1923): 109–67. http://dx.doi.org/10.1080/00045602309356887.
Banner, Stuart. *How the Indians Lost Their Land: Law and Power on the Frontier*. Cambridge, MA: Harvard University Press, 2005. http://dx.doi.org/10.4159/9780674020535.
Baretta, Silvio R. Duncan, and John Markoff. "Civilization and Barbarism: Cattle Frontiers in Latin America." *Comparative Studies in Society and History* 20, no. 4 (October 1978): 587–620. http://dx.doi.org/10.1017/S0010417500012561.
Baronova, S. F., A. N. Bukeikhana, and S. I. Rudenko. *Kazaki: Antropologicheskie ocherki*. Leningrad: Akademiia nauk SSSR, 1927.
Barrett, Thomas M. *At the Edge of Empire: The Terek Cossacks and the North Caucasus Frontier, 1700–1860*. Boulder, CO: Westview, 1999.
Barsh, Russel Lawrence. "Progressive-Era Bureaucrats and the Unity of Twentieth-Century Indian Policy." *American Indian Quarterly* 15, no. 1 (Winter 1991): 1–17. http://dx.doi.org/10.2307/1185205.
Bartlett, Robert, and Angus MacKay, eds. *Medieval Frontier Societies*. Oxford: Clarendon Press, 1989.
Bartold, Vasilii V. *Sochineniia*. Vol. 5. Moscow: Vostochnoi literatury, 1968.
Basin, V. Ia. "Politika Rossii v mladshem i srednem zhuzakh v kontse 50-kh i v 60-kh godakh XVIII veka," *Izvestiia AN KazSSR, seriia obshchestvennaia*, no. 3 (1968): 38–54.
Basin, V. Ia., and U. A. Umurzakov. "Russko-Kazakhskie torgovye sviazi v period prisoedineniia Kazakhstana k Rossii." *Izvestiia AN KazSSR* (1982): 14–18.
Bassin, Mark. "Turner, Solov'ev and the 'Frontier Hypothesis': The Nationalist Significance of Open Spaces." *Journal of Modern History* 65, no. 3 (September 1993): 473–511. http://dx.doi.org/10.1086/244672.
Bater, James H., and R. A. French, eds. *Studies in Russian Historical Geography*. Vol. 1. London: Academic Press, 1983.
Batunskii, Mark. "Islam i Russkaia kul'tura XVIII Veka: Opyt istoriko-epistemologicheskogo issledovaniiakh." *Cahiers du monde russe et soviétique* 27 (January/March 1986): 45–69.

Baudet, E. H. P. *Paradise on Earth: Some Thoughts on European Images of Non-European Man.* Translated by Elizabeth Wentholt. New Haven, CT: Yale University Press, 1965.

Bayly, C.A. *The Birth of the Modern World, 1780–1914: Global Connections and Comparisons.* Malden, MA: Blackwell, 2004.

Beazley, R. "Democratic Factors in Russian History." *Contemporary Review* 161 (March 1942): 139–43.

Becker, Seymour. "The Muslim East in Nineteenth-Century Russian Popular Historiography." *Central Asian Survey* 5, nos. 3–4 (1986): 25–47. http://dx.doi.org/10.1080/02634938608400555.

Bekmakhanov, Ermukhan. *Kazakhstan v 20–40 gody XIX veka.* 1947. Almaty: Kazakh Universiteti, 1992.

Bekmakhanova, N. E. *Rossiia i Kazakhstan v osvoboditel'nom dvizhenii: posledniaia chetvert' XVIII-pervaia polovina XIX veka.* Moscow: Institut rossiiskoi istorii, 1996.

Belich, James. *Replenishing the Earth: The Settler Revolution and the Rise of the Anglo-World, 1783–1939.* Oxford: Oxford University Press, 2009. http://dx.doi.org/10.1093/acprof:oso/9780199297276.001.0001.

Belkanov, Nikolai. "Russian Education for Non-Russian Peoples." *Russian Education & Society* 39, no. 9 (1997): 28–43. http://dx.doi.org/10.2753/RES1060-9393390928.

Belmessous, Saliha. *Assimilation and Empire: Uniformity in French and British Colonies, 1541–1954.* Oxford: Oxford University Press, 2013. http://dx.doi.org/10.1093/acprof:oso/9780199579167.001.0001.

Berkhofer, Robert F., Jr. *Salvation and the Savage: An Analysis of Protestant Missions and American Indian Response, 1787–1862.* Lexington: University of Kentucky Press, 1965.

Berkhofer, Robert F., Jr. *The White Man's Indian: Images of the American Indian from Columbus to the Present.* New York: Vintage, 1979.

Berton, Pierre. *The Impossible Railway: The Building of the Canadian Pacific.* New York: Knopf, 1972.

Betts, Raymond F. *Tricouleur: The French Overseas Empire.* New York: Gordon & Cremonesi, 1978.

Billington, Ray Allen. *Land of Savagery, Land of Promise: The European Image of the American Frontier in the Nineteenth Century.* New York: W. W. Norton, 1981.

Biolsi, Thomas. "The IRA and the Politics of Acculturation: The Sioux Case." *American Anthropologist* 87, no. 3 (1985): 656–59. http://dx.doi.org/10.1525/aa.1985.87.3.02a00140.

Biolsi, Thomas. *Deadliest Enemies: Law and Race Relations on and off Rosebud Reservation.* Berkeley: University of California Press, 2007.

Birzhanov, K. A. "Khoziaistvo prisyrdar'inskikh Kazakhov v seredine XIX—nachale XX v.," *Izvestiia AN KazSSR, seriia obshchestvennaia*, no. 4 (1972): 66–71.

Blakeley, Brian L. *The Colonial Office, 1868–1892.* Durham, NC: Duke University Press, 1972.

Blauner, Robert. "Internal Colonialism and Ghetto Revolt." *Social Problems* 16, no. 4 (Spring 1969): 393–408. http://dx.doi.org/10.2307/799949.

Blegen, Theodore C. "The Pond Brothers." *Minnesota History* 15 (September 1934): 273–81.

Bloch, Marc Léopold Benjamin. *Land and Work in Mediaeval Europe: Selected Papers.* Berkeley: University of California Press, 1967.

Blouet, Brian W., and Merlin P. Lawson, eds. *Images of the Plains: The Role of Human Nature in Settlement.* Lincoln: University of Nebraska Press, 1975.

Bobrick, Benson. *East of the Sun: The Epic Conquest and Tragic History of Siberia.* New York: Poseidon, 1992.

Bodger, Alan. "Abulkhair, Khan of the Kazakh Little Horde, and his Oath of Allegiance to Russia of October 1731." *Slavonic and East European Review* 58, no. 1 (January 1980): 40–57.

Bodger, Alan. *The Kazakhs and the Pugachev Uprising in Russia, 1773–1775*. Bloomington: Research Institute for Inner Asian Studies, Indiana University, 1988.

Bohannan, Paul. *Social Anthropology*. New York: Holt, Rinehart, & Winston, 1963.

Boulger, Demetrius Charles. *England and Russia in Central Asia*. Vol. 1. London: W. H. Allen, 1879.

Bowman, Anne. *Among the Tartar Tents; or, the Lost Fathers*. London: Frederick Warne, 1875.

Brantlinger, Patrick. *Dark Vanishings: Discourse on the Extinction of Primitive Races, 1800–1930*. Ithaca, NY: Cornell University Press, 2003.

Bray, Kingsley M. *Crazy Horse: A Lakota Life*. Norman: University of Oklahoma Press, 2006.

Breyfogle, Nicholas B., Abby Schrader, and Willard Sunderland, eds. *Peopling the Russian Periphery: Borderland Colonization in Eurasian History*. London: Routledge, 2007.

Brezhnev, Leonid Il'ich. *Virgin Lands: Two Years in Kazakhstan, 1954–5*. Oxford: Pergamon, 1979.

Britt, Albert. "Custer's Last Fight." *Pacific Historical Review* 13, no. 1 (March 1944): 12–20. http://dx.doi.org/10.2307/3635735.

Brocherel, Jules. "The Kirghiz." *Scottish Geographical Magazine* 18, no. 8 (1902): 393–406. http://dx.doi.org/10.1080/00369220208733374.

Brockway, Lucile H. "Science and Colonial Expansion: The Role of the British Royal Botanic Gardens." *American Ethnologist* 6, no. 3 (1979): 449–65. http://dx.doi.org/10.1525/ae.1979.6.3.02a00030.

Brodhead, Jane Milliken Napier. *Slav and Moslem: Historical Sketches*. Aiken, SC: Aiken, 1894.

Brooks, James F. *Captives and Cousins: Slavery, Kinship, and Community in the Southwest Borderlands*. Chapel Hill: University of North Carolina Press, 2002.

Brover, I. "K voprosu ob osobennostiakh Rossiiskogo imperializma," *Vestnik Akademii Nauk Kazakhskoi SSR*, no. 7 (July 1953): 21–29.

Brower, Daniel R., and Edward J. Lazzerini, eds. *Russia's Orient: Imperial Borderlands and Peoples, 1700–1917*. Bloomington: Indiana University Press, 1997.

Brown, Dee. *Bury My Heart at Wounded Knee: An Indian History of the American West*. New York: Holt, Rinehart & Winston, 1972.

Brown, Kate. "Gridded Lives: Why Kazakhstan and Montana Are Nearly the Same Place." *American Historical Review* 106, no. 1 (February 2001): 17–48. http://dx.doi.org/10.2307/2652223.

Bryan, Fanny E. "Organization and Work of Missionaries in the Middle-Volga in the Second Half of the Nineteenth Century." *Islam and Christian-Muslim Relations* 6 (1995): 173–86.

Bucke, Charles, and William P. Page. *On the Beauties, Harmonies, and Sublimities of Nature: With Occasional Remarks on the Laws, Customs, Manners, and Opinions of Various Nations*. New York: Harper & Bros., 1841.

Bucko, Raymond A. *The Lakota Ritual of the Sweat Lodge: History and Contemporary Practice*. Lincoln: University of Nebraska Press, 1998.

Burbank, Jane, and Frederick Cooper. *Empires in World History: Power and the Politics of Difference*. Princeton, NJ: Princeton University Press, 2010.

Burgen, Arnold, Peter McLaughlin, and Jürgen Mittelstrass, eds. *The Idea of Progress*. Berlin: de Gruyter, 1997. http://dx.doi.org/10.1515/9783110820423.

Bury, J. B. *The Idea of Progress: An Inquiry into Its Origin and Growth*. London: Macmillan, 1920.
Bush, Barbara. *Imperialism and Postcolonialism*. Harlow, UK: Pearson Longman, 2006.
Cahill, Cathleen D. *Federal Fathers and Mothers: A Social History of the United States Indian Service, 1869–1933*. Chapel Hill: University of North Carolina Press, 2011.
Calloway, Colin G. "The Inter-tribal Balance of Power on the Great Plains, 1760–1850." *Journal of American Studies* 16, no. 1 (1982): 25–47.
Calloway, Colin G., ed. *Our Hearts Fell to the Ground: Plains Indian Views of How the West Was Lost*. New York: Bedford/St. Martin's, 1996. http://dx.doi.org/10.1007/978-1-137-07646-5.
Calvert, Peter. "Internal Colonisation, Development and Environment." *Third World Quarterly* 22, no. 1 (February 2001): 51–63. http://dx.doi.org/10.1080/713701137.
Campbell, Elena I. "The Autocracy and the Muslim Clergy in the Russian Empire (1850s–1917)." *Russian Studies in History* 44, no. 2 (Fall 2005): 8–29.
Campbell, Elena I. *The Muslim Question and Russian Imperial Governance*. Bloomington: Indiana University Press, 2015.
Campbell, Ian. "Settlement Promoted, Settlement Contested: The Shcherbina Expedition of 1896–1903." *Central Asian Survey* 30, nos. 3–4 (September/December 2011): 423–36. http://dx.doi.org/10.1080/02634937.2011.604220.
Cannadine, David. *Ornamentalism: How the British Saw Their Empire*. Oxford: Oxford University Press, 2001.
Cannady, Sean, and Paul Kubicek. "Nationalism and Legitimation for Authoritarianism: A Comparison of Nicholas I and Vladimir Putin." *Journal of Eurasian Studies* 5, no. 1 (January 2014): 1–9. http://dx.doi.org/10.1016/j.euras.2013.11.001.
Carlson, Leonard A. *Indians, Bureaucrats, and Land: The Dawes Act and the Decline of Indian Farming*. Westport, CT: Greenwood, 1981.
Carlson, Leonard A. "Federal Policy and Indian Land: Economic Interests and the Sale of Indian Allotments, 1900–1934." *Agricultural History* 57 (January 1983): 33–45.
Carmichael, Stokely, and Charles V. Hamilton. *Black Power: The Politics of Liberation in America*. New York: Vintage, 1967.
Caroe, Olaf. *Soviet Empire: The Turks of Central Asia and Stalinism*. New York: St. Martin's Press, 1967.
Carr, Helen. *Inventing the American Primitive: Politics, Gender and the Representation of Native American Literary Traditions, 1789–1936*. New York: New York University Press, 1996.
Chatterjee, Partha. *The Nation and Its Fragments: Colonial and Postcolonial Histories*. Princeton, NJ: Princeton University Press, 1993.
Chávez, John R. "Aliens in Their Native Lands: The Persistence of Internal Colonial Theory." *Journal of World History* 22, no. 4 (December 2011): 785–809. http://dx.doi.org/10.1353/jwh.2011.0123.
Chernienko, Denis. "The Rulers of European Nomads and Early Mediaeval Byzantine Historiography." *Acta Orientalia* 58, no. 2 (2005): 171–78. http://dx.doi.org/10.1556/AOrient.58.2005.2.4.
Chernikov, V. S. "Krest'ianskaia kolonizatsiia severnogo Kazakhstana v epokhu kapitalizma." *Istoriia SSSR*, no. 6 (November/December 1982): 132–41.
Cheshire, Harold T. "The Expansion of Imperial Russia to the Indian Border." *Slavonic and East European Review* 13 (July 1934): 85–97.

Chittenden, Hiram Martin. *The American Fur Trade of the Far West: A History of the Pioneer Trading Posts and Early Fur Companies of the Missouri Valley and the Rocky Mountains and of the Overland Commerce with Santa Fe*. Vol. 2. New York: Francis P. Harper, 1902.

Chuloshnikov, A. P. *Ocherki po istorii Kazak-Kirgizskogo naroda v sviazi s obshchimi istoricheskimi sud'bami drugikh tiurkskikh plemen*. Orenburg: Kirgizskoe gosudarstvennoe izdatel'stvo, 1924.

Churchill, Ward. *Kill the Indian, Save the Man: The Genocidal Impact of American Indian Residential Schools*. San Francisco: City Lights, 2004.

Clay, Catherine B. "Russian Ethnographers in the Service of Empire, 1856–1862." *Slavic Review* 54, no. 1 (Spring 1995): 45–61. http://dx.doi.org/10.2307/2501119.

Clifford, James. *Routes: Travel and Translation in the Late Twentieth Century*. Cambridge, MA: Harvard University Press, 1997.

Clow, Richmond. "Bison Ecology, Brulé and Yankton Winter Hunting, and the Starving Winter of 1832–33." *Great Plains Quarterly* 15, no. 4 (Fall 1995): 259–70.

Cocker, Mark. *Rivers of Blood, Rivers of Gold: Europe's Conquest of Indigenous Peoples*. New York: Grove, 1998.

Collier, John. *Indians of the Americas: The Long Hope*. New York: W. W. Norton, 1947.

Collier, John. *From Every Zenith: A Memoir; and Some Essays on Life and Thought*. Denver: Sage, 1963.

Colson, Elizabeth. "Political Organization in Tribal Societies: A Cross-Cultural Comparison." *American Indian Quarterly* 10, no. 1 (Winter 1986): 5–19. http://dx.doi.org/10.2307/1184153.

Colwell-Chanthaphonh, Chip. "When History is Myth: Genocide and the Transmogrification of American Indians." *American Indian Culture and Research Journal* 29, no. 2 (2005): 113–18. http://dx.doi.org/10.17953/aicr.29.2.353j52p005048r81.

Conn, Steven. *History's Shadow: Native Americans and Historical Consciousness in the Nineteenth Century*. Chicago: University of Chicago Press, 2004. http://dx.doi.org/10.7208/chicago/9780226115115.001.0001.

Cooper, Frederick, George M. Fredrickson, and James T. Campbell. "Race, Ideology, and the Perils of Comparative History." *American Historical Review* 101, no. 4 (October 1996): 1122–38. http://dx.doi.org/10.2307/2169637.

Cooper, Frederick, and Ann Laura Stoler, eds. *Tensions of Empire: Colonial Cultures in a Bourgeois World*. Berkeley: University of California Press, 1997. http://dx.doi.org/10.1525/california/9780520205406.001.0001.

Conquest, Robert. *The Harvest of Sorrow: Soviet Collectivization and the Terror-Famine*. New York: Oxford University Press, 1986.

Crews, Robert D. "Empire and the Confessional State: Islam and Religious Politics in Nineteenth-Century Russia." *American Historical Review* 108, no. 1 (February 2003): 50–83. http://dx.doi.org/10.1086/533045.

Cross, Anthony G., and Gerald S. Smith, eds. *Literature, Lives, and Legality in Catherine's Russia*. Nottingham, UK: Astra, 1994.

Cross, Anthony. *In the Lands of the Romanovs: An Annotated Bibliography of First-Hand English-Language Accounts of the Russian Empire (1613–1917)*. Cambridge: Open Books, 2014. http://dx.doi.org/10.11647/OBP.0042.

Curzon, George N. *Russia in Central Asia in 1889 and the Anglo-Russia Question*. 2nd ed. London: Longmans, Green, 1889.

Dakhshleiger, G. F. "Iz opyta istorii osedaniia Kazakhskikh kochevykh i polukochevykh khoziaistv (do massovoi kollektivizatsii sel'skogo khoziaistva)." *Sovetskaia Etnografiia*, no. 4 (July/August 1966): 3–23.

Dal', Vladimir. *Tolkovyi slovar' zhivogo velikorusskogo iazyka v 4 tomakh*. Mocow: Russkii iazyk, 1989–1991.

Darnell, Regna, ed. *Native American Interaction Patterns*. Ottawa: National Museum of Canada, 1988.

Davis, Howard, and Sergey Erofeev. "Reframing Society and Culture in Post-Soviet Russia." *Comparative Sociology* 10, no. 5 (2011): 710–34. http://dx.doi.org/10.1163/156913311X599034.

De Koninck, Rodolphe. "The Peasantry as the Territorial Spearhead of the State in Southeast Asia: The Case of Vietnam." *Sojourn: Journal of Social Issues in Southeast Asia* 11, no. 2 (October 1996): 231–58. http://dx.doi.org/10.1355/SJ11-2C.

DeLay, Brian. *War of a Thousand Deserts: Indian Raids and the U.S.-Mexican War*. New Haven, CT: Yale University Press, 2008.

Deleuze, Gilles, and Felix Guattari. *Nomadology: The War Machine*. New York: Semiotext(e), 1986.

Deloria, Ella. *Speaking of Indians*. New York: Friendship Press, 1944.

DeMallie, Raymond J. "Sioux Ethnohistory: A Methodological Critique." *Journal of Ethnic Studies* 4, no. 3 (Fall 1976): 77–83.

DeMallie, Raymond J. "The Lakota Ghost Dance: An Ethnohistorical Account." *Pacific Historical Review* 51, no. 4 (November 1982): 385–405. http://dx.doi.org/10.2307/3639782.

DeMallie, Raymond J., and Douglas R. Parks, eds. *Sioux Indian Religion*. Norman: University of Oklahoma Press, 1987.

DeMallie, Raymond J., and Douglas R. Parks, eds. *Plains*. Vol. 13, parts 1 and 2, *Handbook of North American Indians*, edited by William C. Sturtevant. Washington, DC: Smithsonian Institution, 2001.

Demko, George. *The Russian Colonization of Kazakhstan, 1896–1916*. Bloomington: Indiana University Press, 1969.

d'Errico, Peter. "Native Americans in America: A Theoretical and Historical Overview." *Wicazo Sa Review* 14, no. 1 (Spring 1999): 7–28. http://dx.doi.org/10.2307/1409513.

Deverell, William. "Fighting Words: The Significance of the American West in the History of the United States." *Western Historical Quarterly* 25, no. 2 (Summer 1994): 185–206. http://dx.doi.org/10.2307/971462.

DeWeese, Devin. "The Influence of the Mongols on the Religious Consciousness of Thirteenth Century Europe." *Mongolian Studies* 5 (1978–1979): 41–78.

Dillon, Richard H. "Stephen Long's Great American Desert." *Proceedings of the American Philosophical Society* 111, no. 2 (April 1967): 58–74.

Diment, Galya, and Yuri Slezkine, eds. *Between Heaven and Hell: The Myth of Siberia in Russian Culture*. New York: St. Martin's, 1993. http://dx.doi.org/10.1007/978-1-137-08914-4.

Dingelstedt, Victor, and N. I. Grodekoff. *Le régime patriarchal et le droit coutumier des Kirghiz*. Paris: Ernest Thorin, 1891.

Dobb, Maurice. *Soviet Economic Development since 1917*. New York: International Publishers, 1968.

Donnelly, Alton S. *The Russian Conquest of Bashkiria, 1552–1740*. New Haven, CT: Yale University Press, 1968.

Donnelly, Alton S. "Peter the Great and Central Asia." *Canadian Slavonic Papers* 17, nos. 2–3 (1975): 202–17. http://dx.doi.org/10.1080/00085006.1975.11091405.

Dorsey, James Owen. "The Social Organization of the Siouan Tribes." *Journal of American Folklore* 4, no. 14 (July/September 1891): 257–66. http://dx.doi.org/10.2307/534012.

Dow, Roger. "Prostor: A Geopolitical Study of Russia and the United States." *Russian Review* 1, no. 1 (1941): 6–19. http://dx.doi.org/10.2307/125427.

Dow, Roger. "Seichas: A Comparison of Pre-Reform Russia and the Ante-Bellum South." *Russian Review* 7, no. 1 (Autumn 1947): 3–15. http://dx.doi.org/10.2307/125328.

Dowler, Wayne. "The Politics of Language in Non-Russian Elementary Schools in the Eastern Empire, 1865–1914." *Russian Review* 54, no. 4 (October 1995): 516–38. http://dx.doi.org/10.2307/131607.

Dowler, Wayne. *Classroom and Empire: The Politics of Schooling Russia's Eastern Nationalities, 1860–1917*. Montreal: McGill-Queen's University Press, 2001.

Doyle, Arthur Conan. *Tales of Sherlock Holmes: Detective Stories*. Three Owls ed. New York: W. R. Caldwell, 1920.

Doyle, Michael W. *Empires*. Ithaca, NY: Cornell University Press, 1986.

Drinnon, Richard. *Facing West: The Metaphysics of Indian Hating and Empire Building*. New York: Schocken Books, 1990.

Dunch, Ryan. "Beyond Cultural Imperialism: Cultural Theory, Christian Missions, and Global Modernity." *History and Theory* 41, no. 3 (October 2002): 301–25. http://dx.doi.org/10.1111/1468-2303.00208.

Eagleton, Terry, Fredric Jameson, and Edward W. Said, eds. *Nationalism, Colonialism, and Literature*. Minneapolis: University of Minnesota Press, 1990.

Eccles, W. J. "The Fur Trade and Eighteenth-Century Imperialism." *William and Mary Quarterly* 40, no. 3 (July 1983): 341–62. http://dx.doi.org/10.2307/1917202.

Edgerton, Franklin. "Notes on Early American Work in Linguistics." *Proceedings of the American Philosophical Society* 87, no. 1 (July 1943): 25–34.

Edwards, Holly, ed. *Noble Dreams, Wicked Pleasures: Orientalism in America, 1879–1930*. Princeton, NJ: Princeton University Press, 2000.

Eklof, Ben, John Bushnell, and Larissa Zakharova, eds. *Russia's Great Reforms, 1855–1881*. Bloomington: Indiana University Press, 1994.

Ellis, Clyde. *To Change Them Forever: Indian Education at the Rainy Mountain Boarding School, 1893–1920*. Norman: University of Oklahoma Press, 1996.

Emerson, Rupert. "Self-Determination." *American Journal of International Law* 65, no. 3 (1971): 459–75. http://dx.doi.org/10.2307/2198970.

Engin, Arin. "Russian Colonialism in Turkestan." *Ukrainian Quarterly* 17 (1961): 158–62.

Englander, David, ed. *Britain and America: Studies in Comparative History, 1760–1970*. New Haven, CT: Yale University Press, 1997.

Enloe, Cynthia H. "Internal Colonialism, Federalism and Alternative State Development Strategies." *Publius* 7, no. 4 (Autumn 1977): 145–60.

Erlich, Victor. "Images of Siberia." *Slavic and East European Journal* 1, no. 4 (Winter 1957): 243–250. http://dx.doi.org/10.2307/304301.

Ermolov, Vladimir Aleksandrovich. "Osobennosti sistemy obrazovaniia v natsional'niykh shkolakh Rossiiskoi imperii: musul'manskie i evreiskie shkoly." *Obshchestvo. Sreda. Razvitie (Terra Humana)* 4 (2009): 100–109.

Eschment, Beate. "Neither Barbarians nor Noble Savages: The Russian View on the Kazakhs of the Empire." Paper Presented at the Central Eurasian Studies Society Annual Conference, University of Michigan, Ann Arbor, September 2003.

Evans, Grant. "Internal Colonialism in the Central Highlands of Vietnam." *Sojourn: Social Issues in Southeast Asia* 7, no. 2 (August 1992): 274–304. http://dx.doi.org/10.1355/SJ7-2E.

Evans, Julie, Patricia Grimshaw, and David Phillips. *Equal Subjects, Unequal Rights: Indigenous People in British Settler Colonies, 1830–1910.* Manchester: Manchester University Press, 2003. http://dx.doi.org/10.7228/manchester/9780719060038.001.0001.

Ewers, John. "When Red and White Men Met." *Western Historical Quarterly* 2, no. 2 (April 1971): 133–50. http://dx.doi.org/10.2307/967751.

Fay, Sidney B. "The Idea of Progress." *American Historical Review* 52, no. 2 (January 1947): 231–46. http://dx.doi.org/10.2307/1841272.

Fear-Segal, Jacqueline. *White Man's Club: Schools, Race, and the Struggle of Indian Acculturation.* Lincoln: University of Nebraska Press, 2007.

Featherman, Americus. *Thoughts and Reflections on Modern Society: With an Introduction on the Gradual Social Evolution of Primitive Man.* London: Kegan Paul, Trench, Trübner, 1894.

Fell, E. Nelson. *Russian and Nomad: Tales of the Kirghiz Steppes.* New York: Duffield, 1916.

Fedorova, Milla. *Yankees in Petrograd, Bolsheviks in New York: America and Americans in Russian Literary Perception.* Dekalb: Northern Illinois University Press, 2013.

Feraca, Stephen E., and James H. Howard. "The Identity and Demography of the Dakota or Sioux Tribe." *Plains Anthropologist* 8, no. 20 (1963): 80–84.

Ferguson, James, and Akhil Gupta. "Spatializing States: Toward an Ethnography of Neoliberal Governmentality." *American Ethnologist* 29, no. 4 (November 2002): 981–1002. http://dx.doi.org/10.1525/ae.2002.29.4.981.

Ferguson, R. Brian, and Neil L. Whitehead, eds. *War in the Tribal Zone: Expanding States and Indigenous Warfare.* Santa Fe: School of American Research Press, 1992.

Fisher, Alan W. "Enlightened Despotism and Islam Under Catherine II." *Slavic Review* 27, no. 4 (December 1968): 542–553. http://dx.doi.org/10.2307/2494437.

Fiskesjö, M. "On the 'Raw' and the 'Cooked' Barbarians of Imperial China." *Inner Asia* 1, no. 2 (1999): 139–168. http://dx.doi.org/10.1163/146481799793648004.

Flandrau, Charles E. "The Inkpaduta Massacre of 1857." In *Collections of the Minnesota Historical Society,* 386–407. Vol 3. St. Paul: Minnesota Historical Society, 1880.

Fleksor, D. *Pereselencheskoe Delo v 1908 goda.* St. Petersburg: Pereselenskoe upravlenie, 1908.

Fox, Dixon Ryan. "Civilization in Transit." *American Historical Review* 32, no. 4 (July 1927): 753–68. http://dx.doi.org/10.2307/1837854.

Fox, Ralph. *People of the Steppes.* London: Constable, 1925.

Fracchia, Joseph, and R. C. Lewontin. "Does Culture Evolve?" *History and Theory* 38, no. 4 (December 1999): 52–78. http://dx.doi.org/10.1111/0018-2656.00104.

Francaviglia, Richard V. *Go East Young Man: Imagining the American West as the Orient.* Logan: Utah State University Press, 2011.

Franks, C. E. S. "In Search of the Savage *Sauvage*: An Exploration into North America's Political Cultures." *American Review of Canadian Studies* 32, no. 4 (Winter 2002): 547–80. http://dx.doi.org/10.1080/02722010209481675.

Frazier, Ian. *Great Plains.* New York: Farrar, Straus, & Giroux, 1989.

Frederickson, George M. "Giving a Comparative Dimension to American History: Problems and Opportunities." *Journal of Interdisciplinary History* 16, no. 1 (Summer 1985): 107–10. http://dx.doi.org/10.2307/204325.

Frederickson, George M. "From Exceptionalism to Variability: Recent Developments in Cross-National Comparative History." *Journal of American History* 82, no. 2 (September 1995): 587–604. http://dx.doi.org/10.2307/2082188.

Galuzo, P. G. "Turkestan i Tsarskaia Rossii—k Voprosu o Kharaktere Kolonial'noi Politiki v Srednei Azii." *Revoliutsionny Vostok* 4 (1929): 94–119.

Galuzo, P. G. *Agrarnye otnosheniia na iuge Kazakhstana v 1867–1914 gg.* Alma-Ata: Nauka, 1965.

Gardner, Lloyd C. "Lost Empires." *Diplomatic History* 13, no. 1 (1989): 1–13. http://dx.doi.org/10.1111/j.1467-7709.1989.tb00041.x.

Gates, Paul W. *The Jeffersonian Dream: Studies in the History of American Land Policy and Development.* Albuquerque: University of New Mexico Press, 1996.

Gates, Paul Wallace. "The Homestead Law in an Incongruous Land System." *American Historical Review* 41, no. 4 (July 1936): 652–81. http://dx.doi.org/10.2307/1842606.

Gellens, Sam I. "The Search for Knowledge in Medieval Muslim Societies: A Comparative Approach." In *Muslim Travellers: Pilgrimage, Migration, and the Religious Imagination*, edited by Dale F. Eickelman and James Piscatori, 50–68. Berkeley: University of California Press, 1990.

Geraci, Robert P., and Michael Khodarkovsky, eds. *Of Religion and Empire: Missions, Conversion, and Tolerance in Tsarist Russia.* Ithaca, NY: Cornell University Press, 2001.

Gerasimova, E. I. "K istorii pereseleniia krest'ian v Ural'skuiu oblast' v nachale XX veka." *Izvestiia AN KazSSR, seriia istorii, arkheologii i etnografii*, no. 3 (1962): 77–87.

Gerhard, Dietrich. "The Frontier in Comparative View." *Comparative Studies in Society and History* 1, no. 3 (1959): 205–29. http://dx.doi.org/10.1017/S0010417500000232.

Gerhard, Dietrich. *Russian Imperialism: The Interaction of Domestic and Foreign Policy, 1860–1914.* Translated from German by Bruce Little. New Haven, CT: Yale University Press, 1987.

Gibbon, Guy. *The Sioux: The Dakota and Lakota Nations.* Malden, MA: Blackwell, 2003. http://dx.doi.org/10.1002/9780470755808.

Giles, Paul. "Reconstructing American Studies: Transnational Paradoxes, Comparative Perspectives." *Journal of American Studies* 28, no. 3 (December 1994): 335–58. http://dx.doi.org/10.1017/S0021875800027626.

Gilman, Rhoda R. "The Fur Trade in the Upper Mississippi Valley, 1630–1850." *Wisconsin Magazine of History* 58, no. 1 (Autumn 1974): 2–18.

Glazov, Yuri. "Chaadaev and Russia's Destiny." *Studies in Soviet Thought* 32, no. 4 (November 1986): 281–301.

Gleason, Abbott. "Republic of Humbug: The Russian Nativist Critique of the United States, 1830–1930." *American Quarterly* 44 (March 1992): 1–23.

Gorbunova, S. V. "Zarozhdenie Russkogo obrazovaniia sredi Kazakhov: shkola pri Orenburgskoi pogranichnoi komissii." In *Kul'tura, Nauka, Obrazovanie: Problemy i perspekivy, Materialy II Vserossiiskoi nauchno-prakticheskoi konferentsii, g. Nizhnevartovsk, 8 Fevralia 2013 goda, Chast' I, Istoriia idei i istoriia obshchestva problemy vseobshchei istorii*, edited by A. V. Korichko, 31–33. Nizhnevartovsk: Izdatel'stvo Nizhnevartovskogo gosudarstvenogo universiteta, 2013.

Gorzhushkin, L. M., ed. *Zarubezhnye ekonmicheskie i kul'turnye sviazi Sibiri (XVIII-XX vv.): Sbornik nauchnykh trudov.* Novosibirsk: Rossiiskaia Akademiia Nauk, Sibirskoe otdel, 1995.

Gould, Eliga H. *Among the Powers of the Earth: The American Revolution and the Making of a New World Empire*. Cambridge, MA: Harvard University Press, 2012. http://dx.doi.org/10.4159/harvard.9780674065024.

Gray, Edward G. "Visions of Another Empire: John Ledyard, an American Traveler Across the Russian Empire, 1787–1788." *Journal of the Early Republic* 24, no. 3 (Autumn 2004): 347–80.

Graybill, Andrew R. *Policing the Great Plains: Rangers, Mounties, and the North American Frontier, 1875–1910*. Lincoln: University of Nebraska Press, 2007.

Green, Elizabeth. "Indian Minorities Under the American New Deal." *Pacific Affairs* 8, no. 4 (December 1935): 420–27.

Greene, Nile, ed. *Writing Travel in Central Asian History*. Bloomington: Indiana University Press, 2014.

Greene, Jerome A. "Out with a Whimper: The Little Missouri Expedition and the Close of the Great Sioux War." *South Dakota History* 35, no. 1 (2005): 1–39.

Greenwald, Emily. *Reconfiguring the Reservation: The Nez Perces, Jicarilla Apaches, and the Dawes Act*. Albuquerque: University of New Mexico Press, 2002.

Gregg, Robert. *Inside Out, Outside In: Essays in Comparative History*. London: Macmillan, 2000.

Grew, Raymond. "The Case for Comparing Histories." *American Historical Review* 85, no. 4 (October 1980): 763–78. http://dx.doi.org/10.2307/1868871.

Grew, Raymond. "The Comparative Weakness of American History." *Journal of Interdisciplinary History* 16, no. 1 (Summer 1985): 87–101. http://dx.doi.org/10.2307/204323.

Grousset, René. *The Empire of the Steppes: A History of Central Asia*. Translated from French by Naomi Walford. New Brunswick, NJ: Rutgers University Press, 1970.

Guettel, Jens-Uwe. *German Expansionism, Imperial Liberalism, and the United States, 1776–1945*. Cambridge: Cambridge University Press, 2012. http://dx.doi.org/10.1017/CBO9781139175920.

Guins, George C. "Russia and the United States in the World Economy." *American Journal of Economics and Sociology* 5, no. 2 (January 1946): 141–58. http://dx.doi.org/10.1111/j.1536-7150.1946.tb01791.x.

Gül, Serkan. "Karşılaştırmalı Tarihte Metot ve Uygulama." *Karadeniz Araştırmaları* 26 (2010): 143–58.

Gump, James O. "The Subjugation of the Zulus and Sioux: A Comparative Study." *Western Historical Quarterly* 19, no. 1 (January 1988): 21–36. http://dx.doi.org/10.2307/969791.

Gump, James O. *The Dust Rose Like Smoke: The Subjugation of the Zulu and the Sioux*. Lincoln: University of Nebraska Press, 1994.

Gunther, Erna. ""The Westward Movement of Some Plains Traits." *American Anthropologist* 52 (April/June 1950): 174–80.

Gustafson, Sandra M. "Histories of Democracy and Empire." *American Quarterly* 59, no. 1 (March 2007): 107–33. http://dx.doi.org/10.1353/aq.2007.0025.

Guthrie, A. B., Jr. *The Big Sky*. New York: William Sloan, 1947.

Hagan, William T. "Private Property: the Indian's Door to Civilization." *Ethnohistory* 3, no. 2 (Spring 1956): 126–37. http://dx.doi.org/10.2307/480525.

Haines, Francis. "The Northward Spread of Horses among the Plains Indians." *American Anthropologist* 40, no. 3 (July/September 1938): 429–37. http://dx.doi.org/10.1525/aa.1938.40.3.02a00060.

Halecki, Oskar. "The Problem of Self-Determination." *Proceedings of the American Philosophical Society* 87, no. 2 (August 1943): 194–98.

Hall, Catherine. *Civilising Subjects: Metropole and Colony in the English Imagination, 1830–1867*. Chicago: University of Chicago Press, 2002.
Hall, Henry Lindsay. *The Colonial Office: A History*. London: Longmans, Green, 1937.
Hallam, Elizabeth, and Brian V. Street, eds. *Cultural Encounters: Representing "Otherness."* New York: Routledge, 2000.
Halliday, R. J. "Social Darwinism: A Definition." *Victorian Studies* 14, no. 4 (June 1971): 389–405.
Hämäläinen, Pekka. "The Western Comanche Trade Center: Rethinking the Plains Indians Trade System." *Western Historical Quarterly* 29, no. 4 (Winter 1998): 485–5C13. http://dx.doi.org/10.2307/970405.
Hämäläinen, Pekka. "The Rise and Fall of Plains Indian Horse Cultures." *Journal of American History* 90, no. 3 (December 2003): 833–62. http://dx.doi.org/10.2307/3660878.
Hambly, Gavin. *Central Asia*. New York: Delacorte, 1969.
Hamilton, Wynette L. "The Correlation between Societal Attitudes and Those of American Authors in the Depiction of American Indians, 1607–1860." *American Indian Quarterly* 1, no. 1 (Spring 1974): 1–26. http://dx.doi.org/10.2307/1184197.
Hannah, Matthew G. "Space and Social Control in the Administration of the Oglala Lakota ("Sioux"), 1871–1879." *Journal of Historical Geography* 19, no. 4 (1993): 412–32. http://dx.doi.org/10.1006/jhge.1993.1026.
Harrison, Brady. "The Young Americans: Emerson, Walker, and the Early Literature of American Empire." *American Studies* 40, no. 3 (Fall 1999): 75–97.
Hasian, Marouf, Jr. "Cultural Amnesia and Legal Rhetoric: Remembering the 1862 United States-Dakota War and the Need for Military Commissions." *American Indian Culture and Research Journal* 27, no. 1 (2003): 91–117. http://dx.doi.org/10.17953/aicr.27.1.t270411632927157.
Hassrick, Royal B. *The Sioux: Life and Customs of a Warrior Society*. Norman: University of Oklahoma Press, 1964.
Hasty, Olga Peters, and Susanne Fusso, eds. *America through Russian Eyes, 1874–1926*. New Haven, CT: Yale University Press, 1988.
von Haxthausen, Baron. *The Russian Empire, Its People, Institutions, and Resources*. 2 vols. Translated by Robert Farie. London: Chapman & Hall, 1856.
Hayes, Carlton J. H. "The American Frontier—Frontier of What?" *American Historical Review* 51, no. 2 (January 1946): 199–216. http://dx.doi.org/10.2307/1839579.
Hays, Robert, ed. *Editorializing "The Indian Problem": The "New York Times" on Native Americans, 1860–1900*. Carbondale: Southern Illinois University Press, 1997.
Haywood, Richard Mowbray. *The Beginnings of Railway Development in Russia in the Reign of Nicholas I, 1835–1842*. Durham, NC: Duke University Press, 1969.
Hazen, W. B. "The Great Middle Region of the United States, and Its Limited Space of Arable Land." *North American Review* 120, no. 246 (January 1875): 1–34.
Headrick, Daniel R. *The Tools of Empire: Technology and European Imperialism in the Nineteenth Century*. New York: Oxford University Press, 1981.
Heaton, Herbert. "Other Wests Than Ours." *Journal of Economic History* 6, no. S1 (January 1946): 50–62. http://dx.doi.org/10.1017/S0022050700052906.
Hecht, David. *Russian Radicals Look to America, 1825–1894*. Cambridge, MA: Harvard University Press, 1947. http://dx.doi.org/10.4159/harvard.9780674492691.
Hechter, Michael. *Internal Colonialism: The Celtic Fringe in British National Development, 1536–1966*. Berkeley: University of California Press, 1975.

von Hellwald, Frederick. *The Russians in Central Asia: A Critical Examination Down to the Present Time of the Geography and History of Central Asia*. Translated by Theodore Wirgman. London: Henry S. King, 1874.

Hertzberg, Hazel W. *The Search for an American Indian Identity: Modern Pan-Indian Movements*. Syracuse, NY: Syracuse University Press, 1971.

Higham, Carol L. *Noble, Wretched, and Redeemable: Protestant Missionaries to the Indians in Canada and the United States, 1820–1900*. Albuquerque: University of New Mexico Press, 2000.

Higham, Carol L. "Saviors and Scientists: North American Protestant Missionaries and the Development of Anthropology." *Pacific Historical Review* 72, no. 4 (November 2003): 531–59. http://dx.doi.org/10.1525/phr.2003.72.4.531.

Higham, Carol L., and Robert Thacker, eds. *One West, Two Myths: A Comparative Reader*. Alberta: University of Calgary Press, 2004.

Hill, Alette Olin, and Boyd H. Hill, Jr. "Marc Bloch and Comparative History." *American Historical Review* 85, no. 4 (October 1980): 828–46. http://dx.doi.org/10.2307/1868874.

Hind, Robert J. "The Internal Colonial Concept." *Comparative Studies in Society and History* 26, no. 3 (July 1984): 543–68. http://dx.doi.org/10.1017/S0010417500011130.

Hine, Robert V. *Community on the American Frontier: Separate But Not Alone*. Norman: University of Oklahoma Press, 1980.

Hirsch, Francine. *Empire of Nations: Ethnographic Knowledge and the Making of the Soviet Union*. Ithaca, NY: Cornell University Press, 2005.

Hoagland, Alison K. "Village Constructions: U.S. Army Forts on the Plains, 1848–1890." *Winterthur Portfolio* 34, no. 4 (Winter 1999): 215–37. http://dx.doi.org/10.1086/496790.

Hobsbawm, Eric. *The Age of Empire, 1875–1914*. New York: Vintage, 1989.

Hobsbawm, Eric. *Industry and Empire: The Birth of the Industrial Revolution*. New York: New Press, 1999.

Hobson, J. A. *Imperialism: A Study*. London: James Nisbet, 1902.

Hodgson, Godfrey. *The Myth of American Exceptionalism*. New Haven, CT: Yale University Press, 2009.

Hoffert, Sylvia D. "Gender and Vigilantism on the Minnesota Frontier: Jane Grey Swisshelm and the U.S.-Dakota Conflict of 1862." *Western Historical Quarterly* 29, no. 3 (Autumn 1998): 342–62. http://dx.doi.org/10.2307/970578.

Hokanson, Katya. *Writing at Russia's Border*. Toronto: University of Toronto Press, 2008.

Holquist, Peter. "'In Accord with State Interests and the People's Wishes': The Technocratic Ideology of Imperial Russia's Resettlement Administration." *Slavic Review* 69, no. 1 (Spring 2010): 151–79.

Home, Henry. (Lord Kames). *Sketches of the History of Man*, 3rd ed., 2 vols. Dublin: James Williams, 1779.

Hopkins, A. G. "Comparing British and American Empires." *Journal of Global History* 2, no. 3 (November 2007): 395–404. http://dx.doi.org/10.1017/S1740022807002343.

Hopkirk, Peter. *The Great Game: The Struggle for Empire in Central Asia*. New York: Kodansha International, 1992.

Howard, Bradley Reed. *Indigenous Peoples and the State: The Struggle for Native Rights*. Dekalb: Northern Illinois University Press, 2003.

Howard, James H. "Some Further Thoughts on Eastern Dakota 'Clans.'" *Ethnohistory* 26, no. 2 (Spring 1979): 133–40. http://dx.doi.org/10.2307/481088.

Hoxie, Frederick E. "The End of the Savage: Indian Policy in the United States Senate, 1880–1900." *Chronicles of Oklahoma* 55 (Summer 1977): 157–79.

Hoxie, Frederick E. *A Final Promise: The Campaign to Assimilate the Indians, 1880–1920.* Lincoln: University of Nebraska Press, 1984.

Hoxie, Frederick E., ed. *Talking Back to Civilization: Indian Voices from the Progressive Era.* New York: Bedford/St. Martin's, 2001.

Hubbard, Lucius F., James H. Baker, William P. Murray, and Warren Upham, eds. *Minnesota in Three Centuries, 1655–1908.* Vol. 1. Mankato: Publishing Society of Minnesota, 1908.

Hudson, Alfred E. *Kazakh Social Structure.* New Haven, CT: Yale University Press, 1938.

Hughes, Thomas. "Causes and Results of the Inkpaduta Massacre." In *Collections of the Minnesota Historical Society,* 263–82. Vol. 12. St. Paul: Minnesota Historical Society, 1908.

Hunczak, Taras, ed. *Russian Imperialism from Ivan the Terrible to the Revolution.* New Brunswick, NJ: Rutgers University Press, 1974.

Hyde, George E. *Red Cloud's Folk: A History of the Oglala Sioux Indians.* 1937. Norman: University of Oklahoma Press, 1975.

Hyde, George. *A Sioux Chronicle.* Norman: University of Oklahoma Press, 1956.

Hyman, Harold M. *American Singularity: The 1787 Northwest Ordinance, the 1862 Homestead and Morrill Acts, and the 1944 G.I. Bill.* Athens: University of Georgia Press, 1986.

Iamzin, I. L., and V. P. Voshchinin. *Uchenie o kolonizatsii i pereseleniiakh.* Moscow: Gos. izd-vo, 1926.

Iggers, Georg G. "The Idea of Progress: A Critical Reassessment." *American Historical Review* 71, no. 1 (October 1965): 1–17. http://dx.doi.org/10.2307/1863033.

Ishboldin, Boris. "The Eurasian Movement." *Russian Review* 5, no. 2 (Spring 1946): 64–73. http://dx.doi.org/10.2307/125160.

"Is It Civilization or Extermination?" *American Antiquarian and Oriental Journal* 22 (January/February 1900): 52–58.

Istoriia Kazakhskoi SSR s drevneishikh vremen do nashikh dnei v piati tomakh. Alma-Ata: Nauka, 1979.

Jackson, Helen Hunt. *A Century of Dishonor: A Sketch of the United States Government's Dealings with Some of the Indian Tribes.* New York: Harper & Brothers, 1881.

Jackson, W. Turrentine. "A Brief Message for the Young and/or Ambitious: Comparative Frontiers as a Field for Investigation." *Western Historical Quarterly* 9, no. 1 (January 1978): 4–18. http://dx.doi.org/10.2307/966887.

Jacobs, Wilbur R. "The Fatal Confrontation: Early Native-White Relations on the Frontiers of Australia, New Guinea, and America: A Comparative Study." *Pacific Historical Review* 40, no. 3 (August 1971): 283–309. http://dx.doi.org/10.2307/3638359.

Jacques, T. Carlos. "From Savages and Barbarians to Primitives: Africa, Social Typologies, and History in Eighteenth-Century French Philosophy." *History and Theory* 36, no. 2 (May 1997): 190–215. http://dx.doi.org/10.1111/0018-2656.00010.

Johnson, Douglas L. *The Nature of Nomadism: A Comparative Study of Pastoral Migrations in Southwestern Asia and Northern Africa.* Department of Geography Research Paper No. 118. Chicago: University of Chicago, 1969.

Jonassohn, Kurt, with Karin Solveig Björnson. *Genocide and Gross Human Rights Violations: In Comparative Perspective.* Piscataway, NJ: Transaction, 1998.

Jones, W. R. "The Image of the Barbarian in Medieval Europe." *Comparative Studies in Society and History* 13, no. 4 (October 1971): 376–407. http://dx.doi.org/10.1017/S001041 7500006381.

Johnston, Sister Mary Antonio. *Federal Relations with the Great Sioux Indians of South Dakota, 1887–1933, with Particular Reference to Land Policy under the Dawes Act.* Washington, DC: Catholic University of America Press, 1948.

Judson, Katherine Berry. *Myths and Legends of the Great Plains*. Chicago: A. C. McClurg, 1913.

Kadioğlu, Ayşe. "The Paradox of Turkish Nationalism and the Construction of Official Identity." *Middle Eastern Studies* 32, no. 2 (1996): 177–93. http://dx.doi.org/10.1080/00263209608701110.

Kakel, Carroll P. *The American West and the Nazi East: A Comparative and Interpretive Perspective*. New York: Palgrave Macmillan, 2011. http://dx.doi.org/10.1057/9780230307063.

Kammen, Michael, ed. *The Past Before Us: Contemporary Historical Writing in the United States*. Ithaca, NY: Cornell University Press, 1980.

Kaplan, Amy, and Donald E. Pease, eds. *Cultures of United States Imperialism*. Durham, NC: Duke University Press, 1993.

Kappeler, Andreas. *The Russian Empire: A Multiethnic History*. Translated by Alfred Clayton. New York: Pearson Education, 2001.

Kasymbaev, Zh. K. "Rol' gorodov vostochnogo Kazakhstana v ukreplenii torgovykh otnoshenii s kochevym Kazakhskim i Russkim krest'ianskim naseleniem v nachale XX veka." *Izvestiia AN KazSSR, seriia obshchestvennykh nauk*, no. 6 (1979): 52–57.

Kasymbaev, Zh. K. *Kenesary Khan*. Almaty, 1992.

"Kazakh Customary Law." *Central Asian Review* 5 (1957): 127–43.

Kellogg, Louise Phelps. "The First Traders in Wisconsin." *Wisconsin Magazine of History* 5, no. 4 (June 1922): 348–59.

Kellogg, Louise Phelps. "Fort Beauharnois." *Minnesota History* 8, no. 3 (September 1927): 232–46.

Kelsey, Harry. "The Doolittle Report of 1867: Its Preparation and Shortcomings." *Arizona and the West* 17 (Summer 1975): 107–20.

Kemper, Michael, and Stephan Conermann, eds. *The Heritage of Soviet Oriental Studies*. London: Routledge, 2011.

Kendirbaeva, Gulnar. "'We Are Children of Alash . . .' The Kazakh Intelligentsia at the Beginning of the 20th Century in Search of National Identity and Prospects of the cultural Survival of the Kazakh People." *Central Asian Survey* 18, no. 1 (1999): 5–36.

Kendirbai, Gulnar. *Land and People: The Russian Colonization of the Kazakh Steppe*. Berlin: Schwarz, 2002.

Kerner, Robert J. "The Russian Eastward Movement: Some Observations on Its Historical Significance." *Pacific Historical Review* 17, no. 2 (May 1948): 135–48. http://dx.doi.org/10.2307/3635513.

Khabizhanova, E., A. Krivkov, and E. Valikhanov, eds. *Russkaia demokraticheskaia intelligentsia v Kazakhstane (vtoraia polovine XIX-nachalo XX vv.)*. Moscow: Russkaia kniga, 2003.

Khalid, Adeeb. "Backwardness and the Quest for Civilization: Early Soviet Central Asia in Comparative Perspective." *Slavic Review* 65, no. 2 (Summer 2006): 231–51. http://dx.doi.org/10.2307/4148591.

Khodarkovsky, Michael. *Russia's Steppe Frontier: The Making of a Colonial Empire, 1500–1800*. Bloomington: Indiana University Press, 2002.

Khoury, Dina Rizk, and Dane Kennedy. "Comparing Empires: The Ottoman Domains and the British Raj in the Long Nineteenth Century." *Comparative Studies of South Asia, Africa and the Middle East* 27, no. 2 (2007): 233–44. http://dx.doi.org/10.1215/1089201x-2007-002.

Kiernan, Ben. *Blood and Soil: A World History of Genocide and Extermination from Sparta to Darfur*. New Haven, CT: Yale University Press, 2007.

Kiesewetter, Alexander. "Klyuchevsky and Russian History." *Slavonic Review* 1, no. 3 (March 1923): 504–22.

Kiparsky, V. "The American Westerner in Russian Fiction." *Russian Review* 20, no. 1 (January 1961): 36–44. http://dx.doi.org/10.2307/126568.

Kisliakov, N. A. *Ocherki po istorii sem'i i braka u narodov Srednei Azii i Kazakhstana*. Leningrad: Nauka, 1969.

Kliuchevskii, V. O. *Kurs russkoi istorii*. Reprint ed. Ann Arbor: University of Michigan Press, 1948.

Kloberdanz, Timothy J. "The Volga Germans in Old Russia and in Western North America: Their Changing World View." *Anthropological Quarterly* 48, no. 4 (October 1975): 209–22. http://dx.doi.org/10.2307/3316632.

Knight, Nathaniel. "Grigor'ev in Orenburg, 1851–1862: Russian Orientalism in the Service of Empire?," *Slavic Review* 59, no. 1 (Spring 2000): 74–100. http://dx.doi.org/10.2307/2696905.

Knight, Nathaniel. "Nikolai Kharuzin and the Quest for a Universal Human Science: Anthropological Evolutionism and the Russian Ethnographic Tradition, 1885–1900." *Kritika: Explorations in Russian and Eurasian History* 9, no. 1 (Winter 2008): 83–111. http://dx.doi.org/10.1353/kri.2008.0002.

Kohn, Hans. "Dostoevsky's Nationalism." *Journal of the History of Ideas* 6, no. 4 (October 1945): 385–414. http://dx.doi.org/10.2307/2707342.

Kohn, Hans, ed. *The Mind of Modern Russia: Historical and Political Thought of Russia's Great Age*. New Brunswick, NJ: Rutgers University Press, 1955.

Kohn, Hans. "Some Reflections on Colonialism." *Review of Politics* 18, no. 3 (July 1956): 259–68. http://dx.doi.org/10.1017/S0034670500009256.

Kol', V. K. "Amerikanskaia gomstednaia sistema nadeleniia pereselentsev' zemleiu, kak sredstvo uspeshnoi kolonizatsii i ekonomicheskago razvitiia russkikh' okrain.'" *Voprosy Kolonizatsii*, no. 10 (1912): 1–34.

Kolchin, Peter. "Comparing America History." *Reviews in American History* 10, no. 4 (December 1982): 64–81. http://dx.doi.org/10.2307/2701819.

Kolchin, Peter. "Some Recent Works on Slavery Outside the United States: An American Perspective." *Comparative Studies in Society and History* 28, no. 4 (October 1986): 767–77. http://dx.doi.org/10.1017/S0010417500014225.

Kolchin, Peter. *Unfree Labor: American Slavery and Russian Serfdom*. Cambridge, MA: Harvard University Press, 1987.

Kosach, Grigorii Grigor'evich. "Ibragim Altynsarin: chelovek v potoke vremeni." *Vestnik Evrazii* 1–2 (1998): 110–31.

Kostenko, L. F. *Sredniaia Aziia i vodvorenie v nei russkoi grazhdanstvennosti*. Saint Petersburg: Tip. V. Bezobrazova, 1871.

Krader, Lawrence. "Principles and Structures in the Organization of the Asiatic Steppe-Pastoralists." *Southwestern Journal of Anthropology* 11, no. 2 (Summer 1955): 67–92. http://dx.doi.org/10.1086/soutjanth.11.2.3628962.

Krader, Lawrence. "Ethnonymy of Kazakh." *American Studies in Altaic Linguistics* 13 (1962): 123–28.

Krader, Lawrence. *Social Organization of the Mongol-Turkic Pastoral Nomads*. The Hague: Mouton, 1963.

Krader, Lawrence. *Peoples of Central Asia*. Bloomington: Indiana University Press, 1971.

Kraft', I. "Priniatie kirgizami russkago poddanstva." *Izvestiia Orenburgskago otdela imperatorskago Russkago geograficheskago obshchestva vypusk'* 12-I (1897): 1–59.

Kreis, Karl Markus. *Lakotas, Black Robes, and Holy Women: German Reports from the Indian Missions in South Dakota, 1886–1900*. Translated from German by Corinna Dally-Starna. Lincoln: University of Nebraska Press, 2007.

Kreyche, Gerald F. *Visions of the American West*. Lexington: University Press of Kentucky, 1989.

Kreindler, Isabelle. "Ibrahim Altynsarin, Nikolai Il'minskii and the Kazakh National Awakening." *Central Asian Survey* 2, no. 3 (1983): 99–116. http://dx.doi.org/10.1080/02634938 308400440.

Kristof, Ladis K.D. "The Nature of Frontiers and Boundaries." *Annals of the Association of American Geographers* 49, no. 3 (September 1959): 269–82. http://dx.doi.org/10.1111 /j.1467-8306.1959.tb01613.x.

Kuderina, Larisa Zh. *Genotsid v Kazakhstane*. Moscow: Skorpian, 1994.

Kuftin, B. A. *Kirgiz-Kazaki: Kulturai i byt'*. Moscow: Izd. Central'nogo muzeia narodovedeniia, 1926.

Kuvakin, Valerii, ed. *A History of Russian Philosophy: From the Tenth through the Twentieth Centuries*. 2 vols. Buffalo, NY: Prometheus, 1994.

Kvasnicka, Robert M., and Herman J. Viola, eds. *The Commissioners of Indian Affairs, 1824–1977*. Lincoln: University of Nebraska Press, 1979.

LaDow, Beth. *The Medicine Line: Life and Death on a North American Borderland*. New York: Routledge, 2002.

LaFeber, Walter. *The New Empire: An Interpretation of American Expansion, 1860–1898*. Ithaca, NY: Cornell University Press, 1963.

Lamar, Howard R. *Dakota Territory 1861–1889: A Study of Frontier Politics*. New Haven, CT: Yale University Press, 1956.

Landes, Ruth. "Dakota Warfare." *Southwestern Journal of Anthropology* 15, no. 1 (Spring 1959): 43–52. http://dx.doi.org/10.1086/soutjanth.15.1.3629003.

Langfur, Hal. "Myths of Pacification: Brazilian Frontier Settlement and the Subjugation of the Bororo Indians." *Journal of Social History* 32, no. 4 (Summer 1999): 879–905. http://dx.doi.org/10.1353/jsh/32.4.879.

Lantzeff, George V. "Beginnings of the Siberian Colonial Administration." *Pacific Historical Review* 9, no. 1 (March 1940): 47–52. http://dx.doi.org/10.2307/3634126.

LaPointe, Ernie. *Sitting Bull: His Life and Legacy*. Layton, UT: Gibbs Smith, 2009.

Larson, Robert W. *Red Cloud: Warrior-Statesman of the Lakota Sioux*. Norman: University of Oklahoma Press, 1997.

Latham, Robert G. *The Native Races of the Russian Empire*. London: Hippolyte Bailliere, 1854.

Lattimore, Owen. *Inner Asian Frontiers of China*. New York: American Geographical Society, 1940.

Lattimore, Owen. "Inner Asian Frontiers: Chinese and Russian Margins of Expansion." *Journal of Economic History* 7, no. 1 (May 1947): 24–52. http://dx.doi.org/10.1017/S0022 5070000053432.

Lattimore, Owen, ed. *Studies in Frontier History: Collected Papers, 1928–58*. Oxford: Oxford University Press, 1962.

Laveille, Father E. *The Life of Father De Smet, S.J.: Apostle of the Rocky Mountains, 1801–1873*. Translated by Marian Lindsay. New York: P. J. Kennedy & Sons, 1915.

Laverne, Léger Marie Philippe. *The Life of Field Marshal Souvarof; with Reflections upon the Principal Events, Political and Military, Connected with the History of Russia, during Part of the Eighteenth Century*. Translated from French. Baltimore: Edward J. Coale, 1814.

Layton, Susan. "The Search for the Primitive in Russian Literature: From Tolstoy to Pasternak." *Dialectical Anthropology* 4, no. 3 (October 1979): 179–203. http://dx.doi.org/10.1007/BF00243820.

Layton, Susan. *Russian Literature and Empire: Conquest of the Caucasus from Pushkin to Tolstoy*. Cambridge: Cambridge University Press, 1994.

Layton, Susan. *Nineteenth-Century Russian Mythologies of Caucasian Savagery*. Bloomington: Indiana University Press, 1997.

Leasure, J. William, and Robert A. Lewis. "Internal Migration in Russia in the Late Nineteenth Century." *Slavic Review* 27, no. 3 (September 1968): 375–94. http://dx.doi.org/10.2307/2493340.

Legters, Lyman H. "The American Genocide." *Policy Studies Journal* 16, no. 4 (Summer 1988): 768–77. http://dx.doi.org/10.1111/j.1541-0072.1988.tb00685.x.

Lemkin, Raphael. *Axis Rule in Occupied Europe*. Washington, DC: Carnegie Council, 1944.

Lenin, Vladimir. *Collected Works*. Vol. 3, *The Development of Capitalism in Russia*. Moscow: Progress Publishers, 1960.

Lewis, G. M. "Changing Emphases in the Description of the Natural Environment of the American Great Plains Area." *Transactions and Papers (Institute of British Geographers)*, no. 30 (1962): 75–90. http://dx.doi.org/10.2307/621303.

Lewis, James I. "The French Colonial Service and the Issues of Reform, 1944–8." *Contemporary European History* 4, no. 2 (July 1995): 153–88. http://dx.doi.org/10.1017/S096077730000337.

Lewy, Guenter. "Can There Be Genocide Without the Intent to Commit Genocide?," *Journal of Genocide Research* 9, no. 4 (2007): 661–74. http://dx.doi.org/10.1080/14623520701644457.

Libecap, Gary D., and Zeynep Kocabiyik Hansen. "'Rain Follows the Plow' and Dryfarming Doctrine: The Climate Information Problem and Homestead Failure in the Upper Great Plains, 1890–1925." *Journal of Economic History* 62, no. 1 (March 2002): 86–120.

Liberty, Margot, ed. *American Indian Intellectuals of the Nineteenth and Early Twentieth Centuries*. Norman: University of Oklahoma Press, 2002.

Lieven, Dominic. "The Russian Empire and the Soviet Union as Imperial Polities." *Journal of Contemporary History* 30, no. 4 (October 1995): 607–36. http://dx.doi.org/10.1177/002200949503000403.

Lieven, Dominic. *Empire: The Russian Empire and Its Rivals*. New Haven, CT: Yale University Press, 2001.

Limerick, Patricia Nelson. *The Legacy of Conquest: The Unbroken Past of the American West*. New York: W. W. Norton, 1987.

Limerick, Patricia Nelson. *Something in the Soil: Legacies and Reckonings in the New West*. New York: W. W. Norton, 2000.

Limerick, Patricia Nelson, Clyde A. Milner II, and Charles E. Rankin, eds. *Trails: Toward a New Western History*. Lawrence: University Press of Kansas, 1991.

Lincoln, W. Bruce. *The Great Reforms: Autocracy, Bureaucracy, and the Politics of Change in Imperial Russia*. DeKalb: Northern Illinois University Press, 1990.

Lincoln, W. Bruce. *The Conquest of a Continent: Siberia and the Russians*. Ithaca, NY: Cornell University Press, 1994.

Lindholm, Charles. "Kinship Structure and Political Authority: The Middle East and Central Asia." *Comparative Studies in Society and History* 28, no. 2 (1996): 334–55.

Lindner, Rudi Paul. "What Was a Nomadic Tribe?," *Comparative Studies in Society and History* 24, no. 4 (October 1982): 689–711. http://dx.doi.org/10.1017/S0010417500010240.

Liubavskii, M. K. *Istoricheskaia geografiia Rossii v sviazi s kolonizatsiei*. 1909. St. Petersburg: Lan', 2000.

Lopatin, Ivan A. "The Extinct and Near-Extinct Tribes of Northeastern Asia As Compared with the American Indian." *American Antiquity* 5, no. 3 (January 1940): 202–8. http://dx.doi.org/10.2307/275279.

Lorcin, Patricia, M.E. *Algeria and France, 1800–2000: Identity, Memory, Nostalgia*. Syracuse, NY: Syracuse University Press, 2006.

Loukianov, Mikhail. "'Rossiia—dlia russkikh' ili 'Rossiia—dlia russkikh poddanykh'? Konservatory i natsional'nyi vopros nakanune Pervoi mirovoi voiny." *Otechestvennaia istoriia*, no. 2 (2006): 36–46.

Lowie, Robert H. ""Reflections on the Plains Indians." *Anthropological Quarterly* 28, no. 2 (April 1955): 63–86.

Lowie, Robert H. *Indians of the Plains*. 1954. Lincoln: University of Nebraska Press, 1982.

Lubetkin, M. John. *Jay Cooke's Gamble: The Northern Pacific Railroad, the Sioux, and the Panic of 1873*. Norman: University of Oklahoma Press, 2006.

Luehrmann, Sonja. *Alutiiq Villages under Russian and U.S. Rule*. Fairbanks: University of Alaska Press, 2008.

Lujan, Carol Chiago, and Gordon Adams. "U.S. Colonization of Indian Justice Systems: A Brief History." *Wicazo Sa Review* 19, no. 2 (Fall 2004): 9–23. http://dx.doi.org/10.1353/wic.2004.0023.

Lyde, L. W. "Types of Political Frontiers in Europe." *Geographical Journal* 45, no. 2 (February 1915): 126–39. http://dx.doi.org/10.2307/1780250.

Lyons, Martyn. *The Writing Culture of Ordinary People in Europe, c. 1860–1920*. Cambridge: Cambridge University Press, 2012. http://dx.doi.org/10.1017/CBO9781139093538.

MacKenzie, John S. *An Introduction to Social Philosophy*. New York: Macmillan, 1895.

Maier, Bernhard. *The Celts: A History from Earliest Times to the Present*. Trans. Kevin Windle. Edinburgh: Edinburgh University Press, 2003.

Malikov, Yuriy. "The Kenesary Kasymov Rebellion (1837–1847): A National-Liberation Movement or 'a Protest of Restoration'?" *Nationalities Papers* 33, no. 4 (December 2005): 569–97. http://dx.doi.org/10.1080/00905990500354137.

Mannheim, Karl. *Ideology and Utopia: An Introduction to the Sociology of Knowledge*. New York: Harcourt Brace, 1936.

Markov, Gennadii. *Kochevniki Azii: struktura khoziaistva i obshchestvennoi organizatsii*. Moscow: Izd-vo Moskovskogo universiteta, 1976.

Marks, Steven G. *Road to Power: The Trans-Siberian Railroad and the Colonization of Asian Russia, 1850–1917*. Ithaca, NY: Cornell University Press, 1991.

Marsh, Rosalind. "The Nature of Russia's Identity: The Theme of 'Russia and the West' in Post-Soviet Culture." *Nationalities Papers* 35, no. 3 (July 2007): 555–78. http://dx.doi.org/10.1080/00905990701368795.

Martin, Janet. "The Land of Darkness and the Golden Horde: The Fur Trade under the Mongols XIII–XIVth Centuries." *Cahiers du monde russe et soviétique* 19, no. 4 (October/December 1978): 401–21. http://dx.doi.org/10.3406/cmr.1978.1337.

Martin, Terry. "The Empire's New Frontiers: New Russia's Path from Frontier to Okraina, 1774–1920." *Russian History* 19, no. 1 (1992): 181–201. http://dx.doi.org/10.1163/187633192X00127.

Martin, Terry. *The Affirmative Action Empire: Nations and Nationalism in the Soviet Union, 1923–1939*. Ithaca, NY: Cornell University Press, 2001.

Martin, Virginia. *Law and Custom in the Steppe: The Kazakhs of the Middle Horde and Russian Colonialism in the Nineteenth Century*. Richmond, UK: Curzon, 2001.
Martin, W. A. P. "The Northern Barbarians in Ancient China." *Journal of the American Oriental Society* 11 (1885): 362–74. http://dx.doi.org/10.2307/592197.
Masanov, Nurbulat. *Kochevaia tsivilizatsiia Kazakhov*. Alma-Ata: Sotsinvest, 1984.
Masanov, Nurbulat. *Istoriia Kazakhstana: narody i kultury*. Almaty: Daik, 2001.
Madsen, Deborah L. *American Exceptionalism*. Jackson: University Press of Mississippi, 1998.
Mason, Robert L. *The Lure of the Great Smokies*. Boston: Houghton Mifflin, 1927.
Mattes, Merrill J. *Platte River Road Narratives: A Descriptive Bibliography of Travel Over the Great Central Overland Route to Oregon, California, Utah, Colorado, Montana, and Other Western States and Territories, 1812–1866*. Urbana: University of Illinois Press, 1988.
Mauro, Hayes Peter. *The Art of Americanization at the Carlisle Indian School*. Albuquerque: University of New Mexico Press, 2011.
Maxwell, John S. *The Czar, His Court and People: Including a Tour in Norway and Sweden*. New York: Baker & Scribner, 1850.
Maybury-Lewis, David, Theodore Macdonald, and Biorn Maybury-Lewis, eds. *Manifest Destinies and Indigenous Peoples*. Cambridge, MA: Harvard University Press, 2009.
McCarthy, Frank T. "The Kazan' Missionary Congress." *Cahiers du monde russe et soviétique* 14, no. 3 (July/September 1973): 308–32. http://dx.doi.org/10.3406/cmr.1973.1179.
McDonnell, Janet A. *The Dispossession of the American Indian, 1887–1934*. Bloomington: Indiana University Press, 1991.
McDonnell, Michael A., and A. Dirk Moses. "Raphael Lemkin as Historian of Genocide in the Americas." *Journal of Genocide Research* 7, no. 4 (December 2005): 501–29. http://dx.doi.org/10.1080/14623520500349951.
McDougal, Judge H. C. "Expansion and Imperialism." Address delivered by Judge H. C. McDougal before the Union Veteran Patriotic League, Kansas City, MO, September 1, 1900.
McFarling, Lloyd, ed. *Exploring the Northern Plains, 1804–1876*. Caldwell, ID: Caxton Printers, 1955.
McGinnis, Anthony R. "Intertribal Conflict on the Northern Plains and Its Suppression, 1738–1889." *Journal of the West* 18 (April 1979): 49–60.
McGinnis, Anthony R. "Strike and Retreat: Intertribal Warfare and the Powder River War, 1865–1868." *Montana The Magazine of Western History* 30, no. 4 (Autumn 1980): 30–41.
McGinnis, Anthony R. *Counting Coup and Cutting Horses: Intertribal Warfare on the Northern Plains, 1738–1889*. Lincoln: University of Nebraska Press, 2010.
McGovern, William M. *The Early Empires of Central Asia*. Chapel Hill: University of North Carolina Press, 1939.
McKee, William Carey, and Georgeen Klassen. *Trail of Iron: The CPR and the Birth of the West, 1880–1930*. Vancouver: Glenbow-Alberta Institute, 1983.
McKenzie, Kermit E. "Chokan Valikhanov: Kazakh Princeling and Scholar." *Central Asian Survey* 8, no. 3 (1989): 1–30. http://dx.doi.org/10.1080/02634938908400671.
McNickle, D'Arcy, and Harold E. Fey. *Indians and Other Americans: Two Ways of Life Meet*. New York: Harper & Brothers, 1959.
Mead, Margaret, ed. *Cooperation and Competition among Primitive Peoples*. 1937. Boston: Beacon, 1961.

Mehta, Uday Singh. *Liberalism and Empire: A Study in Nineteenth-Century British Liberal Thought*. Chicago: University of Chicago Press, 1999.

Meriam, Lewis, et al. *The Problem of Indian Administration: Report of a Survey made at the request of Honorable Hubert Work, Secretary of the Interior, and Submitted to him, February 21, 1928*. Baltimore: Johns Hopkins Press, 1928.

Meserve, Ruth I. "The Inhospitable Land of the Barbarian." *Journal of Asian History* 16, no. 1 (1982): 51–89.

Metcalf, Thomas R. *Ideologies of the Raj*. Cambridge: Cambridge University Press, 1994.

Meyer, Roy W. *History of the Santee Sioux: United States Indian Policy on Trial*. Lincoln: University of Nebraska Press, 1967.

Mikesell, Marvin. "Comparative Studies in Frontier History." *Annals of the Association of American Geographers* 50, no. 1 (March 1960): 62–74. http://dx.doi.org/10.1111/j.1467-8306.1960.tb00333.x.

Miliukov, P. N. *Russia and Its Crisis*. 1905. New York: Collier, 1962.

Miller, David Harry, and Jerome O. Steffen, eds. *The Frontier: Comparative Studies*. Norman: University of Oklahoma Press, 1977.

Milner, Clyde A., II. *With Good Intentions: Quaker Work among the Pawnees, Otos, and Omahas in the 1870s*. Lincoln: University of Nebraska Press, 1982.

Mirsky, D. S. "The Eurasian Movement." *Slavonic Review* 6 (December 1927): 311–20.

Moon, David. "Peasant Migration and the Settlement of Russia's Frontiers, 1550–1897." *Historical Journal* 40, no. 4 (December 1997): 859–93. http://dx.doi.org/10.1017/S0018246X97007504.

Moon, David. *The Plough that Broke the Steppes: Agriculture and Environment on Russia's Grasslands, 1700–1914*. Oxford: Oxford University Press, 2013. http://dx.doi.org/10.1093/acprof:oso/9780199556434.001.0001.

Moore, Charles. *The Northwest under Three Flags, 1635–1796*. New York: Harper & Brothers, 1900.

Morris, Henry C. *The History of Colonization from Earliest Times to the Present Day*. Vol. 2. New York: Macmillan, 1904.

Morris, Ralph C. "The Notion of a Great American Desert East of the Rockies." *Mississippi Valley Historical Review* 13, no. 2 (September 1926): 190–200. http://dx.doi.org/10.2307/1891956.

Morrison, Alexander. "Russian Rule in Turkestan and the Example of British India, c. 1860–1917." *Slavonic and East European Review* 84, no. 4 (October 2006): 666–707.

Morse, Jedidiah. *The American Geography; or, A View of the Present Situation of the United States of America. . . .* 2nd ed. London: John Stockdale, 1792.

Mosely, Philip E. "Aspects of Russian Expansion." *American Slavic and East European Review* 7, no. 3 (October 1948): 197–213. http://dx.doi.org/10.2307/2492130.

Moses, A. Dirk, ed. *Empire, Colony, Genocide: Conquest, Occupation, and Subaltern Resistance in World History*. New York, Oxford: Berghahn, 2010.

Myres, John L. "Nomadism." *Journal of the Royal Anthropological Institute of Great Britain and Ireland* 71, nos. 1–2 (1941): 19–42. http://dx.doi.org/10.2307/2844399.

Nadeau, Remi. *Fort Laramie and the Sioux*. 1967. Santa Barbara, CA: Crest, 1997.

von Nardroff, Ellen. "The American Frontier as a Safety Valve—The Life, Death, Reincarnation, and Justification of a Theory." *Agricultural History* 36 (July 1962): 123–42.

Nasatir, Abraham P. "Anglo-Spanish Rivalry on the Upper Missouri." *Mississippi Valley Historical Review* 16, no. 3 (December 1929): 359–82. http://dx.doi.org/10.2307/1895064.

Nasatir, Abraham P. "The Shifting Borderlands." *Pacific Historical Review* 34, no. 1 (February 1965): 1–20. http://dx.doi.org/10.2307/3636737.

Nasatir, Abraham P., ed. *Before Lewis and Clark: Documents Illustrating the History of the Missouri*. Vol. 2 *Documents Illustrating the History of the Missouri, 1785–1804*. Lincoln: Bison Books, 1990.

Nearing, Scott. *The American Empire*. New York: Rand School of Social Science, 1921.

Newcomb, W. W., Jr. "A Re-Examination of the Causes of Plains Warfare." *American Anthropologist* 52, no. 3 (July/September 1950): 317–30.

Nicholas, Mark A. *Native Voices: Sources in the Native American Past*. Boston: Pearson, 2014.

Nichols, Roger L. "The Canada-US Border and Indigenous Peoples in the Nineteenth Century." *American Review of Canadian Studies* 40, no. 3 (September 2010): 416–28. http://dx.doi.org/10.1080/02722011.2010.496907.

Nikitin, Alexander I. "Russian Eurasianism and American Exceptionalism." In *The Proceedings of the Twenty-First World Congress of Philosophy*. Vol. 2, edited by William L. McBride, 233–38. Ankara: Philosophical Society of Turkey, 2006.

Nisbet, Robert A. *History of the Idea of Progress*. New York: Basic Books, 1980.

Nolan, Mary. "Against Exceptionalisms." Review of *American Exceptionalism: A Double-Edged Sword*, by Seymour Martin Lipset. *American Historical Review* 102, no. 3 (June 1997): 769–74. http://dx.doi.org/10.2307/2171511.

Nugent, Walter. "Frontiers and Empires in the Late Nineteenth Century." *Western Historical Quarterly* 20, no. 4 (November 1989): 393–408. http://dx.doi.org/10.2307/969492.

Nugent, Walter. *Habits of Empire: A History of American Expansion*. New York: Knopf, 2008.

Nurbetova, Gul'nar. *Istoriia "Krasnogo terror" v Kazakhstane (20–30 e gg. XX veka)*. Almaty: Mezhdunarodnogo Kazakhsko-Turestkogo universiteta imeni Kh. A. Iasavi, 2003.

Nurtazina, Nazira. "Great Famine of 1931–1933 in Kazakhstan: A Contemporary's Reminiscences." *Acta Slavica Iaponica* 32 (2012): 105–29.

Nylan, Michael. "Talk about 'Barbarians' in Antiquity." *Philosophy East & West* 62, no. 4 (October 2012): 580–601. http://dx.doi.org/10.1353/pew.2012.0063.

Oehler, C. M. *The Great Sioux Uprising*. 1959. New York: Da Capo, 1997.

Office of Indian Affairs. *Indians at Work* 1. Washington, DC: Office of Indian Affairs, March 1, 1934.

Ohayon, Isabelle. *La sédentarisation des Kazakhs dans l'URSS de Staline: Collectivisation et changement social (1928–1945)*. Paris: Maisonneuve et Larose, 2006.

Okladnikov, A. P., and O. N. Vilkov. "Prisoedinenie zapadnoi Sibiri k Rossii i razvitie ekonomicheskikh sviazei s Kazakhstanom v kontse XVI—pervoi chetverti XVIII v." *Izvestiia Akademii Nauk Kazakhskoi SSR* (May/June 1982): 21–25.

Olcott, Martha Brill. "The Settlement of Kazakh Nomads." *Nomadic Papers* 8 (1981): 12–23.

Olcott, Martha Brill. *The Kazakhs*. 2nd ed. Stanford, CA: Hoover Institution Press, 1987.

Olson, James C. *Red Cloud and the Sioux Problem*. Lincoln: University of Nebraska Press, 1965.

Orth, Samuel P. *The Imperial Impulse: Background Studies of Belgium, England, France, Germany, Russia*. New York: Century Co., 1916.

Osterhammel, Jürgen. *Colonialism: A Theoretical Overview*. Kingston: Ian Randle, 1997.

Ostler, Jeffrey. *The Plains Sioux and U.S. Colonialism from Lewis and Clark to Wounded Knee*. Cambridge: Cambridge University Press, 2004.

Ottoson, Howard W., ed. *Land Use Policy and Problems in the United States*. Lincoln: University of Nebraska Press, 1963.

Pagden, Anthony. *Lords of All the World: Ideologies of Empire in Spain, Britain and France, c. 1500–c. 1800*. New Haven, CT: Yale University Press, 1995.

Pakenham, Thomas. *The Scramble for Africa: The White Man's Conquest of the Dark Continent from 1876 to 1912*. New York: Random House, 1991.

Palat, Madhavan K. "Tsarist Russian Imperialism." *Studies in History* 4, nos. 1–2 (February 1988): 157–297. http://dx.doi.org/10.1177/025764308800400104.

de Palosi, Ervin. "Question de la terre dans la zone des steppes: L'etat des proprieties chez les Kirghizes." *Turan* (October 1918): 472–87.

Pancoast, Henry S. *Impressions of the Sioux Tribes in 1882, With Some First Principles in the Indian Question*. Philadelphia: Allen, Lane & Scott, 1883.

Parker, Geoffrey. *The Geopolitics of Domination*. London: Routledge, 1988.

Parkman, Francis. *Montcalm and Wolfe*. Vol. 1. Boston: Little, Brown, 1912.

Parrish, Peter J. "An Exception to Most of the Rules: What Made American Nationalism Different in the Mid-Nineteenth Century?" *Prologue: Quarterly of the National Archives* 27 (Fall 1995): 219–29.

Patai, Raphael. "Nomadism: Middle Eastern and Central Asia." *Southwestern Journal of Anthropology* 7, no. 4 (Winter 1951): 401–14. http://dx.doi.org/10.1086/soutjanth.7.4.3628514.

Patterson, Palmer. "The Colonial Parallel: A View of Indian History." *Ethnohistory* 18, no. 1 (Winter 1971): 1–17. http://dx.doi.org/10.2307/481590.

Paul, R. Eli, ed. *Autobiography of Red Cloud: War Leader of the Oglalas*. Helena: Montana Historical Society Press, 1997.

Pearce, Roy Harvey. *The Savages of America: A Study of the Indian and the Idea of Civilization*. Rev. ed. Baltimore: Johns Hopkins Press, 1965.

Pease, Donald E. *The New American Exceptionalism*. Minneapolis: University of Minnesota Press, 2009.

Peffer, William A. "Imperialism America's Historic Policy." *North American Review* 171 (August 1900): 246–58.

Petitjean, Patrick, Catherine Jami, and Anne Marie Moulin, eds. *Science and Empires: Historical Studies about Scientific Development and European Expansion*. Boston: Kluwer Academic, 1992. http://dx.doi.org/10.1007/978-94-011-2594-9.

Pianciola, Niccolò. "The Collectivization Famine in Kazakhstan, 1931–33." *Harvard Ukrainian Studies* 25 (Fall 2001): 237–51.

Pianciola, Niccolò, and Susan Finnel. "Famine in the Steppe: The Collectivization of Agriculture and the Kazakh Herdsmen, 1928–1934." *Cahiers du monde russe* 45, nos. 1–2 (2004): 137–92. http://dx.doi.org/10.4000/monderusse.2623.

Pickens, Donald K. "Westward Expansion and the End of American Exceptionalism: Sumner, Turner, and Webb." *Western Historical Quarterly* 12, no. 4 (October 1981): 409–18. http://dx.doi.org/10.2307/968852.

Pidgeon, William. *Traditions of De-Coo-Dah and antiquarian researches: Comprising extensive explorations, surveys, and excavations of the wonderful and mysterious earthen remains of the mound-builders in America. . . .* New York: Horace Thayer, 1858.

Pierce, Richard A. *Russian Central Asia, 1867–1917: A Study in Colonial Rule*. Berkeley: University of California Press, 1960.

Pishchulina, K. A. *Iugo-vostochnyi Kazakhstana v seredine XIV-nachale XVI veka*. Alma-Ata: Nauka, 1977.

Pluciennik, Mark. "The Invention of Hunter-Gatherers in Seventeenth-Century Europe." *Archaeological Dialogues* 9, no. 2 (December 2002): 98–118. http://dx.doi.org/10.1017/S1380203800002142.

Poliakov, Leon. *The Aryan Myth: A History of Racist and Nationalist Ideas in Europe*. Translated from French by Edmund Howard. New York: Basic Books, 1974.

Poltoratzky, N. P. "Nikolay Beryayev's Interpretation of Russia's Historical Mission." *Slavonic and East European Review* 45 (January 1967): 193–206.

Pomerance, Michla. "The United States and Self Determination: Perspectives on the Wilsonian Conception." *American Journal of International Law* 70, no. 1 (January 1976): 1–27.

Pomeranz, Kenneth. "Empire and 'Civilizing' Missions, Past and Present." *Daedalus* 134, no. 2 (Spring 2005): 34–45. http://dx.doi.org/10.1162/0011526053887428.

Pomeroy, Earl S. *In Search of the Golden West: The Tourist in Western America*. New York: Knopf, 1957.

Pomper, Philip. "The History and Theory of Empires." *History and Theory* 44, no. 4 (December 2005): 1–27. http://dx.doi.org/10.1111/j.1468-2303.2005.00340.x.

Pond, Peter. "1740–75: Journal of Peter Pond." In *Collections of the State Historical Society of Wisconsin*, Vol. 18, edited by Reuben Gold Thwaites, 314–55. Madison: State Historical Society of Wisconsin, 1908.

Potanin, G. N. *Materialy dlia istorii Sibiri sobral G. Potanin*. Moscow: Izdanie Imperatorskogo obshchestva istorii i drevnostei Rossiiskikh pri Moscovskom universitete, 1867.

Powell, J. W. "From Barbarism to Civilization." *American Anthropologist* 1, no. 2 (April 1888): 97–124. http://dx.doi.org/10.1525/aa.1888.1.2.02a00000.

Pratt, Mary Louise. *Imperial Eyes: Travel Writing and Transculturation*. London: Routledge, 1992. http://dx.doi.org/10.4324/9780203163672.

Price, Catherine. "Lakotas and Euroamericans: Contrasted Concepts of 'Chieftainship' and Decision-Making Authority." *Ethnohistory* 41, no. 3 (Summer 1994): 447–63. http://dx.doi.org/10.2307/481834.

Priest, Loring B. *Uncle Sam's Stepchildren: The Reformation of United States Indian Policy, 1865–1887*. New York: Octagon Books, 1972.

Prince, Joseph M., and Richard H. Steckel. "Nutritional Success on the Great Plains: Nineteenth-Century Equestrian Nomads." *Journal of Interdisciplinary History* 33, no. 3 (Winter 2003): 353–84. http://dx.doi.org/10.1162/002219502320815163.

Prochaska, David. *Making Algeria French: Colonialism in Bône, 1870–1920*. Cambridge: Cambridge University Press, 1990.

Prucha, Francis Paul. *American Indian Policy in Crisis: Christian Reformers and the Indian, 1865–1900*. Norman: University of Oklahoma Press, 1976.

Prucha, Francis Paul. *The Great Father: The United States Government and the American Indians*. 2 vols. Lincoln: University of Nebraska Press, 1984.

Prucha, Francis Paul. *American Indian Treaties: The History of a Political Anomaly*. Berkeley: University of California Press, 1994.

Pu, Muzhou. *Enemies of Civilization: Attitudes toward Foreigners in Ancient Mesopotamia, Egypt, and China*. Albany: State University of New York Press, 2005.

Pushkin, Alexander. "Nabroski stat'i o russkoi literature," *Polnoe Sobranie sochinenii*. Vol. 11. Moscow: Akademiia nauk SSSR, 1937.

Pyenson, Lewis. "Why Science May Serve Political Ends: Cultural Imperialism and the Mission to Civilize." *Berichte zur Wissenschaftsgeschichte* 13, no. 2 (1990): 69–81. http://dx.doi.org/10.1002/bewi.19900130203.

Quinn, Frederick. *The French Overseas Empire*. Westport, CT: Praeger, 2000.

Reinhardt, Akim D. *Ruling Pine Ridge: Oglala Lakota Politics from the IRA to Wounded Knee.* Lubbock: Texas Tech University Press, 2007.

Roberts, Timothy, and Emrah Şahin. "Construction of National Identities in Early Republics: A Comparison of the American and Turkish Cases." *Journal of the Historical Society* 10, no. 4 (December 2010): 507–31. http://dx.doi.org/10.1111/j.1540-5923.2010.00315.x.

Rabow-Edling, Susanna. *Slavophile Thought and the Politics of Cultural Nationalism.* Albany: State University of New York Press, 2006.

Raeff, Marc. "The Philosophical Views of Count M. M. Speransky." *Slavonic and East European Review* 31, no. 77 (June 1953): 437–51.

Raeff, Marc. *Russian Intellectual History: An Anthology.* New York: Harcourt, Brace & World, 1966.

Ram, Harsha. *The Imperial Sublime: A Russian Poetics of Empire.* Madison: University of Wisconsin Press, 2006.

Rawlinson, H. C. "Observations on two Memoirs recently published by M. Veniukof on the Pamir Region and the Bolor Country in Central Asia." *Proceedings of the Royal Geographical Society of London* 10, no. 4 (1865–1866): 134–53. http://dx.doi.org/10.2307/1799426.

Readman, Paul, Cynthia Radding, and Chad Bryant, eds. *Borderlands in World History, 1700–1914.* New York: Palgrave Macmillan, 2014. http://dx.doi.org/10.1057/9781137320582.

Reilly, Hugh J. *Bound to Have Blood: Frontier Newspapers and the Plains Indian Wars.* Lincoln: University of Nebraska Press, 2011.

Rozhdestvensii, S. V., ed. *Istoricheskii obzor deiatel'nosti Ministerstva Narodnogo Proveshcheniia, 1802–1902.* St. Petersburg: Ministerstvo Narodnogo Prosveshcheniia, 1902.

Riasanovsky, Nicholas V., and Mark D. Steinberg. *A History of Russia.* 8th ed. New York: Oxford University Press, 2011.

Rice, Julian. "'It Was Their Own Fault for Being Intractable': Internalized Racism and Wounded Knee." *American Indian Quarterly* 22 (Winter/Spring 1998): 63–82.

Richards, John F. *The Unending Frontier: An Environmental History of the Early Modern World.* Berkeley: University of California Press, 2003.

Richter, Anthony H. "Father Eugene Buechel and the Lakota Sioux." *Heritage of the Great Plains* 38, no. 1 (Spring/Summer 2005): 4–14.

Rieber, Alfred J. "Russian Imperialism: Popular, Emblematic, Ambiguous." *Russian Review* 53, no. 3 (July 1994): 331–35. http://dx.doi.org/10.2307/131189.

Rieber, Alfred J. "Changing Concepts and Constructions of Frontiers: A Comparative Historical Approach." *Ab Imperio*, no. 1 (2003): 23–46. http://dx.doi.org/10.1353/imp.2003.0104.

Riney, Scott. *The Rapid City Indian School, 1898–1933.* Norman: University of Oklahoma Press, 1999.

Robinson, Doane. *A History of the Dakota or Sioux Indians. . . .* 1904. Minneapolis: Ross & Haines, 1967.

Robinson, Geroid T. *Rural Russia Under the Old Regime: A History of the Landlord-Peasant World and a Prologue to the Peasant Revolution of 1917.* Berkeley: University of California Press, 1969.

Roberts, Henry L. "Russia and the West: A Comparison and Contrast." *Slavic Review* 23, no. 1 (March 1964): 1–12. http://dx.doi.org/10.2307/2492370.

Rochester, Anna. *Lenin on the Agrarian Question.* New York: International Publishers, 1942.

de Rocco, Felix. "Deplacement des Kirghiz en ete." *Revue de Geographie* 39 (1896): 171–74.

Ronen, Dov. *The Quest for Self-Determination.* New Haven, CT: Yale University Press, 1979.

Rose, Deborah Bird. *Hidden Histories: Black Stories from Victoria River Downs, Humbert River and Wave Hill Stations.* Canberra: Aboriginal Studies Press, 1991.

Ross, Frank E. "The Fur Trade of the Western Great Lakes Region." *Minnesota History* 19 (September 1938): 271–307.

Rottier, Peter. "The Kazakness of Sedentarization: Promoting Progress as Tradition in Response to the Land Problem." *Central Asian Survey* 22, no. 1 (March 2003): 67–81. http://dx.doi.org/10.1080/0263493032000108630.

Rozhkova, M. K. "Iz istorii torgovli Rossii so Srednei Aziei v 60-x godakh XIX v." *Istoricheskie zapiski*, no. 67 (1960): 187–212.

Runte, Alfred. "Promoting the Golden West: Advertising and the Railroad." *California History* 70, no. 1 (Spring 1991): 62–75. http://dx.doi.org/10.2307/25158553.

Russell, Peter A. "The Far-from-Dry Debates: Dry Farming on the Canadian Prairies and the American Great Plains." *Agricultural History* 81, no. 4 (Fall 2007): 493–521. http://dx.doi.org/10.3098/ah.2007.81.4.493.

"Russia and the Kazakhs in the Eighteenth and Nineteenth Centuries." *Central Asian Review* 5, no. 4 (1957): 353–59.

Ryskulov, Turar R. *Kazakstan.* Moscow: Gos. izd-vo, 1927.

Rywkin, Michael, ed. *Russian Colonial Expansion to 1917.* London: Mansell, 1988.

Sabol, Steven. *Russian Colonization and the Genesis of Kazak National Consciousness.* London: Palgrave Macmillan, 2003. http://dx.doi.org/10.1057/9780230599420.

Sabol, Steven. "Kazak Resistance to Russian Colonization: Interpreting the Kenesary Kasymov Revolt, 1837–1847." *Central Asian Survey* 22, nos. 2–3 (June/September 2003): 231–52. http://dx.doi.org/10.1080/0263493032000157703.

Sabyrkhanov, A. "Torgovaia politika tsarizma v mladshchem zhuze v vtoroi polovine XVIII veka." *Izvestiia AN KazSSR, seriia obshchestvennaia*, no. 6 (1967): 44–53.

Sabyrkhanov, A. "Zemel'naia politika tsarskogo pravitel'stva v mladshem zhuze vo vtoroi polovine XVIII veka." *Izvestiia AN KazSSR, seriia obshchestvennaia*, no. 2 (1968): 40–48.

Sabyrkhanov, A. "Zemel'nyi vopros v mladshem zhuze vo vtoroi XVIII veka (o predposylkakh uchastiia Kazakhov v krest'ianskoi voine 1773–1775 gg." *Izvestiia AN KazSSR*, no. 2 (1977): 55–59.

Sahni, Kalpana. *Crucifying the Orient: Russian Orientalism and the Colonization of the Caucasus and Central Asia.* Oslo: White Orchid Press, 1997.

Said, Edward W. *Orientalism.* New York: Vintage, 1979.

Sakwa, Richard. "Perestroika and the Challenge of Democracy in Russia." *Demokratizatsiya: The Journal of Post-Soviet Democratization* 13, no. 2 (Spring 2005): 255–75. http://dx.doi.org/10.3200/DEMO.13.2.255-276.

Salzman, Philip C. "Political Organization among Nomadic Peoples." *Proceedings of the American Philosophical Society* 111, no. 2 (1967): 115–31.

Salzman, Philip C., ed. *When Nomads Settle: Processes of Sedentarization as Adaptation and Response.* New York: Praeger, 1980.

Sapargaliev, G. *Karatel'naia politika tsarisma v Kazakhstan (1905–1917 gg.).* Alma-Ata: Nauka, 1966.

Schimmelpennick van der Oye, David. *Russian Orientalism: Asia in the Russian Mind from Peter the Great to the Emigration.* New Haven, CT: Yale University Press, 2010. http://dx.doi.org/10.12987/yale/9780300110630.001.0001.

Schueller, Malini Johar, and Edward Watts, eds. *Messy Beginnings: Postcoloniality and Early American Studies.* New Brunswick, NJ: Rutgers University Press, 2003.

Schusky, Ernest L. "The Evolution of Indian Leadership on the Great Plains, 1750–1950." *American Indian Quarterly* 10, no. 1 (Winter 1986): 65–82. http://dx.doi.org/10.2307/1184156.

Schwarz, Solomon M. "Revising the History of Russian Colonialism." *Foreign Affairs* 30, no. 3 (April 1952): 488–93. http://dx.doi.org/10.2307/20030915.

Seaman, Gary, ed. *Ecology and Empire: Nomads in the Cultural Evolution of the Old World*. Los Angeles: Ethnographics, 1989.

Seaman, G., ed. *Foundations of Empire: Archaeology and Art of the Eurasian Steppes*. Los Angeles: Ethnographics, 1992.

"Seasonal Nomadism." *Central Asian Review* 4 (1956): 226–38.

Seeland, Nicholas. *Les Kirghis. Revue d'Anthropologie* (1886): 25–92.

Senier, Siobhan. "Allotment Protest and Tribal Discourse: Reading Wynema's Successes and Shortcomings." *American Indian Quarterly* 24, no. 3 (Summer 2000): 420–40. http://dx.doi.org/10.1353/aiq.2000.0010.

Sereda, N. A. *Bunt kirgizskogo sultana Kenesary Kasymova, 1838–1847*. 1870. Atyrau: Po zakazu Oblastnogo otniia fonda kul'tury g. Atyrau Respubliki Kazakhstan, 1992.

Sewell, William H., Jr. "Marc Bloch and the Logic of Comparative History." *History and Theory* 6, no. 2 (1967): 208–18. http://dx.doi.org/10.2307/2504361.

S'ezdy sovetov RSFSR i avtonomnykh respublik RSFSR. Vol. 1. Moscow: n.p., 1959.

Shakhmatov, V. F. "K voprosu o razlozhenii Kazakhskoi pastbishchno-kochevoi obshchiny v XIX-nachale XX vv." *Vestnik Akademii Nauk Kazakhskoi SSR*, no. 9 (Sentiabr' 1958): 21–36.

Shannon, Fred A. "Culture and Agriculture in America." *Mississippi Valley Historical Review* 41, no. 1 (June 1954): 3–20. http://dx.doi.org/10.2307/1898147.

Sharp, Paul F. "The American Farmer and the 'Last Best West.'" *Agricultural History* 21 (April 1947): 65–75.

Sharp, Paul F. "Three Frontiers: Some Comparative Studies of Canadian, American, and Australian Settlement." *Pacific Historical Review* 24, no. 4 (November 1955): 369–77. http://dx.doi.org/10.2307/3635321.

Shayakhmmetov, Mukhamet. *The Silent Steppe: The Memoir of a Kazakh Nomad Under Stalin*. Trans. Jan Butler. New York: Overlook/Rookery, 2006.

Shlapentokh, Vladimir. "How Russians Will See the Status of Their Country by the End of the Century." *Journal of Communist Studies and Transition Politics* 13, no. 3 (1997): 1–23. http://dx.doi.org/10.1080/13523279708415351.

Shoemaker, Nancy. "How Indians Got to Be Red." *American Historical Review* 102, no. 3 (June 1997): 625–44. http://dx.doi.org/10.2307/2171504.

Siegelbaum, Lewis. "Those Elusive Scouts: Pioneering Peasants and the Russian State, 1870s–1950s." *Kritika: Explorations in Russian and Eurasian History* 14, no. 1 (Winter 2013): 31–58. http://dx.doi.org/10.1353/kri.2013.0007.

Siegelbaum, Lewis H., and Leslie Page Moch. *Broad Is My Native Land: Repertoires and Regimes of Migration in Russia's Twentieth Century*. Ithaca, NY: Cornell University Press, 2014.

Simms, James Y., Jr. "The Crop Failure of 1891: Soil Exhaustion, Technological Backwardness, and Russia's 'Agrarian Crisis.'" *Slavic Review* 41, no. 2 (Summer 1982): 236–50. http://dx.doi.org/10.2307/2496341.

Singleton, Esther, ed. and trans. *Russia, As Seen and Described by Famous Writers*. New York: Dodd, Mead, 1904.

Skinner, Alanson. "A Sketch of Eastern Dakota Ethnology." *American Anthropologist* 21, no. 2 (April/June 1919): 164–74. http://dx.doi.org/10.1525/aa.1919.21.2.02a00040.

Skliarov, L. F. *Pereselenie i zemleustroistvo v Sibiri v gody stolypinskoi agrarnoi reform*. Leningrad: Leningradskogo universiteta, 1962.

Slezkine, Yuri. "From Savages to Citizens: The Cultural Revolution in the Soviet Far North, 1928–1938." *Slavic Review* 51, no. 1 (Spring 1992): 52–76. http://dx.doi.org/10.2307/2500261.

Slezkine, Yuri. *Arctic Mirrors: Russia and the Small Peoples of the North*. Ithaca, NY: Cornell University Press, 1994.

Slocum, John W. "Who, and When, Were the Inorodtsy? The Evolution of the Category of 'Aliens' in Imperial Russia." *Russian Review* 57, no. 2 (April 1998): 173–90. http://dx.doi.org/10.1111/0036-0341.00017.

Slotkin, Richard. *The Fatal Environment: The Myth of the Frontier in the Age of Industrialization, 1800–1890*. New York: HarperPerennial, 1994.

Smirnoff, Eugene. *A Short Account of the Historical Development and Present Position of Russian Orthodox Missions*. London: Rivingtons, 1903.

Smith, Henry Nash. *Virgin Land: The American West as Symbol and Myth*. 1954. Cambridge, MA: Harvard University Press, 1978.

Smith, J. Russell. "Grassland and Farmland as Factors in the Cyclical Development of Eurasian History." *Annals of the Association of American Geographers* 33, no. 3 (September 1943): 135–61. http://dx.doi.org/10.1080/00045604309357248.

Smith, Sherry L. *The View from Officers' Row: Army Perception of Western Indians*. Tucson: University of Arizona Press, 1990.

Smith, Sherry L. *Reimagining Indians: Native Americans through Anglo Eyes, 1880–1940*. Oxford: Oxford University Press, 2000.

Sneath, David. *The Headless State: Aristocratic Orders, Kinship Society, and Misrepresentations of Nomadic Inner Asia*. New York: Columbia University Press, 2007.

Sokol, Edward. *The Revolt of 1916 in Russian Central Asia*. Baltimore: Johns Hopkins University Press, 1954.

Sorgin, Vladimir V. "Russkiia ideia i Amerikanskaia mechta. Razmyshlenie nad sravnitel'notsivilizatsionnym issledovaniem E. Ia. Batalova." *Obshchestvennye nauki i sovremennost'* 6 (2010): 115–23.

Spiro, Peter J. "The New Sovereigntists: American Exceptionalism and Its False Prophets." *Foreign Affairs* 79, no. 6 (2000): 9–15. http://dx.doi.org/10.2307/20049963.

Spooner, Brian. *The Cultural Ecology of Pastoral Nomads*. Reading, MA: Addison-Wesley, 1973.

Stalin, Joseph. *Sochineniia*, vols. 1–13. Moscow: Gospolitizdat, 1946–1951.

St. Germain, Jill. *Broken Treaties: United States and Canadian Relations with the Lakotas and the Plains Cree, 1868–1885*. Lincoln: University of Nebraska Press, 2009.

Starita, Joe. *"I am a Man": Chief Standing Bear's Journey for Justice*. New York: St. Martin's, 2008.

Stensland, Anna Lee. "Charles Alexander Eastman: Sioux Storyteller and Historian." *American Indian Quarterly* 3, no. 3 (Autumn 1977): 199–208. http://dx.doi.org/10.2307/1184537.

Stephanson, Anders. *Manifest Destiny: American Expansion and the Empire of Right*. New York: Hill & Wang, 1995.

Sterling, Captain Anthony C. *Russia under Nicholas the First*. Translated from German. London: John Murray, 1841.

Stevens, Paul L. "Wabasha Visits Governor Carleton, 1776: New Light on a Legendary Episode of Dakota-British Diplomacy on the Great Lakes Frontier." *Michigan Historical Review* 16, no. 1 (Spring 1990): 21–48. http://dx.doi.org/10.2307/20173209.

Stoler, Ann Laura. "Tense and Tender Ties: The Politics of Comparison in North American History and (Post) Colonial Studies." *Journal of American History* 88, no. 3 (December 2001): 829–65. http://dx.doi.org/10.2307/2700385.

Stoler, Ann Laura, ed. *Haunted by Empire: Geographies of Intimacy in North American History*. Durham, NC: Duke University Press, 2006. http://dx.doi.org/10.1215/9780822387992.

Stoler, Ann Laura, Carole McGranahan, and Peter C. Purdue, eds. *Imperial Formations*. Santa Fe: School for Advanced Research Press, 2007.

Stone, John. "Introduction: Internal Colonialism in Comparative Perspective." *Ethnic and Racial Studies* 2, no. 3 (July 1979): 255–59. http://dx.doi.org/10.1080/01419870.1979.9993267.

Stuart-Fox, Martin. "Evolutionary Theory of History." *History and Theory* 38, no. 4 (December 1999): 33–51. http://dx.doi.org/10.1111/0018-2656.00103.

Sturova, Mariia Viktorovna. "Obrazovatel'naia sreda na territorii Akmolinskoi i Semipalatinskskoi oblastei (50–80-e gg. XIX v.)." *Izvestiia Altaiskogo Gosudarstvennogo Universiteta* 2, no. 4 (80) (2013): 98–102.

Sukhikh, O. E. "'V strane svobodnoi i stepnoi . . .', ili Russkii romantizm nachala XIX v. v poiskakh Kazakhskoi ekzotiki." *Vestnik Omskogo universiteta* 3 (2009): 62–68.

Sultanov, T. I. "Nekotorye zamechaniia o nachale Kazakhskoi gosudarstvennosti." *Izvestiia AN Kaz SSR, seriia obshchestvennaia* no. 1 (1971): 55–56.

Sundetov, S. "K voprosu ob osedanii Kazakhov v nachale XX veka." *Izvestiia Akademii Nauk Kazakhskoi SSR, seriia istorii, arkheologii i etnografii*, no. 3 (1961): 69–70.

Suleimenov, B. *Agrarnyi vopros v Kazakhstane poslednei treti XIX-nachala XX v. (1867–1907 gg.)*. Alma-Ata: Akademii nauk SSSR, 1963.

Stannard, David E. *American Holocaust: The Conquest of the New World*. Oxford: Oxford University Press, 1993.

Stumm, Hugo. *Russia in Central Asia: Historical Sketch of Russia's Progress in the East up to 1873, and of the Incidents which Led to the Campaign against Khiva; with a Description of the Military Districts of the Caucasus, Orenburg, and Turkestan*. Translated by J. W. Ozanne and Captain H. Sachs. London: Harrison & Sons, 1885.

Sunderland, Willard. "The 'Colonization Question': Visions of Colonization in Late Imperial Russia." *Jahrbücher für Geschichte Osteuropas* 48 (2000): 210–32.

Sunderland, Willard. "Peasant Pioneering: Russian Peasant Settlers Describe Colonization and the Eastern Frontier, 1880s–1910s." *Journal of Social History* 34, no. 4 (Summer 2001): 895–922. http://dx.doi.org/10.1353/jsh.2001.0070.

Sunderland, Willard. *Taming the Wild Field: Colonization and Empire on the Russian Steppe*. Ithaca, NY: Cornell University Press, 2004.

Sunderland, Willard. "The Ministry of Asiatic Russia: The Colonial Office That Never Was But Might Have Been." *Slavic Review* 69, no. 1 (Spring 2010): 120–50.

Swift, Jonathan. *Gulliver's Travels into Several Remote Nations of the World*. London: Temple Press, 1939.

Sysoeva, E. K. "Education Policy in Russia from the 1860s through the 1890s." *Russian Education and Society* 39 (1997): 62–76.

Szasz, Margaret. "Indian Reform in a Decade of Prosperity." *Montana: The Magazine of Western History* 20, no. 1 (Winter 1970): 16–27.

Tate, Michael L. "From Cooperation to Conflict: Sioux Relations with the Overland Emigrants, 1845–1865." *Overland Journal* 18, no. 4 (Winter 2000–2001): 18–31.
Teleuova, Elmira. "From History of Nomadic Customary Law." *Sensus Historiae* 7, no. 2 (2012): 169–80.
Tempest, Richard. "Madman or Criminal: Government Attitudes to Petr Chaadaev in 1836." *Slavic Review* 43 (Summer 1984): 281–87.
Terent'ev, M. A. *Istoriia zavoevaniia Srednei Azii*. Vol. 1. St. Petersburg: Tipografiia Komorova, 1906.
Thelen, David. "Of Audiences, Borderlands, and Comparisons: Toward the Internationalization of American History." *Journal of American History* 79, no. 2 (1992): 432–62. http://dx.doi.org/10.2307/2080034.
Thompson, Ewa M. *Imperial Knowledge: Russian Literature and Colonialism*. Westport, CT: Greenwood, 2000.
Thomas, Robert K. "Colonialism: Classic and Internal." *New University Thought* 4, no. 4 (1966): 37–44.
Thornton, A. P. "Colonialism." *International Journal* 17, no. 4 (Autumn 1962): 335–57. http://dx.doi.org/10.2307/40198890.
Thornton, Russell. *American Indian Holocaust and Survival: A Population History since 1492*. Norman: University of Oklahoma Press, 1987.
Thwaites, Reuben Gold, ed. *Collections of the State Historical Society of Wisconsin*. Vol. 18. Madison: State Historical Society of Wisconsin, 1908.
Tillett, Lowell R. *The Great Friendship: Soviet Historians and the Non-Russian Nationalities*. Chapel Hill: University of North Carolina Press, 1969.
Tinker, George E. *Missionary Conquest: The Gospel and Native American Cultural Genocide*. Minneapolis: Fortress Press, 1993.
Tipps, Dean C. "Modernization Theory and the Comparative Study of National Societies: A Critical Perspective." *Comparative Studies in Society and History* 15, no. 2 (March 1973): 199–226. http://dx.doi.org/10.1017/S0010417500007039.
Tleptsok, Ruslan A. "Problema 'imperskogo rasshireniia' Rossii v poniatiiakh i terminakh." *Vestnik Maikopskogo gosudarstvennogo tekhnologicheskogo universiteta* 3 (2010): 1–13.
Tolybekov, S. E. *Kochevoe obshchestvo kazakhov v XVII–nachale XX veka: politik-ekonomicheskii analiz*. Alma-Ata: Nauka, 1971.
Tolz, Vera. "Tolz, Vera. "Orientalism, Nationalism, and Ethnic Diversity in Late Imperial Russia." *Historical Journal* 48, no. 1 (March 2005): 127–50. http://dx.doi.org/10.1017/S0018246X04004248.
Tolz, Vera. "Imperial Scholars and Minority Nationalisms in Late Imperial and Early Soviet Russia." *Kritika: Explorations in Russian and Eurasian History* 10, no. 2 (Spring 2009): 261–90. http://dx.doi.org/10.1353/kri.0.0086.
Tomilov, Nikolaj A. "Ethnic Processes within the Turkic Population of the West Siberian Plain (Sixteenth–Twentieth Centuries)." *Cahiers du monde russe* 41, nos. 2–3 (April/September 2000): 221–32. http://dx.doi.org/10.4000/monderusse.44.
Trafzer, Clifford E., and Joel R. Hyer, eds. *Exterminate Them: Written Accounts of the Murder, Rape, and Enslavement of Native Americans during the California Gold Rush*. East Lansing: Michigan State University Press, 1999.
Treadgold, Donald W. "Russian Expansion in the Light of Turner's Study of the American Frontier." *Agricultural History* 24, no. 4 (October 1952): 147–52.

Treadgold, Donald W. *The Great Siberian Migration: Government and Peasant in Resettlement from Emancipation to the First World War.* Princeton, NJ: Princeton University Press, 1957. http://dx.doi.org/10.1515/9781400877645.

Trennert, Robert A., Jr. *Alternative to Extinction: Federal Indian Policy and the Beginnings of the Reservation System, 1846–51.* Philadelphia: Temple University Press, 1975.

Trexler, H. A. "The Buffalo Range of the Northwest." *Mississippi Valley Historical Review* 7, no. 4 (March 1921): 348–62. http://dx.doi.org/10.2307/1886193.

Trigger, Bruce G. "The Jesuits and the Fur Trade." *Ethnohistory* 12, no. 1 (Winter 1965): 30–53. http://dx.doi.org/10.2307/480866.

Tuna, Mustafa Özgür. "Gaspirali v. Il'minskii: Two Identity Projects for the Muslims of the Russian Empire." *Nationalities Papers* 30, no. 2 (2002): 265–89. http://dx.doi.org/10.1080/00905990220140658.

Turashbekova, D. A. "Pravovye aspekty voenno-diplomaticheskikh deistvii khana mladshego zhuza Abulkhaira." *Al-Farabi Kazakh National University, KazNU Bulletin, Law Series* no. 3 (67) (2013): 3–7.

Turner, Frederick Jackson. *The Frontier in American History.* New York: Henry Holt, 1920.

Turner, Frederick Jackson. *The Significance of Sections in American History.* New York: Peter Smith, 1950.

Tursunbaev, A. B. *Iz istorii krest'ianskogo pereseleniia v Kazakhstan.* Alma-Ata: Akademiia nauk SSSR, 1950.

Tyrrell, Ian. "American Exceptionalism in an Age of International History." *American Historical Review* 96, no. 4 (October 1991): 1031–55. http://dx.doi.org/10.2307/2164993.

Valandra, Edward C. "U.S. Citizenship: The American Policy to Extinguish the Principle of Lakota Political Consent." *Wicazo Sa Review* 8, no. 2 (Autumn 1992): 24–29. http://dx.doi.org/10.2307/1408994.

US Bureau of the Census. *The Indian Population in the United States and Alaska, 1910.* Washington, DC: Government Printing Office, 1915.

US Congress. "An Act to Regulate Trade and Intercourse with the Indian Tribes." In *The Debates and Proceedings in the Congress of the United States; with an Appendix Containing Important State Papers and Public Documents and All the Laws of a Public Nature, With a Copious Index.* Vol. 1. Washington, DC: Gales & Seaton, 1834.

US Department of the Interior. "Letter of the Secretary of the Interior Communicating, in Compliance with a Resolution of the Senate of the 8th Instant, Information Touching the Origin and Progress of Indian Hostilities on the Frontier." 40th Cong., 1st sess. Senate Executive Document 13. Washington, DC: Government Printing Office, 1867.

US Department of the Interior, Office of Indian Affairs, *Annual Report of the Commissioner of Indian Affairs to the Secretary of the Interior. . . .* Washington, DC: Government Printing Office, 1850–1909.

Usenbaev, Kushbek. *1916: Geroicheskie i tragicheskie stranitsy.* Bishkek: Sham, 1997.

Usher, Abbot Payson. "The History of Population and Settlement in Eurasia." *Geographical Review* 20, no. 1 (January 1930): 110–32. http://dx.doi.org/10.2307/209129.

Usselman, Steven W. *Regulating Railroad Innovation: Business, Technology, and Politics in America, 1840–1920.* Cambridge: Cambridge University Press, 2002. http://dx.doi.org/10.1017/CBO9780511511745.

Utley, Robert M. *The Last Days of the Sioux Nation.* New Haven, CT: Yale University Press, 1963.

Utley, Robert M. *The Lance and the Shield: The Life and Times of Sitting Bull.* New York: Henry Holt, 1993.

Utley, Robert M. *The Indian Frontier, 1846–1890.* Rev. ed. Albuquerque: University of New Mexico Press, 2003.

Vaganov, O. A. "Zemelnaia politika tsarskogo pravitelstva v Kazakhstane." *Istoricheskie zapiski*, no. 31 (1950): 71–73.

Vainshtein, Sevyan. *Nomads of South Siberia: The Pastoral Economies of Tuva.* Cambridge: Cambridge University Press, 1980.

Van Alstyne, R. W. *The Rising American Empire.* New York: Oxford University Press, 1960.

Van den Braembussche, A. A. "Historical Explanation and Comparative Method: Towards a Theory of the History of Society." *History and Theory* 28, no. 1 (February 1989): 1–24. http://dx.doi.org/10.2307/2505267.

Vandiveer, Clarence A. *The Fur-Trade and Early Western Exploration.* Cleveland, OH: Arthur H. Clark, 1929.

Vaughan, Alden T. "From White Man to Redskin: Changing Anglo-American Perceptions of the American Indian." *American Historical Review* 87, no. 4 (October 1982): 917–53. http://dx.doi.org/10.2307/1857900.

Vdovina, L. N. "What are 'We'? Russian National Consciousness in Its Historical Context from the Middle Ages to Modern Times." *Russian Studies in History* 37, no. 2 (1998): 25–35. http://dx.doi.org/10.2753/RSH1061-1983370225.

Vel'iaminov-Zernov, V. V. *Istoricheskie izvestiia o Kirgiz-kaisakakh i snosheniiakh Rossii so Srednei Aziei so vremeni konchiny Abulkhair-khana (1748–1765 gg.).* Ufa: Gub. tip., 1853.

Verney, Lady Frances Parthenope. *How the Peasant Owner Lives in Parts of France, Germany, Italy, Russia.* London: Macmillan, 1888.

Viatkin, M. P. *Batyr Srym.* Almaty: Sanat, 1998.

Vikhavainen, Timo. "Sankt-Peterburg glazami finskikh korrespondentov, Vtoraia polovine XIX v." In *Gel'singfors-Sankt-Peterburg, Stranitsy istorii vtoraiia polovine XIX-nachalo XX veka*, edited by T. Vikhavainen and S. G. Kashchenko, 85–108. St. Petersburg: Nestor-Istoriia, 2012.

Vinkovetsky, Ilya. *Russian America: An Overseas Colony of a Continental Empire, 1804–1867.* Oxford: Oxford University Press, 2011. http://dx.doi.org/10.1093/acprof:oso/9780195391282.001.0001.

Walicki, Andrzej. "Russian Social Thought: An Introduction to the Intellectual History of Nineteenth-Century Russia." *Russian Review* 36, no. 1 (January 1977): 1–45. http://dx.doi.org/10.2307/128768.

Walker, James R. *Lakota Society.* Edited by Raymond J. DeMallie. Lincoln: University of Nebraska Press, 1992.

Wardell, John W. *In the Kirghiz Steppes.* London: Galley Press, 1961.

Webb, Walter Prescott. *The Great Frontier.* Boston: Houghton Mifflin, 1952.

Weissleder, Wolfgang, ed. *The Nomadic Alternative: Modes and Models of Interaction in the African-Asian Deserts and Steppes.* The Hague: Mouton, 1978. http://dx.doi.org/10.1515/9783110810233.

Werth, Nicolas. "Stalinist State Violence: A Reappraisal Twenty Years after the Archival Revolution." *Tijdschrift voor Geschiedenis* 124, no. 4 (December 2011): 480–91. http://dx.doi.org/10.5117/TVGESCH2011.4.WERT.

Wessel, Thomas R. "Agent of Acculturation: Farming on the Northern Plains Reservations, 1880–1910." *Agricultural History* 60, no. 2 (Spring 1986): 233–45.

Wheeler, Burton K., with Paul F. Healy. *Yankee from the West: The Candid, Turbulent Life Story of the Yankee-Born U.S. Senator from Montana.* New York: Doubleday, 1962.

Wheeler, Geoffrey. *The Modern History of Soviet Central Asia.* New York: Praeger, 1964.

Wheeler, Marcus. *Oxford Russian-English Dictionary*. Oxford: Clarendon, 1972.
Whelan, Mary K. "Dakota Indian Economics and the Nineteenth-Century Fur Trade." *Ethnohistory* 40, no. 2 (Spring 1993): 246–76. http://dx.doi.org/10.2307/482203.
Whisenhunt, William Benton. *In Search of Legality: Mikhail M. Speranskii and the Codification of Russian Law*. Boulder, CO: East European Monographs, 2001.
White, Bruce. "Encounters with Spirits: Ojibwa and Dakota Theories about the French and Their Merchandise." *Ethnohistory* 41, no. 3 (Summer 1994): 369–405. http://dx.doi.org/10.2307/481831.
White, Richard. "The Winning of the West: The Expansion of the Western Sioux in the Eighteenth and Nineteenth Centuries." *Journal of American History* 65, no. 2 (September 1978): 319–43. http://dx.doi.org/10.2307/1894083.
White, Richard. *The Middle Ground: Indians, Empires, and the Republics in the Great Lakes Region, 1650–1815*. Cambridge: Cambridge University Press, 1991. http://dx.doi.org/10.1017/CBO9780511584671.
White, Richard. "Discovering Nature in North America." *Journal of American History* 79, no. 3 (December 1992): 874–91. http://dx.doi.org/10.2307/2080791.
Wieczynski, Joseph L. *The Russian Frontier: The Impact of Borderlands upon the Course of Early Russian History*. Charlottesville: University Press of Virginia, 1976.
Williams, D. S. M. "Land Reform in Turkestan." *Slavonic and East European Review* 51, no. 124 (July 1973): 428–38.
Williams, Steven Wyn. "Internal Colonialism, Core-Periphery Contrasts and Devolution: An Integrative Comment." *Area* 9, no. 4 (1977): 272–78.
Williams, William Appleman. *Empire as a Way of Life: An Essay on the Causes and Character of America's Present Predicament Along with a Few Thoughts about an Alternative*. Oxford: Oxford University Press, 1980.
Wilson, Angela Cavender. "Walking into the Future: Dakota Oral Tradition and the Shaping of Historical Consciousness." *Oral History Forum* 19–20 (1999–2000): 25–36.
Winner, Thomas. *The Oral Art and Literature of the Kazakhs of Russian Central Asia*. Durham, NC: Duke University Press, 1958.
Wissler, Clark. "The Influence of the Horse in the Development of Plains Culture." *American Anthropologist* 16, no. 1 (January/March 1914): 1–25. http://dx.doi.org/10.1525/aa.1914.16.1.02a00020.
Woeikof, Alexandre Ivanovitch. "Les ressources agricoles de l'Asia Russe." *Annales de Géographie* 18, no. 100 (1909): 369–70. http://dx.doi.org/10.3406/geo.1909.6675.
Wolfe, Bertram D. "Backwardness and Industrialization in Russian History and Thought." *Slavic Review* 26, no. 2 (June 1967): 177–203. http://dx.doi.org/10.2307/2492449.
Wolf, Eric R. *Europe and the People Without History*. Berkeley: University of California Press, 1982.
Wolfe, Patrick. "Settler Colonialism and the Elimination of the Native." *Journal of Genocide Research* 8, no. 4 (December 2006): 387–409. http://dx.doi.org/10.1080/14623520601056240.
Wolfe, Patrick. "After the Frontier: Separation and Absorption in US Indian Policy." *Settler Colonial Studies* 1, no. 1 (2011): 13–51. http://dx.doi.org/10.1080/2201473X.2011.10648800.
Woodward, C. Vann, ed. *The Comparative Approach to American History*. Oxford: Oxford University Press, 1997.
Wright, George Fredrick. *Asiatic Russia*. Vol. 1. New York: McClure, Phillips, 1902.

Wrobel, David M. *The End of American Exceptionalism: Frontier Anxiety from the Old West to the New Deal*. Lawrence: University Press of Kansas, 1993.
Wrobel, David M. *Global West, American Frontier: Travel, Empire, and Exceptionalism from Manifest Destiny to the Great Depression*. Albuquerque: University of New Mexico Press, 2013.
Wunder, John. *"Retained by the People": A History of American Indians and the Bill of Rights*. Oxford: Oxford University Press, 1994.
Wunder, John, ed. *Native American Cultural and Religious Freedoms*. New York: Garland, 1999.
Wyatt, Don J., and Nicola Di Cosmo. *Political Frontiers, Ethnic Boundaries and Human Geographies in Chinese History*. London: Routledge/Curzon, 2003.
Wyckoff, William, and Gary Hausladen. "Settling the Russian Frontier: With Comparisons to North America." *Soviet Geography* 30 (March 1989): 179–88.
Yenne, Bill. *Indian Wars: The Campaign for the American West*. Yardley, PA: Westholme, 2008.
Zaslow, Morris. "The Frontier Hypothesis in Recent Historiography." *Canadian Historical Review* 29, no. 2 (June 1948): 153–67. http://dx.doi.org/10.3138/CHR-029-02-03.
Zakharov, Victor N. "The Russian Empire: Main Features and Particularities." In *Europe and its Empires*, edited by Mary N. Harris and Csaba Lévai. Pisa: Plus-Pisa University Press, 2008.
Zeisler-Vralsted, Dorothy. *Rivers, Memory, and Nation-Building: A History of the Volga and Mississippi Rivers*. New York: Berghahn, 2015.
Zevin, Robert. "An Interpretation of American Imperialism." *Journal of Economic History* 32, no. 1 (May 1972): 316–60. http://dx.doi.org/10.1017/S0022050700075537.
Ziolkowski, Margaret. *Alien Visions: The Chechens and the Navajos in Russian and American Literature*. Newark: University of Delaware Press, 2005.
Zoriktuev, B. R., ed. *Etnicheskaia istoriia narodov iuzhnoi Sibiri i Tsentral'noi Azii*. Novosibirsk: Nauka, 1993.
Zureik, Elia. T. *The Palestinians in Israel: A Study in Internal Colonialism*. London: Routledge, 1979.

Dissertations

Aubakirova, Kh. "Uchastie Sibirskogo Kazachestva v podavlenii natsional'no-osvoboditel'nogo dvizheniia Kazakhskogo naroda pod predvoditel'stvom sultanov Sarzhana i Kenesary." PhD diss., Eurasian University of Astana, 2000.
Bailey, Scott C. Matsushita. "Travel, Science, and Empire: The Russian Geographical Society's Expeditions to Central Eurasia, 1845–1905." PhD diss., University of Hawaii, 2008.
Cameron, Sarah Isabel. "The Hungry Steppe: Soviet Kazakhstan and the Kazakh Famine, 1921–1934." PhD diss., Yale University, 2010.
Doyle, Susan Badger. "Intercultural Dynamics of the Bozeman Trail Era: Red, White, and Army Blue on the Northern Plains, 1863–1868." PhD diss., University of New Mexico, 1991.
Furnish, Patricia Lee. "'Aboriginally Yours': The Society of American Indians and U.S. Citizenship." PhD diss., University of Oklahoma, Norman, 2005.
Kleitz, Dorsey Rodney. "Orientalism and the American Romantic Imagination: The Middle East in the Works of Irving, Poe, Emerson, and Melville." PhD diss., University of New Hampshire, 1986.

Kreindler, Isabelle. "Educational Policies toward the Eastern Nationalities in Tsarist Russia: A Study of Il'minskii's System." PhD diss., Columbia University, 1969.
Lysenko, Iuliia Aleksandrovna. "Missionarskaia deiatel'nost' Russkoi pravoslavnoi tserkvi v Kazakhstane (vtoraia polovine XIX-nachalo XX v.)." PhD diss., Altai State University (Barnaul), 2011.
Malikov, Yuriy Anatolyevich. "Formation of a Borderland Culture: Myths and Realities of Cossack-Kazakh Relations in Northern Kazakhstan in the Eighteenth and Nineteenth Centuries." PhD diss., University of California, Santa Barbara, 2006.
Medvedev, Natasha. "The Contradictions of Vereshchagin's Turkestan Series: Visualizing the Russian Empire and Its Others." PhD diss., University of California, Los Angeles, 2009.
Simon, Michael Pau. "Indigenous Peoples in Developed Fragment Societies: A Comparative Analysis of Internal Colonialism in the United States, Canada, and Northern Ireland." PhD diss., University of Arizona, 1986.
Voorheis, Peter. "The Perception of Asiatic Nomads in Medieval Russia: Folklore, History and Historiography." PhD diss., Indiana University, 1982.

NEWSPAPER AND PERIODICAL POPULAR PRESS

American Journal of Pharmacy. December 1857.
Arthur's Illustrated Home Magazine. February 1874.
Christian Observer. September 7, 1850.
DeBow's Review and Industrial Resources, Statistics, etc. August 1858.
Forum. October 1901.
Friend's Review; a Religious, Literary and Miscellaneous Journal. October 18, 1851.
Friends' Review; a Religious, Literary and Miscellaneous Journal. January 5, 1861.
Graham's American Monthly Magazine of Literature, Art, and Fashion. February 1857.
Hours at Home: A Popular Monthly of Instruction and Recreation. August 1869.
Lippincott's Magazine of Literature, Science and Education. July 1870.
Littell's Living Age. March 28, 1863.
Littell's Living Age. August 4, 1883.
Michigan Farmer. July 21, 1906.
New Englander. January 1875.
New York Evangelist. April 2, 1863.
New York Evangelist. July 5, 1877.
New York Times. June 29, 1873.
Niles' National Register. September 26, 1846.
Scribner's Monthly. December 1876.
Spirit of the Times; A Chronicle of the Turf, Agriculture, Field Sports, Literature and the Stage. May 30, 1846.
Family Magazine, or, Monthly Abstract of General Knowledge No. 4, 1836.
Friend. A Religious and Literary Journal. July 6, 1850.
Friend. A Religious and Literary Journal. January 22, 1853.
Galaxy. A Magazine of Entertaining Reading. February 1, 1867.
Independent. October 10, 1850.
Knickerbocker; Or, New-York Monthly Magazine. May 1847.
Ladies' Home Journal. September 1891.

Ladies' Repository: A Monthly Periodical, Devoted to Literature, Arts, and Religion. January 1870.
Missionary Herald. January 1850.
Phrenological Journal and Science of Health. April 1877.
Western Journal of Agriculture, Manufactures, Mechanic Arts, Internal Improvement, Commerce, and General Literature. August 1850.
Youth's Companion. June 24, 1875.
Zion's Herald. June 25, 1868.
Russkaia starina. No. 99, July 1899.
Zhivaia starina. Vyp. 3–4, 1894.
Russkii Vestnik. No. 7, 1868.

Index

Ablai Khan, 83, 104
Abulkhair (Kazakh khan), 72, 81–83, 86, 89, 105, 112–13, 128–29; Abulkhair's oath (1732), 72, 82–83, 86, 89, 112, 128–29
Abylkhozhin, Zhulduzbek, 47
Acton (Minnesota), 123
Adams, Gordon, 21
Adams, Henry, 108
Adams, John Quincy (President), 152–53
Adas, Michael, 17
Adat, 181. *See also* Kazakh, customary law
Africa, 4, 7, 12, 15, 17, 19, 22, 37–38, 70, 126, 146, 148–49, 154, 171–72, 174, 177, 210, 236, 238, 241
Akmolinsk, 114, 119, 184, 208
Aktau, 119
Alash Orda ("The Horde of Alash"), 219, 222–23, 226
Alaska, 4, 8, 76, 120, 221
alcohol, 103
Alexander I (Russian Tsar, 1801–1825), 109
Alexander II (Russian Tsar, 1855–1881), 120
Algeria, 126, 172–73, 236
allotment, 6, 172, 176–78, 182–83, 185–86, 189–92, 195–96, 208, 215–16, 218–25, 236, 238
American Board of Commissioners for Foreign Missions, 209
American Geographical Society, 174

Americanization, 140, 218, 226
American Revolution, 86
American Social Science Association, 143
American Society for Promoting the Civilization and General Improvement of the Indian Tribes, 211
Amu Darya, 40
Anderson, Benedict, 44, 219
Anderson, Gary Clayton, 46–47, 121
Andrews, Thomas G., 218
Apache (tribe), 6
Arabian Desert, 145
Arabic (script), 215
Aral Sea, 43, 54
Arapaho (tribe), 114, 121–22
Archambault, JoAllyn, 55
Arikara (tribe), 78, 113–15, 122
Asfendiarov, Sandzhar, 40
Asia, 4, 7, 12, 17, 22, 38, 70, 81, 142–44, 146, 148–49, 154, 162, 171–72, 174, 177, 206, 210–11, 238, 241
Asiatic, 53, 75, 84–85, 120, 145, 152, 156
assimilation, 7, 9, 12, 23–24, 111, 129, 146, 156, 187–88, 196, 209–11, 215–16, 218–19, 221, 224, 226
Assiniboine (tribe), 78, 122
Atkins, John D. C. (Commissioner of Indian Affairs), 185, 189–90, 217
Atkinson, Thomas, 53

289

Atlantis, 37
Australia, 15, 206
Austria-Hungary, 182

Bacon, Elizabeth E., 37, 59
Baian-Aul, 114
Bailey, Thomas A., 20
Baitursynov, Akhmet, 219, 222
Baltics, 4
Banner, Stuart, 84, 88, 106
Barbarian, 36, 85, 142–46, 159, 186, 236
Barymta, 160–61
Bashkirs, 4, 70, 75, 80–81, 85, 145
Bassin, Mark, 17
Battle of Geok-Tepe, 105
Battle of the Little Bighorn, 99, 104–5, 126
Bedouins, 36, 145
Belgium, 4, 10
Belich, James, 3, 22, 206
Bell, Captain James, 185
Berbers, 36
Berkhofer, Robert F., Jr., 107, 144, 147, 211
Biolsi, Thomas, 75, 225
Blackfeet, 42, 84, 101
Black Hills, 112, 114, 121, 125–26, 155, 186
"Black Hills' War" (1875–1877), 105, 120
Black Sea, 221
Bloch, Marc, vii, 18
Board of Indian Commissioners (BIC), 187–88
Board of Missions of the Protestant Episcopal Church, 130
Bohannan, Paul, 37
Boilvin, Nicholas (Indian Agent), 111
Bokeikhanov, Alikhan, 44, 192, 221–22
Bolsheviks, 12, 19, 222
Bonaparte, Napoleon, 108–9
Bonin, Gertrude (*Zitkala-Sa*), 156
Bookwalter, John W., 151–52
Bozeman Trail, 124–25, 128, 184, 191
Brazil, 206
Britain. *See* Great Britain
British. *See* Great Britain
Brocherel, Jules, 53
Brodhead, Jane Millikin Napier, 144
Brown, Dee, 46
Brown, Kate, 17
Buddhism, 210
buffalo, 37, 51–54, 71m, 78, 80, 111–12, 127–28, 151, 187
"Buffalo Nation," 39

Bukei Horde, 88, 110, 116. *See also* Inner Horde
Bukei Khan, 110
Bukhara, 43, 70, 73, 81, 102–3, 109, 118–20, 182
Bureau of Indian Affairs (BIA), 173, 178, 181, 185, 187–88, 214, 216–17
Burke, Edmund, 85
Burke Act (1906), 222
Burnaby, Fred, 150

Calhoun, John (US Secretary of War), 113, 115
California, 4, 103, 121–22, 149
Calloway, Colin G., 52, 121
Calvert, Peter, 22
Cameron, Sarah Isabel, 47
Canada, 15, 84, 88, 102–3, 206
Canadian Pacific Railway, 206
Cannonball River, 42
Caroe, (Sir) Olaf, 226
Carr, Helen, 7
Carrington, Colonel Henry, 124
Caspian Sea, 43
Cass, Lewis, 115
Catherine II (Tsarina, 1763–1796, "Catherine the Great"), 85, 88, 109, 159, 209–11, 214
Catholics, 188
Catlin, George, 55
Caucasus, vii, 4, 11, 13–15, 105, 174, 240
Celts, 236
Central America, 20, 70
Central Asia, vii–viii, 4, 11, 16, 37, 40, 46–47, 56, 72–73, 76, 102–3, 105, 109, 118, 120, 142–43, 145, 148, 155–56, 174, 206, 309, 212, 214, 222, 237, 240
Central Asian Revolt (1916), 47
Chaadaev, Peter, 141
Chandler, Zachariah (Secretary of the Interior), 126
Chatterjee, Partha, 23
Chechens, 6
Cherokee Nation v. Georgia (1831), 177
Cheyenne (tribe), 6, 37, 45, 101, 114, 121–22, 126
China, viii, x, 4, 43, 72–73, 76, 80, 83, 103; Chinese x, 3–5, 33, 36, 194
Chittenden, Hiram, 111
Christian, 22–23, 148–49, 156, 175, 184, 187–89, 196, 206, 209–13, 215, 218, 236, 239, 240. *See also* missionaries

Christianity. *See* Christian
Civil War: American, 20, 102, 123, 128, 162, 214; Russian, 12, 222, 226
Clark, William, 108–9, 115
Cocker, Mark, 152, 210
collectivization, 46–47, 224
Collier, John (Commissioner of Indian Affairs), 224–26
colonialism, 3, 5, 7–8, 12, 18–24, 71, 127, 141, 173–74, 235, 237, 241
colonization, vii–ix, 3–24, 33, 42–43, 45–48, 59, 69, 74, 76, 82, 88, 90, 99–102, 104–5, 109, 114, 116, 119–20, 123, 127–29, 139–40, 146–48, 161–63, 171–75, 177–79, 181–83, 185–86, 189, 195, 205, 207–9, 212, 216–17, 219–21, 224, 235–39, 241–42
Colorado, 102, 181, 208
Comanche (tribe), 4, 53
Commissioner of Indian Affairs, 45, 172, 178, 189–90, 215–17, 224
Communist Party Congress (1927), 224
Confederate States of America, 220
Congress (US), 87, 105–7, 113, 130, 176, 178, 183, 183, 187, 209, 213, 224–25
Conn, Steven, 210
Constitution: American, 105, 141, 241; Russian, 106; Tribal, 225
Continental Congress (US), 213
Cooper, Frederick, 239
Cooper, James Fenimore, 14
Crazy Horse, 102, 104–5, 112, 126
Crimean War (1853–1856), 120
Crow (tribe), 37, 70, 84, 101, 113, 122
Cuba, 20, 220
Curzon, George, 142
Custer, Lieutenant Colonel George Armstrong, 39, 126, 155; Custer Expedition (1874), 126, 186
Cyrillic (script), 215

Dakota Superintendency, 45
Dakota Territory, 125, 185
Dartmouth College, 213
Dawes, Charles (Senator), 195
Dawes Act (1887), 45, 189–90, 196, 216, 219, 222–24
De Koninck, Rodolphe, 179
Deloria, Ella, 48
DeMallie, Raymond, 41, 55–56
Denig, Edwin, 54

Department of Justice (US), 124
Department of State (US), 107
Department of the Interior (US), 107, 173, 178, 188
Department of the Treasury (US), 107
Department of War (US), 107, 111, 173, 178, 188, 223
de Tocqueville, Alexis, 5, 141–42
DeWeese, Devin, 37
Divan (Judicial Tribunal), 119
"Divide and Conquer," 100–101, 109–11, 113, 117, 242
Dobb, Maurice, 182
Doolittle, James R. (Senator), 183; Doolittle Commission, 183–84
Dostoevsky, Feodor, 143, 155
Doyle, Arthur Conan, 149
Dulhut, Daniel Greysolon, 77
Duluth (Minnesota), 77, 126
Duma (Russian parliament), 221–22
Dunch, Ryan, 211
Dutch. *See* Holland

Eastman, Charles (*Uhiye Sa*), 156–57, 219, 223
Emancipation Proclamation, Russian, 24, 120, 162, 182, 208
Emerson, Rupert, 224
Eurasia, 36, 39, 41
exceptionalism, 15, 139, 141–43, 239
extinction, 10, 45–46, 139, 146–47, 153–54, 179, 209, 239

Falls of St. Anthony, 109
Far East, 13–14, 143, 207
Father Venegas (Spanish Jesuit), 37
Fay, Sidney, 3, 153
Fetterman, Lieutenant William, 124–25
Fetterman Massacre, 104, 125, 184
Finland, 4, 240
First Russian All-Empire Census (1897), 45–46, 182
Fisk, Captain James L., 172
Fort Atkinson, 114
Fort Jesup, 114
Fort Laramie, 102, 122, 124
Fort Laramie Treaty (1851), 46, 122, 124, 180–81, 186
Fort Laramie Treaty (1868), 125–26, 187
Fort Peck Indian Reservation, 160

Fort Phil Kearny, 125
Fort St. Anthony, 113
Fort St. Antoine, 74
Fort St. Philip, 114
Fort Snelling, 113–15
Fox (tribe), 121
Francaviglia, Richard, 144
France, 4, 10, 74, 77–78, 83, 108–9, 155, 173, 220, 237; French 14, 19, 39–40, 69–75, 77–80, 82–86, 89–90, 103, 108–9, 126, 148, 154, 172–73, 194, 236–37, 241
Fraser, John Foster, 37, 153
Fredrickson, George M., 239
French Revolution (1789), 108–9
Friend (Quaker publication), 171
frontier, 4, 8, 15–17, 21, 46, 76, 82, 85, 89, 102–3, 114–15, 117, 119–20, 122–23, 130, 139, 144, 149, 161, 172, 174–75, 180–81, 186, 188, 211, 213, 220, 225, 236, 239
frontier thesis, viii, 16, 239
fur trade, 48, 71–72, 74, 77–78, 82, 87, 89, 103, 108, 111, 113–14, 121, 176

Gallagher, Hugh D. (reservation agent), 217
Gardner, Lloyd C., 5
Georgia (American state), 177
Georgia (Russian province), 106, 239
General Allotment Act (1887). *See* Dawes Act
genocide, 46–47
Germany, 4, 15; Germans, 154, 172
Gibbon, Guy, 40
Gleason, Abbott, 142
Gold Rush, 15, 46, 103
Gorbachev, Mikhail, 46
Gorchakov, Prince Alexander (Russian Foreign Minister), 120
Governor-Generals (Russian), 107, 113, 115, 118, 173, 175, 184, 192, 241
Gradovskii, Aleksander, 211
Grand River, 42
Grant, Ulysses S. (President and General), 126, 187–88
Grattan Massacre, 104
Grazhdanstvennost' (Russian, "citizenship"), 210
"Great American Desert," 149
Great Britain (England/Britain), 4, 10, 21, 72, 78, 83, 86, 102, 108, 156, 206, 212, 220, 235, 237; British/English, 8, 15, 19–20, 23, 69, 72, 75–80, 82–90, 102–3, 105–6, 108–9, 111, 113, 126, 148, 150, 154, 156, 172–73, 209, 236–37, 240–41
Great Depression, 12
"Great Game," 102, 156
Great Plains, 13, 52, 70, 149–50, 241
Great Sioux Reservation, 125, 186, 190
Greeks, 33, 36, 144, 147
Green, Elizabeth, 225
Greene, Jerome A., 126
Greenwald, Emily, 196
Grigoriev, Vasilii, 81, 112, 195
Gros Ventres (tribe), 122
Grousset, René, 40
Grudzinska-Gross, Irena, 17
Guettel, Jens-Uwe, 172
Guide to the Great Siberian Railway (1900), 207
Guins, George C., 21
Gustafson, Sandra M., 5

Halecki, Oskar, 225
Hämäläinen, Pekka, 53
Hampton Institute, 216
Hannah, Matthew G., 185
Hapsburg Empire, 21
Harrison, Benjamin (US President), 190
Harrison, Brady, 20
Harun Ghazl (Kazakh sultan), 158
Haskell Institute, 216
Hassrick, Royal B., 49
Hawaii, 19, 173
Hayden, Ferdinand, 155
Heart River, 42
Hebrews, 37, 144
Hellwald. *See* von Hellwald
Hennepin, Father Louis, 48
Herndon, Sarah Raymond, 146–47
Herztberg, Hazel W., 226
Higham, Carol L., viii, 18
Hind, Robert J., 22
Hindoos, 213
Hobsbawm, Eric, 206
Hobson, John A., 19
Hokanson, Katya, 151
Holland (Netherlands), 4, 119, 150, 173
Holquist, Peter, 185
Home, Henry (Lord Kames), 154
Homestead Act (1862), 125, 172, 182–83, 186, 190, 194
horses, 35–36, 49–54, 71, 78–79, 84, 88, 102, 114–15, 151, 158, 160, 195

Hottentots, 213
Hudson, Alfred E., 40
Humboldt. *See* von Humboldt
Hunczak, Taras, 3
Huns, 36
Huntington, Ellsworth, 51, 147
Hyde, George E., 115, 196

Ilek, 79
Ilek Line, 114, 117, 128
Ilek River, 117
Illinois, 151
Il'minskii, Nikolai, 214–15; Il'minskii system, 214, 218
Imperial Geographic Society (Russian), 154, 174, 206
imperialism, ix, 3, 5, 10, 12, 16, 18–21, 23, 59, 70–71, 83, 90, 141–42, 148, 171, 209, 221, 235, 237–38, 240–41
Independence (Missouri), 150
India, 12, 172, 206, 209, 236
Indian Peace Commission, 125
Indian Problem, 11, 183, 218
Indian Removal, 177
Indian Reorganization Act (also Wheeler-Howard Act, 1934), 12, 224
Indian Rights Association, 188
Indian Territory, 17, 177, 193, 207
Indian Wars. *See* specific conflicts
Inkpaduta, 123
Inkpaduta's War. *See* Spirit Lake Massacre
Inner Horde, 88, 110. *See also* Bukei Horde
Inorodtsy, 107, 211, 220
Inoverets, 211
Inozemtsy, 211
integration, 22, 24, 172, 206, 210, 226
internal colonization. *See* colonization
Iowa (state), 42, 72, 123, 151, 172
Iowa (tribe), 70, 78
Ireland, 21
Iroquois, 4, 69, 73, 75; Iroquois Wars, 72
Islam, 51, 56–57, 156, 210, 214, 236, 240
Italy, 182

Jackson, Helen Hunt, 130, 195
Jadid, 218
Jamestown, 8
Japan, 221; Japanese, 238
Jaxartes. *See* Amu Darya
"Jay Cooke's gamble," 126

Jefferson, Thomas, 8, 108, 141, 154, 183
Jesuits, 40, 71, 73, 89
Johnson, Douglas L., 37
Joselyn, John, 37
Judaism, 210

Kames, Lord. *See* Henry Home
Kansas, 151, 216, 220
Kaplan, Amy, 3
Karamzin, Nikolai, 210
Karnachev, Ivan, 119
Kashgar, 155
Kazak (newspaper), 222
Kazakh (Kirghis) Steppe, vii, 6–7, 12–17, 24, 43, 46, 53, 59, 69–70, 73–76, 79–83, 87–89, 100–105, 109–10, 112–14, 116, 119–20, 125–28, 130, 139, 143, 145–47, 149, 151, 155–56, 162, 172, 176–78, 181–85, 187, 191–92, 196, 207–9, 211–12, 221, 236, 239–41
Kazakhs: *Aksakal*, 58–59, 82, 84, 88; *Alash* (Kazakh Khan), 43–44; *Aul*, 48–50, 53, 57–59, 88, 116–19, 153, 185; Clan (*ru* and *taipa*), 43–44, 48–49, 57–59, 73, 83, 86, 101, 109–10, 113, 116–19, 130, 161, 194, 242; Customary Law (*adat*), 181; exogamy, 49; *Kalym* ("bride price"), 49; Khans, 40, 46, 58, 82–83, 105, 113, 116, 128–30, 242; Kirghiz, 43, 70, 81, 119, 147, 152, 156, 158; levirate, 49–50; polygamy (see polygamy, of Kazakhs); *Ush Zhuz* ("three hordes") (see *Ush Zhuz*, of Kasakhs); white bone 59
Kazakhstan, vii, ix, 46–47, 81, 156, 226, 239
Kazan, 72, 75, 89
Kazan Theological Academy, 214
Kazan University, 214
Keating, William, 41
Kenesary Kasymov, 101, 104–5, 118–19, 125, 127, 155, 178, 181
Khalid, Adeeb, 240
Khiva, 70, 73, 81, 102, 109, 113, 117, 119–20, 182
Kibitka, 176. *See also* yurt
Kievan Rus', 21
Kiowa (tribe), 4, 112, 114, 121
Kirei, 40
Kivelson, Valerie, 106
Kochevnik, 145. *See* nomadism
Kohn, Hans, 143
Kokand, 43, 73, 102, 109, 118–20, 182
Kokchetav, 114

Kolchin, Peter, 17
Kostenko, Lev F., 56
Kozybaev, Manash, 47
Krader, Lawrence, 41, 43–44, 50
"kulaks," 224
Kumis, 53
Kurt, 53
Kuropatkin, General Aleksei, 192

LaDow, Beth, 220
Lake Mohonk Conference of the Friends of the Indian (1883), 188
Lake Pepin, 74, 109
"land section" (*Zemskii otdel*), 194
Lattimore, Owen, 38
Lazzerini, Edward J., 218
Lea, Luke (Commissioner of Indian Affairs), 178
Leavenworth, Henry (Colonel), 114–15
Lemkin, Raphael, 46
Lenin, Vladimir, 19, 223–24
Leupp, Francis (Commissioner of Indian Affairs), 189
Levshin, Aleksei I., 15, 44, 46, 56, 129–30, 161
Lewis and Clark Expedition, 108–9, 154–55
Lewis, Meriwether, 109, 154–55
Liberty Loans, 223
Limerick, Patricia Nelson, 193
Lincoln, Abraham, 124
Lindner, Rudi, 44, 59
Little Crow (Sioux Chief), 109, 112, 124, 129
Livingston, David, 23
lodge, 44, 55
Long, Stephen, 155
Louisiana: Louisiana Purchase (1803), 108, 155; Louisiana Territory, 4, 84, 108, 114, 154
Lounsbery, Anne, 17
Lowie, Robert H., 52–53
Luehrmann, Sonja, 17
Lujan, Carol Chiao, 21

MacKenzie, John, 5, 236
Madison, James, 141
Maier, Bernhard, 236
Mandan (tribe), 70, 78, 84, 113, 122
Manifest Destiny, 15, 20, 121, 161, 172, 206, 239
Mannheim, Karl, 218
Martin, Terry, 224
Martin, Virginia, 161

Marx, Karl, 20
Mason, Robert L., 8
McGinnis, Anthony R., 42, 160
McGranahan, Carole, 56, 239
Mektep ("native school"), 214
"Meriam Report" (1928), 223–24
Meyendorf. *See* von Meyendorf
Meyer, Roy W., 123
Mexican-American War, 220
Mexico, 4, 20, 102, 220
Middle East, 37–38, 154
Middle Ground, 17, 75
Miliukov, Paul N., 16
Ministry of Agriculture and State Property (Russia), 194
Ministry of Foreign Affairs (Russia), 156
Ministry of Internal Affairs (Russia), 107
Ministry of Overseas France (France), 173
Ministry of State Domains (Russia), 173, 194
Ministry of the Interior (France), 173
Ministry of the Interior (Russia), 194
Ministry of War (Russia), 156
Ministry of Ways of Communication (Russia), 207
Minnesota, 39–42, 71–72, 76, 78, 82–83, 107, 113, 121–24, 126, 151, 172, 208
Minnesota River, 109, 113, 180
Minnesota-Sioux War (1862), 128, 183, 208
missionaries, 24, 45, 50 71, 73, 75, 108–9, 111–13, 121, 175, 177
Mississippi River, 6, 77–78, 84, 87, 108–9, 111–13, 121, 175, 177
Mississippi Valley, 209
Missouri River, 78, 87, 112–14
Mitchell, David (Superintendent of Indian Affairs), 122
Moghul, 37
Mohammedans, 56. *See also* Islam
Mohawks, 37
Mongol, 19, 36–37, 39, 53, 70, 158; Mongolia, 76
"Mongol yoke," 70, 149
Monroe Doctrine, 20
Montana, 42, 72, 102, 124–25, 149, 181, 183, 18, 208, 224
Moon, David, 196
Moreau River, 42
Morgan, Thomas Jefferson (Commissioner of Indian Affairs), 190
Morse, Jedidiah, 5

Moses, A. Dirk, 18
Moslem, 144. *See also* Islam
Muhammed, 56. *See also* Islam
Mussulman, 56. *See also* Islam

Napoleonic Wars, 107–8, 110, 114
Nationality Question, 11, 241
Native American Tribes. *See tribal names*
Navajo, 46
Nearing, Scott, 19
Nebraska, 42, 72, 124–25, 151
"New Deal," 226
New France, 82
New York Times, 206
New Zealand, 206
Nicaragua, 20
Nicholas I (Russian Tsar, 1825–1855), 119
Nicholas II (Russian Tsar, 1894–1917), 221
Nichols, Roger L., 209
Nicollet, Joseph N., 42
Nisbet, Robert A., 153
No Flesh (Sioux chief), 185
"noble savage," 146–47
Nogai-Uzbek-Kazak Confederation, 40
Nolan, Mary, 239
nomadism, 10, 14, 17, 33, 36–39, 52, 176, 178, 192, 195, 224
Northern Pacific Railroad, 126
Northwest Ordinance (1787), 87, 107
Nugent, Walter, 141

Oberly, John H. (Commissioner of Indian Affairs), 217
Office of Indian Affairs (OIA), 225
Ohio, 87, 107–8
Ohio Valley, 84–85, 87
Ojibwa (Chippewa), 40, 78, 86
Oklahoma, 177
Omaha (tribe), 70, 121
Omsk, 79
Omsk Corps of Cadets, 155, 214
Ordinance of 1785, 107
Oregon, 102–3, 148
Oregon Trail, 150
Orenburg, 79, 82, 113–14, 158
Orenburg Frontier Commission, 117, 119
"Orenburg Kirgiz," 116
Orientalism, 143, 148
Orthodox (church), 57, 187, 189, 207, 209–11, 214

Ossetians, 4
Osterhammel, Jürgen, 181, 208
Ostler, Jeffrey, 9, 107, 126, 129, 178
Ottoman Empire, 4, 19, 86, 103
Oxus. *See* Syr Darya
Oytate, of Sioux, 41; Blackfeet, 124; Brulé, 42, 57, 124; Hunkpapa, 42, 57, 124; Mdewakantonwan, 42, 109, 121; Miniconjou, 42, 57, 124; Oglala, 42, 57, 124, 191, 218; Sans Arc, 42, 57, 124; Sisitonwan/Sisseton, 42; Titonwan, 42; Two Kettle, 42, 57, 124; Wahpekute, 42; Wahpetonwan/Wahpeton, 42; Wiciyela, 42

Padgen, Anthony, 23
Palat, Madhavan, 114
Palestine, 21
Parker, Ely, 156
Patai, Raphael, 37
Paul I (Russian Tsar, 1796–1801), 109
Pawnee, 113
"Peace Policy," 187–88
Pearce, Roy Harvey, 146, 153
Peffer, William A., 220
Persia, 19, 72–73, 102–3
Pettigrew, Richard F. (Senator), 191
Philippines, 20, 173, 220
Pidgeon, William 144
Pike, Zebulon, 109, 113, 149, 155, 191
Pilcher, Joshua, 111
Pine Ridge Reservation, 185, 191–92, 196, 217–18
Pogodin, Mikhail, 142
Poland (Poles), 4, 182, 240; Poles, 4, 106
polygamy, of Kazakhs, 49; *Alimuly* 43; *Baiuly* 43; *Chaichkly* 44; *Kangly* 44; *Kereit* 44; *Kongrad* 44; *shezhere* ("genealogy") 43; *Tabyn* 117; *Zhetyru* 43
Ponca, 45, 78, 113, 125
Pond, Gideon, 215
Pond, Peter, 78
Pond, Samuel W., 566, 215
Porter, N. S. (Indian Agent), 160
Powder River, 124
Powder River War (1866–1868), 105, 120, 127, 187
Prairie du Chien, 111, 115; Prairie du Chien Treaty (1825), 121; Prairie du Chien Treaty (1830), 121
Pratt, Mary Louise, 15

296 INDEX

Pratt, Richard Henry, 189, 216
Price, Catherine, 58
Prince, Joseph M., 54
Prisoedinenie ("unification"), 16, 81
Proclamation of 1763, 84, 106
Protestants, 188
"Provisional Statute on the Administration of turgai, Akmolinsk, Uralsk, and Semipalatinsk Oblasts," 184, 186. *See* Steppe Commission
Prucha, Francis Paul, 177, 184
Prussia, 21, 206
Pushkin, Alexander, 146

Qing Dynasty (China), 4
Quakers, 188
Quarterly Journal of the Society of American Indians, 223

Radlov, Vasili, 154
railroads. *See specific railroad*
Red Cloud, 105, 125, 127–28, 191, 196
Red Cloud Agency, 126
"Red Cloud's War." *See* Powder River War
Red Cross, 223
"Regulations on the Siberian Kirgiz," 116
Reid, Mayne, 14
reservations, x, 9, 17, 45, 50, 101, 105, 120, 122–23, 126, 128, 156, 161, 171, 177–80, 182, 184–85, 187–90, 192–93, 196, 214–15, 220, 222, 236, 241
resettlement, viii, 11, 21, 101, 107, 116, 161–62, 172, 176, 178, 181–84, 186–87, 193–95, 207–8, 219, 221
"Resettlement Act" (1889), 194
Resettlement Administration (*Pereselencheskoe upravlenie*), 194–95, 207
resistance, 6, 9, 11, 42, 46, 88, 99–102, 104–5, 112, 115, 119–20, 122, 127–28, 177, 224, 242
Riggs, Stephen R., 40, 44, 44, 212, 215
rivers. *See individual river names*
Robinson, Doane, 112
Robinson, Geroid T., 193
Rocky Mountains, 108, 151, 172
Roman Empire, 19, 33, 236
romanticism, 142, 144, 151, 154
Roosevelt, Franklin, 224–25
Rose, Deborah Bird, 175
Rosebud Agency, 185
Rudy, Charles, 141, 151

rule: direct, 21, 24, 90, 225; indirect, 21, 90
Russian Revolutions: 1905, 221, 238; 1917, 12, 222
Russification, 24, 140, 215, 218, 224, 226

Sacs, 111, 121
Said, Edward W., 143
St. Croix River, 109
St. Germain, Jill, 122
St. Peter's Agency, 115
Saint Petersburg, 81, 85, 156, 186, 241
Samarkand, 103
Samovol'tsy, 85, 193
Sarzhan Kasymov, 117–19
Sblizhenie ("coming together") 16, 24
Schuyler, Eugene, 56, 184
"Scouting" (*khodachestvo*), 194
Scythians, 36–37, 144
Seattle (Washington), 126
sedentary, 35–36, 38–39, 54, 71, 85, 114, 130, 156, 185, 187, 192, 195, 205, 220, 240; sedentarization 12, 17, 191, 196, 215
Select Committee on Aborigines (1837, House of Commons, Great Britain), 212
Semenov, Peter, 154
Semipalatinsk, 79, 184, 208
Semirechie, 43, 119, 181–82, 184, 192
"Semirechie Kirgiz," 116
Senate Committee of Indian Affairs, 191
Seneca (tribe), 156
Serbia, 182
Serfdom (Russian), 24, 85, 120, 142, 162, 182, 208
Sergiopol, 114
Shamil (Imam), 105
Shcherbina Expedition, 192
Sherman, General William Tecumseh, 125, 188
Siberia, 3–4, 11, 13–14, 16, 37, 45, 69–70, 74–76, 79–80, 85–86, 89, 115, 120, 139, 145, 149–51, 153, 172, 174–75, 178, 182–83, 206–7, 210, 221, 241
"Siberian Kirgiz," 116
Siberian Railway Committee, 207
"Silk Road," 771, 103
Sitting Bull, 104–5, 112, 125
"Sitting Bull's War," 120
Skinner, Alanson, 58
slavery, 15, 17, 183
Slavophile, 142–43
Slocum, John W., 211

INDEX   297

Slotkin, Richard, 183
Smith, Henry Nash, 144
Smith, J. Russell, 205
Smith, John Q. (Commissioner of Indian Affairs), 215
Smith, Sherry L., 50, 147, 158
Society for Historians of American Foreign Relations, 5
Society of American Indians, 219, 223
Sioux: *Akicita*, 58; *blotahunka*, 58; Dakota, 39–40, 42, 44–45, 48, 57, 71–73, 86, 109, 111, 121, 124, 187, 215; exogamy, 49; *hakatakus* ("bride price"), 49; *itancan*, 58; Lakota, 39–40, 42, 44, 53, 55, 57, 72; levirate, 49–50; *natowessiwak* (also "Nadoueceronon"), 40; *Oceti Sakowin* ("Seven Council Fires"), 41; *Oyate* (subdivisions) (*see Oyate*, of Sioux); polygamy, 49; Santee, 39, 42, 57, 76, 101, 109, 115, 121, 123; "Sun Dance," 48, 55–56, 217; "sweat lodge," 55; "War Dance" 56; *Tiyospaye* (nomadic community) (*see Tiyospaye*, of Sioux); Teton, 39, 42, 57, 76, 78, 88, 101, 109, 111, 113–15, 121; *Wakiconza*, 58; *Wakicun*, 58; Yankton/Yanktonai, 39, 42, 57, 88, 111, 113–14, 121, 124
Soviet Union. *See* Union of Soviet Socialist Republics
Spain, 4, 84, 102, 220; Spanish 19, 82, 84, 86–87, 102, 108, 220
Spanish-American War, 19, 173, 238
Speransky, Mikhail (Governor-General of Siberia), 115, 122, 175–76, 181; Speransky Reforms (*see also* "Regulations on the Siberian Kirgiz") 122, 175–76, 181
Spirit Lake Massacre (1857), 122
Spooner, Brian, 39
Srym Batyr, 88, 105; Srym Batyr's Rebellion, 99, 105
Stalin, Joseph, 46–47, 224, 226, 240
Stanitsy (Cossack settlements), 114
"Statute on Primary Schools" (Russia, 1864), 215
Steckel, Richard H., 54
Steppe Commission (Russia, 1865), 184
Stoler, Ann Laura, 5–6, 239
Stumm, Hugo, 152
Sultan Kaip-Galii Ishimov, 81, 117
Sunderland, Willard, 173, 207
Sunni Muslims. *See* Islam
Superintendent of Indian Trade (US), 176

Swift, Jonathan (*Gulliver's Travels*), 18–19
Syr Darya, 40, 43, 71, 208
Szasz, Margaret, 223

Taliaferro, Lawrence, 115
Tashkent, 71, 118, 182; Tashkent *Kushbegi*, 118
Tashkent-Orenburg Railway, 207
Tatar (Tartars), 4, 36–37, 56, 75–76, 80, 85, 143–45, 155, 214
Tatarization, 57
Tatimov, Makash, 47
Texas, 4, 181, 208
Thomas, Robert, 129
Thornton, A. P., 237–38
Three Stars, Clarence, 218
Tien Shan Mountains, 43
Tiyospaye, of Sioux, 48, 50, 57–58; *Wicotipi* (camp unit), 48
"Toleration of All Faiths" (Russian edict, 1773), 209
Tolstoi, D. A. (Russia, Minister of Education), 214–15
Trans-Alleghany, 84–85
Trans-Continental Railway, 125, 172, 206
Trans-Kama Line, 74
Trans-Siberian Railway, 172, 206–8
Traverse des Sioux (Treaty, 1851), 122
Treadgold, Donald W., vii–viii, 16
treaties. *See specific treaties*
Treaty of Portage des Sioux (1815), 112
Tsar. *See individual Tsars*
Turgai Oblast, 184, 186
Turkestan (Turkistan), 14, 17, 41, 43, 45, 76, 80, 83, 102–3, 172, 175, 182, 184, 192, 207, 240–41
Turkmen, 4, 6, 80, 105; Turkoman, 237
Turks (Ottoman), 433
Turner, Frederick Jackson, viii, 10, 15–16, 239

Uezd (Russian districts), 9, 185
Ukraine, 4, 239
Union of Soviet Socialist Republics, 12, 15–17, 46–47, 105, 182, 222–26, 239–40
Union Pacific Railroad, 206
Ural Mountains, 69, 74
Ural River, 86, 88, 110, 117, 175
Ush Zhuz ("Three Hordes"), of Kazakhs, 42–44, 49; *Kishi Zhuz* (Little Horde) 43–44, 57, 81–82, 86, 110, 116–17; *Orta Zhuz* (Middle Horde) 43–44, 57, 83, 86, 114, 116, 118, 130;

Uly Zhuz (Great Horde) 43–44, 57, 114, 116, 119
Utley, Robert M., 105, 113–14, 129, 180
Uzbeks, 6, 40, 43, 71

Valikhanov, Chokan, 56, 80, 154–57, 214
vandals, 36
Vernyi, 119, 181, 192
Volga River, 80, 85, 110
Volkonskii, Grigorii (Russian Governor-General), 113
Volkov, D. A. (Governor of Orenburg), 159
Volost' (Russian Administrative unit), 9, 118, 177
von Hellwald, Frederick, 152
von Humboldt, Alexander, 150
von Meyendorf, Baron, 151–52, 158
Voprosy istorii, 47

Wabasha (Sioux Chief), 86, 112
Walicki, Andrzej, 141–42
Walker, James R., 41–42, 51, 55, 57
Washington (District of Columbia), 108, 112, 115, 126, 191, 241
Welsh, Herbert, 188
Welsh, William, 130
Wheeler, Burton K. (Senator), 224–25
Wheeler, Geoffrey, 81
Whelan, Mary K., 48, 50
White, Richard, 16, 52, 70, 75, 77–78, 87, 121, 196, 206, 221
Wilson, Angela Cavender, 124
Wilson, Woodrow (President), 223–24
Wisconsin, 39–41, 71, 74, 76–78, 82, 107, 114, 208
Wolfe, Patrick, 174, 196
Women's National Indian Association, 188
Work, Hubert (US, Secretary of the Interior), 223
World War I, 12, 222–23
World War II, 46
Wounded Knee, 46, 102
Wright, George F., 175
Wrobel, David M., ix, 239
Wunder, John, 23–24
Wyoming, 42, 72, 122, 124, 187

yurt, 44–45, 49, 176

Zhanibek (Kazakh khan), 40, 43, 71
Zheti Su ("Seven Rivers"), 43
Zholaman Tlenchiev ,117–18, 125
Ziolkowski, Margaret, 17, 140

www.ingramcontent.com/pod-product-compliance
Lightning Source LLC
Chambersburg PA
CBHW020246030426
42336CB00010B/642